THE
Offerings
OF THE
Templo Mayor
OF
Tenochtitlan

THE
Offerings
OF THE
Templo Mayor
OF
Tenochtitlan

Leonardo López Luján

REVISED EDITION

TRANSLATED BY
BERNARD R. ORTIZ DE MONTELLANO AND THELMA ORTIZ DE MONTELLANO

University of New Mexico Press
Albuquerque

11 10 09 08 07 06 05   1 2 3 4 5 6 7

Library of Congress Cataloging-in-Publication Data

López Luján, Leonardo.
   [Ofrendas del Templo Mayor de Tenochtitlan. English]
   The offerings of the Templo Mayor of Tenochtitlan / Leonardo López Luján ; translated by
Bernard R. Ortiz de Montellano and Thelma Ortiz de Montellano.
      p. cm.
   Translation and revision of: Las ofrendas del Templo Mayor de Tenochtitlan.
   Includes bibliographical references and index.
   ISBN 0-8263-2958-6 (pbk. : alk. paper)
   1. Templo Mayor (Mexico City, Mexico) 2. Aztecs—Religion. 3. Aztec mythology. 4. Aztecs—
Antiquities. 5. Excavations (Archaeology)—Mexico—Mexico City. 6. Mexico City (Mexico)—
Antiquities. I. Title.
   F1219.76.R45L6713 2005
   972'.53018—dc22

                              2004026815

Book design and composition by Damien Shay
Body type is Minion 10.5/14. Display is Trade Gothic.

To Martha and Alfredo

Contents

Illustrations

FIGURES

PLAN, MATRICES, AND DENDROGRAMS

Foreword

by H.B. Nicholson

In 1519, the greatest urban center in the New World—almost certainly larger than any city in the nation from whence had come those who were about to assail it—was the twin city of Tenochtitlan/Tlatelolco. A remarkable New World Venice, studded with temples, palaces, and markets, it even included a zoo/aviary that might have been the largest in the world at that time. Two years later, in 1521, much of it, especially its central core with its great walled ceremonial precinct containing the principal sanctuaries of its gods, was a devastated ruin. And after its conqueror, Hernán Cortés, established here the capital of New Spain, this sacred enclosure was completely covered by the Metropolitan Cathedral and an adjoining cluster of European-style buildings. Over time, even knowledge of the exact location of its principal shrine, the pyramid temple dedicated to the patron deity of the Mexica, Huitzilopochtli, and Tlaloc, the preeminent rain deity, the Templo Mayor proper, had been lost.

During the colonial period, pre-Hispanic architectural remains, sacred images, and other artifacts were often encountered during construction activities in the heart of the city, culminating in the discovery in 1790/91 of three great stone monuments in the Plaza Mayor: the "Calendar Stone," the colossal Coatlicue, and the Cuauhxicalli of Tizoc. After Independence, further finds of pre-Hispanic material in the Plaza Mayor and its vicinity continued to be made, especially stone sculptures, many of which found their way into the newly established National Museum of Mexico and various collections, both private and public, in Europe and the United States. In 1900, construction of a sewer line along the Calle de las Escalerillas (modern Guatemala), north of the Cathedral, uncovered a mass of pre-Hispanic material, much of it published by Leopoldo Batres and studied most successfully by Eduard Seler. As is now known, this trench—which exposed various offertory caches—sliced through the southern portion of the Templo Mayor.

In 1913, more construction activity just northwest of the Cathedral revealed at least four stages of the stairway at the southwest corner of the Templo Mayor, which effectively established its correct location. Studied by Manuel Gamio, it was left exposed, and, featuring a colossal feathered serpent head projecting from the base of one of the stairway ramps, it became a prominent tourist attraction (on my first visit to Mexico City, in 1946, I was one of those tourists). In subsequent years, a few additional archaeological probes were undertaken in and around the Templo Mayor, and some interesting discoveries were made between 1967 and 1970 during the construction of the Mexico City subway. Then, the great turning point occurred in 1978 when an excavation at the corner of Guatemala and Argentina streets exposed the colossal circular Coyolxauhqui/Chantico monument. This major, much publicized discovery, resulted in government support for the Instituto Nacional de Antropología e Historia's Proyecto Templo Mayor (1978–2005), one of the great landmarks in the history of Mesoamerican archaeology.

Its director, Eduardo Matos Moctezuma, organized a talented, multi-disciplinary team, whose dedicated labors resulted in the complete exposure of all of the construction stages of the premier temple of the Empire of the Triple Alliance and adjacent structures. Numerous publications, by the director, his associates on the project, and many others, resulted from the Proyecto Templo Mayor, including detailed plans, excavation reports, and photographs and drawings of virtually all of the more important finds.

A striking feature of this landmark excavation was the many offertory caches that were encountered in all of the construction stages. Varying greatly in size and location, they contained a remarkable number of different types of offerings, both inorganic and organic. It became obvious that this plethora of sacred caches, deposited at key intervals during the long construction sequence of the Huey Teocalli of Huitzilopochtli and Tlaloc and its surrounding structures, constituted a vital aspect of the rich ceremonial life of the Mexica/Tenochca. Accordingly, meticulous care was devoted to their excavation, recording the precise location of every object and illustrating them with copious photographs and drawings.

As was recognized at the time of its original appearance in 1993, standing out in importance among the multitude of Templo Mayor publications, was Leonardo López Luján's comprehensive monograph dedicated to the description and analysis of the 110 offertory caches encountered during the Proyecto Templo Mayor, plus 8 others that had been discovered earlier. Beginning in 1980, its author was an active participant in the project and was personally involved in the excavation of many of the caches. Recognition of the crucial contribution this study had made to our knowledge of the Templo Mayor led to the publication, a year later, of an excellent English translation by Bernard R. Ortiz de Montellano and Thelma Ortiz de Montellano. In view of its importance, this second edition of the English translation can only be heartily welcomed.

In addition to providing by far the most detailed descriptions of these offertory caches and the relationships between them, expressed mathematically and graphically, López Luján's objective was to elucidate their *symbolic meanings* and the "ritual codes" that account for the choice of items, the temporal sequences followed in their depositions, and their spatial layouts. He fully recognized the challenging difficulties that face the investigator here. He employed a battery of methodological tools in addressing them, including applying some of the insights gained by anthropologists and historians of religion concerning ritual behavior patterns in general. Understandably, his principal interpretative resource was the wealth of ethnohistorical data available concerning the Mexica religious/ritual system at the time of the Conquest.

Owing, above all, to the extensive investigations of the remarkable sixteenth-century Franciscan missionary, Fray Bernardino de Sahagún—which, when pertinent, López Luján employed throughout to good advantage—we possess some of the most detailed accounts of the ritual practices of a non-Western culture ever compiled until modern times. However, aside from rather generalized statements concerning their frequency and importance, Sahagún and the other relevant chroniclers provide very little specific data concerning buried offertory caches of the type deposited in the Tenochtitlan Templo Mayor. In the case of deity images and ritual paraphernalia that display well developed iconography, accurate pantheonic and symbolic identifications can frequently be made by utilizing the considerable knowledge that has been gained concerning this aspect of late pre-Hispanic Central Mexican culture. But satisfactory explanations for the choice of many of the items contained in these caches, including their spatial dispositions, are often much more difficult to come by. López Luján addresses these problems with characteristic thoroughness and perception, carefully examining the available evidence and offering numerous working hypotheses that hopefully can be tested as more relevant archaeological information becomes available.

A typical example of a problem facing anyone attempting to explain and interpret the contents of these offerings is the identification of the ubiquitous stone images of the so-called "horned god." The author examines the question in some detail, recognizing and discussing the various identifications that have been proposed, concluding, in agreement with Matos Moctezuma and other members of the Templo Mayor excavation team, that the best evidence supports an identification as the fire deity, Xiuhtecuhtli/Huehueteotl. I and some others, agreeing with an earlier suggestion of Seler, have instead proposed Tepeyollotl, a terrestrial avatar of Tezcatlipoca—although why this somewhat obscure deity, not even mentioned by Sahagún, should appear so frequently in these offerings is indeed puzzling. López Luján has presented a cogent case for his identification, but I— while still preferring my own—regard the question as still open.

Another of the author's interpretations that I would regard as open to further discussion is his suggestion that the principal ritual focused on the Templo Mayor was Tlacaxipehualiztli, the flaying sacrifice devoted to Xipe Totec. While recognizing the importance of this ceremony within the overall panorama of Mexica ritualism, in my view, Panquetzaliztli, celebrating the birth of the Mexica patron deity to whom the Templo Mayor was dedicated, might be considered a stronger candidate for its preeminent ceremony.

With additional archaeological information becoming available and with the undertaking of more penetrating analyses of the ethnohistorical sources, our understanding of the purposes and significances of these intriguing offertory caches of the Tenochtitlan Templo Mayor should steadily improve. As the author over-modestly concludes, "It is clear that there is a long way to go before reaching a complete understanding of the code of offerings. Practically everything is yet to be done." *The Offerings of the Templo Mayor of Tenochtitlan* constitutes a major advance in this endeavor, while representing a significant contribution to the methodology and analytic strategies of Mesoamerican archaeology in general. Again, its reappearance in this new English edition can only be welcomed most heartily!

Prologue

by Eduardo Matos Moctezuma

Among the most surprising discoveries of the excavations at the Templo Mayor of the Mexica were the rich offerings found there. From the very beginning of our work, we were aware of the importance of these offerings. Because of this, we formulated a specific technique that included extreme care in the process of exploration. This technique allowed us to record clearly the location and internal associations of each object and to document the relationship between a group of offerings in regard to a number of other questions: location in the temple, orientation, similarities and differences with other offerings, and how the location of each was related in some way to the god who presided over the corresponding side of the temple—whether it was Tlaloc or Huitzilopochtli. Each object's relationship to the direction of the universe was determined, as well as its relationship to the gods who reside at the center of the Mexica universe for the Templo Mayor was at the heart of that cosmovision. Not all the offerings came from the same epoch. Appropriate offerings were deposited at different stages of the building's growth.

The study of these materials was complex and difficult, but it was clear that such analyses were the only way to penetrate, even if only partially, that symbolic-mythical-magical-religious world. Due to the particular importance of that world, no specific document was written describing how the objects were deposited, what rituals accompanied them, and when they were placed there. The ancient priests had been careful not to transmit information about something that was of the greatest importance to them because this was not just any building but their principal temple, the heart and center of their universe.

Nevertheless, archaeology allowed us to approach that hidden world, and it has introduced us, after more than five hundred years, to that symbolic universe. The message inherent in the offerings was before us, just as it had been placed there centuries ago. Even though the passage of time had caused some damage and some movement of the objects relative to each other, we could see that their relationship and placement had remained essentially intact. These gifts were the means of communication between humans and the gods, a message expressed in the placement of every object—for no object was placed aimlessly. The ideas expressed in them allow us to participate in the dialogue with the gods, a privilege not given to everyone. With some humility, we accepted the challenge of confronting the language of the gods across the abyss of time and space.

Someone had to begin the task. Considerable time passed from the end of our excavation in 1982 until the results began to appear. Some essays have been written, and there have been some publications about the offerings. Due to the importance of the finds, we wished to be cautious and avoid hasty judgments. However, there were some who, without ever having seen an offering, expressed their opinions. Some could not wait for the opinions of the various specialists who had carried out the research: before the study was completed, they hastened to write about the offerings of the Templo Mayor. They gave opinions without possessing the slightest information about the subject. Some hypotheses were interesting; others showed complete ignorance. We preferred to wait and to choose carefully the person to carry out the interpretation. It had to be a researcher who had participated in the extraction of the offerings and who had seen the complexity of the deposits firsthand. A good knowledge of the Mexica people was also indispensable to the task, as well as the ability to manage modern computer techniques for they would be of great value in carrying out the research. Moreover, such a task required a full time effort and an intense interest in the subject. All these requirements were united in a young investigator who, with enthusiasm and knowledge, took on the task assigned to him. The first results are presented here.

Introduction

For more than five hundred years, the offerings of the Templo Mayor lay unknown underground. As if they were simple minerals, they existed for the greater part of their long history in the midst of rocks, earth, and water. This was the fate of masks, small figures, and ornaments of semiprecious stones, of animals from the outer limits of the *cemanahuac* ("the Aztec domain"), and of ceramic containers, human remains, images of the gods, musical instruments, flint knives, thorns covered with blood, textiles, feathers, food, and, no doubt, more.

After the fall of Tenochtitlan and the violent disappearance of the pre-Hispanic world, centuries went by without the majority of the citizens of the new colonial capital (and later, of the young republic) even imagining the presence of those rich offerings a few meters beneath the daily bustle of the crowds. Little by little, relentlessly, the gifts the Mexica had offered to their gods fell victim to the pressure of buildings, earth movements, water, microorganisms, and rodents. Time had little effect on the more resistant objects; others were deformed, cracked, or disappeared altogether, leaving hardly a trace of their former existence.

That prolonged period of interment contrasts sharply with the brief time of both the religious ritual of the ancient Mexica and the modern archaeological explorations. At one end of the historical chain, during the last years of the post-Classic period, fleeting ceremonies took place to invoke all kinds of divine favors. On more than one occasion—in the midst of ritual dances, the reenactment of mythical scenes, and the sacrifice of war prisoners—a priest must have invoked Huitzilopochtli and Tlaloc with a prayer before placing his gift within the Templo Mayor. Carefully, meticulously, following a preestablished rite, he placed, one by one, the offerings that would carry the message of his hopes. It was his offering and that of his people, the tangible product of one of humanity's greatest desires: to enter into a dialogue with the divinities.

Events at the other end of the historical chain took place between 1978 and 1989, when members of the Templo Mayor Project extracted a good part of what had fallen into oblivion. The offerings recovered their communicative function. Although there was a certain linkage between the two sets of players—the Mexica priests and the modern scientists, separated by an enormous chronological distance—there were vast differences in their values and intents. The message exhumed today reached men instead of gods. The offering, instead of transmitting simple pleas, acquired the value that all human endeavor potentially holds: to be an imperfect synthesis of the epoch in which it was created.

In July 1980 I first participated in the excavation of Mexica offerings. Eduardo Matos Moctezuma, coordinator of the Templo Mayor Project of the National Institute of Anthropology and History (INAH), gave me the opportunity to explore several of the deposits, which I describe in this book. This experience, which lasted nearly two years, allowed me to become directly acquainted with the materials and their contexts. In fact, a considerable number of the hypotheses that guided this research arose at that time. Afterward, on a part-time basis, I continued to collaborate in excavation and laboratory analysis until, in 1988, I fully joined the Templo Mayor Project. That year, I began the study and systematic registration of the 110 offerings discovered by a total of twenty-four archaeologists in nine buildings and three plazas and in the interior of the platform that served as the boundary of the Sacred Precinct of Tenochtitlan.

The main purpose of this investigation was to understand, as far as possible, the religious significance of the gifts excavated in three different field seasons (1978–1982, 1987, and 1989). During the excavations, we perceived that the objects in the offerings were not placed randomly; all had been deposited in an ordered manner. It seemed evident to us that the patterned distribution of the gifts followed a code of expression that could be deciphered by examining the contexts. For this reason, I tried to explain the relationship between the unearthed material and ritual behavior.

This book is the result of the first stage of the investigation. The initial version was used as a thesis for obtaining my title as an archaeologist at the National School of Anthropology and History of Mexico. I am now presenting a revised version of general information on 118 offerings, with special emphasis on the importance of contextual data. The second stage of analysis is in progress.

Throughout the work, I have been able to count on the valuable assistance of teachers, colleagues, and friends. The text and the orientation of the research owe much to continuous conversations with Eduardo Matos Moctezuma and Alfredo López Austin. Both guided the investigation from beginning to end and critiqued the successive drafts of this volume. Diego Jiménez Badillo, Xavier Noguez, and Bertina Olmedo Vera read the entire manuscript and offered valuable comments.

I owe special thanks to those who introduced me to the interesting topic of classification by mathematical methods. At first, Mario Cortina Borja and Maricarmen Serra Puche suggested using numerical taxonomy. Later, Guillermo Espinosa recommended the most appropriate method to be used for this purpose and advised me during the analysis of the data.

I cannot fail to mention those who contributed to this intellectual undertaking by giving me data from their own investigations, lending me publications on the subject, criticizing mistaken or imprecise ideas, and suggesting alternative ways of analysis. Among them are Jorge Angulo, Johanna Broda, Davíd Carrasco, Ximena Chávez, Lourdes Cué, Laura Filloy, Carlos Javier González, Salvador Guil'liem, Elsa Hernández Pons, Francisco Hinojosa, Joyce Marcus, Carlos Martínez Marín, Alejandro Martínez Muriel, Debra Nagao, María Teresa Olivera, Guilhem Olivier,

Bertha Peña Tenorio, Oscar J. Polaco, Juan Román Berrelleza, Antonio Serrato-Combe, Felipe Solís Olguín, Norma Valentín, Constanza Vega Sosa, and Juan Yadeun.

Many of the figures presented in this volume come from the graphics collection of the Templo Mayor Project. Some were drawn expressly to support my arguments. Here I wish to give thanks for the magnificent sketches by the artists Fernando Carrizosa, José Luís García Pérez, Amelia Malagamba, Enrique Mora, Víctor Rangel, Julio Romero, Naoli Victoria Lona, and Alberto Zúñiga, as well as the work of the photographers Salvador Guil'liem and Miguel Morales.

Leonardo López Luján
Mexico City

Translators' Note

To avoid difficulties in pluralizing, names of cultures and native groups have been treated as collective nouns. Nahuatl words are all accented on the next to last syllable; therefore accents, which were used to indicate stress in Spanish, have been omitted on Nahuatl words.

The fusion of the solar principle (fire) and the terrestrial one (water) became the symbol of the Aztec nation. More than a symbol, it was an archetype, a model for society and for the individual... Mexico was born from the union of fire and water. It lives through these elements, and has several times almost died because of them.

— Octavio Paz

CHAPTER ONE

The Excavation and Interpretation of the Offerings in the Center of Mexico City: 1519–1978

HISTORIOGRAPHIC REVIEW

The investigations of Mexica offerings have a long history. The accumulation of drawings, photographs, notes, and unedited information, as well as reports, catalogs, published articles, and books, has increased at different rhythms with the passage of time. It is a peculiar and heterogeneous aggregate that faithfully reflects the changing interests of archaeologists and historians. Therefore, an examination of works dealing with the gifts offered by the Mexica to their gods not only throws light on the practices and concepts of their Mesoamerican society but also reveals a great deal about the evolution of our own profession.

Such a historiographic review is an indispensable instrument for orienting this research. In fact, any previous experience—with its merits and defects—is valuable in carrying out new projects. Unfortunately, this practice has not always been followed in Mexica archaeology, and it has been applied even less frequently in regard to the gifts offered by the Mexica to their divinities. Only four works exist that, to a greater or lesser degree, offer a critical analysis of previous studies and a summary of the evidence they contain. Noemí Castillo and Felipe Solís Olguín's (1975) volume is important because it is the first to gather information about Mexica offerings from various different archaeological explorations. Its authors reported the characteristics of five offerings,

1

assessed their significance, and described the artifacts, which are now lodged in the National Museum of Anthropology. In the introductory chapter to his 1979 publication, Eduardo Matos Moctezuma briefly summarized the history of excavations in the center of Mexico City. He then published representative texts of this history, which previously had been difficult to find. Salvador Mateos Higuera, in Matos Moctezuma (1979a: 205–73), undertook the difficult task of gathering available material on the traces of Mexica culture discovered in the center of Mexico City before 1978. When possible, he gave four important pieces of information for each object: the place where it was found, its formal description, the material of which it was made, and its dimensions. The last part of the article described artifacts of unknown origin that may be offerings. In this same volume, it is useful to peruse Ponciano Salazar Ortegón's "Bibliografía: Vestigios arqueológicos localizados hasta la fecha en el centro de la Ciudad de México." There is no doubt that Debra Nagao (1985b) has written the most ambitious work on the subject until now. In my opinion, its chief value is the abundant bibliography on the excavations and the interpretations of Mexica offerings (Chapters 3 and 7), as well as a useful appendix in which she organized the results of the archaeological finds. When her source permitted, Nagao recorded the place and date of each offering, the archaeological project, the registry number of the deposit, the type of container, the contents, and the publications from which the information was taken. These works are essential to anyone interested in this fascinating topic.

One of the most intriguing aspects of the studies on the Mexica offerings is the evolution of the recovery techniques and the analyses of archaeological data. As I will demonstrate later on, the interpretation of the finding of offerings has depended on how the fieldwork was recorded and on the procedure used for laboratory studies. Interpretation has also been influenced by the development of applicable theories and by the slow accumulation of knowledge generated by other scientific disciplines.

Given the importance of the subject, the rest of this chapter provides a brief historical review of the procedures used in the field and in the laboratory, together with the resulting interpretations. The review will not be exhaustive. It will be limited to the research carried out at the center of Mexico City. Its temporal limits extend from the fall of Tenochtitlan to the inception of the Templo Mayor Project, that is, from 1521 to 1978. Moreover, there will be no detailed description of the discoveries. I refer interested readers to the four publications listed previously and, as far as possible, to each of the ancient works that inspired them.

EXCAVATIONS FROM THE SIXTEENTH TO THE NINETEENTH CENTURIES

Contrary to what might be expected, the greatest number of findings of Mexica offerings occurred during the Spanish conquest and colonial period (1519–1810), particularly during the sixteenth century. Many of these early discoveries were due to chance. Perhaps the first mention of accidental discoveries was in the famous "Relación" by Andrés de Tapia (1963). In it the conqueror told of Hernán Cortés's visit to the Templo Mayor of Tenochtitlan when the city was still governed by Motecuhzoma Xocoyotzin. According to Tapia's account, when Cortés and some of his followers reached the top of the pyramid for the first time, they violated both temples and destroyed several sculptures. Motecuhzoma, to save the statues of Tlaloc and Huitzilopochtli, was forced to replace them with images of Saint Christopher and the Virgin Mary.

> The idols were lowered from their place marvelously well, with good craftsmanship, and they washed the walls. It seemed to the Marquis that, given the outside appearance, there was too little room in the building. He ordered that the front wall be excavated, where they found a deposit of blood, seeds, and an earthenware water jar. They opened it and extracted gold jewels, and there was some gold in a tomb at the top of the tower (Tapia 1963: 70).

In this fragment, it is probable that Tapia, focusing on the presence of the "gold jewels," forgot to mention other objects usually found in this kind of deposit that had no value for him. Although the reference is very brief, it provides valuable information for our purpose.

After a prolonged siege, the Mexica capital fell to the Europeans and was leveled. The conquerors ordered its destruction in order to build a new city over its ruins. One by one, the temples were dismantled, and the images of ancient cults became victims of the religious frenzy. The elimination of any trace of the pre-Hispanic past continued during the entire colonial period. Within a short time, the city was razed by the same indigenous hands that had built it.

Bernal Díaz del Castillo (1982: 194), who participated in the first years of Spanish dominion, gave an exact account of the destruction of the Templo Mayor of Tlatelolco and of the unexpected discovery of offerings.

> From the time we won that fortress and the great city, and the plots of land were distributed, it was proposed that on the site of the great *cu* ["temple"], we should build a church dedicated to our patron and leader, Saint James. Most of the area of the main *cu* was destined for the holy church, and when the foundations were laid bare, in order to make them more solid, they found much gold, silver, jade, pearls, irregular seed pearls, and other precious stones. Similarly, a fellow from Mexico, who had been given another part of the same plot, found the same thing.

On the basis of this testimony, it is logical to suppose that many other people had similar experiences in that period. And from the beginning, the distribution of the wealth from accidentally found offerings created conflicts between the state and the church. As Díaz del Castillo (1982: 194) continued:

> The officials in charge of his majesty's treasury demanded it for his majesty, saying it was his right; and there was a controversy. I do not remember what happened except for the information given by the chiefs and leaders of Mexico and of Guatemuz [Cuauhtemoc], who was still alive then. They said that all the inhabitants of Mexico at that time deposited such jewels and all the rest in the foundations of their temples, and that this was recorded in their books and paintings of ancient things. Because of this, it was retained for the work of the holy Church of Saint James.

During the colonial period, there were also planned explorations for offerings and for pre-Hispanic burials.[1] In some cases, it was the Indians themselves who violated the ancient burial sites, in response to the heavy taxes imposed on them by the colonial government. Toribio Motolinía (Benavente 1971: 26), writing about the plagues that decimated the indigenous population following the arrival of the Spaniards, stated: "The fifth plague was that of the heavy tribute and services imposed on the Indians. Since the Indians had gold, gathered over many years, in their idolatrous temples, in the possession of their lords and leaders, and in their tombs, the Spaniards began to extract great tribute from the natives, and the Indians, terrified after their war with them, gave them whatever they possessed." However, the pillaging was more often the work of the Spaniards. Their searches were not motivated by scientific curiosity but simply by the wish to enrich themselves. We know that innumerable treasure hunters invested huge sums of money in their search for valuable objects in the ancient Mesoamerican territory. Indeed, the systematic European theft of offerings goes back to the days of Juan de Grijalva's 1518 expedition to the Gulf of Mexico.

> Many of these violations occurred at the time of the Conquest, but there were others later, such as the sad story of Captain Figueroa in Oaxaca, who, after acquiring much gold taken from the tombs, sank with his ship, losing both his wealth and his life. These expeditions must have been frequent, and in some cases were legally authorized by the government as shown by a license granted in 1530 to the Count of Osorno, president of the Consejo de Indias, permitting him to locate and open sepulchers for 20 years (Bernal 1979: 40).

In fact, as Ignacio Bernal (1979: 41) pointed out, the plundering of archaeological sites increased to the point where the vice regal government was obliged to legalize the activity, even as it imposed conditions. Apparently, this custom was still in effect in 1774.

In the last years of colonial domination, the ideas of the Enlightenment arrived in New Spain. The novel theories spread rapidly among the Creoles, inspiring the spirit of independence and encouraging a reevaluation of the pre-Hispanic past. At that time, Antonio de León y Gama was probably the most outstanding representative of the vigorous group investigating indigenous life before the Conquest. A physicist and astronomer who was knowledgeable about old monuments, he had the good fortune to examine firsthand numerous remnants of Mexica culture. Most of them had been discovered a short time before, during beautification works in Mexico City as well as other smaller projects. León y Gama (1832: 2nd, 82–83) commented, "Of all that has been found at different parts of the city, while digging ditches for foundations and making other necessary excavations, much has been abandoned as useless by people who are ignorant of their meaning and use at the time of the heathens; but those who have some knowledge and understanding of their history have been able to appreciate them as a fortunate find."

This erudite from New Spain gave careful descriptions of the objects rescued there and also published extensive interpretive studies, such as his *Descripción histórica y cronológica de las dos piedras....* In this monumental work, he gave the most detailed report written until then about an offering. Although León y Gama was not personally present at the discovery made at the Zócalo in January 1791, he described the offering with unusual detail, associating it with the cult to Chantico, the hearth goddess.

A peon named Juan de Dios Morales discovered . . . a sepulcher about 2 varas in length, a little less than a vara in width, made from very well-made tezontle *sillares* ["hewn stone slabs"]. On the inside, filled with very white sand, he found the entire skeleton of an unknown animal, as well as several finely made small clay jars, similar to those of Quautitlan. They contained some copper bells and other trinkets of the same metal. Some people inferred that the large, strong fangs that jutted from the jaws of the animal indicated that it was an extraordinarily large coyote, but I do not know if that conjecture was well founded (León y Gama 1832: 1ˢᵗ, 11–12).

Years later, Alexander von Humboldt (1978: 231) included in his celebrated *Sitios de las cordilleras*. . . . the information given in León y Gama's work, adding the following comment: "It must have been the tomb of a sacred animal, not unusual . . . since the Mexicans built chapels to the wolf, *chantico*; to the tiger, *tlatocaocelotl*; to the eagle, *quetzalhuexolocuauhtli*; and to the snake."

A time of great political turbulence began in the nineteenth century, followed by the struggle for independence and interminable civil wars between federalists and centralists, liberals and conservatives, as well as two tragic foreign interventions. We have not found a single explicit report of explorations of Mexica offerings during that unstable century. However, it is not unlikely that there were discoveries of gifts and that the objects, an easy prey for thieves, augmented both local and foreign archaeological collections. For example, it is quite likely that a good part of the collection accumulated by the Swiss merchant Lukas Vischer between 1828 and 1837, which today forms part of the Ethnographic Museum of Basel, came from the intentional pillaging of offerings (Baer and Bankmann 1990: 11–13). Many of these objects are identical to those found in recent years by the Templo Mayor Project.

EXCAVATIONS IN THE TWENTIETH CENTURY

In the twentieth century, the number of archaeological excavations in the center of Mexico City increased substantially, but data obtained relating to Mexica offerings have been scarce. After a review of field reports compiled in the last ninety years, I find that a large percentage of offerings were examined hurriedly and with the wrong techniques, causing an irreparable loss of information. In general, one cannot determine the chronological development of the works; the accuracy of the information varied. Systematic excavations with good recordings of contexts are limited. Instead, abandoned projects and preliminary reports predominate; in the best of cases, these are kept in the archives of the National Institute of Anthropology and History (INAH). Even worse, the majority of these materials were never analyzed thoroughly. They are still stored, awaiting study.[2]

The same is true for interpretive studies. The few attempts made in this area are chiefly those of historians. Almost all the interpretations are brief and concentrate on the symbolism of specific pieces (usually those of great aesthetic value or with unusual characteristics), without taking into account their association with other objects or monuments. Only recently have researchers attempted broader studies in which the offerings are conceived of as part of major contexts (economic, political, religious, and so on) (Nagao 1985b: 6, 10).

Figure 1:
Discovery number V
made by Leopoldo
Batres, October 16,
1900 (Batres 1902).

A new era of research on Mexica offerings began in 1900 with the work of Leopoldo Batres. Over more than three months, the archaeologist most associated with the Porfirio Díaz period (1876–1911) observed the construction of a sewage system along the ancient street of Escalerillas (now Guatemala Street), between Relox (now Argentina Street) and Santo Domingo (now Brazil Street). During that time, despite serious obstacles, Batres salvaged from the hands of workers and contractors objects belonging to a total of fifteen offerings. It was the richest collection of gifts discovered until then. The results of the excavation, published in a luxurious volume (Batres 1902), were limited to a chronological enumeration of the finds. The focus was on the morphological description of the objects extracted day by day. The descriptions were accompanied by photographs, each one showing, as a trophy of the archaeological enterprise, the aggregate of artifacts belonging to an offering (Figs. 1 and 2). Batres sidestepped, as any of his contemporaries would have done, the importance of stratigraphical and contextual information. He included in his publication a few written references, only three illustrations with oblique views of the objects in situ, and a plan of Escalerillas Street in which the bidimensional coordinates of the finds were marked. The interpretations made by this investigator were short and unsupported. For example, he linked some offerings to cults of the "god of air" and to the "Euterpe [Greek Muse of Music] of the Mexicans."

Batres's discoveries had a great impact on travelers and scholars at the beginning of the century, and comments on his excavations quickly appeared. Antonio Peñafiel (1910) described some of the objects found on Escalerillas Street. Eduard Seler (1903, 1960a; see Nagao 1985b: 6–8) worked out an elaborate study in which he proposed, among other things, to clarify the religious significance of five of the offerings (numbers IV, V, VIII, XXIV, and XXVII) investigated by Batres. With this in mind, he compared the objects found with Mexica sculptures, pictographs, and sources from the

Figure 2:
Two polychrome vessels found by Mrs. Alec Tweedie (1901) and Batres (1902).

sixteenth century, written in the Latin alphabet. In some cases (IV and V), the German sage limited himself to the iconographic identification of unique and elaborate pieces, without taking into account their spatial relationship with other objects in the same deposit. In other cases, he went further in correlating the significance of several gifts in the same offering, linking the whole with cults of specific deities or to periodic rituals. For instance, he suggested that group VIII could be related to the festivals of Tlacaxipehualiztli or Ochpaniztli, group XXIV to the feast of Etzalcualiztli, and group XXVII to the cult of Xochipilli Macuilxochitl. Seler's study is not only a pioneering work in the subject, it is also indispensable for researchers on the religion of the Mexica.

Between 1913 and 1915, Manuel Gamio worked at the intersection of Seminario and Guatemala streets, at a site bordering Batres's explorations. The principal contribution of this excavation was the unexpected discovery of the southwest corner of the Templo Mayor, which disproved numerous hypotheses about the exact location of the building (see Boone 1987). During these excavations, in which stratigraphic techniques were used, an urn "made of stone slabs" was found, containing human skulls. Ceramic receptacles and sculptures, mollusk shells, metallic objects, and quartz beads were also found. Unfortunately, the laconic reports available do not specify the exact location of the objects, nor whether they formed part of an offering (Gamio 1917, 1920, 1979; Noguera 1979).

Twenty years after the Gamio excavations, something similar occurred when Emilio Cuevas started working again at the corner of Seminario and Guatemala. In this case, we also lack the data needed to determine if the excavated objects consisted of discrete groups of gifts. We only know definitely that Cuevas dug a total of eighteen test pits, collecting materials at intervals of 50 cm, in which he recovered artifacts such as knives for human sacrifice, projectile points, prismatic blade cores, and animal and human remains (Cuevas 1934; Noguera 1934).

Eduardo Noguera (1968; see also Solís and Morales 1991) made new discoveries in 1937. That year a great pit was dug at the now-vanished El Volador Square to lay the foundation of what would be the austere Supreme Court of Justice. The discovery of two rich offerings was the most important result of the efforts of this well-known investigator, who, six years before, had found several offerings at Tenayuca (Noguera 1935). The smaller of the two contained a stone vessel; a jar; a *cajete* ("flat earthenware bowl"); a stone urn with many conch shells, shells, coral, greenstone beads, and a rubber ball; and a sculpture with two protuberances on its head, which was identified as an image of the fire god. The larger deposit had more than one thousand vessels of both foreign and local ceramics. As was customary in the archaeology of that period, there was little interest in recording the context: records were limited to a sketch and two oblique photographs, with no scale or directional arrow, in which the objects are vaguely seen in situ. In 1968 Noguera, after analyzing the decoration, style, and function of the artifacts and comparing them with sixteenth-century written sources, concluded that both offerings were part of the ritual of destruction and rebuilding at the time of the New Fire of 1507.

The work of Robert H. Barlow, Antonieta Espejo, and Ponciano Salazar at the ruins of the Templo Mayor of Tlatelolco deserves special mention.[3] Between 1944 and 1945, these investigators unearthed five "type 2" offerings.[4] The records were kept at a very advanced level for that time (Espejo 1945; Martín del Campo 1946; Guil'liem 2003), and the care taken for conservation in the field was outstanding.[5] During the excavations much attention was paid to obtaining a full and complete pictorial record. Espejo's article had different kinds of figures, always accompanied by a scale and a directional arrow: site overhead views and a general profile of the location of the offerings; overhead views, sections, and perspectives, such as oblique photographs of the objects in situ; and photographs of the restored artifacts. In her article, Espejo (1945) explained the way in which a sketch of the plan of an offering was made:

> The method suggested by Doctor Stirling is very simple and practical. After having taken all the coordinates and recording the data in the field notebooks, the objects are removed, placing them in their exact position and sketching them upon a hard surface, preferably a wooden board where the measurement of the box of offerings is traced (we sometimes use paraffin to keep small objects in place), facilitating in this way the exploration of the bottom and the sides of the box and making possible the replacing of the objects in their original position.

Such techniques are not employed today, but because Espejo used them, we have a very complete picture of the original contexts of Tlatelolco.

The description of the offerings is just as precise. For example, the Maertz and Paul color chart, little known at the time, was used. In effect, Espejo, with the assistance of biologists, geologists, and physical anthropologists, indicated for each offering its situation (stratigraphy, location within the building, state of preservation), its description (form, dimensions, fabrication technique, and the orientation of each container), and its contents (quantity, dimensions, technique of manufacture, decoration, state of preservation, and the distribution of the objects, as well as measurements and anomalies of human bones). All these data were provided in a useful, comparative picture (Espejo 1945: fig. 1). Perhaps the only defect in this work is the inadequacy of the interpretive analyses. Espejo barely sketched a supposed association of offerings 1 and 3 with religious ceremonies of the *pochtecayotl* ("merchant guild") of Tlatelolco.

The next recorded finding of Mexica offerings was that of Hugo Moedano Koer and Elma Estrada Balmori in 1948. The description of the find came from a brief report to the Office of Pre-Hispanic Monuments, which was published relatively recently (Estrada Balmori 1979).[6] According to Estrada Balmori, a tunnel was dug in the center of the southern facade of the Templo Mayor for the express purpose of locating an offering. Researchers were greatly surprised when they found not one but two different deposits of gifts. In general, the information about the dig includes complete archaeological descriptions. However, the accompanying diagram is quite sketchy. The principal characteristics of each object (function, raw material used, dimensions, manufacturing technique, state of preservation) and its location (coordinates, orientation, associations) are provided. The physical anthropologist Johanna Faulhaber was in charge of the analysis of bones.

In the 1960s a new and ambitious project was carried out in Tlatelolco. The principal objective was to remove the debris from a large part of the Tlatelolcan Sacred Precinct, a site that would be integrated into the project of the Plaza de las Tres Culturas. For reasons unknown to us, the results published about the explorations of several years were poor and fragmentary (López Luján 1989a; Matos Moctezuma 1988a): there are only indirect references to the offerings recovered,[7] together with some descriptions of isolated objects that probably were gifts (see Flores García 1970; González Rul 1979, 1988).

An exception to this general trend toward incomplete recording was Jorge Angulo Villaseñor's publication (Angulo 1966b).[8] In fact, Angulo gave us one of the most complete investigations until now. In 1966 this archaeologist and restorer salvaged an offering under very difficult circumstances. Because of the haste necessitated by the construction of a sewage drain, he was forced to cover the collection of objects with cheesecloth and plaster in order to extract them in a single block. This allowed him to remove and conserve them in the laboratory with all the care they deserved. His meticulous efforts are reflected in his publication. There we find complete technical catalog cards on each object, iconographic identification, specific identification of animal remains, and two plausible interpretations of the whole. Angulo very cautiously suggested that the offering might be related to the "four hours" of the day or, if not, to the feast of Izcalli. Ten photographs and two sketches of the site clearly show the methods used in extracting the offering, the distribution of the objects in situ, and several isolated artifacts.

Several months after the excavations in Tlatelolco, Angulo, accompanied by Eduardo Contreras, participated in another important find, this time at the Tenochcan Templo Mayor, first discovered by Gamio. While they were consolidating the passageways and installing a walkway, they noticed a stain on a stucco floor. This circular dark stain clearly indicated a rich offering, from which 116 objects were obtained. The fieldwork of excavation, conservation, and recording took two weeks, and during this time, many photographs were taken and an overhead view was made, showing the objects near the surface in situ. Two preliminary reports about this offering were published, thirteen years apart (Angulo 1966a; Contreras 1979b), but neither report provides interpretations.

New and intense explorations of Mexico City took place between 1967 and 1970. Due to the construction of lines 1 and 2 of the subway, a unique opportunity was offered to bring to light the vestiges of ancient Tenochtitlan. Along two trenches 8 m wide, 8 m deep, and several kilometers in length, an unimaginable number of architectural structures, monumental sculptures, sumptuous offerings, and isolated objects were found. "Prehispanic and colonial structures about which nothing was known were revealed, and materials *in situ* were obtained, as well as those recovered in the mechanical excavation" (*Enciclopedia de México* 1977).

This citation, as well as the testimony of various witnesses, indicates that many of the precious objects were destroyed due to the ignorance of the workers. Other pieces met a different fate, becoming objects of illicit trade. With a small group of assistants, archaeologist Jordi Gussinyer, commissioned by the Archaeological Salvage Department of the INAH, fought at the site against the systematic destruction of the patrimony, noting: "The excavation was difficult because of the short time at our disposal. However, the main difficulty was the lack of support by the resident engineers and, above all, the lack of understanding they showed for our work. They were always placing obstacles in our way during the entire task of salvage" (Gussinyer 1968).

In spite of these obstacles, Gussinyer carried out salvage operations from the intersection of Izazaga and Pino Suárez streets to that of Guatemala and Brazil streets. At both corners, he succeeded in getting abundant contextual information, which he published in a fragmentary way in the *Boletín del INAH*. The finding of at least twenty-one offerings is reported there. Sixteen offerings were found at the corner of Izazaga and Pino Suárez, three in structure A, ten in structure L, and three more along Izazaga. Unfortunately, we only know the approximate location of seven of them (Gussinyer 1968: 16, plans 1, 2, 1969, 1970a: 9–12 and fig. 7, 1970b). Five offerings were found on the corner of Brazil and Guatemala (Gussinyer 1972: 20–22, 1979). It is probable that the artifacts located at the intersection of Izazaga and 20 de Noviembre streets are also ritual offerings (Mateos Higuera 1979). However, Gussinyer's reports are very uneven in quality. Although there is a description of the content and context of some offerings, including abundant graphic material, only the existence and approximate location of others were mentioned. His only interpretation of this material focused on the iconographic identification of an anthropomorphic sculpture (Gussinyer 1970b; Heyden 1970).

There are vague references to the discovery of offerings when the foundations of the Metropolitan Cathedral and Sanctuary were reinforced. We know that between 1975 and 1976, 182 tunnels were drilled to reinforce those buildings and that the remains of several Mexica structures were encountered (see Vega Sosa 1979). "Along with the structures, many important offerings appeared. Many were found at the foot of the stairs and before and around altars. When all of them are studied, they will help interpret the function of the foundations and determine to what deities they were dedicated" (Cabrera 1979:56). Only one such cache of gifts is described in reports of archaeological works (Cabrera 1979: 57).

Finally, I will mention the rescue of the circular monolith of Coyolxauhqui—the Moon goddess—at the corner of Argentina and Guatemala streets. The fortuitous finding of this sculpture occurred on February 21, 1978, when workers from the light and power company drilled a hole a few meters from Gamio's excavations. When the discovery was announced, Raúl M. Arana and Angel García Cook, from the Department of Salvage Archaeology, took charge. During a period of seven weeks, a small team of archaeologists and restorers freed the monolith from the debris and recovered materials belonging to five offerings.[9] The preliminary report on the excavations, published in August of that year, contained complete technical descriptions, although it lacked precise drawings of the spatial distribution of the artifacts in situ (García Cook 1978).

The results of the archaeological, osteological, and biological analyses were published some months later (Blanco 1978; Carramiñana 1988; García Cook 1978; Peña Gómez 1978; González Rul 1997).

The discovery of offerings in the historical center of Mexico City continues. Recently, there have been new discoveries on the Zócalo and on Palma, Venustiano Carranza, Moneda, Guatemala, Argentina, and Venezuela streets, as well as in Tlatelolco. (see Hernández Pons 1997; Guil'liem 1999, 2003; Matos Moctezuma 1999, 2000, 2004; Matos Moctezuma et al. 1998; López Arenas 2004).

CHAPTER TWO

The Templo Mayor Project and the Excavation of Offerings: 1978–1991

THE PROJECT AND ITS INNOVATIONS

The shift from the salvage of haphazard discoveries to excavations directed at resolving preestablished problems dates from 1978, the year the Temple Mayor Project was begun by the INAH (Matos Moctezuma 1979b).[1] This project began with the accidental discovery of the Coyolxauhqui monolith, but from the very beginning, a meticulous plan of work was drawn up and a general hypothesis was proposed, which we would try to corroborate through our fieldwork.

In 1978 Mexico experienced a brief period of economic bonanza, due chiefly to the finding and intensive exploitation of oil. The discovery of the moon goddess sculpture in February of that year coincided with that fleeting moment, resulting in one of the most ambitious excavations of recent decades. José López Portillo, president of the republic at that time, visited the site where Coyolxauhqui lay. Fascinated, he observed it carefully and said,

> That February 28, 1978, I felt my full power. I could, if I wished, transform the reality that hid the fundamental roots of my Mexico, precisely at the original center of its history, the mystic sphere of her still unresolved, dialectic tragedy. It seemed to me to be an opportunity to advance its integration, at least as a symbol, and to set up a "twin" plaza to the colonial Zócalo of our independence, so that all Mexicans would understand that we came from Omeyocan—the place of two—a place that we have to accept in order to stand tall and walk on two feet [the Spanish and the Indian] toward

Figure 3:
The Templo Mayor and the Metropolitan Cathedral. (Photograph by Michael Calderwood, courtesy INAH.)

the paths of our future, accepting our mixture as a condition and a source of origin and destiny (López Portillo et al. 1981).[2]

As a result, López Portillo offered unusual support for the complete retrieval of the remains of the Templo Mayor, at the cost of demolishing what he considered to be a "boring accumulation of old, secular, and replaceable urban life" (López Portillo et al. 1981). The financial collaboration

of powerful private enterprises, especially the Fundación Amparo Rugarcía de Espinosa, complemented this controversial presidential caprice. Only in this way could such a project, inconceiv-
able today, have been planned and carried out (Fig. 3).

Fortunately, the members of the INAH knew how to channel the presidential mandate,
devising a strictly scientific archaeological project of great scope. A month later, a small recovery
team belonging to the Department of Salvage Archaeology was replaced by a much larger interdisciplinary group, directed by archaeologist Eduardo Matos Moctezuma.

As a general working hypothesis in line with his own views, Matos Moctezuma (1979b,
1982b) proposed in 1978 that the phenomenological appearance of the Templo Mayor should cor-
relate with the essential causes that led to its construction. In his opinion, the presence of Tlaloc
and Huitzilopochtli in the Templo Mayor—the real and the symbolic seat of Mexica power—was
a superstructural reflection of the economic foundation of that society. The Mexica based their
sustenance fundamentally on agriculture and obtaining tribute from other peoples by military might.
As a result, their economy fostered a cult to the god of water and to a solar, warrior god at their
principal temple in Tenochtitlan. "In the case of the Templo Mayor project we are aware that it
presents a unique opportunity to study an example of Mexica formation, the superstructural, upon
which our project focused, without losing sight of the other areas that compose the social whole,
all of it viewed objectively" (Matos Moctezuma 1979b).

Matos Moctezuma then turned to the task of searching for those manifestations that would
prove his general hypothesis. He was certain that if it were correct, the monoliths and the archaeological material of the offerings, as well as the myths and rituals documented in the sources, would
reflect both the ideology of the dominant group and the military subjugation of other societies.

Like all the large Mexican projects in the 1970s, the Templo Mayor Project included specialists from very diverse areas of knowledge, who combined their best efforts to achieve their mutual
objectives. The new project was organized into five external consultation and support groups and
two internal groups more directly involved in excavation. The first group encompassed the following units (Matos Moctezuma 1979b: 22–23, 26):

1. *Ethnohistory.* Coordinated by Barbro Dahlgren, this unit was responsible for the analysis of information about the Templo Mayor contained in documental sources, and it
produced a monumental anthology (Dahlgren, Pérez Rocha, Suárez Díez, and Valle
de Revueltas 1982).

2. *Historical Monuments.* Headed by Efraín Castro, this unit was responsible for providing information referring to the colonial history of the area.

3. *Laboratories in the Department of Prehistory.* Directed by Lorena Mirambell, this
unit was in charge of dating and petrographic, edaphologic, paleobotanic, and pale-
ozoological analyses.

4. *Physical Anthropology.* Coordinated by Arturo Romano, this unit was in charge of
the osteological analysis of human remains.

Figure 4:
Aerial view of the excavated area. (Courtesy Compañía Mexicana de Aerofoto.)

5. *Soil Mechanics.* Directed by Samuel Ruiz, this unit was responsible for watching the stability of colonial and modern buildings near the excavation area.

Internally, the Templo Mayor Project was divided into two broad areas. The first involved administration, and the second was split into three groups for excavation and six for internal support. Each of the excavation sections had the task of uncovering a portion of the Templo Mayor, in a job that involved about six hundred laborers during its most intense phase (Matos Moctezuma 1979b, 1982c; Matos Moctezuma and Rangel 1982). Section 1, directed by Matos Moctezuma, was in charge of excavating the south and west faces of the building, which extended from the area excavated by Gamio to a parking lot south of Guatemala Street. Section 2, directed by Eduardo Contreras, would excavate the east face, starting from the parking lot of the Secretaría de Hacienda y Crédito Público. Section 3, headed by Hortencia de Vega, would have the task of uncovering the north face, which began at a vacant lot on Justo Sierra Street (Fig. 4).

As stated earlier, there were also six internal supporting sections: Conservation and Restoration, which had a field laboratory;[3] Control of Materials;[4] Photography with a field laboratory;[5] Drawing;[6] Ceramics;[7] and Special Studies.[8]

Once the interdisciplinary staff had been organized, the investigation was divided into three phases (Matos Moctezuma 1982c):

1. An exhaustive compilation and study of the Templo Mayor in historical sources and in the reports from archaeological excavations carried out in the area. Three useful anthologies resulted from this phase (Matos Moctezuma 1979a, 1981c, 1986b).

Figure 5:
First exploration of the Templo Mayor. In the background to the right can be seen the now nonexistent Ethnographic Museum. (Photograph by Salvador Guil'liem, courtesy INAH.)

2. The excavation, carried out principally from March 1978 to November 1982, although work of less importance was done from July to September 1987 and in January and February of 1989. The publications resulting from this phase were a summary of information and research (Matos Moctezuma 1982a) and monthly plans of the advancing excavation (Matos Moctezuma and Rangel 1982).

3. The third and last phase: the analysis and interpretation of the information obtained in Phases 1 and 2. Many works have been published as a result, both by members of the project and by other researchers who have been invited to collaborate on some specific topic.[9] It is likely the third phase will continue for many more years.

The Templo Mayor Project fieldwork began April 15, 1978, only eight weeks after the discovery of the Coyolxauhqui sculpture. From the beginning, the criterion of no reconstruction, contained in the Charter of Venice, was respected. To maintain adequate control of the findings, the area for archaeological work was divided into a rectangular excavation grid, composed of 4-m² squares. Each square was designated by a capital letter (along the E-W axis) and an Arabic numeral (along the N-S axis). The datum point was set at one of the corners of the structure, 2,235.91 m above sea level.

The first months of exploration were marked by a dispute over the projected demolition of buildings covering the Templo Mayor. The ancient quarrels between the indigenists and the Hispanicists were revived, and polemics proliferated between protectors of the cultural patrimony who held antagonistic views. Meanwhile, the excavation was restricted to three lots, which had been used for parking before their expropriation.[10] In several sessions, at which the historical and artistic value of the area was discussed, the Junta Consultiva de Monumentos of the INAH ruled in favor of demolishing a total of thirteen buildings (Matos Moctezuma 1982c)—nine constructed between 1930 and 1950,[11] two built in the nineteenth century and altered in the twentieth,[12] and two others built between the end of the Conquest and the twentieth century.[13] It should be noted here that some architectural details of these monuments were carefully removed and taken to the Office of Historical Monuments (Fig. 5).

During the fifty-eight months of fieldwork, the members of the Templo Mayor Project dug extensively in an area of 1.29 hectares (3.19 acres).[14] The excavations partially affected two blocks, bounded by the streets of Justo Sierra, Moneda, República Argentina, República de Guatemala, Seminario, Licenciado Verdad, and Correo Mayor. The important findings in the area have made us revise many ideas about Mexica society, and they will be an invaluable resource for future researchers. Among the most outstanding discoveries were: fifteen structures (some with several expansions) and 110 offerings (containing more than seven thousand elements),[15] as well as an enormous number of sculptures, mural paintings, fragments of ceramics, and other remains.

In the last few years, the staff directed by Matos Moctezuma has continued its work in research and the dissemination of information. In 1982 the archaeological zone was prepared to make it accessible to tourists. Dismountable walkways and lightweight roofs were built over the ruins of the Mexica buildings,[16] and explanatory signs were posted along the circuits. Since then, the pre-Hispanic structures have undergone intensive conservation treatment, and some sculptures have been stored and replaced by reproductions.[17] Finally, in October 1987, the site museum was opened, and the treasures found in the excavations are now exhibited there in eight halls. Over the last few years, the new building has become the center of the Templo Mayor Project.

THE ARCHAEOLOGICAL TECHNIQUES OF EXCAVATION AND RECORDING

The Templo Mayor Project was characterized by the close cooperation of different kinds of specialists. Among them, the conservators and the archaeologists were in the closest contact. In fact, the technical procedures followed by the conservators and the archaeologists were so interwoven that one group rarely worked without the assistance of the other. However, for practical reasons, I will describe the work of each group separately.

In April 1978 the staff began using a technique for the exploration of offerings that was designed to obtain better information for future research. Obviously, our future investigations would depend to a large extent on the methods used for obtaining adequate and uniform data. The procedure was so careful that work on a single offering sometimes lasted several months.

A total of twenty-four archaeologists[18] participated in the discovery and salvage of 110 offerings between April 1978 and February 1989. Experienced manual laborers, most of whom had worked in other archaeological projects, also collaborated in these efforts.[19]

The finding of offerings became a daily event for the members of the project due to the great number discovered in a relatively small space. Indeed, 110 offerings were found in an area of slightly more than 1 hectare, and when the structures were being unearthed, offerings were

Figure 6:
The circular cracking and color of this stucco floor reveal the existence of offering 10. (Photograph by Salvador Guil'liem, courtesy INAH.)

encountered everywhere. There were several clues to guide the exploration. In some cases, the stucco floors under which the objects lay revealed fractures, sinking, or a different color (Fig. 6). In other cases, an imminent discovery was indicated by the appearance of artifacts in the filling used in the building or on the top sillares of the offering boxes. Once the existence of an offering was confirmed, the boundaries around the area of archaeological material were marked. This was a simple task in the case of offerings contained in the stone boxes or deposited in cavities dug under the stucco floors. Difficulties multiplied if the objects had been deposited among earth and rocks between one building stage and another.

After the boundaries of the offering had been determined, the archaeologists marked the offering on the excavation grid and located it on the master plan. Then its horizontal (x and y) coordinates were recorded on the grid, and its height (z) was calculated relative to the datum point. The offering was then given a name. Almost all offerings were given an Arabic number corresponding to the chronological order of their discovery.[20] However, Matos Moctezuma decided that the offerings found in the North Patio would differ from the others and would be designated by a capital letter.[21]

Before the excavation actually began, some preparatory work was done. First, overhead and cross-sectional views were created, using a 1:10 scale of the zone where the offering had been deposited. Meanwhile, a wood and canvas covering was made; this would protect objects from being stolen during the night, shield them from bad weather, and also allow work to continue in case of rain. Then, on the stucco floor or on a corner of the box, the point of origin (o) from which the coordinates of objects were calculated was marked with a nail: hypothetically, the horizontal x-axis (N-S) and the horizontal y-axis (E-W) intersected there with the vertical z-axis (relative to the datum point level). Finally, photographs were taken, and the stones or slabs that covered the objects were sketched (Wagner 1982).

Figure 7: The archaeologist Diana Wagner excavated offering 11. (Photograph by Salvador Guil'liem, courtesy INAH.)

Figure 8:
General view of the first level of Chamber 3's excavation. (Photograph by Salvador Guil'liem, courtesy INAH.)

Only after completing these steps did the actual salvaging of the deposit begin. Usually, the objects offered by the Mexica were laid one above the other at different vertical levels, a situation that forced the archaeologists to repeat the registration routine at every level. The objects near the surface were given the number 1, those in the next level under it were assigned the number 2, and so on until the lowest level had been reached.

Often the vertical division made by the archaeologist was arbitrary and did not correspond to that of the Mexica. This happened because we only considered objects that were completely visible as belonging to the same level. At times, objects that did not appear clearly on photographs and drawings, although they were part of the preceding level, were recorded at the next lower level. Thus there are clear differences between pre-Hispanic levels and the present levels of excavation.

Exploration consisted of removing the earth and rocks that covered the archaeological material at each level. The space around the offering was normally so small that only one person at a time could work there (Fig. 7). To make sure that work was careful and methodical, the excavation progressed slowly in units of less than 400 cm² (20 cm x 20 cm). Each object detected was cleared little by little until it was fully visible. The basic instruments used were the ones most suited to removing earth in close spaces: small spoons, spatulas, scalpels, probes, bone sticks, dissection needles, sprinklers, fine-haired brushes, artist's paint brushes, and small tweezers. The result of this careful approach was a complete view of the objects in situ at every level, which allowed an examination of spatial associations (Fig. 8).[22]

Once the objects on a given level had been cleaned, the information was recorded. First, the Photography Section took vertical and oblique pictures of the aggregate, as well as of any interesting details. To do this, 35-mm and 6 x 6 cameras, color and black-and-white film, and various systems of lighting were used. Care was taken to ensure that an arrow would be visible in each picture, together with a metric scale showing the cardinal direction and a slate giving the data on the photographic registration.[23]

Afterward, the archaeologists in charge would write their field diaries, and these would later serve as the bases for weekly and monthly reports. The diary recorded the facts related to the contextual location of the offering, the characteristics of the structure containing it, the characteristics of the matrix that covered the material, the quantity and quality of the objects extracted, their tridimensional location, the excavation level to which they belonged, their orientation, their spatial association, and their state of preservation.

Drawing took the most time because of the effort to make the representations as accurate as possible. Usually, in making the drawing, thread, a bubble level, a plumb line, and metric tape were used or, instead, a grid of thread, mounted on an aluminum frame. At each level, a 1:10 scale drawing was made on millimetric draft paper. Then a sheet of transparent paper was placed over the overhead view; upon this, the number of each object and the maximum and minimum depths ($z+$ and $z-$) relative to the point of origin (o) was recorded. The cross section and profile drawings (also at a 1:10 scale) were then created, using the N-S and E-W axes to show the vertical superposition of the objects. Later, all the illustrations of each offering were given to the Drawing Section, where the general plan, the overhead views for the levels, the cross section, and the profiles were drawn in ink and put on a single sheet that combined the graphic information obtained in situ. Sketches of the restored artifacts were also made in the Drawing Section.

The removal of materials was the last step at each level. As the exhumation took place, information was set down on tabular sheets that would be attached to the field diary. There the following data for each item were recorded: the number of the element according to the order of its extraction, a description of the object's form and function, the raw material used, the fabrication techniques, the object's dimensions (length, width, and thickness), its tridimensional location, the level of excavation, the object's association with other objects, the number of the overhead view where it was sketched, other observations, the date of extraction, and the name of the person in charge. At the same time, two labels were made for each object, upon which were written the number of the offering, a description of the contents of the bag or box, the number of the element, the level, the date, and the person responsible. Depending on the object's type, size, weight, and state of preservation, plastic bottles, cardboard boxes lined with cotton, polyethylene bags, or aluminum foil wrappings were used as containers.

The soil removed during the process of excavation and extraction was passed through several different sizes of sieves to recover very small objects and to record the levels to which they belonged.

The objects removed were taken to the Control of Materials Section, where they were assigned an entry number in the general registry and where basic information about them was recorded. Then, depending on the particular case, the object was sent to the Restoration Section, to the Warehouse for Cultural Objects from the project, or to the paleozoology, paleobotany, geology, or dating laboratories, located at that time in the Department of Prehistory of the INAH.

In this way, the basic procedure for excavation at each level came to an end. The process was repeated until the deposit was exhausted. Once it was finished, the general features of the containing structure were recorded, and a sounding of 1 m in depth was made to be sure that nothing remained in the deposit and to determine if another offering might exist below it.

CONSERVATION AND RESTORATION TECHNIQUES

The tasks of conservation and restoration were carried on simultaneously with the excavation. They were done in the archaeological zone, as well as in the field laboratory installed for the purpose in one of the nearby buildings.

Certain physical and chemical conditions in the contexts caused severe deterioration in the objects offered there, a situation that required the speedy cooperation of conservators at the very moment they were found. The degree of damage varied a great deal from one object to another. It seemed that time had no effect on some of them; on others, it caused serious changes in their physical characteristics: deformation, cracks, fractures, separations, or a different coloring from the original. Deterioration was more noticeable in pieces that had undergone changes in their chemical structure through oxidation, hydrolysis, carbonization, organic decomposition, or a similar cause. In extreme cases, some organic materials, such as textiles or feathers, disappeared altogether. We know they existed in the past because of imprints left on the matrices of the deposits.

Three principal factors caused the changes suffered by objects buried over centuries: the characteristics of the earth matrix, the high degree of humidity, and the strong pressure of the upper strata (see Franco Brizuela 1987; Santaella 1982).

Without exception, all the offerings were found inside religious structures. These distinct collections of gifts were contained—either directly or indirectly—in an architectural matrix composed of stones of volcanic origin and a clay-mud material taken from the bed of Lake Texcoco. The soil of the lake was very fine and slightly acid, and it had a high percentage of salts and organic matter; its pH varied between 5 and 6.5, which restrained microbial activity.[24] These factors were the reason why some calcareous archaeological materials, such as bones and marine shells, lost their bonding material and were weakened and sometimes pulverized.

The high level of the water table was another important factor in the deterioration for the underground aquifers are comparatively near the surface in the center of Mexico City. After several years of excavation, we could verify that the rise and fall of their levels were determined by the seasonal variation in rainfall. Because of infiltration and capillary phenomena,[25] water was found everywhere throughout the archaeological zone. It was not unusual to find it less than 15 cm underneath the pre-Hispanic floors. Some offerings were completely submerged, making their recovery extremely difficult. It can be inferred that the archaeological pieces remained for centuries, in an ambiance of high humidity, which at present varies from 60 to 70 percent. In such an environment, some greenstone materials underwent hydrolysis, making them more porous and increasing their fragility. Now the water level of the archaeological zone is stabilized at approximately 4 m in depth by means of a pumping system.

Moreover, the high pressure due to the fill of the architectural expansions during the Mexica period and the construction of colonial and modern buildings caused serious deformation and

Figure 9: Preventive conservation measures in situ. (Photograph by Salvador Guil'liem, courtesy INAH.)

fractures to several offerings. The deposits inside stone boxes were the least affected by the weight of upper layers. Other damaging factors must also be taken into account. There was the settling of the subsoil, earthquake movements, the vibration produced by intense vehicular traffic in the center of the city, temperature changes, and the damage caused by rodents, moss, and fungus.

The routine activities of the conservators of the Templo Mayor Project were divided into: preventive measures for conservation in situ, removal of objects, transportation of objects to the laboratory, and complete treatment for conservation and restoration at the field laboratory (Santaella 1982). Of course, their work depended upon the particular condition of each object recovered. Examples of specific problems are given by Bárbara Hasbach Lugo (1982a, 1982b), Franco Brizuela (1982, 1987), Mercado (1982), Gallardo (1999), Grimaldi (2001) and Marín (2001).

A total of nineteen conservators participated in the work of conservation in situ.[26] Their presence was invaluable. All of them worked diligently to keep the recovered material from suffering more damage, in addition to that undergone during the enormous expanse of time in which they lay buried. It should be mentioned that after a long process of physicochemical transformation, these remains of cultural activity had achieved an equilibrium with the atmosphere where they existed. After being removed, they were exposed to new conditions of humidity, temperature, and light, and as a result, the homeostasis between object and surroundings was broken, reactivating the process of degradation. In this sense, archaeological work inevitably has a destructive effect. But the conservators at the project were always there to minimize deterioration and to avoid the loss of archaeological evidence.

There was a constant interplay between the work of conservation and purely archaeological efforts. Often, the archaeologists had to suspend their tasks so first aid could be given to objects being discovered. Preventive measures were taken practically from the moment the stucco floor that covered the deposit was removed, and a careful maneuver ensured the replacement of the piece of floor after the deposit was emptied. In the case of fragile objects or painted ones, it was the conservators themselves who removed them and cleaned them in situ (Santaella 1982). A thorough cleansing of dirt and salts by spraying with ethanol or distilled water made a magnificent photographic record possible.

Because of the slowness of the excavation process, different kinds of coverings were used to avoid prolonged exposure of the archaeological material to the sun, rain, wind, or dust. Upon contact with the atmosphere, unprotected excavated objects would be exposed to a rapid drying out that could cause internal pressures and changes in size. However, the rapid loss of moisture was prevented by covering objects with damp flannel or other cloth or by directly applying drops of distilled water with an eyedropper. Conversely, if there was excessive dampness in the atmosphere, a fungicide was applied to stop the development of microorganisms on the archaeological material.

When the object showed signs of fragility, lack of cohesion, exfoliation, or pulverization, it had to be consolidated. Usually, an acrylic resin was applied with a common brush, an artist's brush, or a pipette.[27] This solidifying emulsion or solution was very diluted to ensure complete penetration into the object (Fig. 9).

Each conservator had to prepare a technical label describing the preventive work in the field. On it were included archaeological data (location of the offering, description, context,

PROYECTO TEMPLO MAYOR
CONSERVACION DE MATERIALES

FICHA_____
OFRENDA _____
No. ELEMENTO _____
No. ENTRADA _____
No. REGISTRO _____

SECCION_____UNIDAD_____CUADRO_____NIVEL DE OFRENDA _____
PROFUNDIDAD_____ASOCIACION _____

DESCRIPCION DEL OBJETO_____

DIMENSIONES_____MAT. PRIMA_____FECHA:_____
A) descubrimiento_____
B) levantamiento_____

DECORACION _____
PIGMENTO: SI   NO   LOCALIZACION:_____

ESTADO DE CONSERVACION _____

MATRIZ
PH_____HUMEDAD_____CARBONATOS_____SULFATOS_____
FOSFATOS_____TEXTURA_____COLOR_____DENSIDAD_____

TRATAMIENTO IN SITU

MATERIA PRIMA	MATERIAL USADO	PROPORCION SOLVENTE	OBSERVACIONES	FECHA	FIRMA

RECOMENDACIONES: _____

ARQUEOLOGO CON QUE SE TRABAJO   CONSERVADOR RESPONSABLE

Figure 10:
Record for conservation in situ.

registration number, and the person in charge), as well as facts relating to conservation (state, diagnosis, procedure pursued, materials used, proportions, and recommendations for future treatment) (Fig. 10). Only then did the dislodgement of material begin. The conservators intervened when the remains were in poor condition or in the case of objects made up of certain elements (skeletons, mosaics, maguey thorns) that required retention of a particular spatial relationship. Depending on the circumstances, one of three extraction processes was followed: freeing the object by placing metal plates beneath it, using the facing technique (*velado*),[28] or raising the object by means of a plaster covering. Several times, it was necessary to extract the entire container of sillares and remove the offering in the laboratory. In that case, the box was excavated around its

TRATAMIENTO EN TALLER

ANTECEDENTES (Cuando la pieza fue tratada in situ y no se registraron los datos en el anverso): _____

_____

_____

_____

MATERIAL PRIMA	MATERIAL USADO	PROPORCION SOLVENTE	OBSERVACIONES	FECHA	FIRMA

RECOMENDACIONES: _____

_____

_____

FECHA FIN DE PROCESO	RESTAURADOR RESPONSABLE

Figure 11:
Record for conservation in the workshop.

outside periphery, its sides were protected by padding, it was bound with wire, and it was then taken out of its context (Bertha Peña Tenorio, pers. comm., Dec. 1989).

Transportation of the objects was no great problem, considering how near the field laboratory was. The conservators usually made the transfer on foot. In the laboratory, the preventive measures begun in situ were completed, and an entire restoration treatment was given. The first step was a gradual drying of the piece: it was wrapped with polyethylene or damp flannel, then placed next to vessels containing water. When a slower process was required, the object was left for several weeks in a humidification chamber, reducing the percentage of water until it reached 50 percent. During this time, a fungicide was applied to prevent the growth of microorganisms.

When the drying was complete, the conservators performed a second deep and complete cleaning. To remove the dirt, they used sprayers and brushes, distilled water, ethyl alcohol, and a nonionic detergent. They also removed soluble salts[29] and did away with fungus stains.[30] If some fragments had separated from their original support, they were glued together with polyvinyl acetate.[31]

A consolidation of the structure followed.[32] This could be done either at specific places with an artist's brush or an eyedropper or completely by immersion. Consolidant residues were later removed with a scalpel and brush.

In the case of a fragmented piece, the conservator joined the fragments with reversible glues, using presses if deformations appeared.[33] Afterward, the defects and the joinings of the piece were filled and retouched,[34] restoring the original color to each part.[35] Finally, the record of the treatment and restoration (clinical history) was completed, and the article was sent to the Cultural Objects Warehouse (Fig. 11) (see Franco Brizuela 1987).

SEVERAL FOCI OF THE STUDY OF OFFERINGS

In three different periods of fieldwork (1978–1982, 1987, and 1989), a total of 110 offerings were located, distributed among the plazas and the principal buildings (Matos Moctezuma 1987b). In 1983 after the end of the first period of excavations, the Templo Mayor Project team started to analyze the data, and we realized that, in order to research the offerings, the investigators should take into account at least one of the following aspects:

1. *Economic.* The source, manufacture, and circulation of the deposited artifacts; the natural habitat and ways of obtaining the flora and fauna; the age, sex, ethnic affiliation, and possible pathologies of the buried individuals.

2. *Historic.* The particular historical moment in which offerings were given and its effect on the way they were offered.

3. *Religious.* The religious significance of the objects and of the aggregates of offerings and the offering architecture and offering-ritual relationships.

Thus from among the possible choices, two important paths emerged for future research (see Matos Moctezuma 1982b). The first would entail a review of the elements offered at the Templo Mayor that would lead us to a better understanding of the structures and the economic and political dynamics of Mexica society. That is, an analysis of the techniques of manufacture and of the derivation, style, and richness of the materials would increase our knowledge of the ways in which political power was produced among the Mexica and of the relationship over time between Tenochtitlan and other Mesoamerican states (see Rees 1989; Velázquez 1999; Athié 2001; Aguirre 2002; Victoria 2004; López Luján 2005). Another possibility for research would be an examination of the composition and placement of the offerings, which would provide a better understanding of the ideology of the society. The offering is an important part of a ritual moment, and it reflects a code that would be an invaluable source of information if we understood it. Apparently, the vast majority of elements belonging to the 110 offerings we found and unearthed were placed there in strict sequence. Today, unfortunately, we know so little about pre-Hispanic societies that the complexity of the offerings is overwhelming, and a complete interpretation of them is unattainable. Semiotics would certainly help us to understand the ideological value of the elements and of the whole.

A team of investigators from the Templo Mayor Project has begun several studies on the offerings. An important component is a plan for a computerized database in which the enormous accumulation of textual and graphic information generated by archaeologists, conservators, photographers, artists, biologists, geologists, and other specialists will be stored (Jiménez Badillo and López Luján 1989; Jiménez Badillo 1997, 2004). This will, in the near term, allow us to do fast, exhaustive, and systematic analyses. Also in progress are studies about the meaning of the richest and most complex offerings (see Schulze 1997; Del Olmo 1999; Olmedo 2001; Chávez 2002; López Luján 2005), as well as a detailed examination of animal remains (see Polaco 1991; Guzmán and Polaco 2001).

In the following chapters, I offer a first attempt at organizing the general data about the 110 offerings recovered during the last fifty years in the area of the Templo Mayor. It is focused chiefly on the second of the areas mentioned earlier, that is, on the analyses of the composition and placement of the offerings, with the goal of discovering their significance and their ideological value. Readers are thus warned that they will not find, in the following pages, the technological and economical information that is also available from the gifts of the Templo Mayor.

CHAPTER THREE

The Offerings and Ritual Ceremonies

THE OFFERINGS IN THE MESOAMERICAN RELIGIOUS CONTEXT

Each offering should be analyzed as part of a complex of social relationships regulated and expressed in a ritual act, within the framework of a specific religion. This framework has time and interpretive limits. In its strictest sense, it is the Mexica religion, characterized by a mere two centuries of existence in a Mesoamerican society undergoing a rapid process of hegemonic expansion. In a larger sense, the framework is the Mesoamerican religion, following a tradition that goes back to the first agrarian societies and that extended over a vast territory.

The characteristics of Mesoamerican religion are difficult to define due to the religion's breadth. Rather than a collection of elements unchangeable in time and space, it must be seen as a current of concepts and practices in continuous, multisecular evolution and with notable regional differences. For this reason, in spite of the fact that religion is one of the historical aspects that has received the most attention from Mesoamericanists, there are few works that deal with it in a global way and with sufficient depth (see D. Carrasco 1990; López Austin 1990b, 1998).

Because it is necessary to place the study of the offerings in proper historical context, I will cite some of the general elements of Mesoamerican religion that are agreed upon by various experts.

1. Mesoamerican religion touched practically every aspect of social life. It regulated everything from the most insignificant daily acts to relations among the different political entities (Soustelle 1982: 27).

31

2. The regulating nature of Mesoamerican religion in all social relationships made it a very complex institution and difficult to understand from the Western point of view (Conrad and Demarest 1988: 34–35).

3. It was a religion that developed, became strong, and was dogmatized in direct proportion to the increase in social complexity and governmental organization.

4. From the beginning and as one of its most important characteristics, Mesoamerican religion encouraged the faithful to believe in a constant and direct relationship between the human being and the divinities. Ecstatic states were frequent. Mysticism was developed in various ways, and many supernatural situations were attributed to divine possession (López Austin 1988c: vol. 1, 354–55).

5. In spite of individual and familial relationships with the gods, as time went by the government tended to institutionalize and control the principal communal forms of the cult.

6. According to Mesoamerican religious concepts, divine beings were omnipresent in the cosmos, and they were manifested in all the processes of nature as heterogeneous forces in conflict. This led to extreme polytheism. However, the divine personalities did not have sharp boundaries. They were thought to be capable of division and fusion (Thompson 1975: 246–49; López Austin 1983).

7. One of the gods' most important forms of action was their appearance in the world as forces of time. This explains the obsession of Mesoamerican devotees with calendric cycles and hierophanies (Thompson 1978: 59–69).

8. Because of this, Mesoamerican rituals must be understood as ways by which human beings confronted even the most minimal and daily cosmic processes. The rituals were directed toward divine appearances, both "normal" and calendric, and the unexpected. The diversity of the divine beings to which the rituals were consecrated required the creation of specific forms of expression and of complex codes that were carried out in the ritual act and in the nature and distribution of the offered gifts.

Because comprehending the meaning of Mexica rituals involves placing them in their historical context, I will refer here to important concepts in the theory of religion. Some opinions by outstanding theorists that reflect on the particular nature of offerings follow.

THE RITUAL CEREMONIES

Scholars in the study of religion insist on a relationship between the act of oblation, whose material expression is the offering, and (1) other ritual acts and (2) the sacred space where the oblation is performed. These two kinds of relationships are of crucial importance to the topic under study.

According to Jean Cazenueve (1958: 1–34, 366–92, 1972: 29), the offering of gifts to supernatural beings is a special kind of rite or ritual element. Cazenueve (1972:16–19) affirms that a rite is any individual or collective act of a symbolic nature that is repeated following immutable rules (that is, it has a formalized, stereotyped appearance), the effectiveness of which is part of an extraempirical order (that is, it is not perceived to have actual, useful effects). Several writers, among them Pietro Scarduelli (1988: 57), who also proposed emotional connotations as another characteristic of rites, have agreed with Cazenueve regarding the recurring, stereotyped, and extraempirical nature of rites.

The social performance of rituals transmits the knowledge and normative values necessary to the reproduction and survival of a culture. Moreover, it blends in the same corpus cosmological beliefs and the patterns of social order. By pursuing the strict rules of ritual acts, humans seek to communicate with the supernatural. Because of this, a standardized pattern characterizes practically all aspects of the rite (gestures, attitudes, words, and concrete acts). The ideas transmitted are extremely repetitive because repetition through different means is used to assure correct communication and to certify the supposed truth of the message.

Over time, theoreticians of religion have classified rites in different ways. For example, Cazenueve (1972: 29–30) divided them into *pragmatic* or *control rites* (designed to influence natural phenomena), *commemorative rites* (mythical representations), and *bereavement rites* (transformation of the dead into gods). Others have classified rites according to the bond established between humans and the supernatural. In this case, *magical rites* are considered to be coercive and inherently effective in themselves. On the other hand, *religious rites* are held to be supplicating and contingent (Frazer 1956: 74–87).

Henri Hubert and Marcel Mauss (1970) divided rites into two classes on the basis of time of occurrence. For them, sacrificial rites are either *occasional* or *constant*. The occasional ones occur at crucial moments in the life of an individual or society. Among them are the votive, the healing, and the expiatory sacrifices, as well as the rites of passage. The latter, also called *transitional* or *liminal rites*, are carried out when a radical ontological or legal change of status occurs in the life of an individual or society. Examples would be the rites of birth, puberty, matrimony, coronation, and death. In contrast, the constant rites are performed at precise dates on the calendar—for instance, the beginning of artificial chronological cycles or the seasons of the tropical year.

Finally, among many others, I will mention the distinction made by Baal (1976), based on the relationship established between humankind and the gods. *Low intensity rites* are a kind of ideal communication with the supernatural because they indicate a benevolent association between the supernatural and humans. They are usually performed for the purpose of ostentation or at the inauguration of subclans, funeral ceremonies, successful hunts, dedications of buildings, and the beginning or end of agricultural seasons. But when bad luck or disaster convinces humans of the existence of poor relations between themselves and their gods, it is absolutely necessary to establish a *high intensity* communication through rites performed at times of crisis, such as epidemics, disasters, illnesses, and mortal sins. Their purpose is to reestablish normality through complicated ceremonies.

Rites are composed of an enormous variety of verbal and nonverbal elements that are only congruent as a whole. For instance, in a rite of mythical re-creation, verbal communication is enhanced by voice modulations, onomatopoeia, pauses, gestures, and the paraphernalia and costumes of the actors, as well as by the exclamations, laughter, and comments of the spectators and the scenery and the time in which the drama is played.

However, isolated rites are the exception. They are usually performed in a definite time sequence and are called *ritual ceremonies*. Such ceremonies consist of long and complicated spectacles composed of a succession of several rites or ritual elements. Praise prayers, taboos, supplications, games, invocation, sacrifices, magical practices, dances, stagings of myths, purifications, and offerings may all occur in the same ceremony (Cazenueve 1972: 29).

The composition of ritual ceremonies is extremely complicated. Edmund Leach stated, and I agree, that their structure is analogous to that of verbal language. Ritual ceremonies are actually discourses addressed to the supernatural, discourses that can be divided into elements similar to paragraphs, phrases, words, syllables, and phonemes. These elements act as metaphors or metonyms based on specific codes (linguistic, choreographic, gesticular, chromatic, musical, oblatory, and so on). They, in turn, relate to a general code and are presented through a particular syntax. Like parts of speech, the simplest ritual parts have no meaning in themselves. They only make sense when they are combined spatially and sequentially with other elements (Leach 1978: 57–58, 96; Scarduelli 1988: 54–55, 111). The special syntactical organization of ritual ceremonies allows them to transmit very abstract ideas through oral expressions, nonverbal acts, objects, and space. Therefore, deciphering the message of each ritual ceremony presents a real intellectual challenge. An explanation of its meaning involves long and complicated procedures. At the end of Chapter 6, I shall show how the spatial arrangement of the objects offered in the Templo Mayor has a narrative structure resembling that of verbal language and ritual ceremonies.

In my judgment, the study of Mexica ritual ceremonies is the best path to a semantic interpretation of the offerings of the Templo Mayor. In performing this task, one must take into account not only the ritual act itself but also contextual features as different as the place it is performed, the moment of its execution, its time sequence, the objects used by the actors, the attributes that identify them, and the attitudes of the spectators. The ritual ceremony must also be compared with other variations of the same signifying complex, produced by the same world vision and a shared tradition. Both the quantity and the diversity of forms of expression corresponding to basic common codes are important. Offerings and ritual ceremonies are some of these expressive forms. Together with pictographic, sculptural, and narrative materials, they are part of a relatively unified significatory complex. I believe that, in the near future, correlations among those different elements will lead to a broadening of our perspectives. At the same time, such an increased understanding will let us decode the language of the offerings. Besides investigating the message of the offerings, it would be useful to question their originality as particular modes of expression in the totality of rites.

Consequently, it can be inferred that an analysis of context will make the study of a social act—such as the bestowal of gifts, expressed materially in the offerings—more productive. Understanding one part of a ritual ceremony will be greater if the whole is considered. The researcher must examine many variations of the same symbolic "text" in a systematic way. Unfortunately, in the case of Mesoamerica, we possess very few testimonials on the ancient rituals.

RITUAL CEREMONY AND OFFERING

According to Cazenueve (1958; 368, 380), rites of giving, sacrifice, and entreaty are frequently associated with ritual ceremonies because the purpose of all three is to make contact with a superhuman power. Establishing communication through offerings, sacrifice, and prayer is designed to cause a supernatural power to produce a desired effect. I believe that an offering, like a sacrifice, acts as a reinforcement to prayers. Perhaps this close relationship between them is the reason why the Nahuatl verb *huemmana* means both "to sacrifice" and "to offer" (Molina 1944; Siméon 1977; Nagao 1985b: 1).

Offerings and sacrifice have as a common denominator the fact that they are gifts (Baal 1976). Mauss (1971), in his celebrated "Essai sur le don," says that a gift, whether or not it is offered to the supernatural, is not the free and voluntary act it might seem to be. The act of giving involves three subsequent obligations: to give, to accept, and to reciprocate. As Mauss (1971) points out, the last of the obligations (reciprocation) varies according to the individuals engaged in the interchange. For instance, a person of greater status will usually give more than one of inferior rank. The same will be true in the case of a supernatural being involved in the giving because "the gods that donate and give back are here to give a big gift in exchange for a small one." Therefore, the offerings and sacrifices made in honor of the gods are the means for securing greater divine favors. The more abundant the gifts, the greater the expected reward.

In relationships with the gods, the interchange is crucial. With sacrifices and offerings, people "pay" the divinities for their harvests, military success, health, rainfall, and so forth. It is the familiar *do ut des* ("I give so that you will give"). Perhaps this is the reason that, among the Mexica, some of the sacrificial victims were called *nextlahualtin* ("the payments") (López Austin 1990b: 214). Offerings and sacrifices were considered to be gifts, tributes, or payments to the supernatural, as tangible manifestations of the principle of reciprocity seeking a benefit for humans. Moreover, they could be used as homeostatic mechanisms in times of instability.

We can define *oblation* as the ritual act of presenting something (artifacts, vegetables, animals, or humans) to a supernatural being (Baal 1976). The offerings do not have to be live beings, nor do they have to be partially or totally destroyed. According to Nagao (1985b: 1), an offering is a donation or the destruction of a precious possession that serves to propitiate or to render homage to the supernatural and that itself becomes sacred in the act of dedication.

In the case of Mesoamerica, under specific circumstances, some offerings were buried in sacred places (*caches* or *votive caches*) for the purpose of commemorating or consecrating monuments, buildings, and calendric events and to render homage to the deities (López Luján 2001). There is a difference between buried (or "hidden") offerings and mortuary offerings that accompanied the deceased to the great beyond (Espejo 1945; Nagao 1985b: 2). It is probable that the priest, when he deposited offerings inside religious buildings, intended to endow the structure with permanent powers. According to this logic, the gods to whom the temple was consecrated would feed continuously on the gifts, thus establishing an uninterrupted relationship with the faithful.

Sacrifice is defined as a drastic transformation of the offering through violence. A sacrifice is an offering to the gods in which the invisible essence of the offering (artifacts, vegetables, animals, or humans) makes a transition—like that of the soul of a dead person—from "this world" to the "other world." To make the transition possible, its essential nature has to be changed by means of a sudden and violent act (such as killing, destruction, casting out, abandoning, scattering, burning) that results in the death of the offering. Only then is the soul supposedly separated from the material body, similar to what is believed to happen at the death of a human. After a long journey, the sacrificed soul (the essence) will nourish a divinity or, perchance, be converted into it (Leach 1978: 115).

In ancient Mexico, gods were thought to be supernatural entities with limitations (López Austin 1990b: Chaps. 10-12). They were differentiated in part according to the kind of being they could reach and inhabit: the divinities could not take possession of just any being. Here humans served as real mediators. They made certain beings assimilable—transforming them, killing them, interrelating them, and placing them in the proper sites so that the deities could use them.

It is well known that the practice of sacrifice was extremely important to people in the post-Classic Mesoamerican societies. They believed that the blood of a sacrificed victim, made divine by its name (*chalchiuhatl,* "precious water") and considered to be divine food, had life-giving powers. Religious images were anointed with it, thus giving energy to the gods (see González Torres 1985: 116–18). The sun and the earth, opposite principles of the cosmos, were fed with the victims of ritual killing, thereby maintaining, according to Mexica cosmovision, the basic equilibrium of the universe and perpetuating its cyclic course (González Torres 1975: 63–64; Graulich 1988).

However, offering and sacrifice should not be considered to be simple objects of exchange only. They are also the means of establishing relationship and communication with what is sacred. In fact, an offering expresses the existence of a relationship before a material exchange takes place. "All communication is initiated by giving, by offering" (Baal 1976). In many agrarian societies, the gifts to supernatural beings are limited to a few drops or crumbs from the food that is being consumed or to substitutes of little economic value. Sometimes the givers even consume the offering once the ceremony has ended. What is important is not so much who consumes the gift as its indication of the closeness of humans to the supernatural; the intent and the communication are worth more than the object donated. In consequence, the offering symbolizes a part of the donor that acts as a bridge of communication between him or her and the deity. Through this link of sacred relationship, the divine force flows, a constant current of life between the transmitter and the receiver (Leach 1978: 115; Leeuw 1964: 335–40; Baal 1976).

Occasionally, the offering and the rite of oblation are converted into the message itself, a message whose structural logic can be discovered by the researcher. In many cultures, there is a syntax both in the composition and distribution of goods and in the actions of the ones who offer. Here the context serves as a frame for the expression. This will become evident after studying the archaeological offerings in the ambit of the Templo Mayor.

We also find great similarities among the forms of communication with the supernatural and the phenomena of oblation and sacrifice that denote the enormous ties that unite them. In a coherent manner, the two classes of communication defined by Baal (1976), mentioned earlier, are correlated with two kinds of offerings of gifts. The ritual ceremonies of low and high intensity would correspond, respectively, to modest and ostentatious offerings and sacrifices. Baal (1976) emphasized that an offering is a gift to the supernatural that acts as a persuasive and attractive way to establish contacts and improve relationships (see also Mauss 1972: 42–43). When the latter are good, ceremonies of low intensity are performed with relatively modest offerings, and thanks are given for prosperity, health, and long life. But during rites of high intensity, performed at moments of crisis, abundant prayers, sacrifices, and gifts act as homeostatic mechanisms. The offering was conceived, at times, as a gift to the gods but also—and here lies its importance—as a punishment for violation of order, for which the offending person had to pay a price for the forgiveness of sins (Baal 1976).

THE SPACE AND TIME OF RITUALS

The chief purpose of any rite is communication with the supernatural, and to facilitate contact, ritual ceremonies must take place at specific times and places. Many societies believe that hierophany, the manifestation of the sacred, is subject to spatial and temporal rules (Eliade 1967: 19). "This world" and "the other world," the realm of nature and the realm of the supernatural, are conceived in numerous religions as not only different but also opposite areas. The world of humans is by definition "normal," "temporal," "having defined limits," "central," "profane," and "known." Opposed to that, the world of the gods, of the supernatural, is portrayed as "not normal," "nontemporal," "ambiguous," "marginal," "sacred," and "unknown." Such space-time regions are separated by an ambiguous boundary with hybrid qualities, called a *liminal zone*. It is a border area that combines both natural and supernatural elements and exhibits a gradual and continuous transformation toward each of the worlds described. These boundary, delimiting zones are precisely the scenes and centers of ritual activity. It is here that a good part of the hierophanies, the revelations of an absolute and divine reality, occur (Leach 1978: 48, 113). They are the optimal sites for establishing communication with the gods, places where deities should be invoked, worshipped and appeased.[1]

In Mesoamerican thought, this dichotomy has certain peculiarities. All reality is infused with the supernatural, and it is then divided into what is only supernatural—the wholly "light," the divine—and what is mixed—mundane, that which has a combination of natural ("heavy") and supernatural ("light") elements. The latter group includes things with a low concentration of the supernatural and those with a high concentration, which are delicate and dangerous. Therefore, all liminal zones have a high supernatural content.

Leach (1978: 117–18; see also Cerrillo M. de Cáceres et al. 1984: 47–48) distinguished three spatial components in any ritual scenario. The first zone is the sacred place itself. It is part of the "other world." Usually, some iconic symbol is found there, indicating that it is a site of a hierophany. The second zone is contiguous to the first, and the majority of the rites take place there. Both the first and second zones are used exclusively by the priests and religious functionaries. Finally, the third zone is the one occupied by the faithful. It is separated from the holy place by the area of ritual action.

In Mesoamerican cosmovision, several liminal zones existed from which humans could contact the gods. They were dangerous places—"delicate"—protected by monstrous guardians (the *ohuican chaneque*) or by treacherous, difficult-to-cross barriers (lakes, reed fields, brambles, dunes, thickets, or rocky places). Often, ordinary, secular men were unable to see these places (López Austin 1990b: 188). Caves, trees, mountains, precipices, ravines, anthills, springs, abysses, *cenotes* ("water-containing sinkholes"), whirlpools, mountain glades, mountain passes, and crossroads—all of these were part of the numerous Mesoamerican liminal zones (Garibay 1965: 26, 105, 107; Heyden 1981, 1988; López Austin 1973: 84–85; Mendoza 1962: 81; Vogt 1981).

However, in pre-Columbian societies, as in many others, the temple was the sacred place par excellence. This edifice tended to replicate or to simplify the liminal zones of nature. Artificially, it took on the shape of mountains, trees, caves, and other features of sacred geography (Leeuw 1964: 380–81; Eliade 1968: 20–23). Mircea Eliade (1968: 39–44; see also D. Carrasco 1987; Matos Moctezuma 1986c: 32) correctly proposed that the temple symbolized the "center of the Universe" or "the navel of the world." In fact, several worldviews place the temple at the intersecting point of all the paths of the human world, as well as those of the *axis mundi*, the site where the earth, sky, and underworld connect. In other words, all vertical and horizontal axes of the universe meet in the temple, and therefore, it is the site of ontological transformations among the spheres.

According to many religious concepts, a rupture or opening in spatial homogeneity occurs in the temple, which allows the transit of the profane to the higher or lower sacred areas. The temple acts as a cosmic pillar, which, besides holding up the sky, serves as a medium of communication with the divine world. Consequently, it is perceived as a sacred post (*axis mundi, universalis columna*), a ladder, tree, mountain, climbing vine, or any other object linking the three levels of the universe (sky, earth, and underworld).

Regarding this, it should be remembered that people in ancient Mexico believed five enormous trees existed, four at the extreme corners of the earth and one at the center, with their roots sunk deep in the earth and their branches piercing the skies above. They had a dual function: separating the sky from the underworld and containing inside them the forces-destinies-times that flowed from both in ascending and descending directions, to be distributed over the face of the earth. These fluids, hot and cold, masculine and feminine, circulated inside the trees, intertwined spirally (López Austin 1988c: vol. 1, 52–68).

For Eliade, the temple is an *imago mundi* because the world, as a divine creation, is sacred. In many societies, when a ceremonial center was constructed, the avenues, sectors, and buildings that composed it had to follow a pattern of cosmic order. The architects planned the appearance of the principal temple in the image and likeness of the prevailing concepts of spatial configuration regarding the transformation of time in the universe. Therefore, the temple represented or was the summary of the earth. The religious construction could mirror the universe in various ways: by the correspondence of its walls with the four cardinal directions or of its hewn stones with the number of days in the year or by the installation of an icon that represented the *axis mundi*, for example.

A formal resemblance was not the only requisite for becoming a liminal zone or a sacred site. When a temple was dedicated, humans were obliged to perform certain rituals that repeated the primordial act of creating the world for the purpose of guaranteeing the temple's reality and permanence. Thus the ritual ceremony of construction had to resemble the creation of the universe by the gods. Creating the temple meant re-creating the universe and time, acting as in *illo tempore*, or the original time of creation (Eliade 1968: 25–28, 1967: 57, 97; Leeuw 1964: 383–86).

In summary, then, humans held religious festivals in order to approach the divinities. Such overtures were generally made in liminal zones, chiefly in the temples. Both the ritual site and the most suitable time had to be considered for the performance of such ceremonies. In other words, the gods were accustomed to being invoked in sacred places and at the precise moment of their manifestation. In that instant, sacred and profane time coincided and became simultaneous. This was because the influence of the different supernatural entities was governed by cycles that people had to respect if they wished to intersect them ritually (Eliade 1967: 70–71).

Normal, profane time could thus be interrupted by inserting periods of sacred, liminal intemporality. The sacred calendar interrupted daily activities of humankind to cyclically commemorate mythical events. Many rites, as *imitatio dei*, were the eternal return to mythical happenings—their constant reenactment. In each mythical representation, there was an attempt to make human existence resemble the divine, pretending to be contemporaneous with the creating divinities. The religious individual respected cosmogony when he or she created something, initiated a new government, or began a cycle (Eliade 1967: 81–91).

Performing a rite signified receiving the gods in their time and under their circumstances. But not everything was a commemoration of the primordial creative act. Similarly, humans believed they perpetuated the processes of the universe with the repetition of rituals. Religious ceremonies, in calendric order, were believed to be the appropriate means for winning the favor of the gods with sacrifices and offerings, of warding off the forces that irrupt in an orderly fashion into the human world. Humans acted at the opportune moment to carry out specific objectives. And rites required a knowledge of divine regularity (López Austin 1990b: 126, 214).

Returning to the concept of the temple as *axis mundi*, it can be said that whoever entered the precinct caused a break between the profane and the divine, the transitory and the eternal, the human and the supernatural. This step was dangerous and complex. It was indispensable that the person prepare for it through purification or an initiation, that is, through a ritual of ontological transformation. Clearly, not everyone was allowed to undertake the transition to the world of the gods. The ones who could communicate effectively with the powers of the "other world" were the priests, the magicians, the prophets, the shamans, and the hermits who could ritually control the supernatural. They were the individuals with "ritual purity," that is, those who also partook of some of the characteristics of the supernatural.

Communication is established in many ways. In Mesoamerica, relationship with a divinity was initiated with ecstasy induced by hemorrhages, vigils, or pain. It was also possible to reach an ecstatic state by imbibing huge quantities of alcoholic drinks or by using psychotropic drugs. Unusual states such as epilepsy, dreams, accidents, possessions, and visions were also forms of contact (López Austin 1990b: 76–77).

AN ASSESSMENT OF PROBLEMS

I believe it is possible to work out a plan that will permit researchers to decipher the language of the offerings by utilizing a systematic correlation of the archaeological record and documental sources. In my judgment, the key to understanding the meaning of the Mexica offerings, which is the object of this study, rests upon comparing them with the ritual ceremonies that gave them birth and with the symbolic characteristics of the sacred buildings that contain them, noting correlations among the offerings to find recurring features. In fact, if oblation is a fundamental part of ritual ceremonies and if it has a direct link with the religious significance of the buildings where it took place, there should be quantitative and qualitative correlations among the manifestations of three factors: the offerings, the religious architecture, and the ritual ceremony.

It is evident that making a model with these three characteristics will be complicated: the number and complexity of the offerings excavated at the Templo Mayor make it an ambitious project. But I also believe that a cautious approach to this complex study must include different points of view and the use of various techniques. The future analysis of archaeological information must be complemented by data from other scientific disciplines. Purely archaeological work should also further, as far as possible, research in documental sources because the vestiges of material culture and the written texts complement and enrich each other by presenting a linked and continuous vision of the past. In what other way could knowledge of the ritual and religious concepts of the Mexica people be gained? Archaeological materials and their contexts, the pictographs of various post-Classic Mesoamerican societies, the first accounts written by conquerors and missionaries, the texts written in Latin script by indigenous chroniclers, and the ethnographic descriptions written by our contemporaries are only some of the testimonies that illuminate the topic we are researching. The problem must be approached by using converging information from very diverse sources (Bloch 1965: 56–57).

However, the success of such research depends not only on the magnitude and quality of the available data but also on the techniques used. Human deeds are so complex that it is best to analyze them from different directions, with the assistance of tools developed by such disciplines as archaeology, history, ethnography, linguistics, geography, mathematics, and geology. The written texts and the archaeological documents do not "speak" unless one knows how to "interrogate" them with the proper techniques.

The concepts of the theories of religion given in this chapter will serve as a basis for analyzing the functions and meanings of the offerings discovered in the Templo Mayor Project (Chapters 6–8). However, before beginning that analysis, I will review the formal characteristics (Chapter 4) and the symbolic characteristics (Chapter 5) of the site where the oblationary rituals took place—the place where the offerings were buried.

CHAPTER FOUR

The Framework
of the Offerings

THE EXCAVATIONS OF THE INAH
AT THE TEMPLO MAYOR

Over a period of five years, the Templo Mayor Project salvaged one of the most important ritual settings of the Mesoamerican world. The Templo Mayor was the quintessence of the Nahua world vision and by its very name appropriate for propitiating the supernatural. The ruins of the Tenochca *Huey Teocalli* and other surrounding religious structures, excavated between 1978 and 1982, stand as convincing archaeological evidence of the religious fervor of the Mexica people.

Until a few years ago, systematic archaeological information about the twin cities of Tenochtitlan and Tlatelolco was scarce (Figs. 12 and 13). Compared with Teotihuacan and Maya archaeology, there was little architectural evidence and scanty data about the context of the places where remnants of Mexica culture had been salvaged. Obviously, the chief obstacles that limited (and continue to limit) archaeological knowledge of the famous capital of the Central Plateau have been the colonial and postindependence buildings that were erected over the ancient ruins. Consequently, only under exceptional circumstances and in specific areas has it been possible to salvage small portions of the pre-Hispanic city. Thus many of the explorations before 1978 were the result of accidental discoveries, and as a rule, such efforts focused on the rapid recovery of the most outstanding works of art. There was little concern with the recording of contexts (see Chapter 1).

However, we have a very complete picture of Mexica society and of the appearance of Tenochtitlan in the historical writings of the sixteenth century, contrasting sharply with studies of the Maya and particularly those about Teotihuacan. And there is a surprising abundance and depth in the writings about the Templo Mayor. No other monument of ancient Mexico attracted

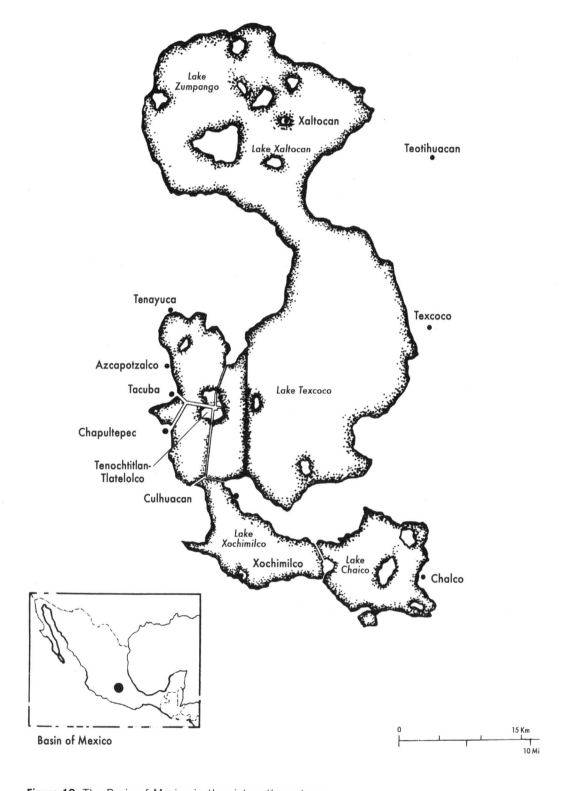

Figure 12: The Basin of Mexico in the sixteenth century.

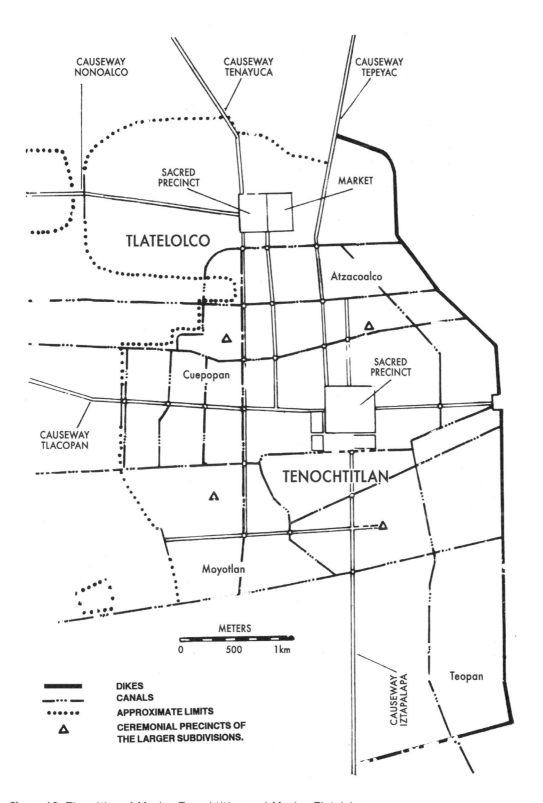

Figure 13: The cities of Mexico-Tenochtitlan and Mexico-Tlatelolco.

Figure 14:
Hypothetical reconstruction of the Sacred Precinct of Mexico-Tenochtitlan after Ignacio Marquina (1951).

the attention of the Spaniards more thoroughly or was the object of such admiration and detailed description as the Templo Mayor. Because of this, we now possess unique documental accounts of the history of the building, from its initial construction through its continuous additions until it was totally razed. Among the collections of historical information about the Templo Mayor, works by the following individuals are outstanding: Dahlgren et al. (1982); León-Portilla (1978, 1981, 1987); and Matos Moctezuma (1981c, 1986b).

Valuable data about the pyramid of Huitzilopochtli and Tlaloc can be found in native pictographs and in Nahuatl texts written in Latin script.[1] They are available in accounts written by the conquerors, who witnessed the functioning and the destruction of the buildings,[2] as well as in the narrations of missionary friars, often based on native tradition.[3] They even appear in the fantastic writings illustrated with wildly extravagant engravings that circulated during and after the sixteenth century.[4]

Through this impressive collection of texts and images, we know not only the history of the buildings but also their forms and dimensions, cult images, sacrificial stones, and the ceremonies performed there throughout the year. Descriptions related to the symbolic meaning of the buildings, their expansions, and the consecration rituals are also important for us because they allow inferences about the economic, social, and political aspects of the Mexica people (León-Portilla 1987).

In contrast, we know very little about the other structures belonging to the Sacred Precinct at Tenochtitlan. Although Fray Bernardino de Sahagún's informants described a total of seventy-eight buildings belonging to the ceremonial quadrangle, information about each one individually was brief and sketchy (Sahagún 1988: vol. 1, 181–89).[5]

The works of Ignacio Marquina testify to the immense wealth of documental information about the Templo Mayor of Tenochtitlan (Figs. 14 and 15). This investigator, after an arduous labor of exegeses and a synthesis of the written sources, made a hypothetical reconstruction of the

Figure 15:
Model of the Sacred
Precinct made in
1999, National Museum
of Anthropology.
(Photograph by
Leonardo López Luján,
courtesy INAH.)

Sacred Precinct that would be proven quite accurate years later. Although he also studied archaeological models and the data obtained in the explorations of Tenochtitlan, Tlatelolco, Huatusco, and Tenayuca, his reconstruction was based chiefly on the graphic portrayals of the sixteenth century. His work resulted in a 25-m² monumental model that re-created the religious life of the site, as well as several plans drawn in ink, various watercolor perspectives, and two very complete descriptions.[6]

Given the abundance of written material about the Huey Teocalli, it is logical to ask: What knowledge did the Templo Mayor Project contribute? What new data came from its explorations? Which of its discoveries offer a different perspective of Mexica society and justify the great expense of the archaeological work? Although some people still insist that the project made no great contribution of scientific value (Cantarell 1984; Molina Montes 1987), the findings speak for themselves. They are so numerous that they will be the subject of research for decades to come. Indeed, I believe that the number of pages written about the Templo Mayor, together with related scientific publications, and the number of investigations in process are the greatest proof of the enormous value of the discoveries made from 1978 to 1989.

It was not until 1978 that researchers confirmed that the building uncovered by Manuel Gamio in 1913 was the temple of Huitzilopochtli and Tlaloc. After the last of the rubbish had been cleared away, it was verified that it was, indeed, the Templo Mayor, a pyramidal structure composed of a great rectangular platform above which rose a base (*basamento*) with several talus structures. This base was topped by two sanctuaries: one to the south, dedicated to Huitzilopochtli, the guardian deity of the Mexica, and another to the north, consecrated to Tlaloc, the Rain God. Each temple had a single entrance. The temples could be reached by two parallel stairways up the principal facade, which were separated by a double *alfarda* ("balustrade") (Fig. 16). The excavations also proved that the Templo Mayor of Tenochtitlan was not unique in its form and construction. It bears a great resemblance to the principal pyramids of Santa Cecilia Acatitlan, Tenayuca,

Figure 16:
Panoramic view from the south of the Templo Mayor and Buildings E and J. (Photograph by Salvador Guil'liem, courtesy INAH.)

and Tlatelolco in the Basin of Mexico and to that of Teopanzolco in the Valley of Morelos (Fig. 17).[7] These temples share most of the following characteristics: (1) they belong to the post-Classic period, from the Chichimec to the Mexica domination; (2) their principal facades are oriented toward the west; (3) they were built in several stages; (4) their two staircases are separated by a double balustrade; (5) the principal temples were the southern ones, which occasionally are taller; (6) the southern temples were dedicated to Huitzilopochtli or to a solar deity; (7) the southern temples could be decorated with red paint, tenons, skulls, or merlons in the form of a fire serpent's tail; (8) the northern temples were dedicated to Tlaloc or to earth or agricultural deities; (9) the northern temples could be decorated with blue or black vertical stripes or with shell or jar-shaped merlons; (10) in the last building stages, the slope of the balustrades changed near the top, becoming almost vertical and forming a kind of pedestal separated from the lower slope by a bow-shaped molding (Barlow 1945; Marquina 1951: 164–77, 180–201, 220–23, 1935; Molina Montes 1987; Pareyón Moreno 1972). There are also several late post-Classic platforms with twin temples in the Central Highlands of Guatemala (Navarrete 1976).

The construction method of the Huey Teocalli of Tenochtitlan was similar in each of its architectural stages (López Luján et al. 2003). The nucleus of the building was made of red and black tezontle, a very porous volcanic stone, thin gray slabs of andesite, basalt stones, and mud-clay material obtained from the bed of Lake Texcoco. Only inside Stage VI could we observe true structural columns that distributed weight evenly. These were great cylinders 170 cm in diameter, reinforced by wooden stakes, in which vertical layers of gray andesite, tezontle, and dirt alternated. The facades of the building were made of blocks of volcanic stone carved on one or several sides. As a rule, tezontle and basalt were used for the facing and hewn pink andesite was used along the edges, at the joining of the two bases, and for drains. There were also basalt tenons jutting from the four facades. The stones on the outside walls were held together with mortar made of

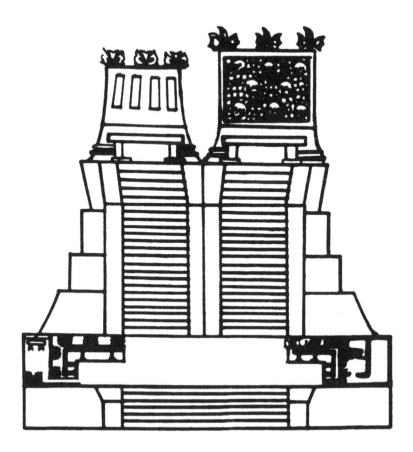

Figure 17:
The Templo Mayor of
Texcoco (*Codex
Ixtlilxóchitl* 1976:
112v).(Drawing by José
Luis García.)

lime and sand or dried mud and sand. Finally, the surface of the building (walls, balustrades, stairways, floors, and pillars) was covered with a layer of white plaster.[8] The treads of the staircases
were hewn, narrow, pink andesite or basalt, and the risers, which were very steep, were made with
irregular pieces of tezontle. The facing of the balustrades was tezontle, and the edging was done
with sillares of pink andesite or basalt. The edging consisted of a series of stones that followed
the slope of the balustrade and stones that penetrated perpendicularly into the fill of the core
(Marquina 1960: 107). The floors of the platforms, as well as those in the rooms themselves, were
made of thick layers of plaster with a thin exterior whitewash or, in exceptional cases, slabs of limestone.[9] The floors of the patios surrounding the great platform of the Temple were laid with gray
andesite flagstones or blocks of pink andesite.

Information about Mexica building methods was also obtained through a study of the dif-
ferential sinking found within the area excavated in the Templo Mayor Project. A visual survey of
the area revealed that several structures had a marked inclination toward the sides and that the
patios slope toward the exterior of the structures. For example, if we analyze Stage VI, we will see
a different sag in each of its parts. The central portion has only sunk 150 cm because it had been
reinforced by the first expansions. In contrast, the settling of the north, south, and eastern facades
hovers around 420 cm. Finally, the western facade shows a settling of approximately 770 cm, caused
by the considerable weight of the staircase. It should be mentioned that the patio surrounding this

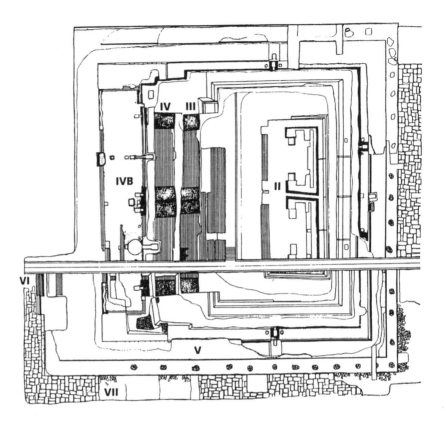

Figure 18:
Building phases of the
Templo Mayor. (Drawing
by Victor Rangel.)

building stage has a 16 percent deviation from the horizontal because the ground is more compressible around the perimeter than under the temples (Mazari et al. 1989).

The asymmetric sinking of the structures is due chiefly to the difference in the solidifying of the clays of the subsoil. Such variation has been caused by the different weights of each part of the structure and by the presolidifying of the subsoil that lies beneath the center of the buildings, resulting from the sum total of the weights of successive building stages. However, the asymmetry is also a result of the different degrees of compressibility of the clays used as filling in the buildings, as well as defects and the speed with which the buildings were erected. The occurrence of settling made it necessary for the Mexica architects to reinforce, correct, and relevel their temples from one stage to the other, a fact corroborated by the archaeological remains (Matos Moctezuma, pers. comm., May 1990). Mazari et al. (1989) believed that the peculiarities of these deformations indicate that the Mexica did not erect their buildings upon the virgin soil of the island of Tenochtitlan but upon an immense artificial platform approximately 11.6 m height. This great platform, called the *Island of the Dogs*, is reflected in the topography of the land today.

According to these researchers, this platform rose 5 m above the surface of the lake in preHispanic times. To support the hypothesis that the terrain was intentionally solidified, they argued that if there had been no artificial underpinning, the soil upon which the Templo Mayor was erected would have shown collapsing beginning in Stage IV; furthermore, the soil would have sunk 9.81 m after the first four increases in weight (Stages I, II, III, and IV), something that did not happen because the settling only amounts to 5.6 m.

Another important contribution of the 1978–1989 explorations was the discovery of several stages of construction of the Templo Mayor that were not known to either the Indians or the Spanish conquerors who lived in Tenochtitlan at the beginning of the sixteenth century (Fig. 18). It was found that the Huey Teocalli was amplified on at least seven occasions on all four sides (Stages I–VII) and that there were five more additions on the western facade (identified by letters of the alphabet: IIa, IIb, IIc, IVa, and IVb).[10] Each of these stages was preserved to a different degree, which is shown by the conservation of only certain parts of the structure. It is best, then, to review all the expansions identified archaeologically; information on each of the building stages of the Templo Mayor can be found in Matos Moctezuma (1981b: 19–37). In Stage I, the oldest known phase, only the floor of the *adoratorios* ("small temples"), a few stair steps, and what appears to be a *chacmool* with facial paralysis were found.[11] These vestiges were discovered after the digging of two pits in the temples and two tunnels in the stairs of Stage II.

Only the upper part of the building corresponding to Stage II could be explored. After the archaeological work, the last two portions of the basamento were visible, with ten of their steps and vestiges of the two temples at the top. Both sites have long benches inside that run from north to south and pedestals where the images of Huitzilopochtli and Tlaloc were almost certainly placed. Mural paintings on both the inner and outer walls of the temples were also found.[12] A coarse black tezontle sacrificial stone (*techcatl*) measuring 120 cm x 40 cm x 10 cm is placed in front of the entrance to the Temple of Huitzilopochtli. A chacmool—measuring 116 cm x 49 cm x 74 cm, carved from violet vitreous andesitic tuff and adorned with red, white, black, blue, and ocher pigments—sits in front of the Temple of Tlaloc. It represents the rain god (López Austin and López Luján 2001). There is a sculpture of a human face accompanied by the glyphs *Tochtli* ("rabbit") and *Calli* ("house") on the riser of the last step and exactly in line with the techcatl (Franco Brizuela 1990: 47–48). The principal facade of Stage II was amplified three times (IIa, IIb, and IIc).

One can see the intermediate part of the pyramidal base and approximately thirteen of the steps of Stage III. A total of nine anthropomorphic sculptures, some of them standard-bearers, were found directly on the stairs, covered with the rubble filling of Stage IV (Hernández Pons 1982). It should be added that several calendric glyphs, particularly *4 Acatl* ("reed"), were discovered on the eastern and southern facades.

Stage IV and its partial additions (IVa and IVb) are doubtless the best preserved. The bottom stage of the pyramidal base was uncovered, as well as the great platform on which it stands. As to the flights of stairs on the lower portion, fourteen intermediate steps from Stage IV, the first three steps of Stage IVa, and the first six steps of Stage IVb were uncovered. On the extreme western side, the platform has a stairway composed of four steps. The platform of the building is adorned with huge attached sculptures; seven serpent heads[13] and an equal number of braziers[14] appear on its four sides. On the southern facade, there is an ophidian head flanked by two braziers decorated with large bows; located on the east side is one head associated with a Tlaloc brazier, and the remains of another. On the northern facade are the remains of the neck of a serpent, a Tlaloc brazier, and the base of another brazier. Four serpent heads were found on the principal facade at the beginning of the balustrades that border the double stairway. Two more with enormous, undulating bodies more than

7 m long flanked the western entrance to the platform and there was another head between these two. In the half of the temple corresponding to Tlaloc, the slope of the platform's stairway is broken by a small altar with two basalt frog sculptures that measure approximately 44 cm x 30 cm x 35 cm and have traces of blue and red paint. A slab 2 m long with an undulating serpent carved in bas-relief on its edge was found on the Huitzilopochtli side, symmetrically related to the frog altar. Elsewhere, the outer walls of the platform are decorated with tenons in the form of small serpent heads. Of course the most impressive sculpture on the platform is the great monolith of Coyolxauhqui, located exactly at the foot of Huitzilopochtli's temple.[15] It should also be mentioned that two calendric glyphs are set in the walls of this building. The glyph *1 Tochtli* was placed on the eastern facade and comes from some construction prior to Stage IVb (that is, at Stage IV or IVa). On the southern facade is the glyph *3 Calli*.

As for Stage V, one can only perceive the remains of the northern, eastern, and southern faces of the platform and part of the floor of the plaza. At present, only a few remnants of platforms of later stages (that is, of VI and VII) remain. From Stage VI, the small heads that seem to emerge from the southern wall of the platform stand out. At this stage, the Templo Mayor reached its widest expansion to the sides. The following Stage VII, atop the platform of Stage VI, only increased its dimensions upward.

THE DATING OF THE BUILDING STAGES OF THE TEMPLO MAYOR

One of the most controversial issues concerning the additions to the Templo Mayor involves efforts to determine their chronology. The controversies are due to contradictions in archaeological data, in the written records of the sixteenth century, and in the kind of markings used to date the buildings. For example, although there are a dozen partial and total amplifications, the Spanish friars reported only four or five. According to Michel Graulich (1987), the pictographs and the written sources mention only (1) the construction of the original modest building with perishable materials, (2) a probable amplification during the reign of Itzcoatl, (3) an enlargement ordered by Motecuhzoma Ilhuicamina, and (4) the addition begun by Tizoc and completed by Ahuitzotl.[16] H. B. Nicholson (cited by Umberger 1987) stated that there were two additions during the time of Itzcoatl (1430 and 1438–1439), two during the time of Motecuhzoma Ilhuicamina (1447 and 1467), and one begun during the reign of Tizoc (1483) and finished during the reign of Ahuitzotl (1487). Matos Moctezuma (pers. comm., Sept. 1990) stated that in the *Crónica X* tradition, there are indications of another expansion corresponding to the reign of Chimalpopoca.

As to archaeological indications of time, very few ceramic remains were found between one constructive level and another during the explorations. And even had ceramics been abundant, they would not have been a good means for fixing dates because the twelve additions mentioned were probably done in a period not exceeding two hundred years. The only indicators of a possibly chronological character are the calendric glyphs set on the facades of Huitzilopochtli's base.

The problem with these calendric notations resides in their multiple meaning. For example, the glyphs *Acatl*, *Calli*, *Tochtli*, and *Tecpatl* ("flint") can refer to 1 day in the 260-day cycle (*tonalpohualli*), as well as to one year in the fifty-two-year cycle (*xiuhmolpilli*). As if that were not enough, the Mexica named each of their gods after the day on which it had been born or had performed some mythical deed (Caso 1967: 189). Generally, a square frame was used to distinguish a glyph referring specifically to a year, but the rule did not apply in all cases and there are many exceptions.

In 1981 Matos Moctezuma (1981b: 50) first published his tentative chronology for the stages of the Templo Mayor. He based it chiefly on the dates given previously by Ignacio Marquina (1960: 60–61) and on the glyphs 2(?) *Tochtli*, 4 *Acatl*, 1 *Tochtli*, and 3 *Calli*, in Stages II, III, IV, and IVb, respectively. Following Alfonso Caso's (1967: fig. 14) correlation of the Aztec and Christian years, he associated these calendric notations with the years A.D. 1390, 1431, 1454, and 1469. On the other hand, for Stages V, VI, and VII, which lack this kind of glyph, Matos Moctezuma chose to stick to the formula of "one stage, one *tlatoani* [king],"[17] linking them to the successive mandates of Tizoc, Ahuitzotl, and Motecuhzoma Xocoyotzin (Fig. 14). Years later, in 1987, Emily Umberger and Graulich published their alternative chronologies separately. Umberger (1987) proposed that all the glyphs at the Templo Mayor referred to exceptional, historic events (deaths or coronations of rulers, military victories, the beginning of some calendric cycles) associated by the Mexica with the presence or absence of the sun. According to this view, glyph 4 *Acatl* commemorates the victory over the Tepanec, the establishment of a political alliance, or the installation of the rulers of the *Excan tlatoloyan* ("Triple Alliance"); the date 1 *Tochtli* celebrates the first year of the Fifth Sun, the first year of the fifty-two-year cycle, or the great drought that occurred in 1454; and the date 3 *Calli* marks the death of Motecuhzoma Ilhuicamina and the ascent of Axayacatl (Fig. 14).[18] Differing from Matos Moctezuma, Umberger believed that after 1431 each ruler attempted (not always successfully, as in the case of Tizoc) an amplification of the building on all four sides and that the glyphs commemorate particular events during the process of the additions. She said: "In addition, the construction finished by Ahuitzotl was supposedly the last major enlargement of the Temple . . . and should therefore correspond to Phase VI, the latest important level excavated. Thus, if Phase IVb was built by Motecuhzoma I and Phase VI by Tizoc and Ahuitzotl, Phase V should pertain to Axayacatl's rather than to Tizoc's" (Umberger 1987: 420).

For his part, Graulich (1987) rejected the idea that the glyphs have a calendric meaning. He argued in favor of a symbolic meaning, always related to the significance of the southern half of the edifice. He proposed that glyph 2 *Tochtli* refers to the calendric name of Ometochtli, the principal god of pulque (fermented agave juice), and he pointed out that several anthropomorphic standard-bearers with attributes corresponding to pulque divinities were also found on the south side of the Huey Teocalli (Stage III). Graulich links the date 4 *Acatl* to the esoteric name of Huehueteotl and with the fire of the hearth, of the sky, of Venus, and of the sun.[19] The sign 1 *Tochtli* refers to the year the earth was created and the beginning of the indigenous cycle of fifty-two years.[20] Because he rejected the chronological value of glyphs, Graulich had no choice but to apply the rule of "one stage, one *tlatoani*." In his opinion, the Mexica rulers, unlike archaeologists, never made a distinction between total and partial additions to the western facade. Thus he attributed the construction of the last eight stages (IIc–VII) to the rulers between Acamapichtli and Motecuhzoma Xocoyotzin; the remaining stages (I, II, IIa, and IIb) were unassigned. As a result of this reasoning, Graulich (1987) proposed a critical revision of Mexica chronology and a substantial setting back of the date for the founding of Tenochtitlan (Fig. 19).

STAGE	GLYPH		PROPOSED CHRONOLOGIES		
		MARQUINA	MATOS MOCTEZUMA	UMBERGER	
I					
II	*? Calli*		Acamapichtli (1375-1395)	Acamapichtli (1375-1395)	
	2? Tochtli		Huitzilihuitl (1396-1417)	Huitzilihuitl (1396-1417)	
			Chimalpopoca (1417-1427)	Chimalpopoca (1417-1427)	
IIa					
IIb					
IIc					
III	*4 Acatl*	(I) Itzcoatl (1427-1440)	Itzcoatl (1427-1440)	Itzcoatl (1427-1440)	
IV	*1 Tochtli*	(II) Motecuhzoma I (1440-1469)	Motecuhzoma I (1440-1469)	Motecuhzoma I (1440-1469)	
IVa					
IVb	*8 Calli*	(III) Axayacatl (1469-1481)	Axayacatl (1469-1481)	Motecuhzoma I (1440-1469)	
	3 Calli				
V		(IV) Tizoc (1481-1486)	Tizoc (1481-1486)	Axayacatl (1469-1481)	
VI	*8? Acatl*	(V) Ahuitzotl (1486-1502)	Ahuitzotl (1486-1502)	Tizoc/Ahuitzotl (1486-1502)	
VII			Motecuhzoma II (1502-1520)	Motecuhzoma II (1502-1520)	

Figure 19: Proposed chronology for the building stages of the Templo Mayor.

The polemic begun by these three researchers continues to this day with little prospect of a solution. Matos Moctezuma, wishing to add new elements to the discussion, has renewed archaeological work inside Stage II, and we hope to have the results of his explorations in the near future. On the other hand, the staff of the Templo Mayor Project has begun a study of other calendric glyphs carved on walls of the Huitzilopochtli's temple, but nothing has been published yet. Almost certainly, this information will be helpful in resolving this interesting problem of chronology.

THE ASTRONOMICAL ORIENTATION OF THE TEMPLO MAYOR

Thanks to the discoveries of the additions to the Templo Mayor, it was possible to calculate the different orientations of the building. We must remember that a number of Mesoamerican ceremonial buildings had a solar nature. This is made clear by the east-west orientation of an enormous number of pre-Hispanic edifices, showing the ancient preference for orienting the buildings toward the points of the rising and setting sun. Thus the axes of the structures indicate the points of their *solar register*—that is, the spot at which the sun appears two times a year in its apparent movement over the Southern Hemisphere and disappears twice yearly in its journey across the Northern Hemisphere. "Expressed in another way the axis of the structure indicates four dates, upon which the sun appears or disappears on the horizon exactly at the point indicated by the axis" (Ponce de León 1982: 8).

In the judgment of several researchers, the particular axial position of the pyramids shows an intention to record and order time. It is quite possible that the orientation of the religious buildings, linked to the solar cycle, was meant to express the concept of a fixed temporal and spatial order. However, the orientation of the buildings varies slightly from one to the other, and in consequence, their solar registers also vary. That is why many researchers have asked why the buildings, in spite of having a general east-west orientation, show variations of several degrees. Among the explanations for this are the ideas that the orientation of the buildings served to mark the beginning of the calendar, to establish important dates of the agricultural cycle, or to indicate the first day of the festival of the divinity to which the temple was dedicated (Tichy 1981; Aveni and Gibbs 1976; Ponce de León 1982: 14–15).

Two years before work began at the Templo Mayor, Anthony Aveni and Sharon Gibbs (1976) estimated that the orientation of Stage VII of the Huey Teocalli was 97°06'. At about the same time, Franz Tichy (1981) estimated the deviation of the building at 97°. Several measurements of the orientation at each of the architectural stages of the Temples of Huitzilopochtli and Tlaloc have been done recently. Those of Aveni, Edward Calnek, and Horst Hartung (1988), as well as those of Arturo Ponce de León (1982), are very accurate.[21] The results of their work are summarized in the following chart:

STAGE	AVENI, CALNEK, AND HARTUNG	PONCE DE LEÓN	
II	96°37' ± 7'	upper 97°25'	lower 98°48'
III	96°19' ± 2'	upper 97°25'	lower 96°02'
IV	97°12' ± 2'	upper 97°25'	lower 96°02'
IVb	96°10' ± 2'	upper 97°25'	lower 96°02'
V	97°22' ± 10'	upper 97°25'	lower 96°02'
VII		upper 97°25'	lower 96°02'
average	96°42' ± 23'	upper 97°25'	lower 96°30'

According to the average measurement of Aveni, Calnek, and Hartung (1988), the sun would rise perpendicularly over the facade of the Huey Teocalli on March 5 and October 9, that is, sixteen days before and after the spring and autumn equinoxes.[22] For their part, both Tichy (1978, 1981) and Ponce de León (1982) affirmed that the solar ephemeris for the Templo Mayor would be set at March 4 and October 10 of each year. Tichy (1978) called attention to the fact that these dates correspond to the first day of the month of Tlacaxipehualiztli and the first day of the month of Tepeilhuitl, according to the calendric correlation of Sahagún.

THE BUILDINGS ADJOINING THE TEMPLO MAYOR

As stated earlier, before the excavations of 1978–1982, very little was known about the buildings bordering the Templo Mayor. Since the explorations our knowledge has increased considerably. Next to the Cu de Huichilobos, fourteen structures were found, some of them with

Figure 20:
View of Buildings A, B, and C. (Photograph by Leonardo López Luján, courtesy INAH.)

several building expansions. These structures were labeled with capital letters. Buildings A, B, C, D, and E are to the north of the Huey Teocalli, on the so-called North Plaza; Buildings F and G are to the south; and Buildings H, I, J, K, L, M, and N lie to the east, in the Patio of the Altars. Almost all of them belong to the period between Stage V and Stage VII, corresponding to 1481–1520 according to Matos Moctezuma's (1981b:50) tentative chronology (see the Templo Mayor General Plan). All these temples were built on the pavement made of gray andesite flagstones or blocks of pink andesite in the patios surrounding the Huey Teocalli.

Figure 21:
Principal facade of
Building F. (Photograph
by Leonardo López Luján,
courtesy INAH.)

Building A is located on the northern patio, next to Buildings B and C; with them it forms
an axis parallel to the northern facade of the Templo Mayor. These structures are oriented longitudinally from east to west. Building A is a base that rises from a socle. It is characterized by two
staircases, oriented to the east and west, respectively. Each one is bounded by two slope balustrades.
In contrast, the north and south facades have a smooth, vertical facing. Building A had no less than
four building expansions (Francisco Hinojosa, pers. comm., Nov. 1989). At present, a visitor can
see the expansions corresponding to Stage VI of the Templo Mayor. Two former constructions can
be detected underneath, one that was also built during Stage VI and another that was related to
Stage V. Of the most recent addition (Stage VII)—torn down in 1981—only the socle, the begin-
nings of the balustrades, and the placings of the facades remain (Fig. 20).

Like Building A, B is a base with vertical facings standing on a socle. On the western side,
there is a stairway with two slope balustrades, decorated with moldings in the form of knots. The
distinctive feature of this structure is visible on the north, east, and south sides, where more than
240 tenons of plastered tezontle representing human skulls adorn the structure—the reason why
the building was named the *tzompantli-altar*.[23] Three construction stages were detected. The oldest
dates from around A.D. 1475; the intermediate one is open to the public and is contemporaneous
with Stage VI of the Templo Mayor; the last, which was dismantled recently, had only the begin-
nings of the balustrades and the facings of the facades (Fig. 20).

Building C is symmetrically placed with respect to Building F, the latter known as the Red
Temple.[24] The form and dimensions of both structures are identical (López Luján 1989b; Olmedo
2002). Before digging began at the Templo Mayor Project, two structures resembling Buildings A
and F were found: one at the corner of Justo Sierra and República Argentina streets and the other
on Guatemala Street just behind the cathedral's apse (Matos Moctezuma 1965; Gussinyer 1970b).

Figure 22:
Building D. (Photograph by Leonardo López Luján, courtesy INAH.)

Figure 23:
Panoramic view of the Templo Mayor and of Buildings E, F, H, and I from the east. (Photograph by Salvador Guil'liem, courtesy INAH.)

They have architectural and decorative details characteristic of the Teotihuacan Classic period, combined with some stylistic features typical of the time they were built. Buildings C and F are made up of two parts, the base of a shrine and a small atrium-like space, that rest on a socle or banquette.[25] The base is clearly reminiscent of Teotihuacan architecture. It is characterized by its outer profile, a short ramp talus as a base supporting a vertical panel terminating in a projecting cornice. The latter consists of a horizontal strip bordered by a narrow frame. The relationship between the height of the talus and the vertical panel is approximately 1:2. The atrium or vestibule has two walls

Figure 24:
Panoramic view of
Buildings C, E, J, K, L,
and O from the east.
(Photograph by Salvador
Guil'liem, courtesy
INAH.)

decorated with stone circles. At the center of the atrium are the remnants of a cylindrical altar made of hewn stone slabs. It is important to mention that purely Mexica stylistic features are added to the Teotihuacan ones. For example, on the eastern side of the platform is superimposed a stairway bordered by balustrades with a typical double slope. On the other hand, the shrines have a rich polychrome ornamentation very similar to the Teotihuacan mural style (Figs. 21, 23, and 24).

Part of a structure designated as Building D was discovered to the north of Buildings A, B, and C. It is a small socle from which rises a base with flat surfaces and a stairway at the western side. It has an enormous semicircular hollow on its upper part that, in Matos Moctezuma's (1984b) judgment, was made for a huge sculpture (Fig. 22).

Building E, better known as the House of Eagles, is splendidly conserved (see Klein 1987; Fuente 1990; Matos Moctezuma 1984a, 1984b; López Luján 2005). It is a large base, whose longitudinal axis runs parallel to Buildings A, B, and C. Its latest structure, corresponding to Stage VI, has two flights of stairs at the western end. One is oriented toward the south and another to the west. Double slope balustrades with moldings in the form of knots flank both stairways. Two polychrome sculptures of eagle heads emerge from the moldings of the western-oriented staircase.

Upon exploring the inside of this addition to Building E, an older structure was found, which was contemporaneous to Stage IV of the Huey Teocalli. It has several interior rooms, and the difference in level between the rooms and the exterior plaza is bridged by two stairways. Thus one enters an immense lobby that must have been covered by a roof of perishable material, as indicated by the base of a L-shaped colonnade. Two full-sized ceramic sculptures of individuals disguised as eagles flank the entrance arch to the first room.[27] From this rectangular room, one enters the next rooms through a door guarded by two ceramic human skeletons. One then arrives at a patio with an impluvium and two chambers located at the end of the north-south axis. The entrances to both are framed by sloping facings with reliefs in the form of four-petaled flowers painted blue and red (Figs. 16, 23, and 24).

Nearly all the inside walls of the precinct have remnants of mural paintings on their upper parts, and there are long benches along the lower parts. The benches are made of two vertical surfaces: the lowest and largest is carved in bas-relief, showing various processions of armed warriors who meet at a *zacatapayolli* ("sacrificial grass bundle"); the upper one is a bas-relief frieze of undulating serpents, painted in red, blue, ocher, white, and black. In front of the benches, there are ten ceramic braziers, which contained charcoal. Eight of them had the face of "weeping" Tlaloc represented in appliqué (*pastillaje*). The remaining two had large protuberances similar to those found in many Mesoamerican braziers. Building E's form and the decorations on the benches recall in some way the Palacio Quemado of Tula and El Mercado in Chichén Itzá.

Building G is located to the south of the Templo Mayor, in the extreme opposite direction from Building E, the House of Eagles. Unfortunately, only a part of the northern facade and of one inside room of this important structure could be excavated. Benches with polychrome bas-reliefs similar to those of Building E were detected; they were decorated with *petates* ("mats") and concentric circles.

Seven other structures were found to the east of the Templo Mayor. The nearest ones, Buildings H and I, are similar to Buildings A, B, C, D, and F. Like those, they are rectangular bases rising from a socle. They have the classic Mexica double slope balustrade, and they are small compared to the Templo Mayor. Buildings H and I are superimposed, and both their staircases are on the western side, but they cannot be considered to be two stages of the same construction. Their relative location, their proportions, their size, and their finish are all different. Building H is the older of the two and seems to correspond to Stage V of the Huey Teocalli. Above this small structure, Building I was built in three phases related to Stages VI and VII but with some sideways displacement. Its oldest phase is the best preserved, and of the two succeeding phases, only part of the socle and the balustrades remain (Fig.23).

A few meters away toward the east there is a very large structure that we have named Building J. It is a platform whose length runs from north to south and extends to areas that could not be excavated. Its eastern and western facades are characterized by a series of balustrades and stairways, although the intercalation of occasional vertical facings can be seen. Matos Moctezuma (1981b, 1984b) suggested it is quite possible that this great platform, instead of the disputed *coatepantli* ("serpent wall") mentioned by the chroniclers, marked the boundary of the sacred precinct of Tenochtitlan. If this is correct, it would have been necessary to mount this platform in order to enter the precinct, climbing up and down the two stairs. This hypothesis is supported by the existence of a structure with the same characteristics on the boundary of the Tlatelolcan civic-ceremonial quadrangle, at least on its northern and eastern sides (Fig. 24) (López Luján 1989a).

During the exploration of Building J, two additions were found, perhaps built at the same time as Stages VI and VII. Unfortunately, the highest part of the platform was destroyed in the twentieth century, and only the first steps of the eastern and western stairways remain intact.[28]

Under the great platform, Eduardo Contreras and Pilar Luna (1982), in charge of the second set of excavations (Section 2), found the so-called Patio of the Altars. There they explored a

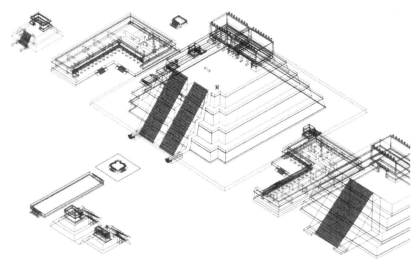

Figure 25:
Hypothetical
reconstruction of
the excavated area.
(Drawing by Antonio
Serrato-Combe 2001.)

much altered and highly confused context with five different levels of construction that these archae-ologists generically called *altars*. These were Buildings K, L, M, and N and several very small structures, some of which are shaped like cubes and might have served as pedestals; this was the case with Altar 15, which supported an enormous pink andesite conch shell. The function of other structures—such as a room with no entrance, with walls of stuccoed tezontle, and with a slab floor—is more difficult to determine (Fig. 24).

As to Building K, we know from the vestiges of a socle, a balustrade, and two stair steps that it was a base similar to Buildings A, B, C, D, F, H, and I and that it was oriented toward the west.

It is possible that Building L, called *Altar 4* by Contreras and Luna (1982), had, indeed, served as an altar. This small rectangular base was built over a layer of sedimentary material reinforced with wooden posts. It was made of tezontle and pink andesite, with a covering of stucco. One interesting fact is the discovery of the traces of four rectangular foundations around Building L. These are located to the northeast, northwest, southeast, and southwest of the building and are oriented longitudinally from north to south. Their function is unknown.[29]

Buildings M and N are true rooms. M is located directly to the south of Building L, and its overhead view looks like a U with right angles. The entrance to this small precinct is toward the north. Building N is made up of two rooms that are very similar to the small temples of Stage II of the Templo Mayor with respect to orientation, size, and proportions. Finally, the inside walls of Buildings M and N are decorated with polychrome murals (Fig. 25).

CHAPTER FIVE
The Symbolism of the Templo Mayor

THE TEMPLO MAYOR AS CENTER OF THE UNIVERSE

The fame of the Huey Teocalli has come to us chiefly through the abundant and colorful narrations of the sixteenth century. Certainly no other pre-Hispanic building in Mexico attracted the attention of the European conquerors as much as this did. However, among the many different aspects of the Templo Mayor reported in the sources, only those referring to its religious significance and to the rituals celebrated there will be discussed in this chapter because these are indispensable to understanding the meaning of the offerings.

The first descriptions of the Cu de Huitzilopochtli were not devoid of the miraculous claims that were typical of the era. A sense of the divine aura that envelops the temple has been there practically since its initial construction. Therefore, it is reasonable to review the most notable aspects of the hierophany that revealed to the Mexica the end of their long wandering and indicated the place to build the temple for their tutelary god. A sequence of three events resulted in the founding of Mexico-Tenochtitlan (Aveni, Calnek, and Hartung 1988).

The first cluster of events is related to the selection and sanctification of the future site of the Tenochcan capital. After a long journey lasting more than two hundred years, the Mexica reached Chapultepec at the end of the thirteenth century. At this lakeside center, a preliminary divine manifestation took place that led to the building of the Cu de Huichilobos. This was the death of Copil, the son of Malinalxochitl. Almost all the sources date this important event as *1 Calli* (A.D. 1285).

An incident during the pilgrimage, in which the evil Malinalxochitl, sister of Huitzilopochtli, and her followers were excluded from the migratory group and abandoned in Michoacán, is well known. The affront impelled Copil to attempt to avenge his mother once the Mexica arrived in Chapultepec. According to some versions, Copil personally accosted the recently arrived group;

63

according to others, he incited the people who lived along the river to attack them (*Anales de Tlatelolco* 1948: 34–35; Chimalpahin 1965: 54–55; Durán 1984: vol. 1, 37–38; *Historia de los mexicanos por sus pinturas* 1965: 48–51). At any rate, the rebel died after a furious battle. Fernando Alvarado Tezozómoc (1949: 43–44) stated that Huitzilopochtli killed Copil in Tepetzinco (later called Acopilco), placed his head on the top of that hill, and gave Copil's heart to Cuauhtlequetzqui, so that he could discard it at the center of the lake at a place called Tlalcocomocco.

> Oh, Cuauhtlequetzqui, come hither. I have here the heart of the villain Copil, whom I went to kill. Run and take it to the middle of the reeds, of the reed-grass field, where you will see a piece of *tepetate* ["porous compacted volcanic ash"] upon which Quetzalcoatl rested when he departed. One of his seats is red and the other black. There you will stand when you cast away Copil's heart (Alvarado Tezozómoc 1949: 43).

Next the Mexica began their long march again, passing through Atlacuihuayan, Mazatlan, Tepetocan, Culhuacan, Tizaapan, Acatzintitlan, Mexicatzinco, Iztacalco, Pantitlan and Temazcaltitlan, finally reaching the island of Tenochtitlan in the year 1 *Tecpatl* (A.D. 1324).[1]

The second sequence of events occurred at that place. There Cuauhtlequetzqui (called Cuauhcoatl in some sources) and Axolohuan (also called Tenoch) entered the thick reed-grass field where Copil's heart had been discarded thirty-nine years before. The first divine revelation took place there, a phenomenon whose characteristics take us back to primordial time. Suddenly everything in the reed-grass field turned white. The two characters found an unusually white great juniper tree, and next to it grew reeds, willows, and cattails that had lost their customary colors and turned white. They saw a spring of transparent water flowing from the roots of the juniper, from which white frogs, snakes, and fish suddenly emerged (Alvarado Tezozómoc 1949: 62–63; Durán 1984: vol. 2, 44; Tovar 1972: 23).

Analysis of the documents from the sixteenth century leave no doubt that the reed-grass field surrounded what I defined in Chapter 3 as a typical Mesoamerican liminal zone. In fact, the site of the divine revelation witnessed by Cuauhtlequetzqui and Axolohuan—the future irradiation center of the city and of Mexica domination—had the attributes of any sacred place. It was a dangerous or "delicate" site, according to indigenous concepts, protected by arduous barriers, such as the lake itself and fields of rushes and reed-grass. Moreover, it possessed presumably excellent avenues for contacting the supernatural. Some sources (Alvarado Tezozómoc 1949: 62–63) mention the presence of a great juniper (cosmic tree?) or an anthill (Alvarado Tezozómoc 1944: 8) precisely in the center of the hierophany. Others (Alvarado Tezozómoc 1949: 62–63) say that under the juniper tree, there were two caves[2] or "two great rocks" (Durán 1984: vol. 2, 44; Tovar 1972: 23) from which rivulets of a dual character gushed.[3]

> And then they saw a double hiding place, a cave. The first hiding place, the first cave faced the east, called Tleatl ("fire water"), Atlatlayan ("place of the burning water"), and the second secret place, the second cave, faced the north. And they intersected each other, one called Matlalatl ("dark blue water") and Tozpalatl ("parrot colored water, yellow water") (Alvarado Tezozómoc 1949: 63).[4]

The documental sources not only repeat the unexpected finding of a tree that emerges from a cave—both of which are related to the sacred geography at the center and corners of the universe (Heyden 1981)—but also insist on the presence of duality. The description of the two rocks that covered a pair of caves from which two springs gushed seems to allude to the forcestimes-fates of Mesoamerican cosmovision that ran, spirally interlaced, inside the cosmic trees—the ascending one hot and masculine, the other cold and feminine (López Austin 1988c: vol. 1, 50–68).

One very interesting fact about these fountains of water comes from Sahagún's (1950–1969: vol. 6, 18–19, 42–43, 88–89) informants. They stated that Xiuhtecuhtli-Huehueteotl—father and mother of the gods, who occupied the "navel of the earth"—resided in *matlalatl-tozpalatl* ("blue water–yellow water"). Therefore, building the key structure of Tenochtitlan on top of these springs meant that it was erected in the center of the universe, exactly over the opening of the delimiting border between the world of men and the dwelling of the gods (Reyes García 1979).

On the other hand, several researchers have emphasized that in sixteenth-century documents, Tenochtitlan is portrayed as geographically analogous to the ancestral home of the Mexica, their point of origin known as Aztlan ("the place of whiteness," of the primordial). The city of the Basin of Mexico shares with its divine archetype its location as an island in the middle of a lake, an ecology marked by abundance, and a site bordering a renowned town called Colhuacan (see López Austin 1973: 85–86; Duverger 1987: 130–32). Besides these traits, the *Historia de los mexicanos por sus pinturas* (1965: 39) showed that there was a hill in Tenochtitlan from which water "that made a river" flowed.

I will not discuss here whether descriptions of the mythical Aztlan are a posteriori rationalizations in the image and likeness of the Tenochcan capital. What is truly important is that official Mexica history makes a strenuous effort to prove that the pilgrimage would not end until a site almost identical to the "birthplace" of the migrants was found. This is corroborated by the example of the unsuccessful attempt to artificially produce a lake environment in Coatepec (Alvarado Tezozómoc 1949: 32–34).

The third and last series of events is related to establishing communication between man and the supernatural in particular space and time. In the year 2 *Calli* (A.D. 1325), the deity told the Mexica the site indicated for the founding of their city. Durán (1984: vol. 2, 48) explained the preamble of the divine message: "They again found the spring that they had seen the previous day, and they saw that the water, which the previous day had flowed beautiful and clear, was flowing red, almost like blood. The stream subdivided into two, and where they parted, the second stream flowed so thick and blue that it was frightening."

Here again, we see the dual aspect of the sacred spring—now shown by the red and blue colors of its waters. Later, these colors would characterize the Temples of Huitzilopochtli and Tlaloc, respectively.

In most descriptions of the founding of Tenochtitlan, the presence of Huitzilopochtli, transformed into an eagle devouring birds of various colors or a serpent on top of a cactus, was the divine signal to settle on the small isle in Lake Texcoco, as received by the Mexica. Durán (1984: vol. 2, 48) continued:

> Seeing that all of this was mysterious, they pressed on, searching for the omen of the
> eagle. Walking to and fro, they saw the cactus and on top of it the eagle with its wings

outspread toward the sunlight, basking in its warmth and the freshness of the morning air and, in its claws, it held an elegant bird with fine resplendent feathers. When they saw it, they humbled themselves, bowing before it reverently as if to something divine. The eagle, when it saw them, acknowledged them, bowing its head to them in every direction.

Durán explicitly stated that the spring and the cactus with the eagle were not located at the same place. Alvarado Tezozómoc (1944: 16) said the opposite, stating that the small Huitzilopochtli shrine was erected "beside the cactus with the eagle and the fountain of water."

Chimalpahin (1965: 55) gave another account, with variations, when he mentioned that the two leaders of the group, Cuauhtlequetzqui and Tenuch, were transformed into divine symbols:

> He again received orders from Cuauhtlequetzqui, "Oh, Tenuche...you must watch over the place you know about, the one in the midst of the reed-grass field and the reeds, lest others dare to come to where you cast the heart we snatched from Copil the magician.... At that place Copil's heart will germinate, and you will go there to watch and keep vigil when a tenuchtli ["rock cactus"] sprouts from Copil's heart, and you will lie in wait for the precise moment an eagle stands on top of the cactus, holding tightly in its claws a half upright serpent, which he will be mauling, wishing to devour it, while it hisses and whistles. And when this appears, Tenuche, because you are that, the Tenuch, the Cactus with the Hard Red Prickly Pear, and the eagle you will see, Tenuche, that eagle will be me, me myself.

Another interesting account about this hierophany is found in the *Códice Aubin*. According to the gloss of these annals, in the year *2 Tecpatl*, Cuauhcoatl and Axolohuan entered the reed-grass field and discovered an eagle perched on a cactus. Immediately after this discovery, Axolohuan submerged himself "where the water looks like blue ink," and Cuauhcoatl gave him up for dead. However, Axolohuan returned to Temazcaltitlan the next day. He told his companions that, inside the spring, he had succeeded in communicating with Tlaloc, who had told him: "Now my son Huitzilopochtli has come. This is his home. He is the only one to be loved, and he will remain with me in this world" (*Códice Aubin* 1979: 95).

As the codex made clear, the Mexica then went to the reed-grass field to clear the space marked by the eagle and approved by Tlaloc—symbols of the sky and of the earth—and to construct an altar at the foot of the cactus. Afterward, they captured Chichilcuahuitl, a Culhua chief, to serve as a sacrificial victim for building the house of Huitzilopochtli. He was ritually sacrificed, and his body was placed on the altar "to serve as its heart."

The end result of these three mythical episodes was the construction of the Templo Mayor and the establishment of the first Mexica capital at the site sanctified by Tlaloc and Huitzilopochtli. The early colonial sources stated that the first modest shrine was erected *on top* of the stone and that the cactus was placed where the eagle had perched (*Historia de los mexicanos por sus pinturas* 1965: 51). They also stated that, like the pyramids of the sun,[5] the moon,[6] and the *tzompantli* ("skull rack") of Chichén Itzá,[7] the primitive Teocalli of

Tenochtitlan was built *above* a cave,[8] the entrance to the terrestrial womb and one of the chief symbols of the *axis mundi* (Broda 1982; Heyden 1975).[9]

> And immediately [the Mexica] went to sell [what they had hunted and caught fishing] and to buy. Then they returned with stone and wood, the first small and the other thin. With them they laid the foundation at the edge of the cave. They placed there the roots of the town, the house and temple of Huitzilopochtli. The shrine was quite small. When the stone and wood arrived, they began construction at once, and they propped it up (Alvarado Tezozómoc 1949: 73).

Thus the original *tlalmomoztli* ("sod altar"), "poorly and miserably built," was located at the middle of the vertical axis of the universe, at the juncture of the earth's surface with the sky and the underworld. Reyes García (1979) found other examples of the Mesoamerican idea that capitals are the magic centers of their respective territories.

Here what I said before becomes coherent. The beings who selected the definite site for the Templo Mayor were Huitzilopochtli and Tlaloc, gods of a celestial and a terrestrial nature, who played opposite and complementary roles at the same time. The Huey Teocalli was placed at the confluence of the upper and lower forces-times-fates that maintained the cosmic order. In other words, it was the ideal location for the offering that would promote contact between the faithful and their most revered deities. This idea is corroborated by the concept of the Mexica capital as "the foundation of the heaven" (D. Carrasco 1981, 1987).

In the historic year of *1 Calli*, the so-called Cu of Huichilobos not only was set in the middle of the vertical axis of the universe but also in the *tlalxicco*, or navel, of the terrestrial surface. The plan of Tenochtitlan, like that of other cities of ancient Mexico, was based on an orthogonal design, imitating the horizontal structure of the cosmos (Nicholson 1971; Heyden 1988: 51–54). It probably followed closely the Tula archetype, described in the sources as a city inhabited by the gods and as a land of eternal abundance and the beginning of wisdom. The Temple of Quetzalcoatl in mythical Tollan, with its four luxurious sanctuaries oriented toward the directions of the universe, seems to have been reproduced in the four-way partition of Tenochtitlan.

After the construction of the primitive temple, the land on which the newly arrived people would settle was marked off into quarters, called *nauhcampan* or *altepexexeloliz* (Zantwijk 1963). The division of the island into four parts recalls the cosmogenic act of the goddess Itzpapalotl in which she fired an arrow toward each of the cardinal points (*Códice Chimalpopoca* 1975: 3, 6). Obviously, the Templo Mayor was at the intersection of these quarter sections. Durán (1984: vol. 2, 50) related that

> the following night after the Mexica finished repairing the shrine where their god was, having drained a great part of the lake as a site for their houses, Huitzilopochtli spoke to his priest or keeper saying, "Tell the Mexica congregation to divide the lordships, each with his relatives, friends and followers, into four districts, with the home you have built for me to rest in at the center, and let each district build in its barrio as it chooses."

The Chichimec had a similar foundation ritual in which they shot arrows in the four directions. Alvarado Tezozómoc (1949: 74–75) commented:

> Again, at night, Huitzilopochtli commanded. He spoke and said, "Harken, oh Cuautlequetzqui…locate, divide, establish the principalities in the four quarters of the earth…It is manifest that you will only establish four sections: "Moyotlan", now called San Juan; "Teopan", now called San Pablo; "Tzacualco", now called San Sebastián, and "Cuepopan", now called Santa María la Redonda.

The Atzacoalco, Cuepopan, Moyotlan, and Teopan quarters were faithful scale models of the pattern that had been commanded by Huitzilopochtli for the entire city. Each of them had at its nucleus a cluster of religious buildings, a market, and an administrative center, and the surrounding area was residential (Calnek 1976).

The thoroughfares of Tepeyac, Iztapalapa, and Tlacopan, which functioned both as organizing axes of urban space and as roads of communication with dry land, intersected when they reached the Templo Mayor (Marquina 1960: 44).[10] In a recent work, Aveni, Calnek, and Hartung (1988) discovered that the east-west axis did not cross through the middle of the building but went through its southern half, that is, through the Huitzilopochtli side. That means that the northern part of the Huey Teocalli, dedicated to Tlaloc, was displaced in an asymmetrical way toward the north of the axis. After this important discovery, these researchers proposed an iconographic subordination of the Rain God to the patron deity of the Mexica.

To summarize, the Templo Mayor represented to the faithful the heart of the sacred precinct, the city, the lake, the basin, and the *cemanahuac* ("earth") (Fig. 26) (Nagao 1985b: 47, 85). In its religious aspect, it was the architectural image of cosmic order. It was also a divine model in the world of humans because at that place the high, medium, and low were articulated with the four directions of the universe (D. Carrasco 1981).[11] Perhaps because of this, Alvarado Tezozómoc (1949: 4) defined Tenochtitlan as the place

> where the eagle tears the serpent apart and devours it; where the fish swims in the blue water, in the yellow water; the meeting place of the flaming waters, in the bracelet (?) of precious plumes. There in that place, in the reed-grass field; in the place of reunion, the waiting place for diverse people from the four directions, where the thirteen "teochichimecs" came to settle, who established themselves miserably when they arrived.

On the economic and political level, the Templo Mayor was nothing less than the materialization of centralized power. Like satellites, the multiethnic populations of the city, of the centers of production, and of the peripheral tributary regions that periodically sent raw materials and finished goods to Tenochtitlan gyrated around it. Consequently, it was "the root, the navel, the heart of all this worldly machine" (Durán 1984: vol. 2, 343). The political and religious powers of the *Huey Tlatocahyotl* ("ruling council") had their origin in the Templo Mayor for it was there the rulers were personified as gods. In other words, the Temple of Huitzilopochtli was the center of centers (Townsend 1979: 37).

Figure 26: The Sacred Precinct (*Primeros memoriales* 1905: 39, fol. 269r.). Drawing by José Luis García.)

THE TEMPLO MAYOR AND THE INTERPRETATIONS OF ITS SYMBOLISM

The historical data about the symbolic connotation of the Templo Mayor are heterogeneous and sometimes contradictory, resulting in varying interpretations by students of the Nahua world. The dual nature of its construction is its most conspicuous trait and the origin of most of the controversies about its meaning (Fig. 27). In spite of the numerous attempts to explain why this great base was topped by two temples, so far there has been no explanation that is completely satisfactory and applicable to other dual temples that date back to the late post-Classic era.

Perhaps the most popular argument is that these kinds of buildings are the result of a process of acculturation. This point of view suggests that the Mexica combined into one the religious system of hunter-gatherers with that of farmers. They added to their original astral cult, customary for northern nomads, the beliefs of the sedentary inhabitants of the Basin of Mexico. This is the reasoning of such reputable investigators as Jacques Soustelle (1982: 36, 58, 83–84) and Graulich (1987), who have tried to explain the combined veneration for Huitzilopochtli, sun and war god, and for Tlaloc, who is tied to rain and to the earth (see also Broda 1971: 246).

Esther Pasztory (1988), also an advocate of this hypothesis, believed that the Mexica must have had overriding reasons to allow Tlaloc to accompany their own tutelary god. She proposed that, through the ancient artistic representations and the historical traditions of the civilized peoples, the Mexica, recently arrived in the Basin of Mexico, came to the conclusion that Tlaloc was not only an important deity of rain, earth, and fertility but also the patron of ruling dynasties, of the great civilizations of the past, and of the Toltecs. However, there are a number of people opposed to these ideas, who base their doubts on the Mesoamerican origin of the Mexica, the existence during their migration of iconographic elements related to Tlaloc, and the difficulty for a recently adopted deity to attain such prominence (Martínez Marín 1964; Ségota 1987; López Austin 1990a).

The second group of proposals is based on the idea that the Huey Teocalli is the material expression of a particular way of life. For example, Gamio (1960: 43–44), toward the end of his life, concluded that a hostile "physical-biological social" ambiance had overtaken Mexica art and mythology. For this distinguished archaeologist and anthropologist, the gods of water and of war were no more than the opposing symbols of the principal enemies the Mexica encountered during their migration—the barrenness of the land they had crossed and the hostility of the people who lived there.

Matos Moctezuma (1979b), for his part, has correlated the phenomenological appearance of the Templo Mayor with what he called its "material determinants." He argued that the consecration of the principal pyramid of Tenochtitlan to the cult of Huitzilopochtli and Tlaloc was a clear superstructural image of an economy based on agriculture and on tribute obtained by the military conquest of other societies. This view has been criticized by Aveni, Calnek, and Hartung (1988), Broda (1987a), and Hers (in press).

A third group of researchers have said that the dual pattern of the Templo Mayor is in full accord with the worldviews of the Nahua (perhaps with those of all Mesoamerica) in that its classification by antonomasia was binary (León-Portilla 1978: 45; Broda 1987a). In fact, division into pairs of opposites has deep roots in the cultural manifestations of ancient Mexico, to

Figure 27:
Templo Mayor of
Tenochtitlan (Durán
1984: vol. 1, pl. 4).
Drawing by José
Luis García.)

the point of becoming a true obsession.[12] For those who defend this hypothesis, the Huey Teocalli is a synthesis of the oppositions and complements of the universe,[13] part of a long tradition of which the sites of Xochicalco and Cacaxtla are outstanding examples (Graulich 1983, 1987, 1990). Because of the interrelation of the two sanctuaries of the Templo Mayor, it has been proposed that the building recapitulates basic oppositions such as the dry season/rainy season, summer solstice/winter solstice, sky/earth, and day/night. Huitzilopochtli's temple is located on the southern half, the direction of the sun's zenith; Tlaloc's temple is on the northern side, in the direction of Mictlan and of night (Aguilera 1982; Graulich 1987).[14]

One of the advantages of this latter view is that the explanation for the dual design depends not upon the specific style of Mexica life but upon religious concepts shared with a large number of post-Classic societies on the Central Plateau. Thus it can be applied to the interpretation of similar buildings constructed during the same era by other peoples.

In a recent work, Dúrdica Ségota (1987) argued that the binary structure of the Templo Mayor is related to the categories of *nature* and *culture*. From her point of view, the left side of the building—the Coatepetl—is a clear allusion to the first warlike actions of the Mexica, an indispensable part of their "cultural patrimony"; on the other hand, the right side represents nature and the powers of earth. In the Templo Mayor, the God of War and the God of Rain enjoyed the same rank because it was believed the mission of both was to preserve the structure of the cosmos—culture and nature—with the help of the so-called precious liquids. Huitzilopochtli had human blood available, and Tlaloc possessed water. Consequently, Ségota based the correspondence upon the system symbolized by Huitzilopochtli and Tlaloc, the iconologic system of blood/water, and the categories culture/nature.

I must point out that, although some sources say the Mexica believed Huitzilopochtli and Tlaloc each "held as much power as the other" (Durán 1984: vol. 1, 20), the preeminence of the cult of Huitzilopochtli is clear in the Templo Mayor. Indications of this supremacy can be seen in (1) the generic designation of the Templo Mayor as the Cu de Huichilobos or Templo de Huitzilopochtli, continuously used in the sources; (2) the location of the southern half of the building exactly at the intersection of the roads of Iztapalapa, Tacuba, and Tepeyac (Aveni, Calnek, and Hartung 1988); and (3) the greater size of Huitzilopochtli's temple, evident in the ruins of the Templo Mayor of Tenochtitlan and of Tlatelolco and in graphic representations from the sixteenth century—for Tenochtitlan, see *Códice Aubin* (1979: 83), *Códice Telleriano-Remensis* (1964–1967: pl. 19), *Códice Vaticano Latino* (1964–1967: pl. 121); for the main temple of Texcoco, see *Códice Matritense* (1906: fig. 2), Durán (1984: vol. 1, pl. 4, vol. 2, 29–30); *Codex Ixtlilxóchitl* (1976: fig. 112v).

Both Matos Moctezuma and Graulich found that the opposition of sky/earth is shown not only in the south/north division of the pyramid but also in a vertical sense. Graulich (1987) related the lower part with dominion over earth, night, and the moon, as indicated by the presence of Coyolxauhqui. The upper part, where the image of Huitzilopochtli was found, was of a celestial nature. That is, the conqueror sun dwelt above, and below lay the conquered moon. Each time an individual was sacrificed at the Templo Mayor, he was dedicated to both deities in order to maintain the movement of the sun and the eternal succession of day and night and of the dry and rainy seasons. Once the victim's heart had been offered to the sun at the top of the edifice, the body was then thrown down the stairs until it reached the Coyolxauhqui monolith, where it was dismembered, the head offered to the earth-moon.

According to Matos Moctezuma (1986c: 71–72, 1988c: 134), the terrestrial level of Mexica cosmovision corresponded to the platform of the Templo Mayor, characterized by great serpent heads and braziers. The celestial levels would be represented by the four main bodies of the base structure, and the *Omeyocan*, or "place where duality resides," was represented by the two shrines at the top. However, it could be asked why the thirteen celestial levels were symbolized by only four sections, especially if we recall that various edifices in ancient Mexico did possess the number of stairs or sections corresponding to the part of the universe they represented. Heyden (1973) accurately proposed that Mexica pyramids symbolized the cosmic levels. In Texcoco, for example, according to Alva Ixtlilxóchitl (1975: vol. 1, 405, vol. 2, 126–27), Nezahualcoyotl built a temple with nine floors that "signified the nine heavens." In Malinalco, one must climb thirteen stairs to reach the temple of Building I, a place replete with elements of duality. In the Mayan world, the temples of Kukulkan in Chichén Itzá and of the Inscriptions in Palenque, which surely represent the nine levels of the underworld, have that same number of stages (Carlson 1981).

Rudolph van Zantwijk (1981) is also among the researchers who have tried to find an answer to this unknown. He argued that

> the Toltecs and the Aztecs imagined a celestial ordering divided into thirteen parts. Each one of these parts was related to a certain type of supernatural phenomena. In full concordance with this vision, the Templo Mayor of Tenochtitlan, which was consecrated in 1487, was composed of four stepped platforms. The three lowest platforms had 3 x 4 = 12 parts facing toward the four cardinal directions, and on the topmost and smallest platform, where the double temple of the gods Huitzilopochtli and Tlaloc was erected, the thirteenth part was found.

However, van Zantwijk unduly adjusted the data to his hypothesis. Why not give the last level the same value as he gave the other three? Obviously if each side corresponds to a sky, as Zantwijk maintained, the total of sixteen levels would not make sense. But let us leave this interesting problem now (it will be broached again in Chapter 8) and examine some theories about the global significance of the Huey Teocalli.

Today there seems to be no doubt that for the Mexica, the Templo Mayor symbolized a sacred hill where their guardian gods resided. An explicit passage that called the Huey Teocalli of Tenochtitlan "temple and hill" is found in Alvarado Tezozómoc (1944: 318). The Temple of Quetzalcoatl was considered to be a true mountain, hollow and full of water (López Austin 1973: 105–6). According to López Austin (1973: 62, 1990b: 197), in Mesoamerican cosmovision, hills were the depository of people prior to their "birth." Once the "birth" had occurred, the communities established towns in which they erected pyramids in the image and likeness of those sacred hills. These replicas—or artificial mountains—served as dwelling places for their divinities intrinsically symbolizing the *altepetl*, or "community."

The testimonies written in the sixteenth century left no doubt that the southern half of the Templo Mayor of Tenochtitlan represented Coatepetl, or the "hill of the serpent"[15]—the setting for the myth about the birth of Huitzilopochtli (for this myth, see Seler 1960–1969: vol. 2, 966, vol. 3, 327–28, vol. 4, 157–67; Broda 1987a; Umberger 1987; Nicholson 1985a; Aguilera 1978: 75; León-Portilla 1978: 24–25). As if that were not enough, the archaeological data gathered during the explorations of the Temple Mayor Project have fully corroborated what was stated in the sources. The following elements, found in the southern half of the Templo Mayor, recall the primordial Coatepec and the myth about the birth of Huitzilopochtli: (1) the position of the images of the gods according to the myth: Huitzilopochtli on top of the pyramid and Coyolxauhqui on the platform; (2) the dismembered and beheaded image of Coyolxauhqui; (3) the possible presence atop the edifice of the sculpture of the mother goddess Coatlicue-Yolotlicue; (4) snake sculptures attached to the base, making it Coatepec ("Hill of the Serpents"); (5) protruding stones on the balustrades that give the appearance of a hill to the pyramid; (6) standard-bearers perhaps related to the Centzon Huitznahua; and (7) skulls of females in offerings associated with the Coyolxauhqui monolith (Matos Moctezuma 1986c: 74–81; León-Portilla 1978: 50; Broda 1987a).

On the basis of this historical and archaeological information, several researchers proposed that the death of Coyolxauhqui at the hands of Huitzilopochtli was reenacted periodically at the Templo Mayor. Yolotl González de Lesur (1968), León-Portilla (1978: 58–65), and Nicholson (1985a) agreed that the theatrical reenactment of the myth took place during the month of Panquetzaliztli.[16] "It was then that Huitzilopochtli was born," Sahagún's informants clearly stated in the *Primeros memoriales*, as they began a description of that period of twenty days (cited by León-Portilla 1978: 60). Matos Moctezuma (1981d) went further by claiming that all the sacrifices performed at the Templo Mayor sought to commemorate that primordial fratricidal act and to celebrate the daily victory of the sun over the moon and the stars.

In contrast, the symbolism of the northern half of the Huey Teocalli is not so clear. Townsend (1982), Matos Moctezuma (1982b, 1988c: 134, 1986c: 71–74, 79–80), and Broda (1987a, 1987b) suggested that this part of the base also represents a hill—the *Tonacatepetl*, or "hill of sustenance," a mythical place where the *tlaloque* ("rulers") guarded maize and where it was stolen from for the good of humanity. It is interesting that plates 24, 25, 32, and 35 of the *Códice Borbónico* have images of Tlaloc's temple sitting directly on top of a hill. But even though this idea is feasible, it lacks historical and anthropological data to support it (see López Austin and López Luján 2004).

Both Broda and Matos Moctezuma believed the Templo Mayor to be a symbolic union of two important mountains: Coatepetl, to the south, and Tonacatepetl, to the north. In two of his latest works, Matos Moctezuma (1986c, 1988c) offered an alternate interpretation, which is compatible with the one outlined previously. In his judgment, the dual design of the hill-temple could have symbolized the first step on the path to Mictlan described by Sahagún: it represented the two hills that collide.

Broda (1987a, 1987b), for her part, concluded that the principal sanctuary of Tenochtitlan represents the sacred mountain, the earth monster that devours human victims. She supported her thesis with some of the excavation data, beginning with the presence of objects of marine origin in several deposits. She said that the offerings are associated more with the total significance of the edifice as a hill-temple than with the two deities to which it is dedicated. Broda (1982) pointed out that

> one outstanding fact of the excavation is the omnipresence of Tlaloc symbols at every phase of the pyramid's construction and above all in the offerings.... The offerings to Tlaloc in the Templo Mayor fall into three categories: 1) the depiction of the god on jars, sculptures, idols and reliefs; 2) the offerings of animals on sculptures and by natural species; 3) the offerings of symbolic objects, for example, the jade beads that were tied in a specific way to the god Tlaloc.

Broda's proposals are very stimulating, but I believe we should examine them to avoid a priori generalizations. Unfortunately, she based her statements on published reports that represent a minimal percentage of the materials obtained between 1978 and 1982. Moreover, Broda could not take into account the relative position of the objects inside each offering, a fundamental key to their meanings. As I shall show in the following chapters, the offerings recovered by the Templo Mayor Project show a great diversity in motives for giving, and therefore they have different functions and meanings.

Broda (1987a) emphasized the earthly character of Tlaloc (as deity of the hills, agriculture, and fertility) in the northern half of the building.[17] As to the southern half, she pointed out the presence of Coyolxauhqui and the similarity of the deity to Coatlicue and Cihuacoatl in the Mexica pantheon, even to the point of considering them slightly varying versions of the same divinity. According to Broda, the general meaning of the Templo Mayor derives from the cults to Tlaloc-Tlaltecuhtli, on the one hand, and to Cihuacoatl-Coatlicue-Coyolxauhqui on the other—that is, to the telluric destructive and generating forces of nature.

OBLATION RITES AT THE TEMPLO MAYOR

The Huey Teocalli of Tenochtitlan was the ritual setting par excellence for the people of the Basin of Mexico during the late post-Classic era. The periodic and exceptional festivities with major social relevance used the impressive monument, symbol of the center of the earth, as a background, and a high percentage of the festivals celebrated there were tied to the solar calendar. Every twenty days, a new religious festival began, so that at the end of the year, there were a total of eighteen. The most noteworthy of the festivities of the xiuhpohualli were Tlacaxipehualiztli, Etzalcualiztli, and Panquetzaliztli.

At the same time as the celebrations of the tropical year, other cyclical rituals took place at the dual pyramid. It is well known that the most important ritual occurred at the end of an era. Thus, after the passing of fifty-two solar years, the New Fire was brought down from the Cerro de la Estrella to the Huey Teocalli, thence to be carried to the other temples and houses of Tenochtitlan and then to all the cities and towns of the empire (Sahagún 1988: vol. 2, 490–91). This ceremony symbolized the renovation of cosmic time at the Cerro de la Estrella and its distribution from the *axis mundi* (the Templo Mayor) to all the limits of the earth's surface (D. Carrasco 1981).

Many other ceremonies were not regulated by time, but their irregular nature did not make them less meaningful. The pomp surrounding the election and investiture of the tlatoque, the funeral rites of lords and leaders, the prayers and gifts to the gods at times of crisis, the dedication of buildings, the victory celebrations, and the consecrations of additions to the edifice were only some of the occasional rituals held at the Templo Mayor.

Usually, the ritual celebrations involved a large number of people. When the tlatoani and the *cihuacoatl* ("snake woman," title of the viceroy) did not take part, the festivities were presided over by the high priests of the double temple, the *Quetzalcoatl Totec tlamacazqui* and the *Quetzalcoatl Tlaloc tlamacazqui* (Sahagún 1988: vol. 1, 229). Only they had the privilege of entering the shrines that topped the pyramid (Conquistador Anónimo 1986: 125). Both of these dignitaries were at the top of the complex hierarchy of servants of the Templo Mayor, composed of hundreds of people who took an active part in the ceremonies (Tapia 1963).

The ritual ceremonies occurred at different hours of the day and night. Depending on the case, they included processions, public dancing, myth reenactment, sacrifices, offerings, the chanting of sacred hymns, the renewal of images, mortifications, ritual games, the eating of special foods, and the representation of divinities by priests, nobles, or sacrificial victims.

Practically all the rituals required offerings of food or of sumptuary objects, most often perishable goods (López Luján 2001a). There are a surprising number of references in sixteenth-century sources to offerings of incense, pulque, cacao, tamales, tortillas, toasted maize, seeds, turkey meat, human and quail blood, tobacco, flowers, amate sprinkled with rubber, balls of rubber, precious feathers, and clothing for the images. These articles were deposited in jars, on dishes, or directly on the altars, and, occasionally, they were burned on a great pyre. Once the rite had ended, the gifts were consumed by those who had offered them or simply left to rot before disposal.

Information about the offerings that were deposited in caves and boxes, on altars, or in temples, however, is extremely scarce. Nevertheless, thanks to a few written references, we know that this kind of gift was buried at least during: the celebration of some festivals of the xiuhpohualli, the performance of certain rituals for social advancement, the ritual preceding the departure of merchants, the funeral of persons of high rank, and the construction or amplification of a building (Olmedo and González 1986).

Broda (1971: 275, 277, 279, 292, 307) found several references to the practice of burying sacrificial victims in caves, boxes, or shrines in the celebrations of the ritual calendar. The majority of the documented cases correspond to celebrations in the cycle of the rain gods.[18]

In the months of this cycle, it was customary to bury rich gifts, as well as human corpses. According to Durán, in the month of Hueytozoztli, the lords of all the towns of the Basin of Mexico, of Tlaxcala, and of Huexotzinco, accompanied by their servants, climbed to the shrine at the top of Mount Tlaloc. There, before the image of the Rain God, they deposited a very rich offering, consisting of clothing, jewels, food, and the blood of a child. At the conclusion of the ceremonies, a troop of one hundred warrior remained there to watch over the precious gifts. "This guard stayed until the food, the baskets and jars had rotted because of the humidity. As for the rest it was buried there and the shrine was walled up until the following year, because priests and ministers did not go to that place, only the guard" (Durán 1984: vol. 1, 83–85).

We also have explicit information about the burying of offerings at noncalendric rituals. Regarding the ceremonies of social promotion, Motolinía wrote that when the son of a Tlaxcaltecan, Huexotzincan, or Cholultecan lord wished to ascend to the rank of *tecuhtli* ("lord"), he had to go through a complicated ceremony. At midnight, he burned incense before the images of the gods and offered a little of his own blood. "Then he walked around the temple and dug in front of the stairs, to the north, south, east and west, and there he buried paper and copal, which is incense, and other things they were accustomed to bury there; and over them he poured the blood he had sacrificed, part of it from his tongue, another part from his ears, another from his arms and his legs" (Benavente 1971: 340).

Merchants performed rituals before departing on commercial expeditions, offering gifts to their tutelary gods. Five banners of paper sprinkled with rubber and human blood were made in the house of one of the leaders as an offering to Xiuhtecuhtli, Tlaltecuhtli, Yacatecuhtli, Ce Coatl Utli Melahuac, Zacatzontli, and Tlacotzontli. Afterward, the banners were burned in the brazier, and the ashes were buried precisely in the center of the patio (Sahagún 1988: vol. 2, 545–46).

As the archaeological registry shows, the Templo Mayor functioned as the principal depository of the offerings of Tenochtitlan. Given the enormous importance of the edifice in Mexica religious life, the victims of sacrifice or some parts of their bodies were placed inside, as were the ashes of the nobles and valuable gifts. There were many reasons for the gifts. Chapter 8 presents evidence that the majority of offerings buried in the so-called Coatepec belonged to exceptional ceremonies, that is, they were *not* periodical.

Referring to the burial of sacrificial victims, Durán (1984: vol. 1, 37) wrote about the cremation in the Huey Teocalli of the corpse of a woman, who personified the goddess Atlatonan, and her belongings, during a ritual dedicated to Chicomecoatl. "Just after she died, they threw her body for that purpose into a well or a subterranean space in the temple [Mayor], with all her clothing and ornaments and the plates and bowl from which she had eaten, and the mats upon which she had sat and slept."

As I will show in Chapter 8, it was also common to bury the incinerated remains of *pipiltin* ("nobles") of major status under the floor of the platform or temples, always accompanied by valuable objects. The written sources often contain descriptions of these ceremonies.

The documents from the contact period also testify to the burial of offerings during the construction of architectural additions to the temple. Durán (1984: vol. 2, 228), for example, said that when Motecuhzoma Ilhuicamina was in power while the Cu de Huichilobos was being enlarged, sumptuous gifts were deposited directly in the filling of the building.

> King Motecuhzoma seeing the speed with which the temple was being built, ordered the lords of the land, in order that his god would be more honored and worshipped, that [they give] many precious stones, many green jades—called *chalchihuites* by them—, beryls [*viriles*], bloodstones, and red agates; that is, all kinds of rich stones and precious jewels and many rich things. And these precious stones and rich jewels were thrown into the mix at each *braza* [1.6 m] expansion of the building.
>
> Thus, paying tribute according to size, each city brought its jewels and precious stones to throw into the foundation, so that they threw so many jewels and precious stones into each *braza* of the building, that it was a wonder. They said that since God was the source of those rich things, it was not unseemly that they be used in his honor, since they belonged to him.

The sources of goods buried in the Templo Mayor can be divided into those obtained by tribute and those obtained outside that system. With respect to the former, the tribute registers include some of the objects found in the offerings, among them marine shells, greenstone necklaces, turquoise masks and mosaics, gold ornaments, lip plugs, copper bells, and copal balls (Molins Fabregá 1956: 48–54; Berdan 1987). Bertina Olmedo and Carlos Javier González (1986: 90–91; see also Nagao 1985a: 48–50, and López Luján 1989b: 61–65) have identified three different types of tributes that might have been used as offerings: customary additional tributes levied for religious ceremonies (see also Durán 1984: vol. 2, 177, 228); extraordinary tributes levied for occasional festivities; and redistributed tributes, that is, parts of the personal tributes of the nobility donated voluntarily for religious ends.[19]

Among the possible ways of acquiring gifts not linked to tribute, we find: obtaining war booty,[20] purchasing on commercial circuits,[21] receiving voluntary gifts, and intentionally searching for sumptuary gifts in burials and offerings of societies that had disappeared (López Luján 1989b: 62–65). However, I should reiterate that these four forms of acquisition are related in one way or another to military expansion or to the Tenochcan economic domination.

Following the last excavations in the center of Mexico City, writers like Matos Moctezuma, Broda, and Nagao studied the general characteristics of Mexica offerings and presented, in broad terms, a hypothesis about their meanings. Matos Moctezuma proposed the existence of ties between the objects offered, the cults to Tlaloc and Huitzilopochtli, and the "two fundamental necessities" of the Mexica: agriculture and war. In addition, he stated that the offerings have a metaphorical language, the meaning of which is directly related to this basic dichotomy of the Mexica economy. In the judgment of the coordinator of the Templo Mayor Project, the images of the Rain God, the remains of marine fauna, and the images of canoes, harpoons, fish, and serpents are linked to Tlaloc, fertility, and agriculture. In a complementary fashion, the objects associated with Huitzilopochtli and indirectly with war and military oppression have to do with death (skulls and human skeletons, sacrificial knives, braziers with bows) and with tribute (raw materials and manufactured goods from foreign sources) (Matos Moctezuma 1987a, 1987b).

Broda and Nagao, differing from Matos Moctezuma, did not emphasize the Tlaloc-Huitzilopochtli dichotomy. Broda (1987a, 1987b) considered that, in some cases, there was little difference between the offerings on the northern half and those on the south. Consequently, she rejected the theory that links the deity on each side of the edifice to the deposit of gifts. In her view, the objects found at the Templo Mayor are related more to the deity to whom they were dedicated than to the total symbolism of the structure as a sacred mountain and as the representation of fertility. She said that although the monumental sculptures, the architecture, and the public rituals legitimize political power, the buried offerings are an expression of the cosmological thinking of the Mexica. She noted that the many objects related to human sacrifice, war, and tribute have as much to do with Huitzilopochtli as with Tlaloc. Broda concluded, based on the predominance of objects with aquatic or fertility significance, that the offerings are part of a "natural philosophy" in which worship of Tlaloc-Tlaltecuhtli and Cihuacoatl-Coatlicue-Coyolxauhqui predominates.

Nagao's (1985b) study of the Mexica offerings is one of the most ambitious carried out up until now. It is a diachronic analysis in which she compared the contents of the buried Mexica offerings with the many deposits discovered in the Maya area, Oaxaca, the Gulf of Mexico, and the High Central Plateau that date from the pre-Classic period to the post-Classic. But even though Nagao's interpretive effort is praiseworthy, I believe that it generalizes too much and has serious problems.[22]

In her conclusions, Nagao affirmed that the Mexica offerings reflect beliefs exclusive to that group of people, as well as pan-Mesoamerican concepts. She proposed that the Mexica compared the burial of gifts with the descending movement, the conceptual equivalent of birth and death (or that of growth and destruction, in a broad sense). She told us that it is possible that the Mexica made a metaphoric analogy: the burial of offerings at the Templo Mayor—cosmic mountain, body of the earth mother—was like the falling of rain that nourished the earth, while the burial of the dead bodies of sacrificial victims was like the sowing of the seed that inseminates it.

In this way, with the burial of gifts, there would be an attempt to nourish and fertilize the earth, that is, to renovate the life-death cycle and to assure the continuity of the solar cycle. Nagao (1985b: 83–85) thus explained the predominance of offerings related to fertility.

In the key part of her argument, she identified the image of the god "with two horns" with Ometeotl.[23] She suggested that the offerings where sculptures of this god are found symbolize the death and regal burial of the supreme creating divinity. She ended by concluding that the presence of this image in the offerings made the Templo Mayor equivalent to Tonacatepetl, or the origin of all sustenance, and made Tenochtitlan the "heart" of the empire (Nagao 1985b: 85–87).

At this point, I will leave the exposition of these latest theories on the global significance of the offerings at the Templo Mayor. In Chapter 8, I will go more deeply into this interesting topic and will give my own opinion there.

CHAPTER SIX
General Characteristics of the Templo Mayor Offerings

THE OFFERINGS AS AREAS OF ACTIVITIES

Considering offerings as archaeological remains, those found at the Templo Mayor can be viewed as *areas of activity* that reflect the past existence of specific and repetitive religious acts. Each offering, like every area of activity, can be seen empirically as a discrete joining of two or more objects and of unrecoverable matrixes. This kind of juncture, always spatially and qualitatively limited, shows internal and structural relationships. To a large degree, the distribution and internal organization are determined by set processes, relationships, and social activities (Manzanilla 1985: 11; Sarmiento Fradera 1986: 33).

Inevitably, when we explore an area of activity, the complex web of ties between its objects and the matrices is disarranged. Thus every archaeological dissection can be characterized as destructive, in the sense that it prevents the conservation of the incorporated whole. Because of this, a careful excavation and an adequate field record are essential to the future analysis of the contexts.

Following Linda Manzanilla's (1985: 11–13) classification, we can consider the offerings of the Templo Mayor to be, through their particular functions, areas of activity of *consumption* or *nonproductive use* appropriate to the *ideological sphere*.[1] The objects that compose the offerings (finished products of various raw materials, human remains, and vestiges of minerals, flora, and fauna) make up morphologically heterogeneous groups. They are related to each other according to the specific function in the ritual act they portray. It is clear that the social significance of any offering depends not only on the intrinsic characteristics of its objects but also on their organization and their spatial ties to larger units of analysis. At the same time, it is important to point out that

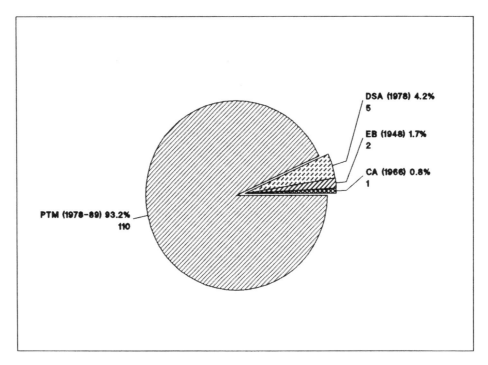

DSA (1978) 4.2%
5

EB (1948) 1.7%
2

CA (1966) 0.8%
1

PTM (1978–89) 93.2%
110

Figure 28: Chart showing analysis of 118 offerings: project and time of excavation.

these particular clusters of gifts occupy the same unity of placement, content, or relationship to some element of an architectural nature (Sarmiento Fradera 1986: 36, fig. 7a).

It is very useful to place areas of activity of the same type in larger, discernible units in order to detect specific social actions. And there is no doubt that studying a group of areas of similar activity helps to determine the prior function of the site where they are found.[2] Later, I will explore how the organization of the archaeological record at the Templo Mayor excavation reveals deliberate patterns of distribution and of association between the offerings and the archaeological structures that contained them.

The excellence of the archaeological record of the Templo Mayor is very crucial. In fact, the impressive recording of contexts made the detection of areas of activity relatively easy. We who participated in the excavations there can testify that, in general, the gifts buried in the different buildings had maintained their original distribution: indeed, an enormous number of offerings were found almost as they had been deposited by the Mexica priests centuries before. In other words, the majority of the contexts explored were *primary*. Many of the boxes of offerings were sealed, and the gifts placed in the building fill were protected by fine soil and stone slabs. Nor was the disposition of the objects substantially affected by the frequent movements and readjustments of the subsoil.[3]

Only ten offerings were severely altered after their placement (79, 90, D, M, C, 77, 2, 36, 32, and 55; see the description of Complex Q in Appendix 2). Thus, only in these cases did we find *secondary contexts*. Human's destructive action is evident in several of the offerings: two were violated in the pre-Hispanic era, one in colonial times, and four during last century. Several natural factors also changed some offerings. In one instance, rodents used one of them as a burrow.[4] Two deposits were found to be empty, probably as the result of an attack of microorganisms and fungi or of the effect of oxidation-reduction on organic materials.[5] With the exception of these cases, the contexts of the Templo Mayor were in an excellent state of preservation.

THE STUDY SAMPLE

After five years of continuous labor, the Templo Mayor Project excavated an area of 1.29 hectares. As shown in Chapter 2, the circumstances of 1978 made possible an accumulation of data never before imagined about the remains at the Sacred Precinct of Tenochtitlan. Those circumstances were ideal for carrying out a detailed recording of the archaeological contexts. Thanks to this work, we have, for the first time, an itemized report of more than one hundred offerings. This new vision of the whole gives a general perspective of the giving behaviors in the building with the greatest ritual and cosmological implications in the city.

The analysis given in the following chapters includes the 110 offerings explored by the Templo Mayor Project up to 1989. It also includes eight previously discovered offerings in the same area. Moreover, there is enough information available about them to allow a valid comparison between earlier finds and these new discoveries (Estrada Balmori 1979; Angulo 1966a; Contreras 1979b; García Cook and Arana 1978). Consequently, my study includes a total of 118 offerings discovered in four archaeological projects in the Templo Mayor and in nine adjoining buildings (Fig. 28).

Estrada Balmori-Moedano/INAH (1948)	2	offerings (B1 and B2)
Contreras-Angulo/INAH (1966)	1	offering (CA)
DSA/INAH (1978)	5	offerings (1–5)
PTM/INAH (1978–1987)	110	offerings (6–94; A–Q; Chamber 2–Chamber 3; Burial 1)
Total Sample	118	offerings

In spite of the fact that the offerings under study make up a highly complex and heterogeneous aggregate, it was possible from the beginning to detect, with simple techniques, several contextual regularities. After a visual analysis augmented by descriptive statistics, we were able to discern different gift patterns that were perhaps linked to different functions and meanings of the offerings. We also identified different patterns that followed criteria of time (the date of the ritual), space (the location within the building), container (the type and dimensions of the receptacle), contents (the abundance and variety of the gifts), and the internal distribution (the placement of the objects).

A specific procedure was followed to find the contextual regularities of the offerings observed. The first step was to select the contextual attribute[6] that would define each of the 118 offerings (or entities)[7] being studied. To do this, fifteen attributes were chosen.

Matrix of Contexts

NUMBER OF ATTRIBUTE	OFFERINGS 1, 2, 3, 4, . . . 118
1	x-coordinate of excavation
2	y-coordinate of excavation
3	Building
4	Building stage
5	Vertical location
6	Horizontal location
7	N-S dimension of the offering
8	E-W dimension of the offering
9	Vertical dimension (Z)
10	Orientation
11	Number of levels excavated
12	Proposed number of real levels
13	Kind of container
14	Range of elements
15	Number of elements

Once the attributes had been determined, the possible states for each were specified. To this end, a table of alternative states with their numerical equivalencies was set up.[8]

Afterward, the contextual information for each object was sought in various registers and publications (Estrada Balmori 1979; Angulo 1966a; Contreras 1979b; García Cook and Arana 1978: 36–65).[9] The data obtained were standardized and placed numerically in a matrix, in which fifteen contextual attributes were related to the 118 offerings (15 attributes x 118 entities = 1,770 entries).[10]

Finally, two procedures, suggested by Guillermo Espinosa, were followed to detect the most evident patterns. First, a statistical analysis of the context matrix was done. Second, the spatial distribution of the different states of each attribute was visually inspected. To do this, offerings that shared the same state were painted the same color on the General Plan. Thus each attribute was put on a separate General Plan.[11]

Table of Possible States and Numerical Equivalencies

BUILDING	
Templo Mayor South (Temple of Huitzilopochtli)	1
Templo Mayor North (Temple of Tlaloc)	2
Union of Templo Mayor (Huitzilopochtli-Tlaloc)	3
Building A	4
Building B	5
Building C	6
Building D	7
Building F	8
Building J	9
Building I	10
Building L	11
Outside Patio	12
Eastern Plaza (rear)	13
Building E	14
North Plaza	15

BUILDING STAGE	
II	1
III	2
IV	3
IVa	4
IVb	5
V	6
VI	7
VII	8

VERTICAL LOCATION	
Floor	1
Platform	2
Main body	3
Stairway	4
Temple	5

HORIZONTAL LOCATION	
Center	1
Center-north	2
Center-south	3
East	4

Table of Possible States and Numerical Equivalencies *(continued)*

West	5
North-northeast	6
North-northwest	7
South-southeast	8
South-southwest	9
Northeast corner	10
Northwest corner	11
Southeast corner	12
Southwest corner	13

ORIENTATION

North	1
South	2
East	3
West	4
East-west	5

ORIENTATION

North	1
South	2
East	3
West	4
East-west	5
Undetermined	6

CONTAINER

Building fill	1
Stone urn	2
Box of sillares	3
Building fill, under floor	4

RANGE OF ELEMENTS

0–50	1
51–100	2
101–150	3
151–200	4
201–250	5
251–300	6
More than 300	7

THE SPATIAL DISTRIBUTION OF THE OFFERINGS

Our excavations were very successful in terms of finding gifts. One of the principal results was the discovery of an unusual density in the number of offerings: if we divide the number of offerings by the area of the excavation, there was an average of 1 deposit for each 110 m² of space. This gives some idea of the enormous concentration of offerings in such a small area. However, it is obvious that the offerings were not placed in a uniform fashion; rather, specific distribution patterns were observed.

Apparently the location, as well as the quality and quantity of the gifts, depended upon the importance of the building, of the principal architectural axes, and of the semiotic value of each part of the construction. There are obvious groupings in the General Plan that are clearly governed by the different importance of the buildings where they are found. The 118 offerings under study came from eight different buildings, three plazas, and the interior of the platform that served as the limit of the Sacred Precinct. In the Templo Mayor, the perfect setting for Tenochtitlan's gift-giving rituals, the richest gifts were buried under its floors and platforms, inside its stairways, inside its main bodies, and in its two temples.

This phenomenon is apparent in the unusual number of offerings discovered in the principal edifice of Tenochtitlan—eighty-six (72.9% of the total). It is interesting to note that the number of offerings recovered on the Tlaloc side (forty) was nearly equal to that on the Huitzilopochtli side (thirty-nine) and that the number of deposits (seven) at the union of both bases was small (Fig. 29). The total contrasts strongly with the number of offerings found in the other architectural structures. Falling far behind in importance are Buildings I, A, and E, with nine, six, and five offerings, respectively (Fig. 30).

From a casual visual analysis of the General Plan, it is easy to see that almost all of the offerings are distributed following imaginary axial lines (Fig. 59). The greater part of the offerings were deposited along the three principal axes that cross the Templo Mayor from east to west. The first and second pass through the middle of each of the two temples and their respective stairways; the third runs exactly through the middle of the building where Tlaloc's and Huitzilopochtli's bases unite. The offerings on the north and south facades also follow an axial distribution. Most of them form an axis that passes through the middle of the Templo Mayor, joining the heads of serpents and the braziers. Moreover, a good number of the deposits were concentrated at the four corners of the structure (Matos Moctezuma 1987b, 1988c). The thirty-two offerings of the adjoining buildings were no exception. They followed similar patterns to the ones just described (see the General Plan).

It is noteworthy that several deposits were closely associated with important sculptured monuments of the Templo Mayor. For instance, there are eight offerings beneath and at the sides of the Coyolxauhqui monolith (1–6, 92, and 93), one under the chacmool (94), and one under the techcatl of State II (38). It is evident that the proximity of the gifts is due to gift rituals directly related to that specific sacred figure.

An analysis of the context matrix also showed the existence of patterns in the horizontal location of the offerings. The Tenochca buried the majority of their gifts on the eastern facade (23.5%) and the western facade (29.4%) of the temples, clearly a distribution with a solar significance. The most important concentrations of offerings were observed on the western facades of the structures, which often were the principal ones. Following these in terms of abundance

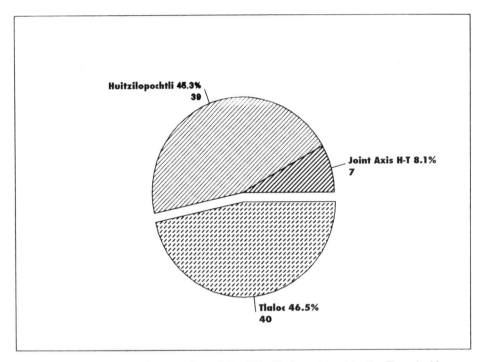

Figure 29: Chart showing building location of the 86 offerings found in the Templo Mayor.

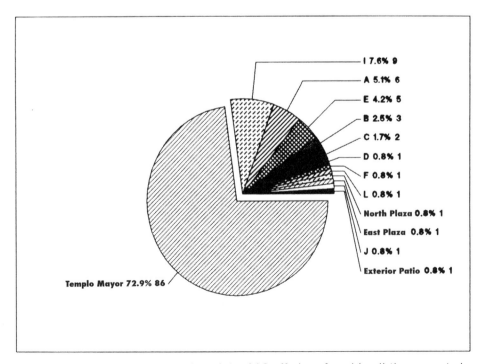

Figure 30: Chart showing building location of the 118 offerings found in all the excavated area.

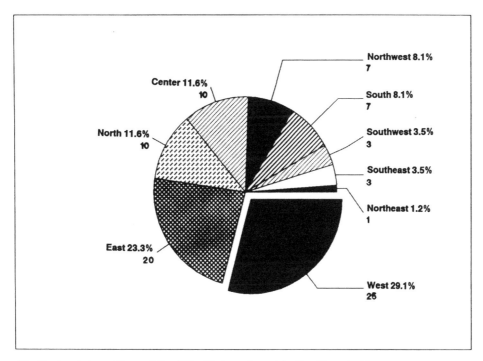

Figure 31: Horizontal position of the 86 offerings found in the Templo Mayor.

were the ones situated in the center of the buildings on the northern and southern facades and at the corners (Figs. 31 and 32).[12]

The horizontal location of the offerings with respect to the architectural structures determined the orientation of the gifts. This means that the placing of the gifts in relation to the cardinal directions depended in general upon which face of the edifice they were deposited.[13] For example, all the offerings on the facades that faced south were oriented toward the south, and a high percentage of those on the northern facades were oriented toward the north. On the other hand, the offerings located on the eastern and western facades and inside the temples that topped the base were preferentially oriented toward the west. Because of this, almost 50 percent of the 118 offerings were oriented westward (Figs. 33 and 34). There are a few exceptions to these patterns, but their number is not significant. Perhaps the most obvious of the deviations are the five offerings that, in spite of being situated on the principal facade of the Templo Mayor, are oriented toward the south (Fig. 35).

The offerings also had a vertical location, which differed relative to the architectural construction. During the excavation, they were discovered at different heights. Deposits of objects appeared under the floors of plazas surrounding the buildings, on the platforms of pyramidal structures, on stairways, inside the different architectural masses, and on top, usually inside the temples. The highest percentage came from floors (28%) and platforms (37.3%), and those located on stairways and main bodies were less abundant (Figs. 36 and 37). It would seem that this particular statistical distribution was not the result of ritual patterns but due instead to the difference in preservation of the excavated buildings. A walk through the archaeological zone shows us that the Spanish

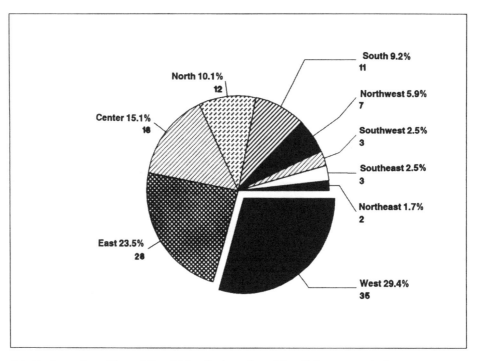

Figure 32: Horizontal position of the 118 offerings found in all the excavated area.

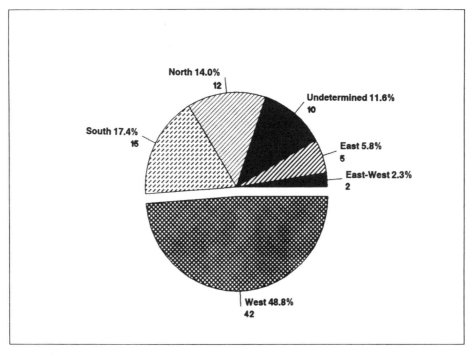

Figure 33: Orientation of the 86 offerings found in the Templo Mayor.

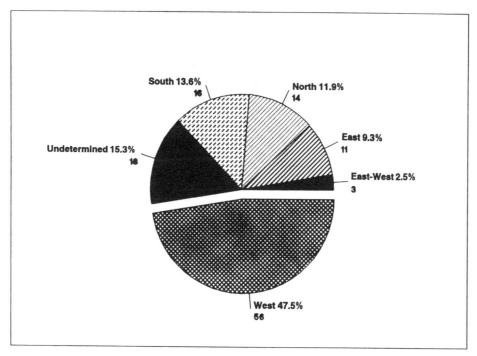

Figure 34: Orientation of the 118 offerings found in all the excavated area.

destruction of the Sacred Precinct of Tenochtitlan primarily affected the middle and upper sections of the constructions. In the case of the Templo Mayor, only the temples of Stage II were saved, due to their height (only slightly lower than the level of demolition) and to the fact that they were preserved under a considerable number of superimposed structures. The General Plan shows a clear predominance of floors, platforms, and first stair steps of what was the main temple.

A similar situation is found in the distribution of offerings by building stage.[14] Of course, the greatest accumulation of gifts was found in the more completely preserved expansions. Nearly half of the offerings extracted from the Templo Mayor (49%) belong to Stage IVb (Figs. 38 and 39). The differing concentrations of excavated offerings between one building stage and another are also due to technical limitations of the Templo Mayor Project. For example, it was not possible to clear the rubble from the platform corresponding to Stage II of the Huey Teocalli because the discovery of groundwater very near the surface prevented a deeper excavation (Fig. 40). But logically, there should be several offerings at the bottom of that expansion. A verification of this assumption will have to wait for the development of new procedures to surmount present barriers to exploration.

With current techniques, digging deeper into Stages III and IV to detect additional offerings would have meant removing the stairways of Stage IV and the platform of Stage IVb, respectively. It was also impossible to find the principal facade of the Templo Mayor at Stages V, VI, and VII—such an effort would have threatened the stability of the closest colonial buildings, as can be seen in the General Plan. In short, the statistical distribution of the offerings by vertical

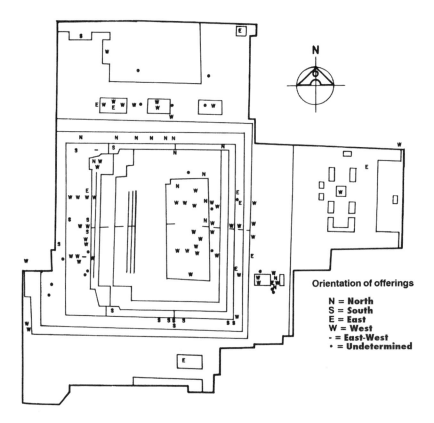

Figure 35:
Sketch showing the orientation of each offering.

Orientation of offerings

N = North
S = South
E = East
W = West
- = East-West
• = Undetermined

location and building stage was modified by the different destruction of the contexts and the technical limitations of the excavation.

These two facts become more significant when we try to compare the offerings of different epochs (Graulich 1987), each of which could be dated according to the building stage directly above it.[15] In my view, diachronic studies of the offerings are very risky. For instance, it has been proposed that the predominance of funerary remains with valuable objects in Stage II, of blue water jars in Stage III, and of complex offerings in Stage IVb is the result of a gradual change in ideology. But in the first place, one would have to question such abrupt changes in the lapse of only one hundred years. And before making that kind of assumption, the diverse vertical location of the gifts at each stage should be considered. All the offerings from Stage II come from temples, those of Stages III and IV were located in the main body of the building, and those of IVa on the platform. On the other hand, at Stages IVb, VI, and VII, the offerings came from the floor and the platform, and in Stage V from the main body and the platform. In my opinion, therefore, the cause for the difference in the quantity and quality of the objects offered should be sought not in a chronological change in ideology but in the different semiotic value of each part of the edifice.

It seems more logical to look for a political and economic change to explain the offerings of different eras. Some writers have argued that the copious offerings of Stage IVb (1469–1481), with foreign objects that possibly came from recently conquered areas, are radically different from those of earlier stages (Olmedo and González 1986: 79–82; Matos Moctezuma 1988c: 91). In their

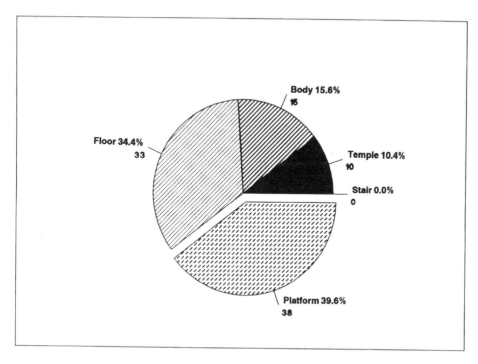

Figure 36: Vertical location of the 86 offerings found in the Templo Mayor.

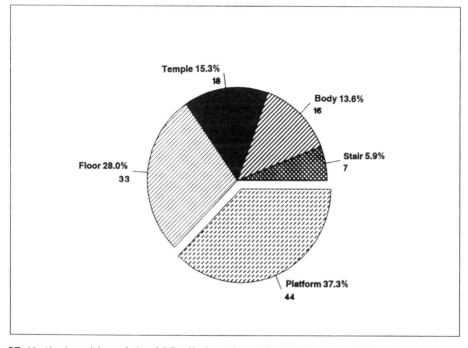

Figure 37: Vertical position of the 118 offerings found in all the excavated area.

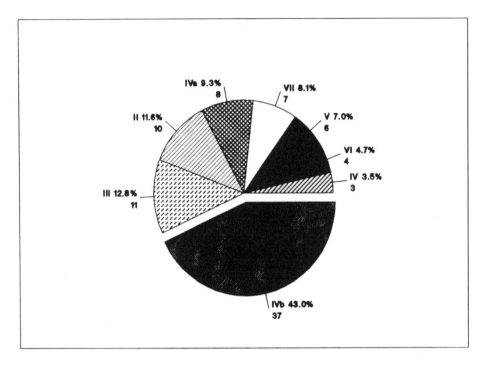

Figure 38: Building stage of the 86 offerings found in the Templo Mayor.

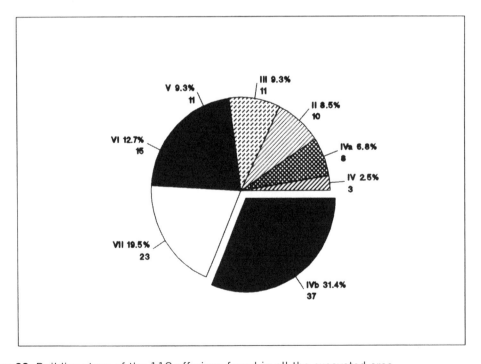

Figure 39: Building stage of the 118 offerings found in all the excavated area.

Figure 40:
Appearance of the groundwater level on the stairway of Stage II of the Templo Mayor. (Photograph by Salvador Guil'liem, courtesy INAH.)

view, this difference in wealth indicated a sudden expansion of the empire. Although these theories are plausible and suggestive, I believe we should be careful in assigning a time scale to the practices of oblation.

THE TYPES OF CONTAINERS

The 118 offerings under investigation were ultimately buried under the plaza floors or directly inside the buildings. As we found out during the excavation, the gifts were placed in different receptacles or containers, the size of which were in direct proportion to the amount of each offering. Matos Moctezuma (1979b, 1987b) identified three kinds of containers.

> 1. *Offerings in the fill.* In 57.7% of the cases, the objects were placed directly in the earth and tezontle stone building fill used in the structures. Often, the gifts that lay in the core of the buildings had been placed upon a thin layer of fine soil and protected with dirt, stone slabs, or fragments of tezontle hollowed on one side. I believe the offerings in the filling can be subdivided into two groups: those that were placed in the filling during the construction or enlargement of the building (29.7%) and those that were introduced by perforating the floors when the building was in full operation (28%) (Figs. 41 and 42).
>
> Usually, the offerings of the first subtype were poor (Fig. 9). They were located at secondary places of the Templo Mayor, in the eastern, northern, and southern facades of Stage III, on the southern face of IVb, and on the eastern and western facades of Stages V and VII. They were also placed inside Buildings A, B, C, and I,

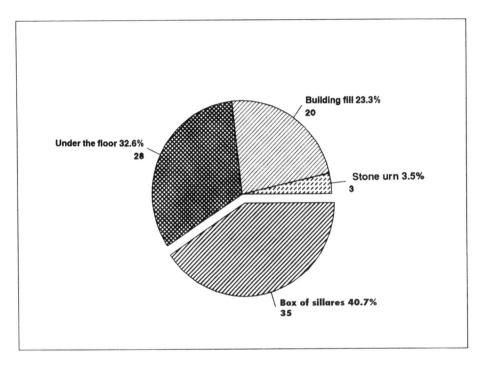

Figure 41: Type of container of the 86 offerings found in the Templo Mayor.

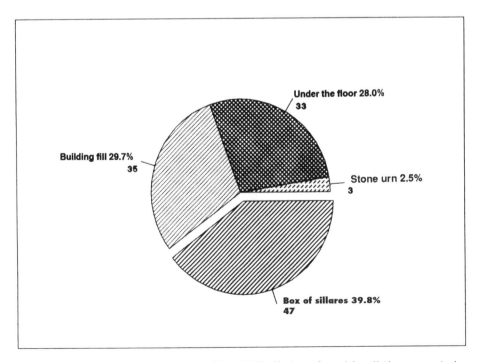

Figure 42: Chart showing type of container of the 118 offerings found in all the excavated area.

Figure 43:
Offering 58 was found in the fill under the stucco floor. (Photograph by Salvador Guil'liem, courtesy INAH.)

as well as on the stairways of Building E (Fig. 47). Offerings of the second subtype, those placed under the floor, were richer, and they also revealed a regular distribution (Fig. 43). They were found in places of major importance in the Templo Mayor: inside the temples of Stage II and along the principal axes and corners of Stage IVb. Similarly, they were found in the North Plaza between Buildings A and B and in Building I (Fig. 47).

2. *Offerings in boxes of sillares.* Offerings in boxes of sillares with square or rectangular sides enclosing parallelepiped volumes followed in frequency (39.8%). The size and materials of these containers varied. The bottom of the box was normally made with

one or more slabs, although some were made of sillares of tezontle or quarry stone or a thick layer of stucco (Fig. 44).

As a rule, the sides were made with several layers of assembled tezontle sillares, hewn on one side and adjusted for good seating and joining. Sillares of the same row were of equal height, although different rows could be of different heights, and the rough side faced the inside. However, the richest offerings had sides made with real quarry stone sillares.[16] Both the rows of tezontle bricks and the quarry stone sillares could be joined with or without mortar. In the case of a few offerings, slabs placed in a vertical position acted as walls. Sometimes, the bottom or the inner sides or both were covered with a layer of plaster, which was occasionally painted.

Once the gifts had been deposited inside, the box was covered with large slabs supported on the upper edges of the walls or directly over the objects. The outer side of the cover was, in some cases, also covered with plaster. Other offerings were simply covered with dirt and small pieces of tezontle.

Generally speaking, the boxes of sillares were made in the fill, near the surface, during the construction or expansion of the building. Almost all the offerings found in boxes were probably deposited at the consecration festival of the new temple, although there are also indications that some were made while the Templo Mayor was in full use. For example, see the discussion of the causes leading to offering 48 in Chapter 8.

Large boxes of sillares were the receptacles for the most sumptuous offerings (Fig. 45). They were concentrated in the axes of the buildings, in the principal facades, and at the corners. In the Templo Mayor, boxes of sillares were found in the temples of Stages II, in the north and east facades of Stage III, in the principal axes of the four sides of IVb, and on the western facade of Stage VII. They were also found in the most prominent places of Buildings A, B, C, F, and L (Fig. 47).

3. *Offerings in stone urns.* Only three offerings (18, 19, and 29) were completely contained in stone urns (2.5%). The urns were carved from basalt or tezontle and consisted of two pieces with flat surfaces: the vessel itself and the cover. The box was a prismatic monolith whose upper border was raised for a better fit of the cover. The interior had a fine plaster covering (Fig. 46). Another urn was found inside the box of sillares in offering 41, containing most of the materials in the offering. This urn differed from the others because it had carved surfaces and was decorated with blue paint, representing Tlaloc, together with the glyphs *13 Quiahuitl* ("rain") and *13 Acatl* (González 1982; see also Appendix 3).

The stone urns were in very different places. That of offering 29 was deposited at the core of the Templo Mayor at the time Stage III was being erected; those of 18 and 19 lay under the floor of the western platform of Stage IVa, and that of offering 41 was on the platform corresponding to Stage IVb. The last three contained objects associated with the Tlaloc cult (Fig. 47).

Figure 44:
Offering 56 was found inside a box of sillares. (Photograph by Salvador Guil'liem, courtesy INAH.)

THE TYPES OF CONTENTS

The archaeological materials from the 118 deposits are extremely diverse (Matos Moctezuma 1988c: 85–121; Nagao 1985b: 48–82; Wagner 1982). Thanks to Nagao's (1985b: 48–62) study, we know that the contents of the Mexica offerings were, to a certain degree, similar to the offerings of other Mesoamerican societies. According to Nagao, the Mexica shared with many other groups the custom of burying as gifts figures and ornaments of greenstone and other semiprecious stones, carved obsidian artifacts, ceramic containers and braziers, the remains of sacrificed humans and of birds, marine shells, conch shells, burned materials, mutilated sculptures, and

Figure 45:
Chamber 2 has one of
the most sumptuous
offerings of all those
analyzed. (Photograph by
Salvador Guil'liem,
courtesy INAH.)

perishable objects. These kinds of gifts are found so often in such different space and time contexts that many of them can be considered as universal in the oblation rites of Mesoamerica.

However, Nagao (1985b: 62–82) said that the Mexica offerings also show certain innova-
tions that give them a character of their own. Differing from the offerings of other regions and
times, those deposited in Tenochtitlan and several other Mexica sites included flint sacrificial knives,
standardized statues of deities, stone containers, stone masks, divine insignia (scepters, earspools,
noseplugs, and breastplates), miniatures (of houses, braziers, canoes, tools, and musical instruments),
copper bells, and marine sand.

Matos Moctezuma (1979b, 1988c: 91) estimated that around 80 percent of the gifts found
in the Templo Mayor are of foreign origin. The archaeological record shows that the Mexica imported
from remote areas a large part of the finished goods and animal species they offered to the gods

Figure 46:
Offerings 18 and 19 were deposited inside stone urns. (Photograph by Salvador Guil'liem, courtesy INAH.)

of the Huey Teocalli. Most of the materials came from the tributary provinces dominated by the Triple Alliance, especially those located in the present states of Puebla, Oaxaca, and Guerrero, as well as from the coastal regions of the Gulf of Mexico. Comparatively speaking, the number of Mexica products is small (Matos Moctezuma 1987b, 1988c: 88–91).[17]

Animal remains predominate among the 118 offerings.[18] The analysis and specific identification of these samples have not been completed because of the huge accumulation of remains recovered.[19] At present, we have the partial results from a study of fifty-five offerings (1, 3, 5, 6–9, 11–13, 15, 17–24, 30–31, 33, 36, 38, 41, 48–52, 56–62, 64–65, 68–70, 81, 83–85, C2–C3, A–B, H, K–L, and N), and eleven zoological groups have been identified, representing nearly two hundred species (Polaco, Butrón, and Cárdenas 1989).

The biologists who undertook this arduous task have found, among other things, that the vast majority of materials belong to species whose natural habitats lie a considerable distance from Tenochtitlan. The animals identified came from four different ecological zones: the temperate zone of the Central Plateau, the tropical forests, the coral reefs, and the coastal estuaries and lakes (Matos Moctezuma 1988c: 115–18; Polaco et al. 1989; Polaco 1991; Guzmán and Polaco 2001).

Invertebrates predominate in the animal collection. They belong to five different phyla: Arthropoda, Equinoderma, Parazoa, Coelenterata, and Mollusca. The first three phyla are represented by a few species.[20] From the coelenterates, eight species of hard coral and soft coral that inhabited the reefs of the Atlantic Ocean have been identified.[21] And from the last phylum, the shells of mollusks provide the most abundant remains of invertebrates found in the offerings. These animals were collected on land,[22] in sweetwater,[23] and in marine areas. According to the analysis of offerings 1, 3, 5, and H, more than 75 percent of the marine mollusks came from the Atlantic coast

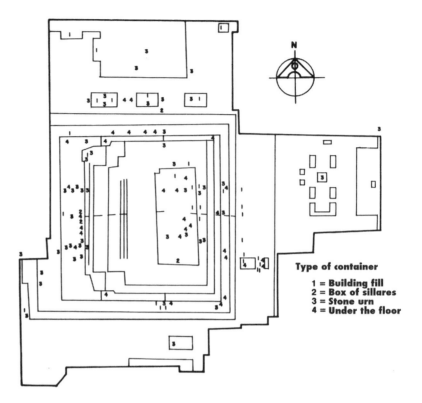

Figure 47:
Sketch of the type
of container for
each offering

Type of container

1 = Building fill
2 = Box of sillares
3 = Stone urn
4 = Under the floor

(Jiménez Badillo 1991; López Luján and Polaco 1991; Polaco 1982; Carramiñana 1988). These are sub-divided into polyplacophores,[24] gastropods (conch shells),[25] and lamellibranchs (bivalves).[26] A high percentage of the periostracii of the mollusk shells show no signs of wear or breakage, an indication that the animals were collected alive in their natural habitats. There are also some that were probably gathered on beaches, showing marks of abrasion by sand and retaining fragments of other invertebrates inside them.[27] In spite of the fact that most of the species are edible, the presence of opercula on several shells shows that they were not eaten.

The next most abundant remains after the mollusks come from the chordate phylum (Alvarez and Ocaña 1991; Alvarez 1982). About 58 percent of them belong to four different kinds of land vertebrates: amphibians, reptiles, birds, and mammals. The toad is the only amphibian; four *Bufo* sp. specimens were found (Alvarez and Ocaña 1991). It is interesting that no complete reptile examples were discovered. Moreover, only certain parts of each animal were deposited: turtle shells (Fig. 48), the skulls and skins of serpents, and the skulls and skin plaques of alligators (Fig. 49).[28] A significant number of birds also appeared in the offerings of the Templo Mayor;[29] the most common were quail, perhaps sacrificed during oblation rituals. Usually, the Mexica buried the entire bird, although in the case of certain birds of prey, only the head, wings, and claws were found. Although there are few signs of their existence, it is likely that many feathers were also offered.[30] Mammals are the last kind of vertebrates deposited as gifts.[31] A significant percentage of the remains belong to animals like mice, rats, gophers, and sheep, which clearly indicates that they belonged to later levels that intruded into pre-Hispanic contexts.

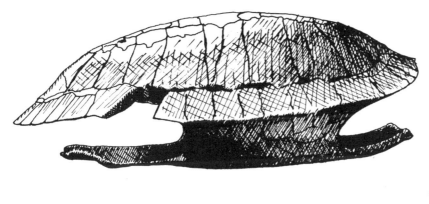

Figure 48:
Turtle shell offering.
(Drawing by Amelia
Malagamba.)

Forty-two percent of the chordates belong to two classes of aquatic vertebrates: fish and elasmobranchs (Alvarez and Ocaña 1991). Almost all the identified specimens came from the estuaries and reefs of the Gulf of Mexico;[32] the grouper is the only one from the Pacific Ocean.[33] Paradoxically, the sweetwater species that lived in the lakes of the Basin of Mexico hardly appear in the archaeological record.[34] Starting with the presence of specific characteristics in the examples studied, we can infer selective fishing. We know these were not food offerings because the number of edible species is only 30 percent.[35] To the contrary, poisonous fauna predominated, which is enormously important for symbolic analysis. Fish like the porcupine fish, fugu fish, puffer fish, trunkfish, and the barracuda are toxic when eaten; the scorpion fish and the ray inject poison into the victim. Additionally, most species had strange peculiarities: sharp teeth (shark, sawfish, and barracuda), strange bodies (needlefish and half-beak), bright colors (angelfish and parrot fish), or strong bristles (porcupine fish, trunkfish, and angelitos [*Prionotus cf. evolans*]). The predominance in the excavated contexts of dental, premaxillar, preopercular, and neurocranial remains and the absence of vertebrae or hipural plates is meaningful. This means that, in many cases, the Mexica did not deposit the bodies of the fish but only their heads and scales. All this is evidence that the Mexica observed strict rules in selecting animal material and prepared it in various ways before it was deposited.

Because of their perishability, relatively few remnants of the offerings of flora have endured until now. We found the remains of seeds and ears of corn, agave stalks and thorns, flowers,[36] grass, squash, wood copal,[37] charcoal, and rubber. Through decay, most of the vegetable matter has lost its original form, although in a few cases, we could detect precisely the original shape of the wooden objects—for example, zoomorphic representations, scepters, sheets, and bars, cylinders, spheres and anthropomorphic figures made from copal.

The raw minerals brought to Tenochtitlan from remote regions deserve special mention. Because of their quantity and wide distribution, marine sands and muds from lakes, coastal lagoons, and river outlets stand out (Carramiñana 1988). With these materials, the priests made homogeneous beds inside the receptacles, where they later placed all kinds of gifts.[38] Also discovered, although

Figure 49:
Offered alligator skull.
(Drawing by Amelia
Malagamba.)

fewer in quantity, were small unworked fragments of turquoise, jet, alabaster, and greenstone, as well as a kaolin obtained near the present city of Pachuca, Hidalgo.[39]

Another important kind of offering was human remains. Some individuals of high rank were ritually buried in the Templo Mayor after their bodies had been incinerated: we have their ashes and some of their partially burned bones (Chávez 2002).[40] By contrast, the remains of other people, sacrificial victims, were buried at the foot of the Templo Mayor. Osteological analysis shows that the sacrificed were infants killed in honor of Tlaloc[41] and decapitated adults.[42]

As mentioned before, the most abundant offerings of fabricated goods found in the deposits of the Templo Mayor were of foreign origin. Most of them came from the states of Guerrero, Oaxaca, Puebla, and Veracruz and could have come to Tenochtitlan as a result of tribute, commerce, donation, or pillage. I should emphasize that they were not unique pieces but relatively standardized, sumptuary articles imported in great quantities. Among the most important are: some 160 masks and two hundred anthropomorphic, full-size figures, as well as many greenstone animal and plant representations, coming from the state of Guerrero (Olmedo and González 1986: 117); two orange ceramic cinerary urns from Toluca Valley (Matos Moctezuma 1983, 1988c: 106–9; Chávez 2002); 203 sculptures—among them the ones known as "penates" (household gods)—and the votive portrayals of musical instruments, perhaps from the Mixteca (Urueta Flores 1990); two large water jars and several sculptures of travertine from the Puebla-Tlaxcala region (Matos Moctezuma 1988c: 102–13); and an impressive number of copper bells and greenstone beads, pendants, and earplugs of still undetermined origin.

The discovery of true antiques from the pre-Classic and Classic periods should also be mentioned. The Mexica, like the other Mesoamerican groups, buried in their own religious buildings rich, fabricated goods they took out of graves and offerings that had belonged to previous societies. During the excavations at the Templo Mayor, we found several Olmec objects, forty-one Teotihuacan pieces (Fig. 50), and twenty-three other pieces in the style known as Guerrero-Teotihuacanoid (Matos Moctezuma 1979c; López Luján 1989b; 2001b). Almost all these relics are beautiful works of carved stone or clearly religious ceramic vessels. They were made between twenty-two and seven centuries before they were offered at the Huey Teocalli.

Although the objects made by the Mexica are not as numerous as the imported goods, they do add up to a considerable total. For the most part, they are objects with a religious function, the most outstanding being the divine images in traditional form that were apparently made

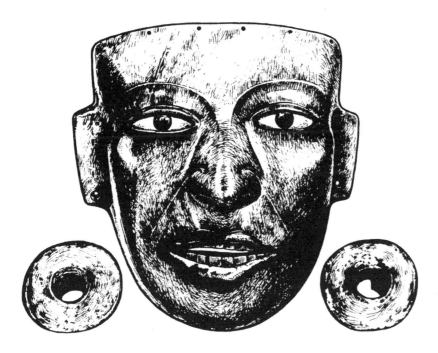

Figure 50:
Teotihuacan mask found in offering 82. (Drawing by Enrique Mora.)

expressly to be buried as offerings.[43] Other commonly found objects were the so-called skull-masks (Fig. 51), religious insignia (in stone, shell, or ceramic),[44] ceramic cosmic symbols,[45] small braziers, jars and boxes of orange ceramic, incense burners of polychrome ceramic, depictions of musical instruments,[46] blood letters made of bone, and carved stones.[47]

THE RICHNESS OF THE OFFERINGS

The number and variety of elements constituting an offering differed enormously (Fig. 52). The poorest offerings were limited to a single object: a cylinder of copal (offering 75) or ash remains (offering G). There were also offerings composed of objects of the same kind: four ceramic incense burners (offering 76), seven sacrificial knives (offering 76), a stack of maguey thorns (offering 72), and so on. Nevertheless, the most common offerings assembled very diverse materials (for example, blood letters, copal, quails, beheaded skulls, alligators, shells, braziers, and images of Tlaloc), occasionally reaching a total of up to 364 elements grouped in twenty-nine different categories.

The richness of the offerings is inversely proportional to the number of offerings. Seventy-four of the deposits studied (62.7%) had between zero and fifty elements.[48] The plots of the range of elements show that the number of offerings is fewer as their splendor increases (Figs. 53 and 54).

There was, however, an exact pattern of distribution for the offerings in the buildings, with respect to the number of elements contained. Usually, the offerings with few elements were grouped in the oldest constructive stages, at the corners, and in the secondary facades of the edifices. On the other hand, the most abundant were concentrated in the more recent stages, particularly in the principal facades and the central axes of the structures (Fig. 55).

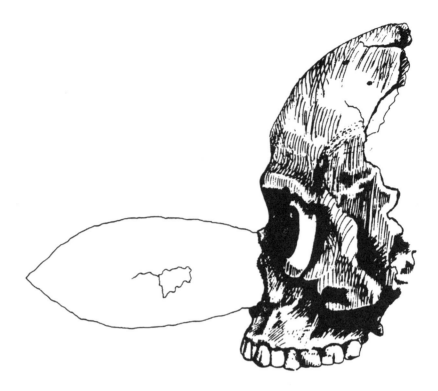

Figure 51:
Skull-mask offered in
the Templo Mayor.
(Drawing by Amelia
Malagamba.)

THE MANAGEMENT OF INNER SPACE

The meticulous recording done by the members of the Templo Mayor Project was very beneficial. One of the most significant results of this careful and methodical work was the discovery of the complex arrangement of gifts on the inside of containers. We became aware that each of the seven thousand elements offered was arranged in a premeditated and orderly fashion (Matos Moctezuma 1987b). Clearly, the species of flora and fauna, the products brought from remote regions, the Olmec and Teotihuacan "antiquities," and the Mexica manufactured objects were not placed randomly inside the architectural structures. And the purposeful placement of the materials should be understood as the intentional result of a ritual act, which was tied to the religious ideology of the individuals who performed it.

It is easy to verify the existence of internal spatial patterns—all it takes is an analysis of the photographs and plans that show each offering in situ. The gifts formed patterns in relation to the imaginary horizontal axes, the clusters of similar objects, and the vertically superposed levels.

The most noteworthy pattern in the gifts is their organization about horizontal axes (Fig. 60). The objects of each deposit are distributed along imaginary axes that run in a longitudinal and transverse direction, and often these paths serve to separate two symmetrical spaces. The same kind

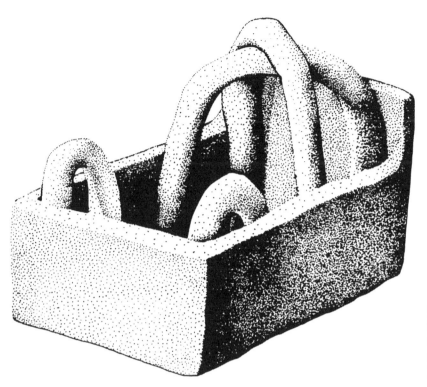

Figure 52:
Ceramic representation
of a deforming cradle.
(Drawing by Germán
Zúñiga.)

and number of objects are found on both sides of the axes. However, the organization of the materials was not limited to a simple bilateral symmetry. Objects that, according to Nahua cosmovision, had an opposed or complementary character were placed at the extreme ends of the principal axes. For example, flutes and horizontal drums, braziers and Tlaloc jars, and images of Xiuhtecuhtli and Tlaloc were found in opposite ends within the horizontal plane of the offering.

We also found that objects with the same characteristics of shape and form tended to be grouped together, spatially associated in well-defined groups (Fig. 61). Groupings of shells, conch shells, fish, quail, representations of musical instruments, sacrificial knives, projectile points, anthropomorphic sculptures, thorns for self-sacrifice, and such were very common. Moreover, these clusters generally had a number of significantly repetitive components. For example, there were groups of 2, 3, 4, 5, 8, 9, 13, 18, 40, and 120 elements. We know some of these numbers—2, 3, 4, 5, 9, and 13—were of great importance in the Mexica model of the universe (see López Austin 1988c: vol. 1, 50–68 for their significance). The number 18 is related to the calendar for it represents the total of twenty-day months that make up the Nahua *xihuitl* ("year"). It is harder to see the meaning of numbers such as 8, 40, and 120, although they could be multiples of the numbers associated with the cosmos.

Moreover, a marked layering of the materials offered is added to the complex horizontal distribution; 60.2% of the offerings had objects placed one above the other on different levels (Figs. 56 and 62). Although the offering and the burial of gifts were almost always performed on a single occasion,[49] the presence of vertical placement levels for objects indicates their correspondence with particular ritual moments of the same ceremony.

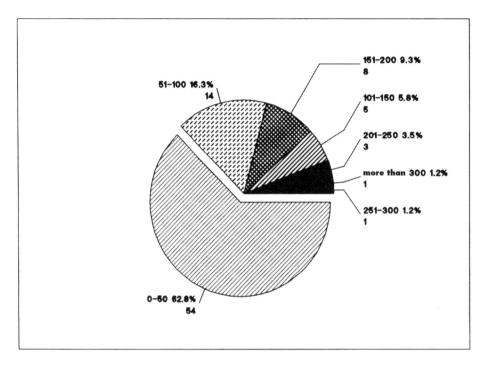

Figure 53: Range of the number of elements found in the Templo Mayor.

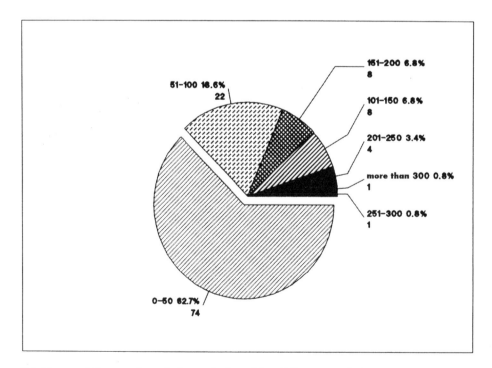

Figure 54: Range of the number of elements found in all the excavated area.

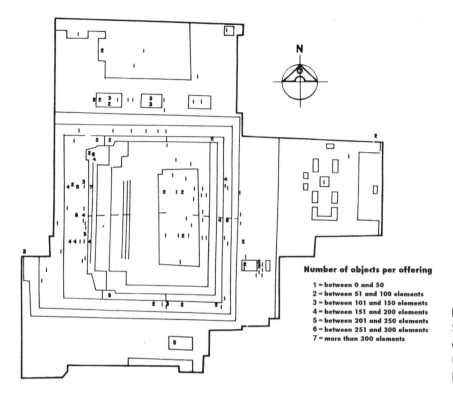

Number of objects per offering

1 = between 0 and 50
2 = between 51 and 100 elements
3 = between 101 and 150 elements
4 = between 151 and 200 elements
5 = between 201 and 250 elements
6 = between 251 and 300 elements
7 = more than 300 elements

Figure 55:
Sketch showing the distribution of the number of objects per offering.

The simplest offerings had a single level of objects; the more complicated might have had up to six layers. Each vertical level was composed of objects so similar to each other that strict taxonomic criteria must have been followed during the gift ceremonies (Fig. 63). It seems evident that the classification in a vertical sense obeyed a religious system. For instance, in the most sumptuous offerings the deepest levels, which were the first to be deposited, were composed of elements closely associated with the aquatic world of Mesoamerican cosmovision (such as shells, conch shells, corals, sculptures of greenstone, and portrayals of Tlaloc). The intermediate level basically contained the skin parts of fish, reptiles, and felines. Finally, the highest levels were characterized by images of deities, divine symbols, and ritual paraphernalia. In Chapter 8, I will discuss the possibility that segments of the cosmos were represented by layering objects with corresponding traits: on the lower level, aquatic objects; on the intermediate level, terrestrial objects; and on the upper level, celestial objects. In other offerings, we also encountered homogeneous levels: of mammals, greenstone beads, sacrificial knives, musical instruments, ceramic objects, and so on.

According to my statistical analysis, the single level offerings are the most numerous, 39.8% of the total. The offerings with two or three layers follow and are equally abundant (14.4%). The remainder have four, five, and six levels (Figs. 56 and 57).[50] If we review the distribution of offerings in the buildings in relation to the number of layers, we find a similar spatial pattern. The offerings with few vertical levels are primarily found in the oldest building stage and on the secondary facades of the buildings. Conversely the complex deposits with the greatest number of layers are

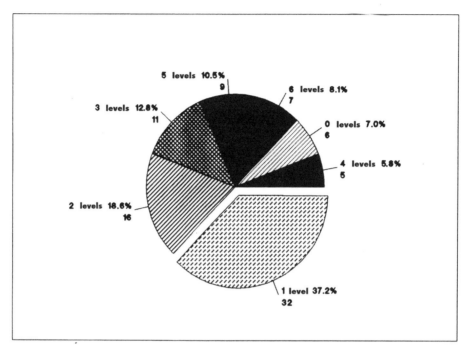

Figure 56: Proposed number of levels for the 86 offerings found in the Templo Mayor.

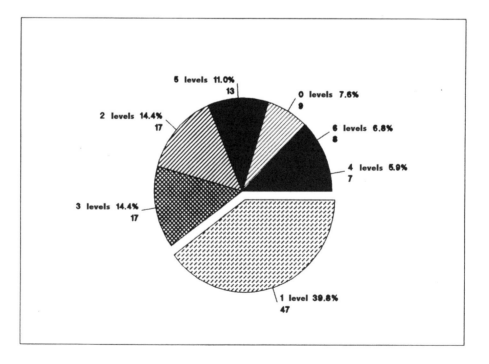

Figure 57: Proposed number of levels for the 118 offerings found in all the excavated area.

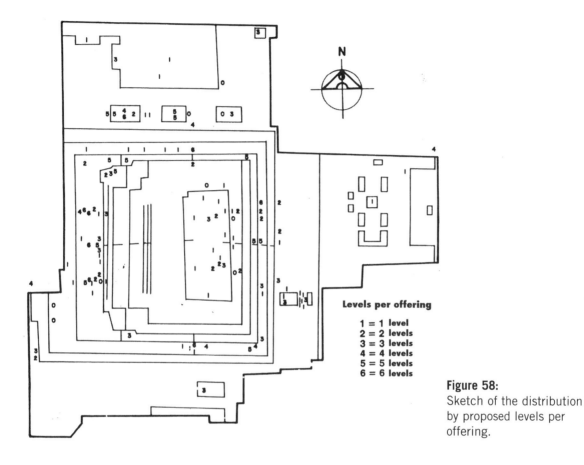

Figure 58:
Sketch of the distribution by proposed levels per offering.

Levels per offering

1 = 1 level
2 = 2 levels
3 = 3 levels
4 = 4 levels
5 = 5 levels
6 = 6 levels

grouped at the most recent stages, especially on the principal facades, on the central axes, and at the corners of the structures (Fig. 58).

PROPOSALS FOR ANALYSES

The preceding information demonstrates that not all of the offerings were buried with similar rituals nor for the same reasons. The diverse locations, contents, and internal distribution denote different purposes for the oblations. The placing of gifts in the earth and stone filling, between one building stage and another, was evidently tied to the work of expanding the edifice. It seems that other offerings were given at times of crises.[51] Many others are related to the cult of Huitzilopochtli or of Tlaloc, the deities to whom the temple was dedicated, and were linked to periodical or exceptional festivities. Finally, the other clusters of gifts could be related to the total significance of the Templo Mayor.

The complexity and diversity of Mexica offerings is such that, until now, their meaning has been obscured. The different principles evident in the spatial organization of the offerings follow a code that is difficult to decipher. We have a long way to go before reaching a final answer. It is clear that a rigorous and systematic method is needed for this task.

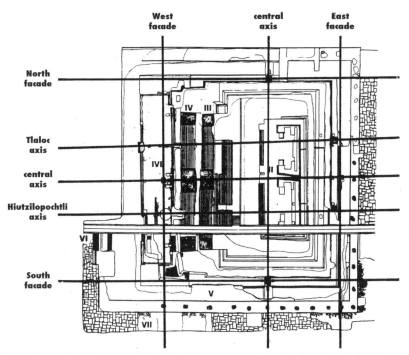

Figure 59: Imaginary axial lines marking the places where the Mexicas buried their offerings. (Drawing by Victor Rangel.)

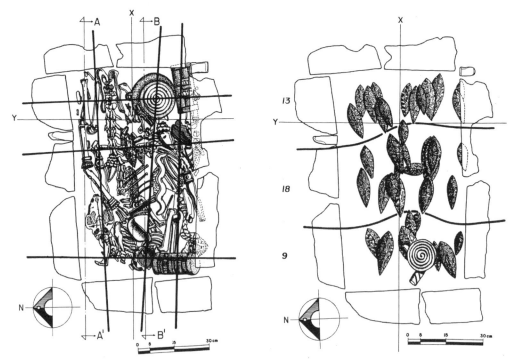

Figure 60: Imaginary horizontal axes. Offering H, excavation level 1. (Drawing by Leonardo López Luján.)

Figure 61: Groupings of 13, 18, and 9 sacrificial knives. Offering H, excavation level 3. (Drawing by Leonardo López Luján.)

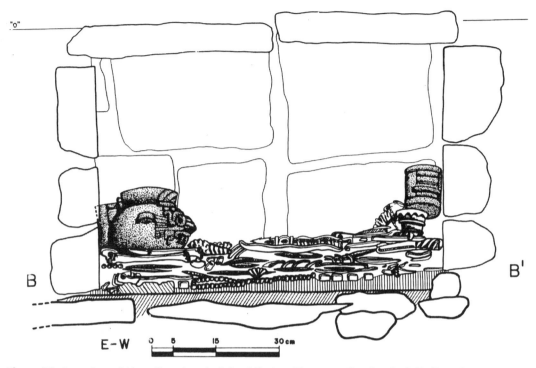

Figure 62: Layering of the offered materials. Offering H, excavation levels 1-5. (Drawing by Leonardo López Luján.)

From my viewpoint, a study of the offerings should go beyond a simple analysis of their contents. To sidestep the question of the relative position of the objects implies that relationships of complementarity, contradiction, superiority, subordination, and so forth are equivalent. But the objects are not isolated. They are parts of groups that functioned in specific cultural contexts. A gift acted as a sign or a symbol,[52] transmitting information only when it was combined with other gifts. Some objects probably had multiple semantic values, each one of which was expressed differently depending upon the context in which it was found. In a complementary way, it is possible that different kinds of objects shared the same meaning and were used as alternatives or synonyms.

The information in this chapter shows that archaeological contexts have a great similarity to ritual syntax and to verbal language. If this is correct, we will find two kinds of archaeological syntax: an "internal" one, corresponding to the distribution of objects within a container or receptacle, and an "external" one, related to the arrangement of the offerings with respect to architectural structures. In this sense, we could speak of a "language" of the offerings that resembles the basic principles of writing—a language not only expressed in signs and symbols, but also with grammatical (or contextual) rules.

For Ian Hodder (1988: 151), the term *contextual* refers to the presence and location of archaeological entities "in their respective texts." "The general idea here is that 'context' can refer to those parts of a written document that come immediately before and after a particular paragraph, connected in such a close fashion with its significance, that the meaning would not be clear if we separated them."

Figure 63:
Level composed of a jaguar and a wolf. Offering H, excavation level 2. (Photograph by Leonardo López Luján, courtesy INAH.)

Leach (1978: 15), in his book *Culture and Communication*, agreed with this idea. After an interesting discussion, he reached the conclusion that "*all* the different non-verbal dimensions of culture . . . are organized in structured groups in order to incorporate information coded in an analogous manner to the sounds, words and declarations of a natural language."

From this standpoint, such an analogy would be the logical consequence of the existence of a common code employed by the different human senses at a highly abstract level. This allows the conversion of sound messages to visual, olfactory, or tactile messages and vice versa (Leach 1978: 15).

Fortunately, as both Hodder and Leach maintained, the symbols of material culture are simpler, more enduring, and more flexible than their verbal homologues. To this is added the relative simplicity of the syntactic rules of nonverbal language, as compared with those of writing—something that is encouraging for any attempt at "reading" archaeological contexts.[53] However, the fundamental problem of understanding the meaning of material culture (for example, that of the offerings) rests on the fact that we do not yet have adequate "dictionaries" or "grammars."

I believe that the first attempt at approximating the language of the offerings should begin with two kinds of analyses: an offering can be studied as a unit by itself or as part of a greater unit of analysis. In the first case, the offering is considered as a discursive unit in which three basic syntactical factors stand out: the *horizontal space,* which determines the association of the objects (imaginary axes and groups of similar elements); the *vertical* space, related to the placement of objects in certain patterns tied to the time of the ritual oblation (the pieces are distributed successively in levels of superposition); and the *tridimensional space,* resulting from the accumulation and joining of horizontal levels during the course of the rite.

On the other hand, the offering can also be understood as a part of a larger unit of analysis, included within two different kinds of complicated complexes. Consequently, the offering should be studied as:

1. Part of a series of ritual patterns, that is, in relation to the long duration of the ritual tradition, religious belief, and cosmovision.[54] Here it is indispensable to analyze each offering in terms of its location in the ceremonial site and in comparison with the other offerings, particularly those that correspond to the same historical moment.

2. Part of the historical phenomena, that is, in relation to factors in the long, medium, or short time period (structural time, time of confluences, and time of events)—including institutions; economic, political, and social changes; famines; epidemics; and conquests. In this context, one must take into account the fact that the objects usually offered can be substituted by equivalents at certain historical moments when access to them would be difficult or, inversely, when other objects of better quality are available.

CHAPTER SEVEN

The General Taxonomy of the Templo Mayor Offerings

CLASSIFICATION IN ARCHAEOLOGY

Once the patterns perceived by a simple inspection or by descriptive statistics had been found, a more detailed analysis of the 118 offerings under study was needed. In Chapter 6, I referred to the more obvious characteristics. In this chapter, I will classify the material by means of complex techniques that will confirm the rough primary groups,[1] find precise criteria for division, and even discover new groups not apparent by means of the manual analysis of the data. These groupings will simplify the discovery of the offerings' syntax.

Since the eighteenth century, the distribution of archaeological entities into groups has been a fundamental part of our discipline. At present, a large part of the time and budget for a project is devoted to the classification of the different entities (attribute, artifact, artifact type, assemblage, culture, and cultural group) (Clarke 1978: 22–24). Indeed, this task has become so habitual that many investigators think of it not as a means but as the ultimate end of their search.

Why do archaeologists dedicate so much time to the work of classification? The answer lies in not considering taxonomy as a mere diversion or as an obsession of any scientist, for a well-understood classification yields many benefits. The first of them is of a practical nature. Imagine an archaeologist who wishes to communicate his or her findings and who had to describe each and every one of the entities discovered without the advantage of the groupings derived from proper classification (Orton 1988: 31). From that comes a second advantage: classification implies the creation of models needed for the organization and study of archaeological data. Complex situations are simplified when numerous entities are grouped, ignoring, for the moment, data that do not fit.

Classification can also become a valuable instrument for detecting regularities.[2] As is well known, various archaeological entities often show similarities due to nonrandom processes. Uniformity in archaeological material is caused by certain conditions or impositions of both physical and social action. Often the resemblances observed in material remains derive from certain patterns of social behavior, although they are not an immediate reflection of them; many archaeological regularities result from specific human activities. This is why the archaeologist uses material culture as a way of understanding the total cultural system. Furthermore, the search for patterns and their causes is a good procedure for reaching general statements, establishing predictive models, and generating new hypotheses (Clarke 1978: 21–22; Orton 1988: 32–33). These advantages justify the effort to classify the 118 offerings. After a cursory review of some of the deposits, we found great regularities in the spatial distribution of the gifts—regularities that would allow them to be grouped. Although the members of the project did not find identical offerings, we saw degrees of similarity among them. In other words, we discovered that they could be grouped in *polythetic groups*. "A polythetic group is a cluster of entities of which each one possesses a great number of the attributes of the group and each attribute is shared by numerous entities, while none of them is at the same time sufficient and necessary to assure its state as a member of the group."[3]

Before proceeding on the subject of the taxonomy of the offerings, I would like to mention some other problems relevant to this topic. One involves the *etic* or *emic* nature of archaeological typologies. That is, do archaeologists make artificial (and sometimes subjective) interpretations in their classifications, or do they approximate the taxonomy of societies that have disappeared? This is an old problem that has provoked disputes for decades. An example is the polemic started by J. A. Ford (1954) and Albert Spaulding (1953). As Hodder pointed out in a provocative book (1988: 160–61), most archaeologists have had to acknowledge a certain amount of subjectivity in their classifications. This is good because acknowledging the problem allows us to minimize the role of the observer. The conscious definition of criteria, the use of mathematical and computerized techniques, and the accumulation of the maximum possible information about the reasons for the resemblances and differences of archaeological entities are the approaches modern archaeologists have used to reduce this common bias. Perhaps because of this, there are now an increasing number of practitioners who consider taxonomy merely a heuristic method—an exploratory tool to analyze the structure of the data in a systematic way.

The number of possible classifications available to modern investigators, as well as people in the past, is infinite. The characteristics of each classification depend on the conscious or unconscious selection of attributes from an equally unlimited number of reasons for classification. Therefore, for our classifications to mean something, they must be congruent with the context of the problem we are trying to solve. With this in mind, the classification of the 118 offerings in the following pages will approximate, as far as possible, the indigenous taxonomy that classified gifts for the purpose of the rituals. The intent of the proposed grouping is limited to finding the logic behind Mexica ritual actions. In other words, I wish to use my own taxonomy as a heuristic method with semiotic value.

It is useful to explain the three steps in any classifying process (Orton 1988: 67). The first step is archaeological. It consists of defining the relevant attributes of the study. Here it is very important to define the criteria that guide the selection of the characteristics of each entity to be recorded. The second step is the classification itself. At this time, the study sample is divided into subunits, following certain indispensable norms for good partitioning.[4] The archaeological entities are grouped mathematically according to their similarities and differences. Thanks to computer science, this process is now faster and more objective than in the past. The final step consists of defining the groups, a task in which both the classificatory design and the reasons for such groupings should be made clear. As I will show later, a good example of this step is the partitioning of the dendrograms. This stage should be seen as the beginning of an interpretation of the results in a sociocultural context.

NUMERICAL TAXONOMY

I used *numerical taxonomy*, which has been employed productively for more than forty years, for grouping the offerings. This method was developed in 1963 by Peter H. Sneath and Robert R. Sokal for resolving problems of biological systematics and population biology.[5] However, neither scientist imagined that numerical taxonomy would rapidly transcend the boundaries of their discipline to become very popular in other fields of knowledge. Today numerical grouping is practiced in many areas, as shown by the yearly publication of more than one thousand titles (Doran and Hodson 1975: 159; Lock and Wilcock 1987: 37).

The first successful application in archaeology was Hodson, Sneath, and Doran's (1966) use of numerical analysis with a cluster of bronze fibulas. Since then, this productive method has become an indispensable taxonomic instrument in our field. Mexican archaeologists, among others, have successfully employed this method. Some praiseworthy examples are works by Espinosa and Manzanilla (1985), Janet Long Solís (1977), Olmedo and González (1986), and Maricarmen Serra Puche, Jean Pierre Laporte, and Espinosa (1978).

The acceptance of numerical taxonomy in academic circles is due largely to the fact that it allows the classification of huge aggregates of entities in a fast, explicit, and objective way. Numerical taxonomy is made up of a set of mathematical procedures that enable us to form groups with minimal internal variation and with relative differences from other groups of the same classification. The entities are grouped according to attributes shared at the moment of study (*phenotypic relationships*), without regard to the origin and evolution of their similarities (*genetic relationships*) (Martínez Malo 1979). The resemblance between two entities is expressed numerically in a *similarity coefficient*.[6]

Numerical taxonomy, like all other classificatory procedures, requires as a first step the selection of the total of entities that will be analyzed and the explicit choice of relevant attributes. Here it is recommended that the archaeologist (1) choose the largest possible number of attributes;[7] (2) include only attributes with two or more alternative states;[8] and (3) assign the same weight to each state.[9] There are two different scales for attributes: qualitative scales that can be subdivided into nominal scales, in which the entities differ by units of the attribute (present/absent, discrete), and ordinal scales, in which the entities differ in the magnitude of the attribute either discretely or continuously.

Quantitative scales that can be expressed with either discrete or continuous values are divided into ratio and interval scales. In numerical taxonomy, the states of attributes are always given in ciphers, but in a ratio scale, these units have no arithmetic value (Martínez Malo 1979).

The next step consists of a description of the entities according to the chosen attributes. The results of the description should be recorded in numerical terms on a data matrix. On the matrix, the entities are placed on the columns, and the attributes are set down on the rows. After the analysis of the study sample, the numerical value of the states of the attribute are recorded at the corresponding intersections of rows and columns.

Once this operation is completed, the similarity between each pair of entities is computed according to the number of common attributes. The observed similarity is expressed by a numerical coefficient. The nature of this coefficient depends on the study's purposes and the nature of the scale employed. An association coefficient will be used in the case of a qualitative scale of attributes.[10] If a quantitative scale is required, a coefficient of dissimilarity or distance should be used.[11] With a computer, it is possible to make a fast calculation of the similarity among all possible pairs of entities: the result is a symmetrical square matrix (of association or of distance). The entities now appear both in the columns and in the rows, and the measure of similarity or dissimilarity between a pair of entities lies along the diagonal running across the intersection of the corresponding column and row. Depending on the coefficient used, the largest similarity or the smallest dissimilarities lie on the diagonal where each entity crosses with itself.

Unfortunately, the taxonomic structure of this matrix is not apparent at a simple glance. The problem is how to simplify the matrix to make it comprehensible without distorting it. There are at least three techniques that solve the problem in different ways: cluster analysis, multidimensional scaling, and an analysis of the principal components.[12] The best-known numerical taxonomy packages use cluster analysis, and only the principles of those methods will be described here.

Two different types of classification are obtained by the analysis of the similarity matrix using cluster analysis. Nonhierarchical methods result in a single division of entities into classes. Hierarchical methods produce a series of divisions, which are represented iconically with dendrograms, or trees, of the entities. On any dendrogram, the entities with the greatest similarity values are located on nearby branches, and differing entities are on the more distant branches. Note that the branches of the dendrogram represent levels of similarity between entities, rather than genetic descent.

Usually, hierarchical methods construct the tree from its branches back to the trunk.[13] The nature of the dendrogram (that is, of the links among the entities) depends directly on the clustering method chosen. Although there are several methods, three of them are used most frequently: single linkage clustering, average linkage clustering, and complete linkage clustering.

The simplest procedure and the only one of a continuous nature is that of the simple linkage clustering.[14] Initially, each entity constitutes an individual grouping. Next, the pair of entities whose coefficient of similarity is the highest in the similarity matrix is found. These two entities make up the first group. Then the matrix is examined to find the next highest coefficient. If it occurs between an entity of the first group and a third entity, the latter joins the group. On the other hand, if it is found between another pair of entities, those two form another group. These two groups are fused if the next highest coefficient occurs between an entity of the first group and one of the second. The process continues in this way until the dendrogram is completed, with the number of groups slowly reduced (Anderberg 1973: 137; Doran and Hodson 1975: 176; Sneath and Sokal 1973: 216–22; Orton 1988: 51–56).

The principal problem with single linkage clustering is that it generates chaining among the entities: once the links are formed, they will not be broken. The consequences are long groups whose extremes can be very different. Because of this, many archaeologists prefer to use one of the other two methods.

Average and complete linkage clustering methods were developed to avoid the problem of chaining (Anderberg 1973: 138–40; Doran and Hodson 1975: 176–77; Sneath and Sokal 1978: 222–40). Both produce dendrograms that better represent the taxonomic structure of the similarity matrix. The groups are small and compact, and they give reliable information about the linkages at the middle of the dendrogram. Just as in single linkage clustering, the two most similar entities in average and complete linkage clustering form the first group. However, the rules for attaching other entities onto existing groups are different. In complete linkage, for instance, an entity is joined to a group if its similarity to the group is equal to that of its most dissimilar member. Two groups are joined when their two most dissimilar entities—one in each group—are both united by a similarity to one another. Average linkage clustering calculates the arithmetical mean of the similarity between the entity and the members of the group to which it is to be connected or between the members of two groups to be united.

One of the inconveniences of the average and complete linkage methods is that they require a greater number of mathematical calculations, consuming more computer time and memory. They also are discontinuous, which means that a minimal change in the similarity coefficient of two entities can affect their immediate proximity on the dendrogram and even the entire model (Martínez Malo 1979; Orton 1988: 56). In spite of these limitations, the average and complete linkage methods together yield better results than those of single linkage clustering because they do not lead to chaining of the entities. One the other hand, it should be pointed out that the results of both methods are often quite similar.

Traditionally, the results of cluster analysis are presented in the form of dendrograms.[15] This kind of model compresses into two dimensions the taxonomical structure of the similarity matrix. The abscissa of the dendrogram represents the similarity coefficients that unite the entities. The ordinate joins, at the extremes of its branches, the entities classified. Therefore, the intersection of an abscissa and an ordinate indicates the degree of similarity between the two branches joined there. In this way, the dendrogram shows a series of increasingly inclusive groupings, from the specificity of entities themselves to the generalization of the trunk or the single group.

There are several ways to partition a dendrogram, but none is completely satisfactory. Two of them are based on mathematical intuition: either a set number of groups are chosen and a horizontal line is traced on the dendrogram so that it will intersect the same number of branches or a similarity coefficient is selected and the existing branches are cut at that level. An alternate form in which the branches are separated at different levels is better because it is based on archaeological intuition; a "good" group is one where the members join on a lower part of the dendrogram and do not join another group until quite a bit later (Dunnell 1971: 101; Orton 1988: 58–59).

The last step of numerical taxonomy is the interpretation of the dendrogram, that is, the search for the meaning of the groupings according to the attributes selected and to the initial hypothesis. The validity of the groups and the identity of the states of attributes that define each cluster should be verified visually at this crucial stage (Orton 1988: 59; Espinoza and López 1980: 65).

THE PROCESS EMPLOYED

Having explained the fundamentals of numerical taxonomy, I will describe the specific process followed in classifying the offerings. In our study sample, encompassing 118 offerings, each offering was conceived of as an entity susceptible to grouping.

The chief problem lay in selecting the attributes of the offerings on the basis of an analysis with an acceptable degree of objectivity. As with any other entity, an offering has an infinite range of attributes, which makes it impossible to include all of them. In our study, a few archaeologically significant attributes were explicitly selected for the investigation, using as a guide my frame of reference, my personal concept of the problem, and even my prejudices. The purpose of this work was to find the religious significance of the offerings. In my judgment, this task would be successfully completed if the original role of each object in the offerings was taken into account. Thus, characteristics such as the raw material, size, and techniques of manufacture of artifacts may not be relevant in certain circumstances: it all depends on the semiotic value in a particular context. Therefore, an attribute of an offering is any object type to which a semiotic value is given in a ritual act. *Object type* in this context does not have the usual meaning of *type* in archaeology.

It is evident that there are levels of objectivity involved in the selection of attributes (such as those due to experience gained in daily work) that are difficult to state explicitly. And any selection of attributes can, of course, be improved. In this case, we tried to reach a balance between criteria in which the objectivity was obvious and criteria that assumed the significance of an object in the ritual. One way to reduce error in classifications is to select a large number of attributes, thereby diluting the negative effect of the ones that are incorrectly chosen. For purely operational purposes, a prior classification was made, which served as a guide in developing the list of attributes. The following fifteen groups, chosen in advance, were useful in the first stage but did not influence the computerized process. I will list them only as a simple explanation of the process.

1. Divine images (attributes 1–15). Included were anthropomorphic portrayals clearly attributed to a god, particular images whose identification has not been possible, and objects that were used generically to represent different divinities.

2. Divine symbols (attributes 16–28). These are objects associated with the different divinities, such as scepters and distinctive attire.

3. Localizators (attributes 29–35). These attributes indicate the segment of the cosmos to which the offering refers. They are masses of materials that reproduce the domain where the god is located.

4. Faunal remains (attributes 36–61). These include complete or partial bodies of animals, some of which have an environmental function similar to that of the objects in the preceding group.

5. Sculptural representations of flora and fauna (attributes 62–68).

6. Cosmic symbols (attributes 69–71). These are stone and ceramic objects that refer to the circulation of forces through the universe.

7. Penitential instruments (attributes 72–75). These are objects directly or indirectly related to self-sacrifice.

8. Sacrificial instruments (attributes 76–77). These are artifacts directly or indirectly related to ritual killing.

9. Sacrificed human remains (attributes 78–79).

10. Remains of birds used in sacrifice (attribute 80).

11. Clusters of gifts and objects given as offerings (81–88).

12. Votive representations (attributes 89–93). Included in this group are representations of musical instruments and votive miniatures.

13. Sumptuary gifts (attributes 94–103). These are gifts of precious materials.

14. Funerary material (attributes 104–107). These include human remains and mortuary objects.

15. Unidentified objects (attributes 108–109). These are all kinds of decayed material.

With this as a guide, a total of 109 attributes or different object types were chosen. These were, indeed, significant in the numerical taxonomy analysis, that is, they had a direct influence on the formation of groups. According to the selection criteria, any of these object types had to give semiotic information about the offering and had to be present in at least one offering. All object types were given the same value. A list of them follows:

Matrix of Contexts

ATTRIBUTE NUMBER	OBJECT TYPE (ATTRIBUTE)
1.	Xiuhtecuhtli
2.	Tonacatecuhtli
3.	Mictlantecuhtli
4.	Tlaltecuhtli
5.	Tezcatlipoca
6.	Ehecatl
7.	Tlaloc
8.	Chalchiuhtlicue
9.	Skull-mask

Matrix of Contexts

ATTRIBUTE NUMBER	OBJECT TYPE (ATTRIBUTE)
10.	Anthropomorphic mask
11.	Anthropomorphic figure
12.	Penate
13.	Personified knife
14.	Deity portrayed on a jar
15.	Deity made of copal
16.	Xiuhcoatl scepter
17.	Deer head scepter
18.	Scepter in form of a serpent
19.	Chicahuaztli scepter
20.	Scepter termini (snake rattle and serpent head)
21.	Obsidian earplug and scepter
22.	Representation of a deforming cradle
23.	Brazier with a bowknot
24.	Split-end noseplug typical of Xipe Totec
25.	Oyohualli
26.	Perforated shell circle
27.	Perforated obsidian circle
28.	Tzicolnacochtli or ehecacozcatl
29.	Sand
30.	Rubber
31.	Greenstone bead
32.	Fragment of raw greenstone
33.	Fragment of raw travertine
34.	Fragment of raw turquoise
35.	Fragment of raw jet
36.	Jaguar
37.	Puma
38.	Lynx
39.	Wolf
40.	Armadillo
41.	Rabbit
42.	Eagle
43.	Hawk
44.	Crow
45.	Toucan
46.	Heron
47.	Pelican
48.	Turkey
49.	Alligator
50.	Serpent
51.	Turtle
52.	Toad
53.	Shark

Matrix of Contexts

ATTRIBUTE NUMBER	OBJECT TYPE (ATTRIBUTE)
54.	Sawfish
55.	Fish
56.	Conch shell
57.	Shell
58.	Crustacean
59.	Chiton
60.	Sea urchin
61.	Coral
62.	Representation of a feline
63.	Representation of a bird
64.	Representation of a serpent
65.	Representation of a turtle
66.	Representation of a fish
67.	Representation of a conch shell
68.	Plant representation
69.	Ceramic ollin
70.	Helicoidal bead
71.	Spiral
72.	Bone or agave bloodletter
73.	Manta ray spine
74.	Prismatic obsidian blade
75.	Obsidian core
76.	Sacrificial knife
77.	Blank
78.	Decapitated human skull with first vertebrae
79.	Sacrificed child's skeleton
80.	Quail
81.	Ceramic incense burner
82.	Potsherd
83.	Brazier
84.	Jar
85.	Cajete
86.	Charcoal
87.	Copal
88.	Seed
89.	Representation of a musical instrument
90.	Representation of a miniature canoe with fishing gear
91.	Representation of miniature atlatl
92.	Representation of an axe or club
93.	Projectile point
94.	Gold necklace beads
95.	Turquoise necklace beads
96.	Rock crystal necklace beads
97.	Greenstone necklace beads

Matrix of Contexts

ATTRIBUTE NUMBER	OBJECT TYPE (ATTRIBUTE)
98.	Stone pectoral or pendant
99.	Earplug or noseplug
100.	Copper or silver bell
101.	Remains of textiles
102.	Traces of feathers
103.	Olmec or Teotihuacan relics
104.	Incinerated human remains
105.	Unburned bone remains
106.	Funerary urn
107.	Stone bead in the mouth
108.	Amorphous wood remains
109.	Turquoise mosaic

After the 109 attributes (object types) were defined, a two-state nominal scale was chosen. This means that each kind of object could only have two alternative states: "absence" or "presence," numerically represented as 0 and 1, respectively, although they do not have any arithmetical value. The selection of this kind of scale was due to the heterogeneity of the field records consulted. In many cases, the exact quantities of the objects contained in each offering were lacking; a single "element number" was given a group of objects without noting the total of its components. The choice of scale was also influenced by the lack of semiotic value for the total number of each object type. As I demonstrated in the last chapter, objects of the same type are associated horizontally in several groups for which the numbers of the respective elements have a clear religious significance. When these numbers are added together, the resulting total is meaningless.

Later, the information concerning the object types that comprised each offering was collected. To do this, both the publications concerning the excavations of 1948, 1966, and 1978 (Estrada Balmori 1979; Angulo 1966a; Contreras 1979b; García Cook and Arana 1978) and the different field records of the Templo Mayor Project (1978–1989) were consulted. The information obtained was manually entered into a matrix, relating 109 object types with each of the 118 offerings (12,862 entries). It is important to add that the completed matrix showed a high index of absences (recorded as 0) due to the predominance of uncommon object types (see the General Matrix of Presences/Absences).

The General Matrix of Presences/Absences was entered for analysis into an IBM PC/AT microcomputer. Initially, the data were entered using the Lotus 1-2-3 spreadsheet (version 2.01). The great versatility of this package allowed continuous entry, correction, and organization of the data. After repeated comparisons of the handwritten matrix and the computer version, the latter was exported in a binary form, with the help of an interface, to a statistical program for the purpose of calculating the dissimilarity by means of mathematical coefficients. For this, we used the package UCINET (*Microcomputer Package for Network Analysis*), version 3.0 (1987).[16]

Once the information was in the UCINET, the dissimilarity coefficients were calculated, measuring the existing Euclidian distance between each pair of offerings, on one hand, and that between each pair of object types, on the other. This procedure consisted of counting the number of attributes without common states, that is, the number of discrepancies or unshared presences/absences (0,1 or 1,0) between two entities. The result was two dissimilarity matrices. Later, the resulting matrices were squared in order to learn the exact number of unshared states (0,1 or 1,0).[17]

Next the complete linkage (diameter) method was applied to the two dissimilarity matrices in order to avoid chaining. In a short time, UCINET drew up two clustering structures that were the basis for the offerings and object types dendrograms. All the information processing was done by the Institute for Investigations of Applied Mathematics and Systems of the Universidad Nacional Autónoma de México (UNAM), under the skillful supervision of Guillermo Espinosa.

The partition of both dendrograms was done at different dissimilarity levels. The groupings were considered to be satisfactory when their members joined on the lower part of the dendrogram and did not combine with another group until fairly high on the tree, forming well-differentiated branches. All the groupings defined in this first attempt at division were compared visually with the excavation plans. The offerings from the same group were compared to each other with respect to the contextual location, the number of objects contained, and the internal distribution. By looking at the plans, it was relatively easy to analyze the degree of coherence in the dendrogram groupings at different levels of hierarchy. Thus it was decided if a grouping was correct, if it was possible to subdivide it further, or if it could be enlarged by adding more members. The hierarchical structure of the dendrogram was always respected in this process.

A study of the plans for excavation helped us, among other things, to see that some branches should be partitioned very early on the dendrogram. This was the case for deposits with only one kind of object. For example, the computer joined the offerings of copal, ashes, and maguey thorns almost at the base of the dendrogram. Despite their radical differences, the machine considered them to be very similar to each other because they shared the state of absence (0) in 108 of the 109 object types. Consequently, I had to cut the dendrogram at the level of 1 unshared presence/absence (see the Dendrogram of Offerings).

Another way to verify the internal coherence of the groupings was to define which attributes (object types) had a greater frequency in those groupings. The original Lotus 1-2-3 matrix was redone according to the sequence of objects and object types indicated on the dendrograms (see the Reordered General Matrix). This reorganization grouped the presence states (1) into "clouds" that made it easier to see which of the attributes defined each group. The frequencies of the "present" states were calculated in all the groups in order to find the values that exceeded a certain level of significance, thus establishing the principal attributes of each group (Figs. 64-66).[18] The presence of an object type was considered relevant when it was recorded in all or in the majority of the members of the group. Major importance was given to the presence of those object types that, besides defining a group, were absent from the rest of the sample.

From my point of view, the detailed analysis of the Dendrogram of Offerings and the visual comparison of the members of each group resulted in a good classification. Generally, the groups of offerings obtained, called complexes, are homogeneous and compact. They often share the same internal distribution of objects and a similar spatial location. On the Dendrogram of Offerings, 102 of them can be classified into twenty complexes,[19] and 16 are isolated. The latter

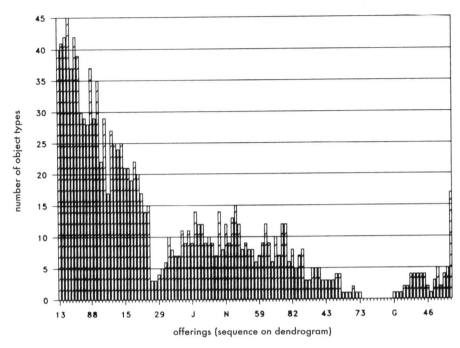

Figure 64: Graph showing the variety of offerings (number of object types) according to sequence on the dendrogram.

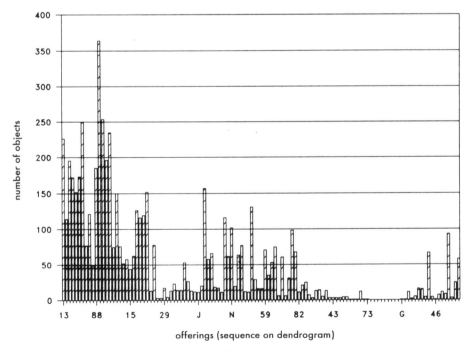

Figure 65: Graph showing the richness of the offerings (number of elements) according to the sequence on the dendrogram.

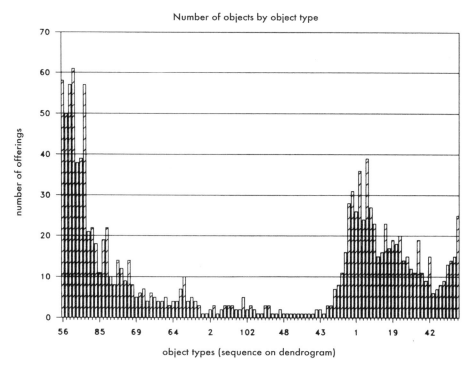

Figure 66: Graph showing frequency of object types according to the sequence on the dendrogram.

present such a diversity in the quantity, quality, and distribution of the objects contained, as well as in their contextual location, that they can be considered unique offerings.[20]

Similarly, the Dendrogram of Object Types was used to analyze the attributes that defined the groups of offerings and to better understand the object types that were repeatedly associated. After an analysis of the dendrogram, I obtained thirteen complexes of object types.[21]

Appendix 2 has a detailed description of the twenty complexes obtained, and Appendix 3 describes the sixteen unique offerings. For each complex of offerings, information will be given about: (1) the general characteristics of the complex (members, hierarchical grouping structure within the dendrogram, and complexes of object types that determine the groupings); (2) the richness of the offerings (quantity and diversity of the objects obtained in each deposit); (3) the context of the offerings (time and spatial location), together with the type and dimensions of the container and the number of levels of excavation; and (4) the internal distribution of the objects (general orientation, vertical levels of superimposition, orienting horizontal axes, and the most conspicuous groupings). The description of each group will be accompanied by a sketch of the architectural structures, showing the spatial distribution of the offerings.

CHAPTER EIGHT

Approach to the Meaning of the Offerings

ANALYSIS OF THE MEANING

After a long search for the logic, structure, and meaning of the offerings, it is now time to tie up some loose ends. Using the systematic correlation of the archaeological record, the historical sources, and ethnographic testimonies, I will try to elucidate the religious significance of two unique offerings and of thirty-four others, which are grouped in seven different complexes. I believe that the key to this analysis lies in the correlation of the offerings with descriptions of the ritual ceremonies that created them, in the comparison with the symbolic characteristics of the buildings in which they were placed, and in an internal comparison to find recurring traits. However, I am convinced that a complete understanding of the offerings discovered in the Templo Mayor Project is an extremely ambitious enterprise that will require long years of concerted effort by numerous specialists. Obviously, the study of these rich deposits of gifts must be carefully done, using various perspectives and different kinds of information.

Several approaches are used in the explanation that follows. First, I will analyze offerings 16 and 48 separately—offerings that can be considered unique because of their exceptional characteristics. After that I will examine the poorest offerings according to numerical taxonomy (O, P, and R). These are deposits that contain only one object type. Later, I will describe the blue jars complex (N), the stone urns complex (F_1), and the funeral deposits complex (E). Finally, I will explore the general significance of the consecration offerings complex (A), which is the richest of all.

OFFERING 16

THE CHARACTERISTICS OF OFFERING 16

This offering is made up of three different deposits.[1] It is located inside Building L, one of the fifteen structures found around the Huey Teocalli. The chief relevance of offering 16 to our analysis lies in its clear symbolic correlation with the surrounding architectural structures. The gifts that compose it show, in an unusual way, an internal spatial distribution similar to the one that Building L has, with its four surrounding altars (Fig. 157).[2]

Offering 16 was found under the western base of that building. In Chapter 4, I mentioned that this small and deteriorated rectangular building is contemporaneous with Stage VI of the Templo Mayor. It is surrounded by the traces of four altars that were perhaps torn down by the Mexica themselves, located toward the northeast, northwest, southeast, and southwest. Just as in Building L, the four altars have a rectangular base and are oriented longitudinally from east to west. Unfortunately, we have only a few indications about what the function of this building complex might have been.

Offering 16, one of the poorest in our study, has only three different object types. If we study the computer-generated dendrogram, we will see that offering 16 occupies a branch next to offering 91 (see the Dendrogram of Offerings). However, it was not possible to group the two deposits because offering 91 could not be completely excavated (see Appendix 2).

A quarry stone sillar box protected the modest gifts of offering 16. The most interesting object was a red tezontle anthropomorphic sculpture characterized by two protuberances on the head. The image was found at the extreme east, facing westward. It was surrounded by five greenstone beads distributed uniformly at the corners (northeast, northwest, southeast, and southwest) and the center of the box. Curiously, the central bead was a little larger than the others. A prismatic obsidian blade also lay in the central section (Figs. 67 and 68).

Continuing our exploration toward the eastern side of the box, we found a hewn quarry stone niche, which was labeled 16-A. Inside were another five greenstone beads distributed exactly as those of offering 16, one in the center and one in each corner, but here the central chalchihuite was smaller than the other four. A third deposit, which I have provisionally named "annex" (see description in Appendix 3), was discovered on the central facade of Building L (Contreras and Luna 1982). It was only a small, polychrome vessel adorned with the face of Tlaloc, containing twenty-four greenstone beads (see the blue jars complex).

The images with two protuberances on their heads

As the first step to understanding the meaning of offering 16, I will look at the principal object in the offering, the anthropomorphic image with two projections on its head (Figs. 69 and 70). This is not an unusual image—many specimens of this type were found in the twentieth century in the ruins of Tenochtitlan. They are sculptures with very stereotyped traits that always form part of offerings. Until now, archaeologists have reported a total of forty-one figures with that feature, coming from thirty-one offerings, and they are still being cataloged.[3] We do not know the context for a few

Figure 67:
Offering 16. (Photograph by Salvador Guil'liem, courtesy INAH.)

others, all of which belong to collections in North America or Europe.[4] It is quite likely that they come from similar deposits, and it is logical to believe, as Nagao (1985b: 64) did, that they were made expressly to be buried in religious buildings.

In general, the Mexica sculptors used basalt or tezontle for these images. Their dimensions and proportions are standard, and all of them are between 30 and 40 cm tall. The invariable presence of the *maxtlatl* ("breechcloth") leaves no doubt that they represent males. A reclining position, although not unique to these deities, is present in every case. "They are seated with their legs apart, facing front and with bent arms placed on the knees one over the other, marking off the internal space" (Solís Olguín 1985).[5]

Without exception, their eyes seem to be blind or closed, and they have a delicate mouth from which only two rectangular teeth protrude over the lower lip.[6] They wear earplugs in the shape of rectangular plaques with dangling pendants. On their heads, they wear diadems adorned with large concentric circles. From the center of each diadem, an undulating form, which may represent a stylized animal, emerges. A smooth paper fan is tied to the nape, and several elements that appear to be ribbons, bands, or locks of hair adorned with what seem to be stylized turtle shells hang from the shoulders. However, the most characteristic attribute of each of these images is the two block-shaped protuberances with four edges that emerge from the head.

A high percentage of the sculptures retain traces of coloring, which obviously contributed to the iconographic identification of the personage represented. The majority of sculptures have black pigment on the lower half of the face and red around the mouth and ears. Two examples of this unmistakable facial decor can be seen in Rubén Bonifaz Nuño (1981: 127) and Matos Moctezuma (1986c: 107). Some also have remains of blue coloring on the upper part of the face. The bands on the diadems were painted red, and the concentric circles and central elements were blue.

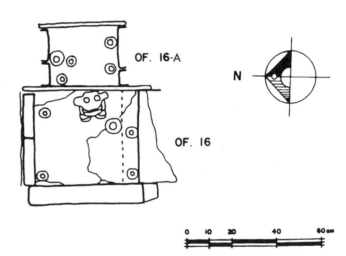

Figure 68:
Cross section and
overhead view of
offerings 16 and 16-A.
(Drawing by
Germán Zúñiga.)

The protuberances on the heads had traces of ocher, and the forms hanging over the backs were blue.[7] The earplugs were blue with red horizontal bands.

It is astonishing that all the pieces have such standardized features. Only two of them show noticeable differences from the others, differences that probably mark them as specific advocations or as different gods. The first one is piece number IVb 649 at the Basel Ethnographic Museum (Fig. 71c). In contrast to the others, it shows an individual with: a beard, a descending plumed serpent emerging from the diadem, circular earspools, two protuberances shaped like tortoise shells,[8] a pleated paper fan, and a tortoise shell on its back. The second piece was discovered in Chamber 2 of the Templo Mayor (Fig. 71b).[9] Several features characterize this sculpture: it is made of travertine, the individual is in a seated position with his hands along his sides holding onto his knees, there is a cord in the diadem, the individual has circular earspools, there are two protuberances shaped like tortoise shells,

Figure 69: Photograph of anthropomorphic sculpture with two protuberances on its head. (Photograph by Miguel Morales, courtesy INAH.)

Figure 70:
Different views of
an anthropomorphic
sculpture with two
protuberances on
its head. (Drawing by
José Luis García.)

there is a pleated paper fan, and a tortoise shell is on the figure's back. These two exceptional pieces have elements that, tentatively, might relate them to earth and fertility.[10]

An old polemic

Until now, scholars of pre-Hispanic Mexico have not agreed about who the sculptures with the two protuberances on the head represent. This argument, which has been going on for almost a century, hinges upon a number of problems of interpretation. The first concerns the pose of the image. Several investigators have seen its state of repose as the distinctive trait. However, a seated position with hands resting on knees is a characteristic of countless gods; many sculptured deities are in this position. Among them are Ehecatl-Quetzalcoatl,[11] Macuilxochitl,[12] Mictlantecuhtli,[13] Tlaloc,[14] Chalchiuhtlicue, Tonatiuh,[15] and, of course, the personage with the two protuberances on his head.

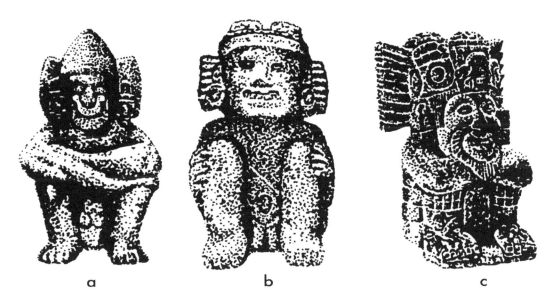

Figure 71: (a) Anthropomorphic sculpture in offering 6 at the Templo Mayor; (b) white stone anthropomorphic sculpture in Chamber 2 of the Templo Mayor; (c) figure number IVb 649 in the Museum für Völkerkunde in Basel. (Drawing by José Luis García.)

Some pictographic representations have important clues as to the specific meaning of such a body pose. In them, small seated gods—perhaps simple divine images—are seen on the inside of temples, receiving gifts of copal, rubber, wood, maize, and iguanas from the hands of gods who are standing (see *Códice Dresde* 1988: pl. 8c; *Códice Madrid* 1985: pls. 11c, 51b, 68a, 95b, and 96a; *Códice Fejérváry-Mayer* 1964–1967: pls. 33 and 34). From this, it would seem that a particular position indicates that gods who are receiving offerings are in a state of inactivity. This hypothesis seems to be supported by Alain Ichon's (1973: 161) comments about the religious concepts of contemporary Totonac.

However, we can now come to a conclusion about how the Totonacs conceived the actions of their gods. The formula of *standing/sitting* characterizes every act of their gods, and by extension, of the person officiating. We have seen how the Sun God of Maize created the world "by rising" in the East. On foot, or raised, seems to characterize the creative activity of gods, or the act of a Semi-God: Thunder, Wind, Fire, who carries out their function. *Seated or sitting, to the contrary, characterized the inactive, but not passive, god, since he is in the position to receive the offerings given to him for work performed (or damage avoided). When he is seated he is given "to eat and to drink"* (emphasis L.L.L.).

All this shows that the distinctive attributes of each deity should be sought not in the body's posture but in the head: the facial features, the decoration on the face, the headdress, and the earplugs.

The second problem is the mix of the attributes of different gods in the sculptures under study. It seems reasonable to suppose that such variations express the indigenous intent of representing fusions, doublings, advocations, or particular episodes of the deities. Above all, the mixture of attributes has complicated the work of researchers.

The third problem comes from studying these images as isolated, unique objects. Most of the interpretations sidestep archaeological information. In the best of cases, the analyses are based minimally upon partial data or on that from dubious sources.

There are at least five proposals for identifying the images with two protuberances on the head.[16] They have been related principally to: deities of mountains, rain, and water (Seler 1960a); Tepeyolotl (Estrada Balmori 1979: 186; Nicholson, in Heyden 1970; Nicholson 1983, 1985b; Nicholson and Quiñones Keber 1983: 87–89); Nappatecuhtli (Heyden 1970); Ometeotl-Tonacatecuhtli (Nagao 1985a, 1985b: 66–70); and Xiuhtecuhtli-Huehueteotl (Seler 1903; Peñafiel 1910: Huehueteotl plate; Castillo Tejero and Solís Olguín 1975: 18; Wagner 1982; Matos Moctezuma 1987b, 1988c: 92–94).

In a 1901 pioneering study, Eduard Seler (1960a) formulated the first hypothesis: that there was a connection between the nine sculptures discovered by Batres in 1900 and the deities of mountains, rain, and water.[17] He based this iconographic identification upon only two characteristic attributes: the paper ornament on the neck and "two large wild boar teeth." Following this line of thought, Seler (1960a: 850) conjectured that the pair of protuberances on the head "perhaps represented the crests and peaks of mountains."

Nicholson and E. Quiñones Keber are the main proponents of the second hypothesis (Nicholson 1983, 1985b; Nicholson and Quiñones Keber 1983: 87–89). In one of their articles, they based their statements on a study of piece number IVb 649 in the Basel Ethnographic Museum (Fig. 71c). Although this sculpture does have certain likenesses to the ones found in the Templo Mayor, it does not share other important attributes that define the complex as a whole. The image in the Swiss museum shows clear differences from those found in an archaeological context during the twentieth century. In Nicholson and Quiñones's opinion, the presence of a beard and what might be two locks of hair linked this piece to the representations of Tepeyolotl ("the heart of the mountain") on plate 14 of the *Códice Borgia*. They suggested that the sculptures discovered in the Templo Mayor are "versions" of the same deity or, in other words, prototype images of Tepeyolotl. These sculptures, they told us, could have functioned as "hearts" of the offerings in the same way that the Huey Teocalli symbolized the ritual "heart" of the Triple Alliance.

In my view, this interesting proposal presents some problems. First, it establishes a possible relationship between the Basel sculpture and Tepeyolotl based upon only two shared attributes. Second, the Basel sculpture has important morphological differences from those of the Templo Mayor. And third, the same authors underscored the contradictory fact that Tepeyolotl was scarcely mentioned in sixteenth-century documents and that the sculptures they related to this deity abound in the offerings. Doris Heyden (1970) briefly criticized Nicholson.

Heyden (1970) identified a beautiful piece, unearthed during the works at the Metro, as Nappatecuhtli, an advocation of Tlaloc corresponding to the four corners of the universe. She based the identity of the sculpture on: its general adornment with blue paint; certain features marked with black pigment, "possibly *ulli* (rubber)"; the paper headdress; the ulli-stained maxtlatl; and, very importantly, the central position of the sculpture in relation to a group of five boxes of offerings oriented in the four cardinal directions. However, Heyden also saw attributes belonging to Xiuhtecuhtli-Huehueteotl in the Metro image: the two protuberances on the head that "have a clear resemblance to a *mamalhuaztli* (fire drill)," the black and red paint around the mouth, and the signs of old age, such as "the tired eyes and the teeth that come out from the mouth in the same way as from old people's gums."

The fourth and most recent hypothesis is Nagao's (1985a, 1985b: 66–70). She associated the Templo Mayor sculptures with Tonacatecuhtli ("lord of our sustenance"), a supreme creator deity also known as Ometeotl ("God Two"). According to Nagao, the stone images buried in offerings have iconographic indications of both supreme status and fertility, a combination she described as unique to Ometeotl-Tonacatecuhtli. Nagao pointed out that (1) the two protuberances on the head may be abstract representations of duality, hills, or fire drills, "all symbols of creation and origin"; (2) the supposed ears of corn or tortoise shells on the protuberances of only two sculptures and on the back of most of the others are linked to sustenance and fertility;[18] (3) the diadem (*chalchiuhtetelli*) with precious greenstones and *xiuhtototl* ("lovely cotinga") proclaims the high status of the divinity; (4) the toothlessness refers to the advanced age of the god; (5) the paper headdress is associated with fertility, rain, and sustenance; (6) the rectangular earplugs are related to Tlaloc and the pulque deities, "also clearly connected to fertility and abundance"; and (7) the assumed position for giving birth or of bisexuality is a characteristic of Tonacatecuhtli.[19]

Nagao concluded that the presence of Ometeotl-Tonacatecuhtli in the offerings "probably symbolizes his death and burial as a sacrificial victim and as seed to assure future sustenance." She said the images formed part of fertility rituals. Finally, she thought the sculptures deposited in Stage IVb may have been put there because of the great drought of the year 1 *Tochtli* (1454).[20]

I believe that among all the identifying features developed by Nagao, only three are unquestionably related to the descriptions and images of Ometeotl-Tonacatecuhtli (the others have only indirect links with this deity, as well as with others also associated with high rank and fertility).[21] I refer to the signs of old age, the paper fan on the nape, and the protuberances supposedly in the form of ears of corn. However, there is some confusion regarding the latter, perhaps due to the poor photographs used by Nagao. A close examination of the protuberances on the sculpture in the Basel Museum and the sculpture in Chamber 2 of the Templo Mayor will clearly show that they are convex and that they represent, with polygons on only one side, the five longitudinal series of tortoise shell bone plaques: a central series, formed by medium-sized hexagonal elements; two wider ones to the side; and another two marginal ones (Figs. 71b and 71c).

One must also question the burial in the Templo Mayor of effigies of the god "who had no temple or to whom no sacrifices were made because it is said he did not want them in order to be more majestic" (*Códice Vaticano Latino 3738* 1964–1967: pl. 15). In fact, there is no festival, sacrifice, or rite dedicated to the supreme god of the Mexica. This fundamental fact is congruent with the absolute lack of sculptures of Ometeotl-Tonacatecuhtli, as well as the scant pictographic representations.[22] Regarding this, Juan Bautista Pomar (1964–1968: vol. 1, 175) said: "And many ancient songs of which only a few fragments are known today testify to this, because in them are many honored names and titles of God, like the statement that there was only one, and that he was the creator of heaven and earth. That he sustained everything made and created by him, that he was at the top of the nine tiers, and *that he had never been seen in human form or in any other shape*" (emphasis L.L.L.). In the light of such strong evidence, Nagao (1985b: 69) was forced to argue, without proof, that the sculptures in question were not made to exhibit in public but were to be buried "as a sacrifice."

Most researchers who have analyzed the sculptures with the two projections on the head support the fifth hypothesis that identifies the images with Xiuhtecuhtli-Huehueteotl, the Old God of Fire, Turquoise, and the Year (Seler 1903; Peñafiel 1910: Huehueteotl plate; Castillo Tejero and Solís Olguín 1975: 18; Matos Moctezuma 1987b, 1988c: 92–94).[23] As I will show, this interpretation is based on a greater number of analogies among the sculptural images, descriptions from the time of contact, and representations in codices. This hypothesis is the only one that makes sense in the light of the contextual information gathered during the archaeological works.[24]

There is no doubt that Xiuhtecuhtli-Huehueteotl was one of the oldest and most revered of the indigenous pantheon (López Austin 1985a). The great transcendence of the Old God of Fire in the Aztec era is shown by the frequent mention of him in the texts of the sixteenth and seventeenth centuries. Through them, we know in detail the attributes of Xiuhtecuhtli. Among the Spanish chroniclers, Sahagún (1950–1969: bk. 1, fol. 12r) gave the most accurate description. According to the Nahuatl text of his indigenous informers,

> The array [for Xiuhtecuhtli] was: *The lower part of his face was painted black. He owns an [ornament] with chalchihuitl stones.* He owns a paper crown with [blue feathers] of the *xiuhtototl*; he has a spray of quetzal feathers. *He owns an arrow headdress; he owns a dart headdress.* He owns fire serpent earplugs. He owns a pectoral crossed by yellow paper. He also has copper bells. He has rattles. His shield has turquoise mirror mosaics. He owns a staff with the viewing devise (translation and emphasis L.L.L.).

Additional facts about Xiuhtecuhtli's apparel can be found in Sahagún's (1988: vol. 1, 49) Spanish version of the Nahuatl passage:

> The image of this god was painted as *a nude man*, who had *a beard stained with a resin called ulli, which is black, and a red stone labret on his chin.* On his head he had a paper crown painted with different colors and motifs. On top of the crown there were sprays of green feathers, like flames from a fire. He had feather tufts to each side, like pendants, toward his ears. He had earplugs in the holes of his ears, carved in turquoise mosaics. On his back he had plumage resembling a dragon's head, made of yellow feathers with marine conch shells. He had copper bells tied to the insteps of his feet. In his left hand he held *a shield with five greenstones, called chalchihuites, placed in the form of a cross* on a thin gold plate that covered almost all the shield. In his right hand he had a kind of scepter that was a round gold plate with a hole in the middle, and topped by two globes, one larger than the other, the smaller one had a point (emphasis L.L.L.).

Further on, Sahagún (1988: vol. 1, 171) stated that, during the tenth day of Izcalli, the priests crowned the image of this god in the following manner:

> They placed a crown which they called *quetzalcomitl* on his head. It was made of rich feathers; the bottom was narrow, fitting the roundness of his head, but it became

wider toward the top.... *The crown also had two feather sprays, one on the left and one on the right, which emerge together from the temples like horns bent forward. At their top are many fine feathers called quetzalli which emerge from small bowl-like containers. These two sprays or horns are called cuammamalitli.* A mane of long, blond hair was sewn to the lower rear of the crown and hung over his shoulders. The hair was clipped evenly at the ends. It seemed as if this hair was natural and came from underneath the crown (emphasis L.L.L.).

Unlike images of Tepeyolotl and Ometeotl-Tonacatecuhtli, the image of Xiuhtecuhtli-Huehueteotl was, for centuries, frequently reproduced throughout the Mesoamerican territory in ceramics, stone, and pictographs. This rich artistic assortment is, of itself, proof of the importance the fire cult had among Mesoamerican people (Fig. 74).

If we compare the numerous representations of Xiuhtecuhtli-Huehueteotl with the sculptures discovered in the offerings at the center of Mexico City, we will find at least seven shared attributes: (1) an almost nude body,[25] (2) old age shown by eyes that seem blind or closed and the presence of only two teeth,[26] (3) black pigment on the lower half of the face and red around the mouth,[27] (4) red pigment on the ears,[28] (5) blue pigment on the earplugs,[29] (6) a crown decorated with concentric circles (precious stones?)[30] and with an undulating element[31] that perhaps represents a xiuhtototl,[32] and (7) two projections emerging from the head (with traces of ocher coloring) that could be the sticks used to make fire by friction (*ome cuammamalitli*) or the pair of reeds/arrows that Xiuhtecuhtli displays on his headdress (Figs. 75 and 76).[33]

On the other hand, it should be remembered that the sculpture found by Batres in Deposit Number V has three rhomboidal elements or flowers on the crown instead of the typical concentric circles. Ordinarily, these elements adorn the sides of the cylindrical braziers carried upon the backs of the Teotihuacan images of Huehueteotl. A good sketch and a detailed description of the sculpture found by Batres can be located in Seler (1960a). Seler defined the rhombus as a flower (Figs. 72 and 73).

It is not surprising that Xiuhtecuhtli bears the insignia of the aquatic and fertility gods, such as the smooth paper fan and the rectangular earplugs with a central pendant.[34] Scholars have long emphasized that this fire deity also has aquatic qualities, among them acting as the patron of the day Atl ("water") (López Austin 1985a: 260, n. 3; Spranz 1982: 364). We still have no convincing answers on the meaning of the tortoise shells over the god's back. However, there are Mixtec images of a sacrificer named "turtle-*xiuhcoatl*" (stucco of Tomb 1 of Zaachila; *Codex Nuttall* 1975: pls. 12, 19b, 44; *Codex Selden* 1964: pl. 2; *Códice Selden (Roll)* 1964–1967: pl. 4). This sacrificer was attired with a helmet shaped like a "fire serpent" and had the tail of this same mythical animal and a turtle shell; occasionally, he had black paint over the lower part of his face and red paint around the mouth.[35]

Xiuhtecuhtli-Huehueteotl in the Mesoamerican religious context

The cult of the God of Fire, of the Year, and of Turquoise perhaps began as far back as the middle pre-Classic period. At the time of the Spaniards' arrival, Xiuhtecuhtli was one of the most revered deities of the Mexica pantheon, in spite of the fact that the *Florentine Codex* listed him among

Figure 72:
Old-fashioned Mexica
Fire God with rhomboidal
elements. (Photograph by
Salvador Guil'liem,
courtesy INAH.)

the gods of secondary importance (title page, chapter 13, of Book 1). This apparent contradiction disappears when we realize that this list was not present in the original Nahuatl text, given in folio 37v of the *Primeros memoriales*.

The importance of Xiuhtecuhtli is apparent not only in the wide spatial-temporal distribution of his cult but also in the magnitude and quality of family and public rituals dedicated to him, the number and size of his temples, the concept of his supposed infallible transforming power, and his direct relationship with the governing class (López Austin 1985a).

Xiuhtecuhtli-Huehueteotl was closely associated with time and the marking of annual, quadrennial, eight-year, and secular periods. Two festivals of the *xiuhpohualli* ("count of the days," or solar year)—Xocotl Huetzi and Izcalli—were dedicated to the death and the resurrection of this god, respectively. Xiuhtecuhtli was worshipped as Lord of the Year during that last month. On the tenth day of Izcalli, during the festival called *huauhquiltamalcualiztli* ("eating of the amaranth leaf tamales"), the New Fire was lighted on Tzonmolco Calmecac (Sahagún 1988: vol. 1, 187),

Abb. 51. Idol aus Te-
zontle, einen Berggott
darstellend,
am 16. Oktober 1900 in
der Calle de las Es-
calerillas gefunden.

Figure 73:
Xiuhtecuhtli with
rhomboidal elements
found by Batres
(Seler 1960a.)

signifying the imminent change of the annual cycle and the rebirth of the fire deity (Sahagún 1988: vol. 1, 98, 171–72, and 176–77). The Izcalli rituals grew in importance every four years. Victor Castillo Farreras (1971) suggested that this was because the leap-year correction was made at that time: the last day of the month was forty-eight hours long. Every eight years, a great celebration was held for Xiuhtecuhtli because that was when the cycle combining the 584 days for Venus and the 365 days for the Sun was completed (Caso 1953: 56). Finally, the well-known festival of the New Fire was held every fifty-two years, marking the close of the cycle of 18,980 days produced by combining the 260-day and 365-day periods (Caso 1953: 56; Sahagún 1988: vol. 2, 488–92).

In historical sources, there are many names for the God of Fire, something that surely reflects his supposed capacity for doubling. According to López Austin (1985a), some of these names refer to

Figure 74:
Xiuhtecuhtli (*Códice Borbónico* 1979: pl. 9). (Drawing by José Luis Garcia.)

Figure 75:
Xiuhtecuhtli (*Códice Tudela* 1980: pl. 99r). (Drawing by José Luis Garcia.)

Figure 76:
Xiuhtecuhtli (*Códice Borbónico* 1979: pl. 20). (Drawing by José Luis Garcia.)

the correspondence between his advocations and the pre-Hispanic division of the cosmos: thus he was known as Tocenta ("Our Single Father"), as supreme divinity of the universe; Teteo Innan-Teteo Inta ("Mother, Father of the Gods"), as the binary and polar division of the cosmos; Nauhyotecuhtli ("Lord of the Group of Four"), as the partition of the earth's surface into quarters; and Chicnauhyotecuhtli ("Lord of the Group of Nine"), as the vertical division that includes the underworld.

The Mexica thought that this god, in his advocation as Xiuhtecuhtli, resided on the *axis mundi*, that is, on the three fundamental levels of the cosmos: Ilhuicatl, Tlalticpac, and Mictlan (Seler 1963: vol. 1, 93; Paso y Troncoso 1979: 238).[36] According to several written sources, Xiuhtecuhtli dwelt in the center of the universe, in the navel of the world, in the place where the dual springs known as matlalatl-tozpalatl (see page 65) came together: "the Mother of the Gods, the Father of the Gods, suspended in the place of the navel of the earth, inside the enclosure of turquoise stones, fortifying himself with turquoise bird water, the ancient god, Ayacmictlan, Xiuhtecuhtli" (*Códice Florentino* 1979: bk. 6, fols. 71v–72r).

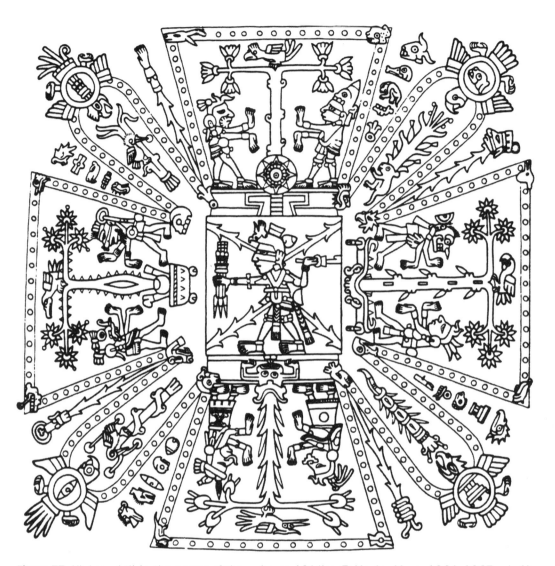

Figure 77: Xiuhtecuhtli in the center of the universe (*Códice Fejérváry-Mayer* 1964–1967: pl. 1). (Drawing by José Luis Garcia.)

This quotation agrees perfectly with some pictographs. For example, in the famous representation of the universe on plate 1 of the *Códice Fejérváry-Mayer*, Xiuhtecuhtli can be seen precisely on the central compartment, in the center of centers (Fig. 77).

The central position of Xiuhtecuhtli within the cosmic structure has been pointed out repeatedly (Matos Moctezuma 1988c: 94). Caso, one of the investigators who have emphasized this topic, wrote:

The god of fire undoubtedly represents one of the oldest concepts of Mesoamerican peoples. He is the god of fire in relation to the cardinal directions, just as the *tlecuil* or brazier for lighting fire is the center of the house or the indigenous temple. That is why the figure of a cross is seen frequently on the priests of this god, it is also found decorating the great incense burners called *tlemaitl,* literally "fire hands", with which the priests offered incense to the gods (Caso 1953: 55; cf. Seler 1963: vol. 1, 92).

Here Caso emphasized the central position of the deity but in close association with the cardinal points, synonymous with the four extremes of the earth's surface.[37] With this meaning, the Nahua invoked Xiuhtecuhtli by saying, "*Tlalxictenticaé, Nauhiotecatlé,*" that is, "he who fills the navel of the earth, he of the group of four" (Sahagún 1988: vol. 2, 545). Moreover, the periodic enactment of a sacrificial ritual was performed in the Tzonmolco, a temple dedicated to Xiuhtecuhtli. Each year in the month of Izcalli, four slaves were killed there. The victims were dressed in the image and likeness of the God of Fire, although each wore a color alluding to a cardinal direction: green (Xoxouhqui Xiuhtecuhtli), yellow (Cozauhqui Xiuhtecuhtli), white (Iztac Xiuhtecuhtli), and red (Tlatlauhqui Xiuhtecuhtli) (Sahagún 1988: vol. 1, 187).

As a side note, I might add that there is an interesting small Teotihuacan figurine that represents the Old God of Fire with a headdress of quincunxes (Sejourné 1957: 104, fig. 3).

The images in their archaeological context

The comparison of graphic and written testimony supports the link proposed by several scholars between the two protuberance sculptures and Xiuhtecuhtli-Huehueteotl. This hypothesis also agrees completely with the archaeological evidence. We should include in the comparison the discovery made by Noguera (1968; see also Solís and Morales 1991) in what was formerly the Plaza de El Volador. In 1937 this archaeologist found a pair of offerings in the fill of an enormous platform. We now know that the major deposit had more than one thousand ceramic containers, many of them decorated with death symbols. Next to this impressive deposit was found a box of sillares that held three containers, a stone urn, shells, conch shells, corals, greenstone beads, a rubber ball, and a sculpture with two protuberances on its head. After making a brief analysis of the artifacts and comparing them with sixteenth-century documentary sources, Noguera concluded that both offerings were buried in the ritual of disposal and renovation of the New Fire ceremony of 1507. In his opinion, the image with the two protuberances on its head represented the Old God of Fire, symbol of the time cycle that ended that year.

Gussinyer (1970a) reported a similar find at the intersection of Izazaga and Pino Suárez streets, inside structure L-3—a structure with a circular base and an attached adjacent rectangular body. This structure is characterized by the presence on one of its rafters of the glyph *2 Acatl,* the date on which the Mexica celebrated the last New Fire. Exactly in the center of the construction was a box whose slabs were decorated inside with red pigment and with four year and directional markers with the number 13 (13 x 4 = 52): *13 Calli* (facing the east), *13 Tochtli* (facing the north), *13 Acatl* (facing the west), and *13 Tecpatl* (facing the south). Inside was an offering composed of flint knives, maguey thorns, a miniature brazier with ashes, a sculpture of a frog, the spine of a sawfish, a rubber container, and four "loaves of copal." Under the offering was a box of sillares containing a figure with protuberances on its head (oriented to the west) (Heyden 1970), a blue vessel, greenstone beads, and copal residues. Four similar but smaller boxes were around this offering, placed respectively to the north, south, east, and west of the central offering. Among other things, they contained flint knives, greenstone beads, and copal (Gussinyer 1970a, 1970c). The characteristics of structure L-3, as well as the form and contents of the offerings, could also be related to the New Fire festival.

The identification with Xiuhtecuhtli-Huehueteotl is also corroborated by the archaeological records of offerings 16 and 16-A excavated by the Templo Mayor Project. Let me review the original context: (1) the deposits of Building L had a central position in regard to four altars; (2) in each of the two boxes (offerings 16 and 16-A), there was a cluster of five chalchihuites distributed in a manner analogous to that of Building L and the four surrounding altars; and (3) the sculpture with the two protuberances presided as the principal offering (see López Luján 2005). Recall the similarity between these three clusters of five elements (one architectural and two artifactual) and the well-known Mesoamerican quincunx, the symbolic representation of the five points of the earth's surface.[38] Similarly, recall the "shield with five greenstones" that Xiuhtecuhtli carried, according to Sahagún's (1988: vol. 1, 49) text.

The link between Xiuhtecuhtli-Huehueteotl and the sculptures with two protuberances makes sense in other contexts explored by the Templo Mayor Project.[39] These peculiar sculptures appear in 26 of the 118 offerings in the study sample,[40] and without exception, the figures occupy a prominent place. As a rule, they were placed at the head of the deposit, on its highest level. Curiously, in twenty-two offerings (84.6% of the cases), the images that I identify as Xiuhtecuhtli-Huehueteotl shared their privileged position with sculptures of Tlaloc. It can be said that both presided over the donation (see the General Plan).[41]

This link clearly shows that a considerable number of offerings at the Templo Mayor were dedicated to two divinities of enormous importance in Mesoamerican religion, whose cult goes back to the pre-Classic period. On one side, there is the image of the Old God of Fire and the Year, associated with the masculine, hot, diaphanous, and celestial half of the universe; on the other side is the representation of the God of Rain, associated with the feminine, cold, humid, dark, and terrestrial half. Thus fire and water (*atl-tlachinolli*) are together, a basic unity of opposed and complementary elements, around a temple of dual construction placed at the center of the universe: the Huey Teocalli.

In conclusion, I believe there is enough evidence to say that offerings 16 and 16-A were dedicated to Xiuhtecuhtli-Huehueteotl as the god who inhabited the navel of the cosmos. The evidence not only proves the importance of the Fire God but also shows the place he occupied in the universe.

OFFERING 48

THE CHARACTERISTICS OF OFFERING 48

This is a unique deposit, made up of an unusual accumulation of children's skeletons. Interest in this multiple burial derives from the relative scarcity of human remains in the various contexts excavated by the Templo Mayor Project.

Offering 48, together with offerings 18, 19, 89, 69, 49, 50, J, and 84, forms part of Complex F. The computer joined these nine deposits in a polythetic group because most of them contain seashells, conch shells, corals, copal residues, statues of Tlaloc, Mixtec penates, and representations of musical instruments. Nevertheless, Complex F shows little internal coherence in terms of the quantity and the placing of gifts within each deposit (see the detailed description of Complex F in Appendix 2).

Among all the offerings of the complex, it is 48 that has the greatest number and variety of objects. This fact is reflected on the dendrogram. Offering 48 is the last one in the complex, almost at the middle of the dendrogram.[42] In general, the number of differences in this offering in relation to the other members of Complex F is greater than the shared characteristics. Therefore, I will analyze this deposit separately.

Offering 48 was discovered at the northeast corner of the Templo Mayor, in the half of the building belonging to Tlaloc (Fig. 137) (see Appendix 2). The children's skeletons were in a huge box, the inside of which was plastered (see a detailed description of offering 48 in Appendix 2). Unfortunately, the original context had been partially altered by the foundation of a colonial building: the upper layers of the box and some materials had been destroyed, especially the northwest corner. In such a confused context, it was only possible to note that the offering box had been improvised on top of a small altar located on the Templo Mayor platform corresponding to Stage IVa. The upper surface of the altar served as the bottom of the box.[43]

The objects of offering 48 were superimposed in five vertical levels, each corresponding to a specific part of the rite (Figs. 78–82).[44] First, the supplicants spread marine sand in a thin homogeneous layer on the bottom of the box. It is plausible that they were trying to symbolically create a fragment of the cosmos with aquatic characteristics. This idea is strengthened by the many visual Mesoamerican expressions, which are used as tropes.[45] If this is the case, we would find a kind of physical synecdoche here, a part standing for the whole—the aquatic world of the tlaloque represented by marine sand. Sahagún's informants seemed to confirm this idea. In the marginal annotations to a song in honor of Yacatecuhtli, the expression *xalli itepeuhyan* ("scattering of sand") was used as a synonym for Tlalocan (Fig. 80) (*Veinte himnos sacros de los nahuas* 1978: 200–8).

In the next step of the rite, those in charge placed numerous corpses of the sacrificed on the layer of sand. Most of the bodies were in a bent dorsal decubitus position with no particular orientation. Several skeletons wore necklaces made from tiny greenstone beads. In contrast, two other skeletons displayed rich, disklike pieces at breast level—a pair of wooden disks (27 and 34 cm in diameter, respectively) with appliquéd turquoise mosaics and turtle shell. Greenstone beads were found in the mouths of five individuals (Figs. 80 and 81).

The next level of the offering was made up of another assemblage of numerous children's bodies. However, in contrast to the bodies of the second level, those on the third level had been sprinkled with blue paint during the ritual. The donors then placed a fourth layer of objects of mostly organic origin in an irregular manner. During the explorations, greatly deteriorated remains of copal, wood, birds, small conch shells, worked shells, and possibly squash containers were extracted, as well as a prismatic obsidian blade (Fig. 79).

The fifth and last level was composed of eight tezontle sculptures imitating Tlaloc jars (Fig. 78). These coarse sculptures were of several sizes, and each had a base like a truncated cone, a round body, a high neck, a hardly distinguishable spout, and a plaited handle. On its side, in relief, was

Figure 78:
Offering 48 (excavation level 1). (Drawing by Germán Zúñiga.)

the face of the God of Rain (with the typical rings around his eyes, curved plaited nose, mustache, and fangs), a headdress of folded paper, and a crown of feathers. All the pieces were plastered and decorated with white, black, blue, and red colors, and ten of the eleven jars were found in the southern half of the box. It is interesting that they were all intentionally placed on their sides in an east-west direction, simulating the pouring of water.[46]

PHYSICAL ANTHROPOLOGY DATA

After a very careful study of the bone remains, physical anthropologist Román Berrelleza (1986) was able to determine the number of children sacrificed, and he attempted to ascertain their ages, sex, pathologies, and causes of death. In the sample, he identified a minimum of forty-two individuals between two and seven years of age.[47] Twenty-two were male, six female. It was impossible to determine the sex of the other ten (Román Berrelleza 1986: 98–113).

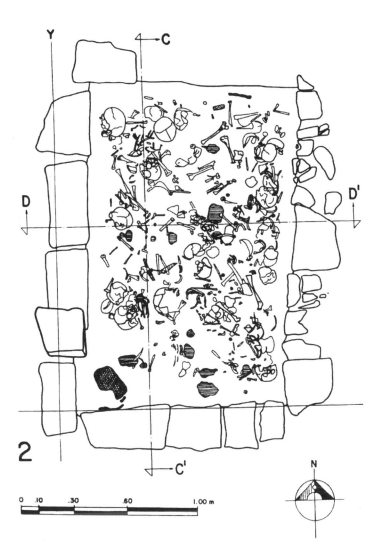

Figure 79:
Offering 48 (excavation level 2). (Drawing by Germán Zúñiga.)

The bones of twenty-one children (50%) had signs of hyperostosis, a defect caused by nutritional-related problems such as anemia due to iron deficiency, the imperfect assimilation of nutrients, gastrointestinal ailments, and parasites (Román Berrelleza 1986: 114–26). Román Berrelleza (1986: 126–31) also detected circular caries in five individuals, apparently the direct consequence of prenatal problems or malnutrition after birth. Thirty-two skulls had signs of intentional deformation: flattening of the lambdoid region in twenty-seven cases and tabula-erect in the other five (Román Berrelleza 1986: 135–41). After a microscopic inspection, no signs of cut marks were found on bones, leading to the conclusion that the children had their throats cut.[48]

RECONSTRUCTION OF THE RITUAL

It is evident that the religious meaning of offering 48 is related to the cult of the Rain God. This seems to be verified by the burial of the offering on the western side of the Templo Mayor, as well

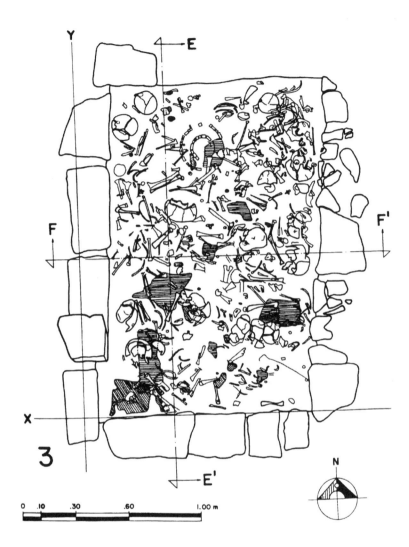

Figure 80:
Offering 48 (excavation
level 3). (Drawing by
Germán Zúñiga.)

as by the predominance of objects symbolizing the aquatic world of Nahua cosmovision: sea sand, blue pigment, shells, conch shells, possibly squash containers, Tlaloc jars, and the corpses of sacrificed children who in life had suffered serious illnesses.

The death of children is an unmistakable element in the ritual ceremonies offered to the tlaloque, and for obvious reasons, the religious chroniclers of the sixteenth century commented at length on the deep-rooted Mesoamerican custom of sacrificing children. In their writings, the description of this particular holocaust was given as much space as their condemnation of it. According to the Spanish friars, the sacrifice of children was ordained in certain festivities of the 365-day calendar. Sahagún (1988: vol. 1, 84) mentioned the months of Atlcahualo, Tlacaxipehualiztli, Tozoztontli, and Hueytozoztli, although if we take into account other sources, the months of Atemoztli (Benavente 1969: 36) and Izcalli (Durán 1984: vol. 1, 292) should be added to the list. This means that the practice was limited to the dry season.

Children were sacrificed to assure abundant rain for the next agricultural cycle. The petition for water was addressed to Tlaloc and his helpers, who supposedly lived in the mountains and hills

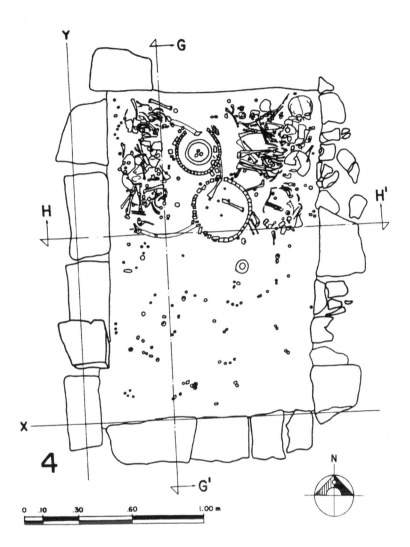

Figure 81:
Offering 48 (excavation level 4). (Drawing by Germán Zúñiga.)

where they controlled the rainfall (Broda 1987a). The most precious gift consecrated to these aquatic deities was a child who had two cowlicks in his or her hair and who had been born under a propitious sign. Broda (1971: 273) stated that the children selected personified the tlaloque—divinities described in the sources as "dwarf agents." With this in mind, the victims were dressed in the image and likeness of these divinities and were named for the hill where they were to be sacrificed.

Good or bad omens were believed to depend to a large degree on the attitude of the children during the ceremony. "When they took the children to be killed, if they cried and shed many tears, those who were taking them rejoiced, because it was an omen of heavy rain that year" (Sahagún 1988: vol. 1, 81).

The archaeological information gathered by the Templo Mayor Project coincides with the historical record as to the age and sex of the children. Spanish documents state that both girls and boys between three and seven years old were sacrificed. They also agree with the physical anthropologists' analysis that the children were killed by having their throats cut (Pomar 1964–1968: 168–69;

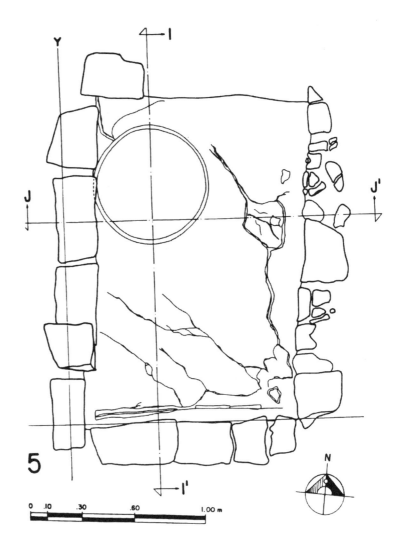

Figure 82:
Offering 48 (excavation level 5). (Drawing by Germán Zúñiga.)

Benavente 1969: 35; Durán 1984: vol. 1, 83–86). Some friars also spoke of drowning (Benavente 1969: 36; Sahagún 1988: vol. 1, 105: Mendieta 1945: vol. 1, 111), extracting the heart (Sahagún 1988: vol. 1, 81, 104), and abandonment in caves (Benavente 1969: 36).

In spite of these interesting similarities, the historical and archaeological records do not agree completely. For example, the archaeologists' total of forty-two individuals in offering 48 is much greater than the number given by the chroniclers: Durán (1984: vol. 1, 83–86) and Motolinía (Benavente 1969: 35–36) estimated from one to four sacrifices, depending on the ceremony. Pomar (1964–1968: 168-69) wrote of between ten and fifteen victims, and Sahagún (1988: vol. 1, 83, 104) spoke vaguely of "many."

Moreover, no text identified the Templo Mayor as the site for the sacrifice and burial of children. Instead, the places where the victims lost their lives were said to be several islands and hills in the Basin of Mexico,[49] as well as the Pantitlan whirlpool (Benavente 1969: 36; Durán 1984:

vol. 1, 86, 90; Sahagún 1988: vol. 1, 104–5; Mendieta 1945: vol. 1, 111). Afterward, the corpses were taken to various locations. They were thrown inside caves (Pomar 1964–1968: 168–69), tossed into Pantitlan (Durán 1984: vol. 1, 86, 90), buried in a "stone box like an ancient sarcophagus" (Benavente 1969: 35), or simply cooked and eaten by the participants in the ceremony (Sahagún 1988: vol. 1, 104–5). However, finding offering 48 in the rubble of the Templo Mayor is not surprising. The Huey Teocalli, as a fit dwelling for Tlaloc and as an artificial model of a sacred hill, would also be a proper place for such ceremonies.

Based upon the preceding statements, we can affirm that offering 48 is the tangible product of a massive and exceptional sacrificial rite, performed in an atypical place. The characteristics of this impressive deposit of children's corpses do not seem to correspond to those of one of the six periodic rituals mentioned in the chronicles. If they had, there would surely have been other similar discoveries during the 1978–1989 explorations.

In his bachelor's thesis, Román Berrelleza (1986: 164) proposed that the multiple sacrifice in honor of Tlaloc might have been part of the solemnities for the consecration of the Templo Mayor. However, the context in which offering 48 was discovered offers little to support this theory. Beyond that, there are great formal differences between offering 48 and the other deposits that have been associated with consecration ceremonies. At the end of this chapter, I will analyze the consecration offerings of Complex A, which, among other things, are outstanding for their internal coherence, the enormous richness of their contents, and their equal distribution on both sides of the structure. In my opinion, the motive for a massive and exceptional sacrifice at an atypical site—as shown in offering 48—should be sought in a singular historical event. In Chapter 4, I pointed out that the glyph *1 Tochtli*, associated with Stages IV and IVa, is the only possible chronological reference. This basalt tablet, imbedded on the eastern side of the Templo Mayor, has a full figure of a rabbit and the numeral 1 framed by a raised square. Archaeological information tells us that the plaque was placed before the building of Stage IVb, with which it was finally buried. Thus it seems reasonable that the Mexica would have engraved the glyph *1 Tochtli* to commemorate an important historical event that occurred during Stage IV or IVa.

The chief problem in interpreting the *1 Tochtli* glyph is that it can correspond either to one of the days of the tonalpohualli (sacred 260-day calendar) or to one of the years of the xiuhmolpilli (fifty-two-year cycle). The problem is further complicated because the Nahua gave to each deity the calendric name of the day he or she was thought to have been born or upon which the deity had performed some deed worthy of recording (Caso 1967: 189). Considering this possibility, Graulich (1987) believed the glyphs engraved on the walls of the Templo Mayor have no calendric meaning. The Belgian investigator suggested that the date *1 Tochtli* refers to a mythical event: the year the earth was created, beginning the xiuhmolpilli.

However, if we assume that the Huey Teocalli glyphs are specific calendric dates, it is possible that the date *1 Tochtli* commemorates an exceptional event. The Mexica typically used a framing square to show that the glyph referred specifically to a year, although, according to many scholars, this is not always the case. Indeed, there are numerous exceptions. But it is quite likely that the use of a square frame for the notation *1 Tochtli* does indicate a year. According to Caso's (1967: table 15) correlation of Aztec and Christian years, that date could have corresponded to the years A.D. 1402, 1454, and 1506.

---

156 • CHAPTER EIGHT

For their part, Matos Moctezuma (1981b: 37) and Umberger (1987) were inclined to give a chronological character to these bas-reliefs. Umberger thought the glyphs refer to historical phenomena that the Mexica linked symbolically to the presence or absence of the sun. She argued that *1 Tochtli* is a date with multiple meanings: the first year of the Fifth Sun, according to Nahua mythology; the change of the cycle of fifty-two years, that is, the rebirth of the sun;[50] and the famine of 1454. "I do not think, however, that the Mexica would have placed this date in the temple just for its negative connotations, that is, to commemorate the famine. In other words, the date 1 Rabbit probably meant to refer to the beginning of the Fifth Era and commemorate the cycle change, and as a secondary connotation it recalled the disastrous famine" (Umberger 1987).

I disagree with Umberger because I believe there is sufficient proof that this date commemorates the great drought of 1454, instead of the origin of the Fifth Sun or the beginning of the century. As Rafael Tena (1987: 92–99) has demonstrated, beginning in 1351, the Mexica no longer lighted the New Fire on *1 Tochtli* but on *2 Acatl*, a year later. In fact, numerous sources record that the new cycle transition during Motecuhzoma Ilhuicamina's reign was celebrated on *2 Acatl*, that is, 1455 (*Anales de Cuauhtitlan* 1975: 52; *Anales de Tlatelolco* 1948: 57; *Códice Vaticano Latino 3738* 1964–1967: pl. 110; *Códice Telleriano-Remensis* 1964–1967: pl. 8; Chimalpahin 1965: 100, 201).

On the other hand, there is a great deal of evidence to show that the Mexica erected monuments consecrated to transcendental historical events at various places in their dominion (Nicholson 1972a; López Luján and Morelos 1989). The tlatoque were definitely prone to mark for posterity important moments of their existence, including those with "negative connotations." Durán told how Motecuhzoma Ilhuicamina, for example, ordered a memorial carved on the cliffs of Chapultepec, recording, among other things, the fateful year of 1454.

And then [Tlacaelel] summoned all the best carvers and stone cutters that could be found in all the provinces to carve in the most lifelike manner possible the figure of the king and of himself. He spoke to them thus, "The great king Motecuhzoma [Ilhuicamina], my brother, seeing that he is now old and that his days, as well as mine, are numbered, wishes and designs, so that the memory of both of us will endure, that you carve our images on the best stone that can be found in Chapultepec, and that there be no delay, but that you begin work at once. And simultaneously, you will represent the year Ce Tochtli, when the former famine began. Go then and look for the best stone to be used for that purpose" (Durán 1984: vol. 2, 245).

If the date *1 Tochtli* was engraved on Chapultepec, why not also record this tragic event on the walls of the Templo Mayor? We know that the drought affected all the inhabitants of the Basin of Mexico equally for it is recorded in writings from diverse places in the area (López Luján and Jiménez Badillo 1987).

According to Durán (1984: vol. 2, 241–44),

the drought was so severe the springs dried up, fountains and rivers no longer flowed, the earth burnt like fire, and the dryness caused great fissures and cracks. . . . The people began to grow weak and to walk, withered and thin, from the hunger they were undergoing and others became ill by eating things harmful to their health. Others, through sheer necessity, abandoned the city, their houses, wives and children, fleeing to more fertile places in search of relief.

The devastating effects of the lack of rain were set down in practically all the annals that describe the pre-Hispanic history of the valley.[51] In his *Tercera Relación* Chimalpahin (1965: 99–100) said that 1454 was the year

> when it was said, "the people rabbited themselves," according to the ancients, the fourth year in which there was nothing to eat. Because of this the ancient Mexica sold themselves.... Many people died throughout the land, and many suffered from attacks of wild beasts and carnivorous vultures. The expression "the people rabbited themselves" was also said in another way: "The people became Totonacs," due to the fact the Totonacs bought the Mexica with maize. There, in Cuextlan, the Mexica went to sell themselves in exchange for corn. Until it rained again, that was used as money.

The situation was so desperate at that time that the Mexica dedicated rich gifts, invocations, and supplications to the gods of rain.[52] Motolinía (Benavente 1969: 36) and Torquemada (1969: vol. 1, 121) stated that the sacrifice of children in honor of the tlaloque began on the fateful *1 Tochtli*.

> This Sacrifice to the God of Water began the way many others began in that World, among the ancient Gentiles.... Because at a certain time, when it didn't rain during four years, the fields dried up and there was hardly a green thing to be found. Some Oracle whom they consulted about the great disaster they were experiencing, must have told them that their misfortune would ease if they would sacrifice children to Tlaloc, the God of Water (Benavente 1969: 36).

In summary, there is strong evidence that offering 48 was a response to the great drought that desolated Tenochtitlan, beginning with the year *1 Tochtli*. The exceptional and massive character of the holocaust, as well as the atypical place of its occurrence, perhaps indicates the desperate attempt of the Mexica to establish high-intensity communication with their gods, as Cazenueve described it (see Chapter 3). Perhaps the principal purpose of offering 48 was to reestablish the coveted normality by means of sacrifices and abundant gifts designed to serve as homeostatic mechanisms.

THE COMPLEXES WITH THE SIMPLEST OFFERINGS (COMPLEXES O, P, AND R)

Complexes O, P, and R have the poorest offerings in terms of type, with just one object type each. The only offerings in Complex O were cylinders of copal; Complex P has an irregular accumulation of maguey thorns; and Complex R has a layer of ashes (see the Reordered General Matrix).

Because of this, the three complexes join nearly at the bottom of the dendrogram (see the Dendrogram of Offerings).

THE OFFERING OF COPAL (COMPLEX O)

Offerings 67, 75, and 63 make up this complex, following the division proposed in Appendix 2 (which provides a detailed description of Complex O). Their classification (100% frequency in Complex B of object types) was determined by the sole presence of a cylindrical mass of copal (see the Reordered General Matrix).[53] Besides their identical contents, these offerings have a similar spatial arrangement, and all were found at the extreme northern part of the Templo Mayor (Fig. 150) (see Appendix 2). It is interesting that the donors placed the masses of copal at equal distances forming an axis in line with the northern facing of the Huey Teocalli. The three offerings were buried under the building fill of Stage IVb, 160 cm below the flagstones that formed the floor of the sacred precinct (Fig. 83) (see the General Plan). This leads us to believe that the rite of oblation occurred during the construction of Stage IVb. During the 1978–1989 explorations, the flagstones located symmetrically to the extreme south of the building were not removed. It is quite possible that objects similar to those of Complex O are located there, as well.

Offerings 67, 75, and 63 rested upon a layer of compacted soil and were protected by sillares placed in no particular order. As stated, each offering was composed of a cylindrical mass of yellow copal, approximately 30 cm in diameter and 30 cm in height. At the time of excavation, the center of the upper face of the cylinders had a 3-cm depression (Figs. 84 and 85).

I feel it is too risky at this point to give a definite conclusion about the meaning of Complex O. We should be cautious for two important reasons: first, because copal, along with conch shells, is the material most frequently mentioned in the archaeological records of the Templo Mayor;[54] second, because the Mexica offered this resin to their gods with remarkable constancy, as recorded in the historical sources of the sixteenth century. We know that huge quantities of copal were periodically brought to Tenochtitlan as tribute,[55] and the greater part of this valuable cargo was destined to be used in religious performances. Like amate paper and rubber, copal was deposited in sacred places as an offering to the supernatural (Sahagún 1988: vol. 1, 127). However, the general practice among the Nahua was to burn the resin as incense to produce its typical sweet-smelling aroma. In practically all rituals, both public and private, copal incense was used. Sahagún (1988: vol. 1, 189), in describing things offered in the temples, said:

> The priests offered incense in their temples at certain hours day and night. They used incense burners made of baked clay that had as a crucible, a medium sized receptacle with a hollow shaft about a *vara* [0.84 m], or a little less in width, and about a *codo* [forearm, 0.42 m] in length, and inside were small pebbles that rattled. The vessel was carved like an incensary with designs that pierced the vessel itself from the middle to the end. They got coals from the fire with it, threw copal on the coals, and then went before the statue of the Devil lifting the incense burner to the four corners of the universe. They also incensed the statue. This done, they returned the coals to the hearth. Everyone in the city did this in their houses, once in the morning and again

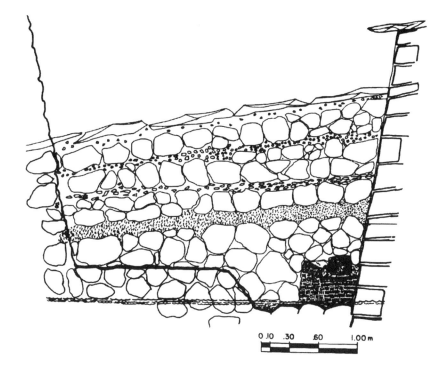

Figure 83:
Offering 63 (north-south cross section). (Drawing by Germán Zúñiga.)

at night, incensing the images they had in their places of prayer or in their court-yards.... For the incense offering, or copal, the Mexicans and everyone in New Spain used a white gum called *copalli*, which is still used a great deal, to incense their gods.... Judges also used it when they were performing some official act. Before begin-ning, they cast copal on the fire in reverence to those gods and to ask their assistance. It was also used by singers at their festivals. Before singing, they threw incense on the fire in honor of their gods and asked for their help.

Besides its religious use, copal was also employed by doctors, who valued the resin highly for its many healing qualities (Martínez-Cortés 1970: 41).

Because of the omnipresence of *copalli* in the religious life of the Mexica, we can only spec-ulate on the significance of the offerings of Complex O. Perhaps an explanation of its meaning lies in the architectural context of the cylinder. It is probable that the burial of copal in the building fill of Stage IVb indicates a rite due to the enlargement of the Templo Mayor.

Complex O has strong links with offering 70, something that, unfortunately, is not com-pletely clear in the dendrogram (see the location of offerings 63, 67, 75, and 76 in the Dendrogram of Offerings). As can be seen in the General Plan of the excavation, offering 76 was located on the northeastern corner of the Templo Mayor, on the same axis as the three copal deposits. The offering is composed of four ceramic incense burners placed in the building fill, 87 cm below the flagstone layer of Stage IVb. These incense burners, very similar to those described by Sahagún, have serious fractures and deformities caused by the heavy pressure they have withstood during

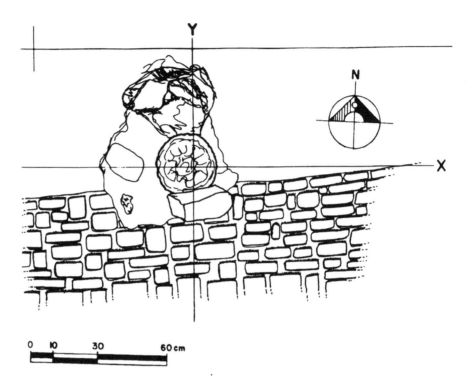

Figure 84:
Offering 63
(excavation level 1).
(Drawing by
Germán Zúñiga.)

the centuries of their burial.[56] Traces of white, blue, and black paint can be seen on their outer sides, and a chip of a gray obsidian that may have served as an instrument of self-sacrifice was found directly associated with incense burners (cf. Heyden 1972).

THE OFFERINGS OF MAGUEY THORNS (COMPLEX P)

Offerings 72 and 73 make up Complex P (a detailed description of Complex P is in Appendix 2). They join near the bottom of the dendrogram because both have an amorphous accumulation of maguey thorns.[57] The two deposits were found under the flagstone floor at the eastern end of Building I (Fig. 151) (see Appendix 2). Apparently, they were placed on a bed of soil in the building fill *during the work of expansion* of the Templo Mayor in Stage VI (see the General Plan).

Offering 72 consists of an irregular cluster of thorns measuring 87 cm long, 60 cm wide, and 18 cm thick (Fig. 86). Offering 73 was smaller: 20 cm long, 20 cm wide, and 5 cm thick. In both cases, they were distributed in an irregular manner. They lacked the circular arrangement that would indicate the gradual decomposition of a *zacatapayolli* ("plaited grass ball") into which they might have been inserted. Such an arrangement can be clearly seen in the offerings of Complex A. The maguey (*Agave salmiana*) thorns of Complex P are long, gray, and conical.[58] Their length varies between 5 and 8 cm. The thorns of offering 72 were associated with some remains of the outer skin of the maguey plant leaves (Aguirre 2002).

We have a great deal of information about the function of maguey thorns in the societies of pre-Hispanic Mexico. Often the thorns of the agave were used as needles and pins. However,

Figure 85:
Offering 63 (perspective).
(Drawing by
Germán Zúñiga.)

their most extensive use was as instruments of ritual self-sacrifice. The documents written when the Spanish arrived say that body-piercing and bloodletting were done for the dual purpose of inflicting pain on the individual and obtaining the precious liquid to be offered to the divinities. Maguey thorns were used on the most delicate parts of the bodies of children, youths, and adults, such as the tongue, lips, ears, eyelids, fingers, teats, fleshy parts of the arms, genitals, and calves. There were multiple reasons for self-sacrifice: to obtain divine favors, to avoid harm from supernatural forces, to expiate sins, for moral and physical strengthening of the individual, and so on. This kind of self-sacrifice was required for magicians, priests, and those in charge of academic education and ritual (Heyden 1972; López Austin 1988c: 380–81).

Through an analysis of the sources that describe self-sacrifice, Heyden (1972) concluded that the maguey thorns, together with reed splinters, serpent fangs, and prismatic obsidian blades, were used by the laypeople, priests, and youths at the temple-schools. Usually, the blood-covered thorns were inserted into grass balls as a gift to the gods. In contrast, piercing instruments made from the bones of eagles, felines, and deer were used exclusively for the penitence of the tlatoque and the nobles.

As in the case of Complex O, it is difficult to determine the kind of ceremony involved in offerings 72 and 73. This is complicated by the great number of rituals where self-sacrifice was practiced. The fact that only thorns were found in these offerings is not enough information to be able to define the basic outlines of a ritual. From the archaeological findings, it can only be said that a

Figure 86:
Offering 72 (excavation
level 1). (Photography by
Salvador Guil'liem,
courtesy INAH.)

massive act of mortification was carried out during the remodeling of Building I. If this is true, the maguey thorns were buried simultaneously with a gift of blood to consecrate the future construction.

THE OFFERINGS OF ASHES (COMPLEX R)

Complex R is composed of offerings O and G (see a detailed description of Complex R in Appendix 2). Like the offerings of Complexes O and P, these two deposits joined early in the dendrogram. The only attribute and the common denominator of the group is a layer of ashes mixed with clay-mud and small fragments of charcoal.[59]

Although both deposits have the same kind of contents, they differ substantially in their spatial location and probably in their function. Offering O was discovered inside Room B of Building E (the House of Eagles). Offering G was found at the North Plaza between Buildings A and B (see the General Plan). Both offerings date to the construction of Stage V of the Templo Mayor (Fig. 153) (see Appendix 2).

Offering O is inside a stone box, whose top was at exactly the same level as the stucco floor of the room.[60] The inside walls of the box have been exposed to fire, and the content was only a layer of ashes varying between 2 and 15 cm in depth. In my opinion offering O is not really an offering, but a *tlecuil* ("fire pit"), used daily to heat the large chambers of the site. I base this theory on four different factors: (1) the form and size of the box, which is similar to that of other archaeological hearths; (2) the signs of fire on its inner faces; (3) the fact that the deposit of ashes was not definitively sealed with the stucco floor with which it was associated;[61] and (4) the location of the box inside the House of Eagles (see López Luján 2005).

Offering G was inside a cylindrical cavity (73 cm in diameter and 42 cm deep) dug below the flagstones of the Eagle Plaza. This cavity contained a 42-cm-deep layer of ashes with a volume of 0.175 m^3. In this case, the relatively large accumulation of ashes and the location lead us to believe that a large fireplace was lighted during a ceremony such as the one described by Sahagún (1988: vol. 1, 191) in book 2 of his *Historia general*:

> When they had to go to some battle, first of all the soldiers went to the hills to gather wood, which was used in the temples, and they laid heaps of it in the monasteries of the priests, and from it they took some to burn, which was consumed in great quantities between night and day *in the patios of the temples, or on the high pyres that were made for this purpose in those same patios.* At other times the ministers of the temples and those who dwelt in the *calmecac* were in charge of bringing wood. They called this *teucuauhquetzaliztli* (emphasis L.L.L.).

THE COMPLEX OF OFFERINGS OF BLUE JARS (COMPLEX N)

Complex N is noticeable by the great similarity among its offerings, in terms of spatial distribution as well as the type and placement of the artifacts. The group is composed of six deposits: offerings 28, 43, 26, 25, 35, and 47 (a detailed description of Complex N appears in Appendix 2). The deposits join practically at the base of the dendrogram, an indication of the internal cohesion of the cluster (see Dendrogram of Offerings).

The offerings are relatively poor because they have only three or four object types. For this reason, they are found on the dendrogram together with other deposits with little content diversity. Thus they are related to the copal offerings (Complex O), maguey thorns (Complex P), altered offerings (Complex Q), ashes (Complex R), Burial 1, and offerings 71, 76, and 30.

Offerings 28, 43, 26, 25, 35, and 47 were easily grouped because they had three object types in common: a round jar, a cajete (both belonging to object types of Complex E),[62] and several greenstone beads (the kind of object type in Complex A). Offerings 35 and 47 also had traces of copal (see the Reordered General Matrix).

The six offerings of Complex N also show similarities in their distribution: a neat pattern of spatial distribution can be easily seen by examining the location sketch (Fig. 149). Without exception, all were located on the northern half of the Templo Mayor, that is, the part corresponding to the Tlaloc sanctuary. Offerings 28 and 35 were located on the north wall of the building, and offerings 43, 26, 25, and 47 on the east wall. All were in the building fill of one of the two bodies of Stage III. This means that the Mexica deposited them next to the facing of Stage II, during the work of the third enlargement (see the General Plan).

The objects in each deposit were carefully protected with fine soil and, in some cases, with flagstones and sillares before being buried by the nucleus of the foundation (Fig. 87). According to the field reports, the objects were placed on a single vertical level. A round jar and a small cajete, both of Aztec monochrome orange ceramics, were the most noteworthy gifts in

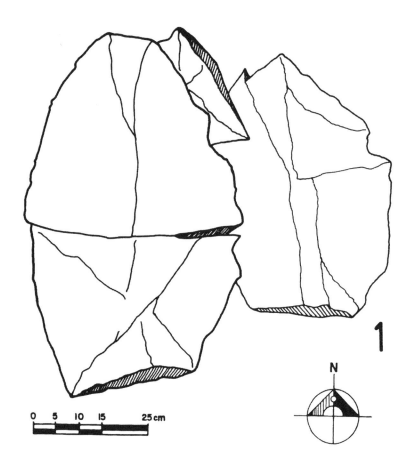

Figure 87:
Offering 43 (excavation level 1). (Drawing by Germán Zúñiga.)

0   5   10   15   25 cm

N

1

each one of these deposits (Figs. 88 and 89). Before their burial, the jars and cajetes were randomly sprinkled with a blue pigment and decorated with pairs of black stripes.[63]

The association of round water jars with the cult to the God of Rain seems unquestionable. The connection comes, first, from their presumed function as containers of liquid and their celestial color. Second, the northerly position of these artifacts in relation to the Huey Teocalli must be noted, a fact that is corroborated by documents from the sixteenth century in which the Temple of Tlaloc is topped with merlons shaped like water containers.[64] It must be pointed out, however, that what is illustrated there are not exactly jars but pitchers.[65] Nevertheless, round jars are seen in at least a couple of representations of the month Etzalcualiztli, the principal religious festivity dedicated to Tlaloc (*Códice Mauricio de la Arena* in Barlow 1943; *Códice Vaticano Latino 3738* 1964–1967: pl. 60; *Codex Magliabechiano* 1983: 34r). On one of them, plate 60 of the *Códice Vaticano Latino 3738*, the face of the deity is seen, and he is carrying a jar in his right hand and a corn plant in his left.

Sahagún, speaking of the rituals of Etzalcualiztli, confirmed the role played by jars similar to those discovered during the archaeological work. The Franciscan said that when the celebrations were almost over, the priests sacrificed those who had personified the tlaloque during that twenty-day period. "And then they opened the person's breast, the chest cavity was opened, the

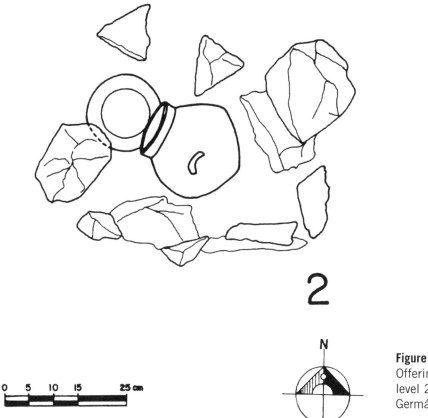

2

N

0 5 10 15   25 cm

Figure 88:
Offering 43 (excavation
level 2). (Drawing by
Germán Zúñiga.)

heart removed. They put it in *a jar painted blue, called "cloud jar," painted on all sides with rubber.*
And their wrappings were paper sprinkled with rubber, much rubber, full of rubber. This is what
they do to all those who were the images [of the tlaloque]; they throw all their hearts there."[66] After
the sacrifice, the priests went in canoes to the Pantitlan whirlpool, where they threw in the jars with
the hearts and countless "fine greenstones."

A somewhat similar ceremony took place when an individual contracted a disease attributed to aquatic causes. To get rid of the suffering, squash containers filed with pulque were offered
to the tlaloque. "It is said that these were jars of precious stones called chalchihuitl" (Sahagún 1988:
vol. 1, 61–62). The oblation was done when the squash vessels were thrown into the Pantitlan
whirlpool, in the same manner as that of the "jars of clouds."

Evidently, the jars were associated with Tlaloc and with his small helpers not only in
graphic depictions and in Mexica ritual cycles but also in their cosmovision. One of the better-
known descriptions of the world of the rain divinities is in the *Historia de los mexicanos por sus*
pinturas (1965: 26).

They say about the god of water [Tlaltecuhtli] that he has a dwelling with four rooms
and in the center a large patio where there are four great barreñones of water:[67] one

Figure 89:
Offering 26 (excavation level 2). (Photograph by Salvador Guil'liem, courtesy INAH.)

of them is very good, and when rain falls from it, it is good weather and corn and seeds grow. The other is bad and when it rains from it, the corn gets spider-webbed and mildews; When it rains from another, it freezes; When it rains from the last, no grain is formed and [the crop] dries up. And in order for it to rain, the god of water created many tiny helpers, who were in the rooms of the house. They have *alcancías* [clay money boxes] in which they carry water from the barreñones in one hand, and sticks in the other. When the Rain God orders them to rain somewhere, they take their containers and sticks and shower down the water as they are ordered. When they break the container with their sticks, it thunders and when there is lightning, it had been held inside or was a part of the water container.

Returning to archaeological materials, we should not forget the last of the attributes in Complex N: greenstone beads, always found inside the round jars. Depending on the offering, the chalchihuites were found in groups of three, four, or five beads; thus it is doubtful that they were originally part of necklaces.[68] In fact, previous excavations had found greenstone beads inside shells and various other kinds of containers. Seler (1960a), commenting on such findings, concluded that the chalchihuites in that context symbolize small drops of water. Walter Krickeberg agreed with that idea.[69]

There is little debate about the pre-Hispanic meaning of the chalchihuites today. Sahagún (1988: vol. 2, 222–23), in book 11 of the *Florentine Codex*, recorded the indigenous belief that the greenstones prized by the *pipiltin* ("nobles"), such as the *quetzaliztli*, the *quetzalchalchihuitl*, and the *chalchihuitl*, both attract and exude moisture. Discussing how these materials were obtained, he said, "There is another indication of where the precious stones are found, especially the ones called chalchihuites. At the place where they are created the grass that grows there is always green. And this is because these stones always exude a fresh, moist exhalation. When they find this, they dig and find the stones where these chalchihuites are made" (Sahagún 1988: vol. 2, 789).

The aquatic significance of greenstone probably comes from its color, its brilliance, and its texture. However, the metaphoric meaning of the chalchihuite seems to go further. Nagao (1985b: 51) thought it functioned as one of the symbols par excellence of fertility. Proof of such a proposal may be seen in the famous *tepetlacalli* found in Tizatlan,[70] which is now a part of the collection of the National Museum of Anthropology. On one of its inner walls is an image of a chalchihuitl from which plants of corn emerge (López Austin and López Luján 2004: 426).

The apparel of the water gods is another important fact about the chalchihuite-fertility connection. In his long account of the indigenous pantheon. Sahagún (1950–1969: bk. 1, 7, 22; see also Durán 1984: vol. 1, 81) only referred to the green bead necklaces as a divine attribute in the chapters dedicated to Tlaloc and Chalchiuhtlicue. However, thanks to the writings of Sahagún and other friars, we know that the chalchihuites were repeatedly offered to the tlaloque (López Austin 1985b: 235; Durán 1984: vol. 1, 82).

I have discussed the possible symbolic connotations of the artifacts that define Complex N. But the meaning of the whole cannot be found merely by summing up the parts. We also require information about the contextual relations of the objects. The key to the significance of the six offerings in question rests on the complementary positions of jars, cajetes, and beads.

Based on the archaeological record, it is easy to conclude that all the jars were purposefully placed on their sides in a regular manner: the mouths of the jars in offerings 26, 25, 28, and 35 are intentionally oriented toward the north, and those in offerings 43 and 47 have their mouths toward the west. The cajetes are always in a horizontal position, precisely under the open end of the jars (Fig. 90). In other words, we found a jar decorated with blue pigment, containing greenstone beads, laid on its side, and with its opening associated with a cajete.

Considering that, it is logical to conclude that these offerings represented jars of the tlaloque in a position that simulated the pouring of precious water—chalchihuites—into cajetes. The cajetes represented the surface of the earth. These objects were probably placed there as an act of propitiation that gave the new building the attributes for a residence of Tlaloc—a room from which to generate rains and thus fertilize the earth.

Before concluding, I will give some evidence to support my position. The first is a fragment of a tepetlacalli in London's British Museum (Fig. 91). The Mexica box is dated to the year

1499,[71] and on one side is a depiction of Tlaloc in a horizontal position with his legs bent. The extended arms of the deity hold a jar adorned with a large chalchihuite. Ears of corn and streams of water terminating in chalchihuites and conch shells flow copiously from the jar. Nicholson (1972a) believed that this tepetlacalli (which also has bas-reliefs with images of two *ahuitzome* ["fantastic aquatic animals"], the glyph 7[?] *Acatl*, and the Earth Monster) could have been Ahuitzotl's cinerary urn, which alluded to the consecration of the Acuecuexcatl aqueduct and the flood that caused the ruler's death.

The second proof is a mural painting that covers the northern doorjamb of Building A of Cacaxtla (Fig. 92). The building has been tentatively dated to A.D. 750. A figure clad in a short jaguar-skin skirt and a blue pectoral is the principal motif of the painting. In his right arm, he holds a green jar decorated with a mask of Tlaloc, from which come streams and drops of water. In his left hand, he holds a serpent with green volutes and yellow flowers. According to Sonia Lombardo de Ruiz (1986: 233, 236), one of the interpreters of the symbolism of these murals, the act of pouring water from the jar is linked to the propitiation rituals of water and the earth's fertility.

In two Mayan pictographs, the *Códice Dresde* (1988: 36c, 39b, 43b, 74) and the *Códice Madrid* (1985: pls. 9, 13, 30), Chaac, the Old Red Goddess of Weaving (in her advocation as Lady of the Jars) is seen pouring water on the earth's surface from the jar. According to the religious tradition of the ancient Maya, these divinities stored rain in ceramic containers, which were probably known by the name *buleb, buleu,* or *zaayan buleb* (*Códice Dresde* 1988: 242, 252). Significantly, almost all the scenes in question are located in sections dedicated to farmers' almanacs and to the glory of the rainy season (*Códice Dresde* 1988: 214–16, 242, 245, 252).

THE COMPLEX OF OFFERINGS OF STONE URNS (SUBCOMPLEX F₁)

The offerings of Subcomplex F_1 are conspicuous because of the enormous similarity between them, particularly in their location and in the kind and placement of the artifacts they contain. According to the proposed classification, only two offerings compose the grouping: numbers 18 and 19.[72] These two offerings join practically at the base of the dendrogram, thus confirming the internal coherence of the pair.[73]

The two offerings of Subcomplex F_1 contain seven and eight different kinds of objects respectively. In our classification dendrogram they group with offerings 89, 69, 49, 50, J, 84, and 48 to constitute Complex F. The computer rapidly grouped offerings 18 and 19 because they had six kinds of objects as a common denominator: conch shells and greenstone beads (object types of the F Complex); amorphous pieces of copal (object types belonging to the B Complex); prismatic obsidian blades and ceramic fragments (object types belonging to the D Complex).[74]

These and other objects were found inside and on top of two cubical stone urns (*tepetlacalli*) whose surfaces had been smoothed with a thin layer of whitish stucco.[75] These urns were buried under the floor of the west platform of Stage IVa of the Templo Mayor, while this structure was being used (Fig. 46). A pit was excavated exactly midway between the two monolithic serpent heads that terminate the central balustrades of the Templo Mayor, and exactly at the junction of Huitzilopochtli's

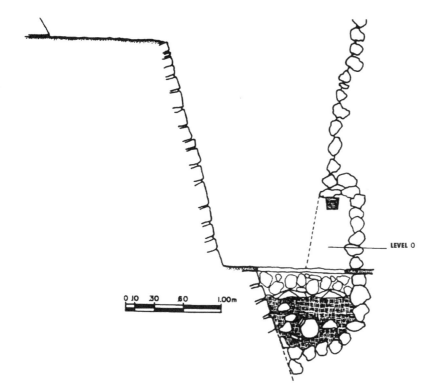

Figure 90:
Offering 43 (west-east
cross section). (Drawing
by Germán Zúñiga.)

and Tlaloc's temples. Offering 18 lies south of offering 19.[76] It is clear that both offerings were part
of a simultaneous ceremony that took place about A.D. 1469, during the reigns of Motecuhzoma
Ilhuicamina or Axayacatl.

To start with, a number of materials related to fertility and to the aquatic world were
deposited: 1,041 conch shells in offering 18 and 1,118 in offering 19; 173 greenstone beads in offering 18 and 109 in offering 19; 1 shell in offering 18 and 1 seed in offering 19. As we saw in the previous section, together with the mollusk shells and the seeds, the greenstone beads were some of the
most important fertility symbols (Nagao 1985b: 51). Sahagún's informants stated the following:

> The greenstone beads, the bracelets, the fine turquoises are precious. Only they are
> precious: they are what brings life to the world, what nourishes it, what gives it vital-
> ity. What is alive—through them, lives, talks, is happy and laughs. (Sahagún 1979: bk.
> VI, ch. 8, f. 29).

After that, thirteen anthropomorphic greenstone statuettes of the M-4 Mezcala type were
carefully placed on top of this bottom layer (see Gay and Pratt 1992: 44–55). Before placing them,
the Mexica had painted these statuettes with blue, black, red, white, and ocher pigments. They had
been given the attributes of the rain gods by painting headdresses, goggles, moustaches, and mouths
on their smooth surfaces. When they were found, the thirteen sculptures were still standing facing south, leaning in two ranks on the north wall of each box. Two irregular lumps of copal were

Figure 91:
Tlaloc with water jar.
Stone box at the
British Museum.
(Drawing by José
Luis García.)

Figure 92:
Personage on the north
doorjamb of Building A
of Cacaxtla. (Drawing by
José Luis García.)

placed before them. At the end of the ceremony, the urns were closed with the lids, and a prismatic obsidian blade and several pot shards thrown on the top.

The religious meaning of offerings 18 and 19 is revealed by a prayer to Tlaloc recorded by Sahagún in Nahuatl. The prayer emphasizes the cruelty of the rain deities who hide the rain and sustenance in their stone subterranean warehouse, leaving humans without food. I quote:

> O Master, O Our Lord, O Giver, O Green, O Lord of Tlalocan, O Lord of Yauhtli, O Lord of Copal. Truly, now the gods, the providers, the lords of rubber, the lords of yauhtli, the lords of copal—our lords—*have gone into the box, they have hidden themselves in the coffer. They have hidden for themselves the green stone beads, the bracelets, the fine turquoises*... (Sahagún 1979: bk. VI, ch. 8, f. 28; see Sullivan 1965).[77]

This passage refers to a well-known myth about Huemac, the haughty ruler of Tula. Huemac beat the tlaloque in a ball game and spurned the maize that they offered him after being defeated. The tlaloque were offended and answered him thus: "Well then, now we will hide our *chalchihuites* [precious stones]; now the Toltecs will undergo hardships..." After this, they caused a terrible freeze and a drought that lasted four long years (*Leyenda de los Soles* 1975: 126–27).

In my opinion, these well-known fragments found in sixteenth-century sources are explicit enough to allow us to infer that our two offerings (urns containing beads, shells, and the rain gods) were part of a ceremony conferring Tlalocan's characteristic as the warehouse of sustenance on the Templo Mayor. Depictions of boxes in aquatic and fertility contexts support my analysis. For example, in plate 26 of the *Códice Telleriano-Remensis* (1964–1967) a *petlacalli* ("reed box") decorated with a necklace of green beads floats atop the current of water that emerges from Chalchiuhtlicue's skirt. Similarly, on plate 28 of the *Códice Borgia* (1963) the earth looks like a *tepetlacalli* ("stone box") in the scene representing the year 1 *House*; while on plate 61, Tonacatecuhtli (Lord of our Sustenance) is shown giving birth to a box of treasures.

The ceremonies, that contemporary Nahuas from the State of Morelos carry out in honor of the "owners of water" (dwarf spirits called *ahuauhque*), are just as relevant (Grigsby 1986). Every year at the beginning of May, the inhabitants of Tlaxictlan[78] offer food, toys, miniature utensils, and flowers to these spirits. To do this, they undertake pilgrimages to seven sacred locations. Three of these are springs found to the north in Chalchiuhtlan ("The Place of Green Stones") Hill. The fourth sanctuary is a well and a fissure located in the village itself. The three remaining sites are caves on the sides of Tepepolco, literally "The Place of Many Hills." It is extremely interesting that the inhabitants of the region conceive of these caves as warehouses full of maize, and, simultaneously, as places from which water emerges as clouds. What is really surprising is that these seven sanctuaries of the aquatic deities are called by the generic name *tepetlacalco*, literally "the place of the stone coffer or box."

Up to now, I have not been able to find a satisfactory explanation for the repeated occurrence of the *thirteen* statuettes of the tlaloque inside each urn. However, there are interesting clues both in pre-Hispanic iconography as well as in the ethnography of modern Mexico. Thus, for example, the Classic Maya depicted the God of Number Thirteen as a bizarre serpent, which sometimes had the *Tun* (a 360-day time unit) glyph on its head, and was directly related to water (Thompson

1978: 135–36; Taube 1994).[79] Today, Nahuas in the Northern Puebla mountains designate the locality closest to the *Talocan*, the world of the rain deities, with the number thirteen and Talocan itself as number fourteen (Knab 1991: 47–49). Another suggestive hint is the ceremony that the inhabitants of Xcalakoop, Yucatán carried out in 1959 to plead with the rain deities not to punish the Tulane archaeologists who had excavated, and thus desecrated the Balankanche Cave (Andrews IV 1970: 72–164).[80] During an extremely long prayer, the "thirteen chak lords (rain deities)," the "thirteen holy balaams (jaguars)," and the "thirteen lords of the spring" who dwelt inside the cave were repeatedly invoked—all of this taking place in the "place of the thirteen springs."[81]

FUNERAL DEPOSITS COMPLEX (COMPLEX E)

THE ARCHAEOLOGICAL EVIDENCE

Complex E is one of the most interesting in our analyses. It is not exactly a cluster of offerings but a group of deposits that contain funeral remains and mortuary material.[82] To avoid confusion and to simplify the explanation, I will follow the nomenclature of the Templo Mayor Project, which calls this kind of deposit *offerings*.

According to numerical taxonomy, Complex E consists of a total of eight deposits—offerings 34, 39, 44, 74, 29,[83] 10, 37, and 14 (a detailed description of Complex E is in Appendix 2). Because of its great internal coherence, this group is clearly set apart on the dendrogram.[84] It is only linked by a branch near to Complex D (formed by offerings 3 and 5). Among the attributes that determine Complex E are cinerary urns, human ashes, and perforated obsidian circles (belonging to the Complex G object types) (see the Reordered General Matrix). These attributes possess a dual quality: they have high degrees of frequency in the complex (79.16%),[85] and they are almost completely absent in the other offering complexes.

The spatial distribution of the eight mortuary offerings shows important regularities. The most conspicuous feature is that all, with the exception of number 74 (which is in Building I), are located in the southern half of the Templo Mayor, the part belonging to the cult of Huitzilopochtli (Fig. 136) (see Appendix 2). Moreover, these offerings, except for 29 (which lies in the building fill), are found under stucco floors, a sign that the Mexica buried the cinerary urns while the building was being used (Fig. 93). To do this, the grave diggers broke through a small portion of the floor, dug a cavity where they placed the urn and, if needed, the funerary offering, covered it with fine soil and flagstones, and then replaced the damaged floor.

The deposits of Complex E were put there at four different architectural stages. Offerings 34, 39, 44, and 37 were found in Stage II, just inside the Temple of Huitzilopochtli and next to the pedestal that supported the image of that god (see the General Plan). As a rule, the objects were placed in small cavities. Offering 29 was on the southern side of the base corresponding to Stage III. Offerings 10 and 14 were on the western platform of Stage IVb. Finally, offering 74 belongs to Stage VI; it was found on the southeast corner of Building I's platform.

The type of material and the spatial placement inside the offerings of Complex E also followed rigid patterns. For instance, the objects in each deposit were predominantly oriented

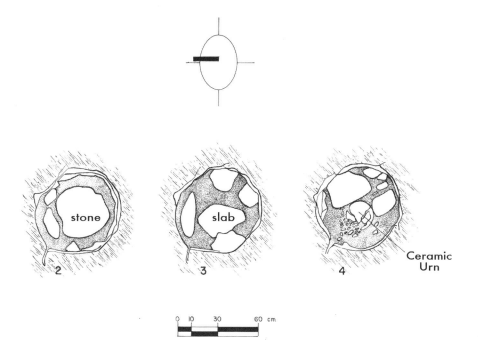

Figure 93:
Offering 10 (excavation levels 2-4). (Drawing by Julio Romero.)

toward the west. Depending on the case, they were placed in one or two vertical levels. The objects of offerings 44, 74, 29, 10, 37, and 14 were distributed at a single level. The central piece for each of these six deposits was an urn containing ashes and partially burned human bones. The raw material, the form, and the size of the funerary urns differed from one offering to another: a plumbate ceramic container shaped like a dog with a flat clay cajete as a lid (offering 44); an orange ceramic jar (offering 74); a tepetlacalli, or basalt box, with a lid of the same material (offering 29); an orange ceramic vase with bas-reliefs representing deities in profile, armed with an atlatl and a bundle of darts (offerings 10 and 14);[86] and a tripod cajete of orange ceramic with blue pigment (offering 37) (Figs. 93–99).[87]

Different artifacts were mixed with the incinerated remains inside the urns in offerings 29, 10, 37, and 14.[88] Most of these objects showed signs of having been in a fire. Greenstone and gold beads predominated, as well as piercing-cutting instruments (bone bloodletters, prismatic obsidian blades, projectile points of obsidian, and flint). There were also an obsidian necklace composed of fourteen beads in the form of duck heads and two helicoidal beads in the container for offering 14, a necklace of thirty turquoise beads in the cajete of offering 37, and a greenstone pectoral representing a rattlesnake crossing a polygon perforated at the center in the jar of offering 10 (Figs. 97 and 98).

The objects in offerings 34 and 39 were placed at two vertical levels, which differed from the other six offerings.[89] Polished stone objects in no apparent order predominated at the deepest level. Beads of different shapes and materials (greenstone, travertine, rock crystal) predominated. Helicoidal beads stood out among them (two beads in offering 34 and two clusters of five beads in offering 39). Closely associated with the beads we found obsidian and greenstone earplugs, perforated obsidian disks, anthropomorphic sculptures of greenstone, and also metal artifacts.

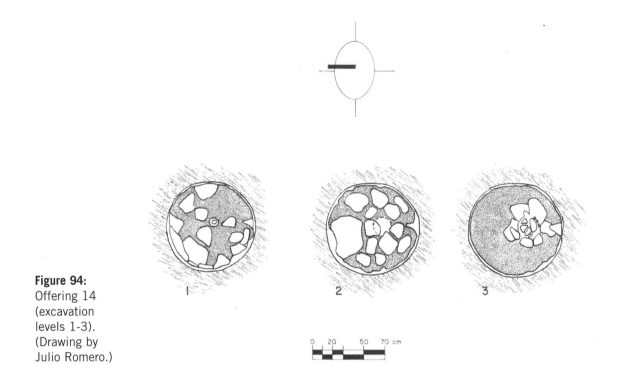

Figure 94:
Offering 14
(excavation
levels 1-3).
(Drawing by
Julio Romero.)

On the first level of offering 34 there was also a sculpture in the form of a duck head and a knife, both made of flint.

The highest level was topped with a funerary urn. In offering 34 we found an obsidian container and lid. The stylized representation of a human skull in high relief was on its sides. It contained burned remains, a silver mask,[90] and a gold bell with the glyph ollin. In offering 39, the urn is of travertine with an obsidian lid and has a still unidentified god in high relief (Fig. 99). Inside there were human ashes, a gold bell, and two greenstone circular plaques with a circular perforation in the center. I should mention here that two other deposits not belonging to Complex E are related to it because of their funerary character. These are offering 3 and Burial 1 (a detailed description of offering 3 is in Appendix 2, and that of Burial 1 is in Appendix 3). The first was deposited in a cylindrical box of tezontle sillares, located on the platform of Stage IVb. Inside, there was a lot of material, most of which had undergone intense cremation: copal; worked shell; coral; sponges; sea urchins; remains of the bones of humans, fish, quail, turkey, opossum, stingrays, serpents, falcon, and alligator; and the remains of gold, silver, and copper bells. Burial 1 contained the only unburned, complete adult skeleton found during the excavations of the Templo Mayor Project. It was from a direct, primary burial of a woman, who lay in a reclining position in the building fill of Building 1. An Aztec ceramic plate placed in front of her chest was the only mortuary offering.

HISTORICAL AND ETHNOGRAPHIC EVIDENCE

The archaeological evidence obtained during the excavations of the Templo Mayor Project is clarified by comparing it with historical sources of the sixteenth and seventeenth centuries

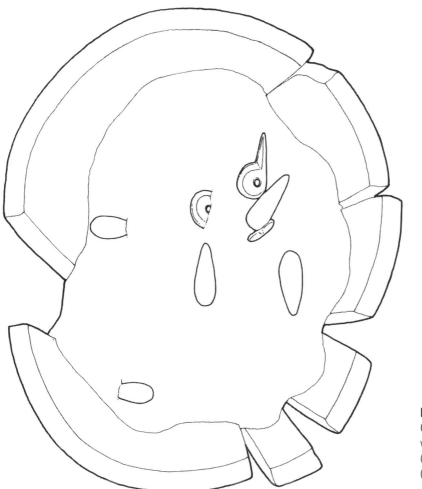

Figure 95:
Objects deposited inside
vessel in offering 14
(excavation level 1).
(Drawing by
Julio Romero.)

and with ethnographic reports of the twentieth century. In fact, our perspective on the total meaning of Complex E completely changed after consulting the chronicles in Latin script about the concepts of death and the funerary practices of the ancient Mexicans.

The Nahua of the sixteenth century conceived of death as the disintegration of the elements that constitute the human being during his or her earthly existence: the body, the blood, and the animic forces (*tonalli*, *teyolia*, and *ihiyotl*) (López Austin 1988c: vol. 1, 313–16). López Austin (1988c: vol. 1, 317), who has made an in-depth study of these beliefs, suggested that plate 44 of the *Códice Laud* might represent such a disintegration (Fig. 100). It shows four serpentlike figures emerging from a corpse. Two of them with serpentlike heads emerging from the crown of the head and the abdomen of the individual would allude to the separation of the tonalli and the ihiyotl; another one of them, which comes from the chest and has the head and arm of Ehecatl, would be the teyolia; and the remaining skeleton would symbolize the corpse.

Figure 96:
Objects deposited inside
vessel in offering 14
(excavation level 2).
(Drawing by
Julio Romero.)

According to prevailing ideas of that era, after a person's death, the teyolia, or soul of the heart, was destined for the so-called worlds of reward and punishment. The cause of death determined, on one hand, the final destiny of the teyolia and, on the other hand, the ritual treatment of the cadaver. After a number of archaeological discoveries, we know that, except on a few occasions, cremation was limited to post-Classic Mesoamerica. At that time, the custom of burning human corpses was the most common funerary practice of the Mexica (Ruz Lhuillier 1968: 69–70, 199–200). They only buried directly those who were destined to dwell in Tlalocan and Chichihualcuauhco.

Warriors who died in battle and people who died of a common illness (*tlalmiquiztli*, or "earthly death") were incinerated (Nagao 1985b: 38).[91] However, the teyolia would follow a different route because death in war was held to be glorious and that of the tlalmiquiztli was thought to have no privileges. The teyolia of the warrior, after leaving the body, supposedly journeyed eighty days in order to reach Tonatiuh Ilhuicac, where it would serve the sun for four years. However, the other teyolia would descend eight levels over four long years, until it reached, if it did not vanish, the ninth-level place called Mictlan or, more precisely, Chicnauhmictlan (López Austin 1988c: 318–21, 330–36).[92] Some written sources hint

Figure 97:
Bas-relief of the ceramic vase discovered in offering 10. (Drawing by Fernando Carrizosa.)

0   5 cm

at a view that the tlatoani had a teyolia that could divide: it seems that part of this animic force went to Mictlan and part to the world of the sun (López Austin 1988c: vol. 1, 320–21).[93]

It was believed that the cremation of the corpse and the giving of rich offerings played a decisive role in the passage of the soul. Fire served as an effective means of communication between the human world and the traveling teyolia. Through transmission by fire, the person's soul received from his or her relatives offerings for Mictlantecuhtli, as well as the things necessary for its survival—the souls of its servants and a dog that would make the journey less hazardous (López Austin 1988c: vol. 1, 320–21). It may even be that burning the body was believed to contribute to the liberation of the soul. Following this logic, the cremation of the corpses of those who were going to Tlalocan was not needed because after burial, they entered directly into the domain of the lords of vegetation and rain.

It would not be illogical to speculate that the soul of the deceased followed the same path as that of forces-times-destinies, that is, the helical paths that intertwine the sky and the underworld.[94] Unfortunately, we lack the references necessary to support that theory and we have only ethnographic indications of this possible past belief. For instance, present-day Maya in Yucatán open a round hole in the palm-leaf roof just above the dead person to facilitate the departure of the spirit. This is because the Maya believe that each of the seven skies above has a hole through which a tree or a reed ladder passes; the soul can ascend this tree or ladder to the place of the Great God (Tozzer 1982: 180).

Figure 98:
Bas-relief of the ceramic vase discovered in offering 14. (Drawing by Fernando Carrizosa.)

0   5 cm

Another clue comes from the modern Nahua in the Sierra of Puebla, who depend on Lord Santiago to recover the lost soul of a relative. They say he does this by traveling in a circle—the only way of finding, controlling, and capturing a soul (Signorini and Lupo 1989: 238–40). Another piece of evidence comes from a Pipil myth recorded in El Salvador in the 1930s. There it is said that ascending and descending to the world of the gods is done by following a helical path, by means of a twisted reed ladder or the coils of a snake's body or by flying in a helix around a tree (López Austin 1988a).

Returning to the time of Mexica splendor, one of the principal ends of funeral rites was to prepare the deceased for life after death. A complicated ritual sequence was essential to accomplish this. It is likely that before their cremation, the burned corpses found in Complex E had undergone a ceremony similar to the one Motolinía told about in his *Memoriales.* The Franciscan devoted a chapter to a description of the funerals of native lords (Benavente 1971: 304–07).[95] He wrote that four days after death, a precious stone was placed in the mouth of the deceased,[96] and a forelock was cut from the crown of his head. This hair was placed in a box, together with a lock of hair cut at the time of his birth.[97] Afterward, the face of the corpse was covered with a mask and the body was wrapped in rich cloths[98] and adorned with the paraphernalia of the god in whose temple he was to be buried.[99]

Motolinía stated that the mortuary bundle was taken to the foot of the main temple on the same day, where it was burned with copal and torches.[100] A great number of servants and slaves

Figure 99: Cinerary urn of offering 39. (Photograph by Salvador Guil'liem, courtesy INAH.)

Figure 100:
Possibly a portrayal of the separation of the souls taking place after death (*Códice Laud* 1964–1967: pl. 44). (Drawing by José Luis García.)

were sent to the sacrificial stones;[101] later, their bodies would feed the great funeral pyre, and their souls would accompany that of their master (*Codex Magliabechiano* 1983: fol. 65v; Sahagún 1988: vol. 1, 222). A reddish-colored dog was also killed. It was supposed to help the deceased cross the gorges and waterways during the journey to Mictlan (Sahagún 1988: vol. 1, 221). Rich dishes, chocolate, pulque, tobacco, flowers, and paper[102] were given to the dead to make his stay in the other world more pleasant.[103]

After the fire had consumed the mortal remains of the lord, the priests placed his ashes and the half-burned bones in the box with his hair and the precious stone (the chalchihuitl-heart).[104] Just above the funerary container, they placed a sculpture of the lord,[105] offering him rich gifts for four days. After that they buried the box. New sacrifices and offerings would make up part of the numerous mourning ceremonies that would end four years after his death.

Unfortunately, Motolinía said little about the actual burial of the box. He only mentioned, in an aside, that the lords' ashes were buried in the temples. In the work of other chroniclers, there is more detailed information, although at times it is contradictory. Evidently, these differences are due to the fact that the burial place depended upon the status the decreased held in life.

In general terms it can be said that the Mesoamerican custom was to bury the dead in places where it was believed the soul could begin its journey easily or where the remains would preserve a beneficial force for the relatives. These places corresponded to some of the main liminal zones of the native cosmovision. Both written sources and archaeological records attest that individuals of the highest rank were buried in caves (Torquemada 1969: vol. 1, 60–61; Heyden 1981; Ruz Lhuillier 1968: 157), in the courtyards of palaces,[106] and in the main bodies of platforms, bases, and pyramids (Ruz Lhuillier 1968: 153).[107]

According to Cervantes de Salazar (1936: vol. 2, bk. 4, 40–41), the temples on top of the bases were reserved for the governors of the highest rank. "The shrines served as burial sites for the rulers, because others were buried in the ground, around the temples and in their patios."

Díaz del Castillo wrote briefly about a truly regal mausoleum next to the tzompantli at the Sacred Precinct of Tlatelolco.[108] And a great deal was written about the burial places of the Tenochcan tlatoque. We find contradictory versions of the resting place of Motecuhzoma Ilhuicamina: Durán (1984: vol. 2, 248) said that his remains were buried in the patio of his house, but Alvarado Tezozómoc (1944: 174) stated that they were taken to "the house of the superstition *tetzahuitl Huitzilopochtli*."

Information about the funeral rites of the next three tlatoque is a little clearer. According to the *Crónica X* group, the mortuary bundle and the image of each lord were taken to the top of the Templo Mayor for cremation. Durán (1984: vol. 2, 299, 311, 394), writing about the image of Axayacatl, noted, "They placed it before the idol Huitzilopochtli, and they put his dead body beside it." Tizoc's cadaver was burned "before the statue of Huitzilopochtli," and that of Ahuitzotl "was taken up to the feet of the idol." Alvarado Tezozómoc (1944: 242, 265, 391) was less specific in his *Crónica mexicana*, merely stating that they burned the corpses of these lords "next to Huitzilopochtli's feet."[109]

After sacrificing a considerable number of slaves and burning them on the royal pyre, the priests buried the remains of the tlatoani (Durán 1984: vol. 2, 300, 394; Alvarado Tezozómoc 1944: 392). There is no doubt that they were buried in the shrine of the tutelary god of the Mexica or in the *Cuauhxicalco*. Regarding Axayacatl, Durán (1984: vol. 2, 300) wrote,[110] "After killing all the male and female slaves and the dwarfs and hunchbacks—sometimes exceeding fifty to sixty people— blood was thrown on the fire, which extinguished the burning ashes. Grave diggers gathered it all, dug a hole at the feet of Huitzilopochtli and buried it there with all the hearts of the dead, together with the rich jewels, feathers and mantles that had been offered to him."

Tizoc's ashes were treated in the same manner, according to Alvarado Tezozómoc.[111] Both authors agreed that the remains of Ahuitzotl were buried next to the *cuauhxicalli* or *Cuauhxicalco* (Alvarado Tezozómoc 1944: 392; Durán 1984: vol. 2, 395). Eighty days after the funeral of each of these lords, another wooden image was made, more slaves were sacrificed, and many gifts were offered. All were burned and buried (Alvarado Tezozómoc 1944: 243; Durán 1984: vol. 2, 311).

Unlike his predecessors, Motecuhzoma Xocoyotzin did not receive the funeral rites befitting his rank because of the particular circumstances at the time of his death. One source said that his subjects threw his corpse in a temple that had been demolished by Cortés and that, after burning the body, they drank his ashes (Costumbres, fiestas, enterramientos 1965).[112]

When other members of the royal family died, their bodies were treated in a way similar to that of the tlatoque. For instance, it was said of Tlacaelel, the most famous cihuacoatl in Mexica history, that his ashes were buried "next to the sepulchers of kings" (Durán 1984: vol. 2, 369). In the case of Motecuhzoma Xocoyotzin's three brothers, who were slain in combat, it is said that, in the absence of mortal remains, three statues were carved and were burned before the image of Huitzilopochtli and that the ashes were buried in the *cuauhxicalli* (Durán 1984: vol. 2, 436).

Finally, I would like to mention a valuable reference about a similar practice carried out in Acolhuacan. Alva Ixtlilxóchitl (1975: vol. 2, 188) said that Nezahualpilli was cremated and that the gold coffer containing his ashes was buried in the Templo Mayor of Texcoco.

Figure 101: Atl-tlachinolli (malinalli) of the huehuetl of Malinalco and a helicoidal bead of a funerary offering. (Drawing by José Luis García.)

THE FUNERAL DEPOSITS IN THE TEMPLO MAYOR

After a brief review of documental sources and ethnographic reports, it is possible to come to some basic conclusions. In the first place, it is evident that Complex E is composed of funerary deposits belonging to persons of the highest rank, who were cremated so that their teyolia could go to the Tonatiuh Ilhuicac or Mictlan. The burial of seven of the deposits in the southern half of the Templo Mayor and their orientation toward the west tie the dead directly to the cult of the sun and to Huitzilopochtli. It should be remembered that both the warriors and the tlatoque were frequently associated with that astral body and that the tlatoani acted as the earthly personification of the Mexica tutelary god.

This particular distribution of burials was not exclusive to the so-called people of the sun. This is shown by the findings of Eduardo Noguera (1935) on the last expansion of the dual temple of Tenayuca. Like offerings 10 and 14, the three ceramic cinerary urns discovered in the 1930s lay at the foot of the southern stairway of the building, the half dedicated to the worship of the sun.[113] These containers had been placed inside 150-cm-deep round cavities, which contained a lot of calcinated earth. One urn was adorned with a geometric decoration, another had no adornment, and the last was shaped like an opossum. The contents were not very different from those of the urns at the Huey Teocalli of Tenochtitlan.[114]

If we accept as true the information contained in the many sixteenth-century sources, the cremated remains in the deposits of the Templo Mayor belong to individuals at the top of the Mexica social ladder. Only they had the privilege of being buried in the Cu de Huichilobos. Of course, the status of people buried inside Huitzilopochtli's chapel, right "at the foot" of the pedestal supporting the god's image, was even greater. Therefore, it is plausible that the urns found at Stage II contained the mortal remains of the first Tenochcan rulers, the cihuacoatl, the chief priests or members of the royal family (see Chávez 2002). The relative poverty of these burials, in comparison to the ones described in the era of Spanish contact, could be due to the status of the Mexica as vassals before 1430. In my opinion, the dignitaries of Stage II died of tlalmiquiztli, or a common, ordinary disease. This idea is supported by the presence of chalchihuite-hearts, inside urns in the form of Mictlantecuhtli, or of a reddish dog, as well as by the act of cremation itself.

On the other hand, it is probable that the two individuals buried in offerings 10 and 14 held places of less importance on the social scale, due to their burial on the platform of Stage IVb and the relative poverty of the funeral offering (Matos Moctezuma 1983; Chávez 2002). There is the remote possibility that the images of armed gods engraved on both containers refer to the death of an officer in battle.[115]

Last, I would like to propose that the eight deposits of Complex E contain objects associated with the journey of the teyolia and its stay in the worlds of reward and punishment. Several of the offerings include jewels (earplugs and necklaces)—perhaps used by the individual before his demise, perhaps given by allied lords and tributaries during the rites. Moreover, almost all the deposits include cutting-piercing instruments (sacrificial knives, points, and bloodletters), which may have been the means of obtaining the blood that would strengthen the soul during its journey or that would be given to the god of the dead upon arrival in Mictlan. It is possible that these objects were bloody when buried. The recurring presence of helicoidal beads,[116] as well as a gold bell with the glyph ollin, could be linked to the representation of the spiral path and the gyrating movement followed by the soul (Fig. 101). The numerous obsidian and greenstone disks, each with a hole in the center, as well as rattlesnakes traversing a perforated polygon or a chalchihuite topped with four concentric circles quite plausibly symbolize the passage from the human world to that of the gods.

One should also emphasize the repeated finding of depictions of duck heads—duck were thought to be the souls of the dead (López Luján 2005)[117]—and heads of what could be monkeys and opossums, found in Tenayuca and Tlatelolco. These three animals were *naguales* ("animal doubles") of Ehecatl-Quetzalcoatl. This god, apparently associated with the separation of the teyolia, has been characterized in a recent work as the extractor of the forces-times-destinies of the helical pillars that cross the cosmos and as the traveler par excellence from the profane world to the divine (López Austin 1990b: 305–39; López Austin, López Luján, and Sugiyama 1991).

To summarize, I believe that the archaeological information (spatial distribution and content of the offerings) and the historical and ethnographic data make more sense when analyzed together.

THE COMPLEX OF CONSECRATION OFFERINGS
(COMPLEX A)

I have intentionally left the richest and therefore the most complex group of offerings until the last.[118] This group presents the greatest obstacles to deciphering the significance of the offerings. But in spite of what might be expected, the spatial regularity of these deposits and the extraordinary diversity of the materials they contain allow us to be precise about their religious meaning.

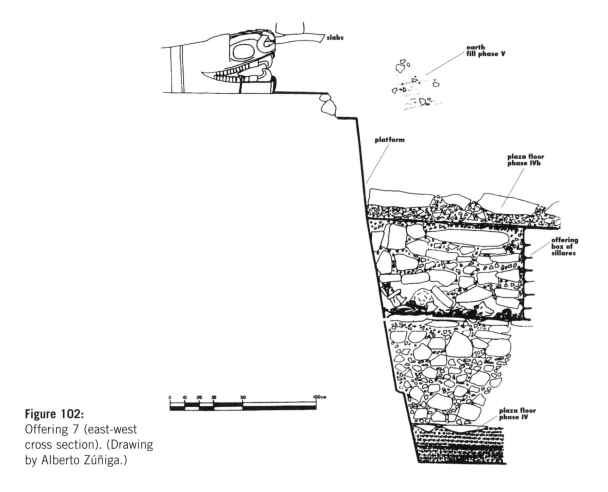

Figure 102:
Offering 7 (east-west
cross section). (Drawing
by Alberto Zúñiga.)

Furthermore, I would venture to state that Complex A offers the greatest possibility for study by comparing it with historical and ethnographic data.

DESCRIPTION AND ANALYSIS OF THE COMPLEX

According to the proposed grouping, Complex A is made up of offerings 13, 17, 11, 20, 6, 1, 23, 60, 7, 61, and 88 (a detailed description of Complex A is in Appendix 2). These eleven deposits join together very late on the dendrogram (see Dendrogram of Offerings). This is due not to the great dissimilarity among the offerings but to their exceptional richness. Complex A occupies a branch of the tree clearly isolated from the other complexes, which means that the grouping is meaningful.[119] But despite its isolation on the dendrogram, the offerings of Complex A have spatial and content affinities with Complexes B (Chambers 2 and 3) and C (offerings 22, 58, 24, 15, 62, 70, and CA), as well as with offerings 83, F, P (from Complex J), and L.[120]

The computer grouped offerings 13, 17, 11, 20, 6, 1, 23, 60, 7, 61, and 88 because they share an important number of attributes (see the Reordered General Matrix). The common denominator of these offerings is the presence of materials belonging to seven different object type

Figure 103:
Offering 7 (excavation
level 1). (Drawing by
Alberto Zúñiga.)

complexes: A (composed of conch shells, shells, and greenstone beads), B (copal only), C (copper bell, wood remains, and a sacrificial knife), J (fish and quail remains), K (statues of Xiuhtecuhtli and Tlaloc, copal deity, and coral), L (a shell circle, pectoral, and pendant), and M.[121] Additionally, several deposits have earplugs, deer head scepters, noseplugs (?) with Xipe Totec's split ends, and ceramic incense burners.

The homogeneity of the offerings of Complex A is also apparent in their spatial distribution. By looking at the location sketch, one can see the regularity of their placement around the Templo Mayor (Fig. 130) (see Appendix 2). All the offerings were discovered at Stage IVb—three on the northern half, four on the southern half, and four more at the axis of union of the bases of Tlaloc and Huitzilopochtli. According to the field records, then, all eleven offerings are the result of the same ritual: they were all buried simultaneously during the consecration ceremony of this new expansion.

Figure 104:
Offering 7 (excavation level 2). (Drawing by Alberto Zúñiga.)

The offerings were found at the corners of the building and on its principal axes (the three axial lines that cross the base in an east-west direction and the central line that crosses in a north-south direction, according to a strict bilateral symmetry). Curiously, the offerings that were paired by the computer because of their high index of similarity were located at the opposite ends of the same axis, with bilateral symmetry. This is true of offerings 11 and 20, 7 and 61, 13 and 17, and 23 and 60 (see the General Plan). I should mention that offerings 7 and 61, located on the northern and southern face, respectively, are nearly identical.

Another easily perceived regularity involves the vertical position of the deposits. The five offerings on the principal facade and offering 20 (located at the center of the back side) were inside the platform; the five offerings of the secondary facades (north, east, and south) were found under the flagstone floor that served as a placing for that platform (Fig. 102).

Figure 105:
Offering 7 (excavation
level 3). (Drawing by
Alberto Zúñiga.)

In every case, the donors opened pits large enough to hold a significant number of gifts. Eight offerings were found in spacious boxes of sillares, almost always covered with flagstones. The other offerings were located inside irregular cavities made in the building fill. When two offerings of this complex were found in the same area, one of them was contained in a box of sillares and the other set directly in the fill. This is the case in offerings 11 and 13, 1 and 6, and 17 and 20 (see the General Plan).

The placement of the gifts with respect to the cardinal directions depends upon the face of the building in which they were buried. For instance, the materials of offerings discovered on the southern side were oriented toward the south, and those found in the northern side faced the north. Offerings 17 and 20 were the exceptions because, although they were located on the eastern face, their objects were predominantly oriented toward the west.

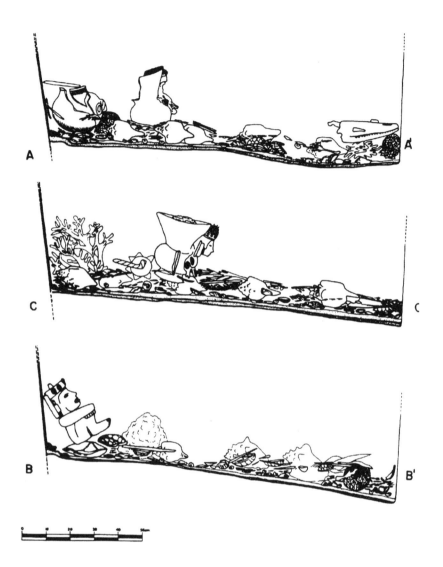

Figure 106:
Offering 7 (different east-west cross sections). (Drawing by Alberto Zúñiga.)

The spatial distribution of the material on the inside of the receptacle also followed rigid patterns. The materials were stacked vertically in five or six levels, corresponding to different moments of the rite (Figs. 103–112).[122] Evidently, the marked superposition of objects corresponds to the complexity of the expressed discourse.

The lowest level was formed by a homogeneous layer of marine sand that never exceeded 4 cm in depth (Figs. 105 and 112). In some cases, the sand included material such as gravel, conch shells, shells, sea urchins, and fish bones. As I pointed out in discussing offering 48, it is quite possible this layer symbolically re-created a portion of the cosmos with aquatic characteristics: the Tlalocan or xalli itepeuhyan.

The donors placed the second level, composed of small shells and conch shells, on top of the sand. We found a homogeneous bed of these mollusks, mostly from the Atlantic coast, in seven offerings. Four offerings had small deposits (at this level), and there were sea urchins, greenstone

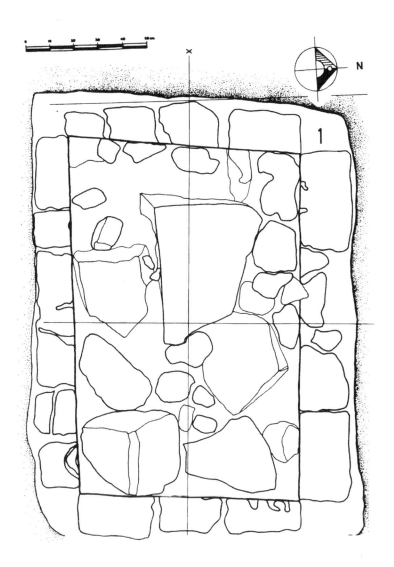

Figure 107:
Offering 23 (excavation level 1). (Drawing by Alberto Zúñiga.)

beads, copper bells, and copal anthropomorphic figures in several offerings. Regarding the significance of this level, it should be pointed out that the Mexica considered marine animals, metals, and stones to be cold and humid beings, coming from the underworld (López Austin 1990b: 372). Moreover, the conch shell was compared to the female uterus as a symbol of fertility and birth (Figs. 105, 106, and 111).

The third level was also composed of marine animals but of a larger size. Gastropods and corals predominated: the *Strombus* and *Xancus* conch shells, as well as lace corals, were distributed along the longitudinal axis of the offering. In contrast, the deer antler corals were found only in the corners (Figs. 104, 106, and 110).

Next the donors laid down a fourth level, made up exclusively of fish, reptiles, and, to a lesser degree, mammals. In spite of the abundance of animal remains found in this context, it is remarkable that not a single complete example was discovered. In fact, after a careful biological

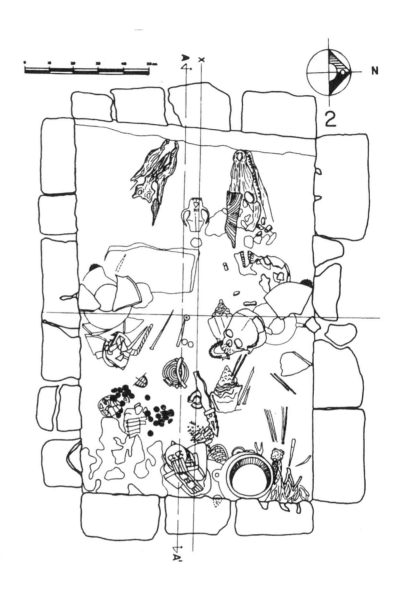

Figure 108:
Offering 23 (excavation
level 2). (Drawing by
Alberto Zúñiga.)

analysis, we know that the Mexica deposited only certain anatomical parts of each animal: dental
remains, premaxillas, preopercula, and the neurocrania of fish; turtle shells; the crania and dermal
plates of alligators;[123] the nose cartilage of sawfish;[124] the crania and skin of serpents; and the skin
of the puma (Figs. 103, 106, and 109).[125] The complete absence of vertebrae and of hipural plates
of fish indicates that the donors eliminated the trunks and buried only the heads and scales. Similarly,
only the heads of serpents and alligators were buried. In the case of turtles, the presence of shells
with no skeletons or drumsticks, which would indicate a musical function, emphasizes the premeditated and selective act of offering the shell, perhaps seen as the symbolic equivalent of the
skin of fish, alligators, and mammals. At any rate, at this level, we see a preference for separating
and burying the head and skin of dead animals while they were still fresh.

For an approximate idea of the fourth level's aspect, the reader should mentally reconstruct the exact moment when it was placed there by the Tenochcan priests. The image would almost

Figure 109:
Offering 23 (excavation level 3). (Drawing by Alberto Zúñiga.)

certainly be a uniform "skin" layer that physically and visually separated the deepest levels with aquatic significance (first, second, and third) from the one nearest the surface (the fifth). This intermediate layer must have had a rough and corrugated texture, due to the prevalence of reptile skins and a large proportion of fish with monstrous bodies, strong skin spines, or sharp teeth.

Without going too deeply into the subject, we can affirm that, in diverse contexts, the Mexica associated the serpent (Gutiérrez Solana 1987: 46), the tortoise, and the puma with earth and fertility. We must remember that Cipactli, the original feminine and aquatic monster that symbolized earth and its abundant production, occurs repeatedly in pre-Hispanic art as an alligator-like beast, a sawfish (*acipactli*), or an ophidian. One of the most beautiful cosmogonic myths recorded in the *Historia de los mexicanos por sus pinturas* (1965: 25–26) told of Cipactli's form and the role it played in primordial times. "And then they created the skies, beyond the thirteenth, and they made water and *created a great fish, called Cipactli, that is like a crocodile, and from this fish they*

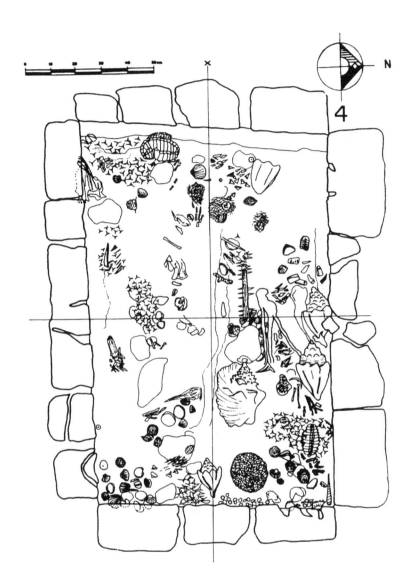

Figure 110:
Offering 23 (excavation
level 4). (Drawing by
Alberto Zúñiga.)

made the earth, as will be told. . . . Afterwards, when all four gods were together, they made the earth from the fish Cipactli, which they called Tlaltlecuhtli, and they painted it as god of the earth, *lying on top of a fish*, since it was made from it."

This cross between an alligator and a fish that, after the creative act, became the earth also appears in the *Histoire du Mechique* (Garibay 1965: 108):

Two gods, Quetzalcoatl and Tezcatlipoca, brought down the goddess Tlaltecuhtli. . . . And before she came down, *there already was water upon which she walked, but nobody knows who created it.* . . . and they squeezed her so hard she split in the middle, and from the back half they made the earth; and they took the other half to the sky, which caused the other gods to be very ashamed. . . . And to compensate [for it], they made trees, flowers and grass from her hair; from her skin small herbs and tiny flowers; from

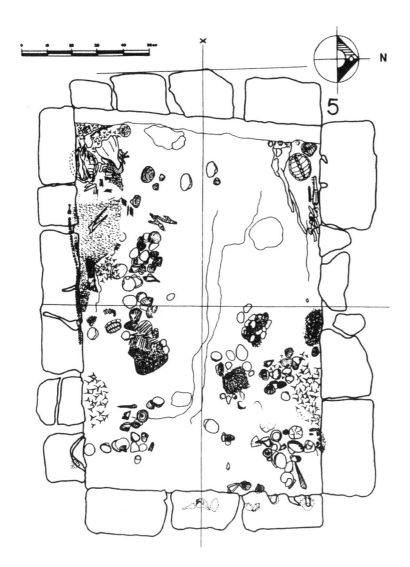

Figure 111:
Offering 23 (excavation level 5). (Drawing by Alberto Zúñiga.)

her eyes, wells and springs and small caves; from her mouth, rivers and small caverns; from her nose, valleys and mountains (emphasis L.L.L.).

The exclusive presence of large pieces of skin, belonging to animal species with a terrestrial significance and covering layers of sea sand, shells, and conch shells, suggests, I propose, that the fourth level, like those preceding it, symbolizes an important part of the cosmos. In this case, it is the surface of the earth—that is, the circular crust of a world that is filled by the waters of Tlalocan (Sahagún 1950–1969: vol. 11, 247–48), the reptilian covering that floated on the sea.

The fifth level was the richest of all. It was composed fundamentally of images of gods, representations of divine paraphernalia, cosmic symbols, cutting-piercing instruments, and the skulls of decapitated persons (Figs. 103, 106, 108, and 113). The most important of all the objects at this level were the statues of Xiuhtecuhtli-Huehueteotl and the jars with Tlaloc's

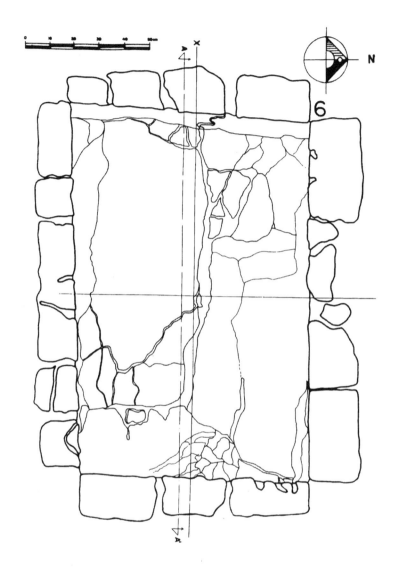

Figure 112:
Offering 23 (excavation level 6). (Drawing by Alberto Zúñiga.)

face. The images of the God of Fire and the God of Rain were always together at the head or in the center of the deposits, in the act of presiding over the gift. In most of the offerings, there was a sculpture of Xiuhtecuhtli and one of Tlaloc. In three cases, two sculptures of each of these deities were found. In the central part of some deposits, there were, in varying proportions, copal figures, skull-masks,[126] full-body sculptures, Mezcala-style masks, Mixtec penates, Teotihuacan masks, and even an Olmec mask. Large ceramic braziers with an effigy of a fertility goddess, probably the maize goddess,[127] were located at the extremes of the transversal axis of the offerings (Fig. 114).

As to the divine paraphernalia, four objects seem to be spatially related, together playing a fundamental symbolic role.[128] They are the small representations of emblems carved on flint, white stone, obsidian, and greenstone: scepters shaped like a deer's head, serpent scepters, the *chicahuaztli* ("rattle stick"), and the noseplug (?) with a "swallow-tail" split end.

Figure 113:
Offering 61 (excavation level 1). (Photograph by Salvador Guil'liem, courtesy INAH.)

The first pair of objects (the deer head and the serpent scepters) make up a unit composed of two symbolic elements that are, at the same time, opposed and complementary. The deer represents the sun and fire (Seler 1963: vol. 2, 135). In various myths of pre-Hispanic[129] and modern Mexico,[130] this mammal is closely tied to solar and fire deities; this connection is also seen in old pictographs. In the *Códice Borgia* (Seler 1963: pls. 33, 55), for example, the deer carries the sun on its back, and Iztac Mixcoatl, the ancient God of Fire, wears a deer disguise. In other native codices (*Códice Telleriano-Remensis* 1964–1967: pl. 33; *Códice Vaticano Latino 3738* 1964–1967: pl. 54; see also *Códice Borbónico* 1979: pl. 20) Xiuhtecuhtli and Xochiquetzal (*Tonalámatl de Aubin* 1981: pl. 20) carry staffs in the form of a deer head, very similar to those in our offerings (Fig. 115).

Figure 114:
Incense burner with
effigy of a fertility
deity. (Drawing by
Amelia Malagamba.)

The serpent scepter, on the other hand, is intimately linked to the aquatic world. Often the undulating body of a snake symbolizes currents of water and the fertilizing lightning bolts, one reason why it is among the most characteristic attributes of the gods of rain (Durán 1984: vol. 1, 82; Gutiérrez Solana 1987: 30; Graulich 1990; Pasztory 1975: 27). Because of this, pictographic and sculptured images of Tlaloc (*Codex Magliabechiano* 1983: fols. 89, 91; *Códice Borbónico* 1979: pls. 7, 23, 24, 25, 26, 32, 35; *Tonalámatl de Aubin* 1981: pl. 7; Durán 1984: pl. 15, fig. 22; *Códice Laud* 1964–1967: pls. 21, 23), of Chalchiuhtlicue (*Codex Magliabechiano* 1983: fol. 92), and of Nahui Ehecatl (*Códice Telleriano-Remensis* 1964–1967: pl. 12; *Códice Vaticano Latino 3738* 1964–1967: pl. 27) holding a snake or a serpent scepter are frequent. Like the deer head scepter, the depiction of a serpent scepter is not exclusive to Mexica culture. Examples include the images in the north jamb mural of Building A in Cacaxtla and mural 1 of corridor 23 at Tetitla, Teotihuacan (Fig. 116) (Miller 1973: 126).

The combining of the opposites water-serpent/fire–deer head in the Complex A offerings can also be found in several pictorial representations.[131] The most interesting one is in the *Códice Borbónico*. In the center of plate 21, Oxomoco and Cipactonal are seen inside a rectangular frame that has two openings. Two staffs in the form of a deer head flank the upper opening, and an undulating stream of precious water flows from the lower one (Fig. 117).

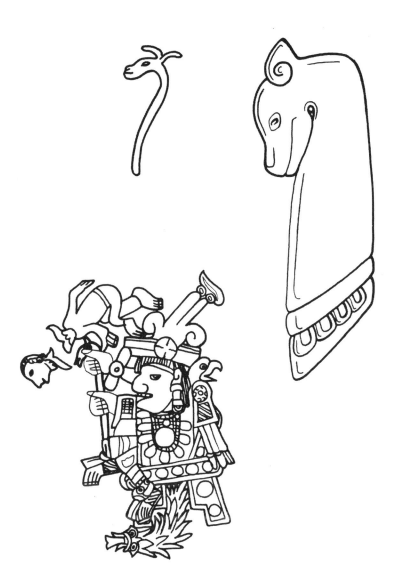

Figure 115:
Deer head scepter in the Templo Mayor and its pictographic portrayals (*Códice Borbónico* 1979: pl. 20; *Tonalámatl de Aubin* 1981: pl. 19). (Drawing by José Luis García.)

The pair composed of the chicahuaztli and the split-end noseplug have undeniable links to Xipe Totec. The chicahuaztli is still used in religious ceremonies, representing the *coa* ("hoe") that pierces the earth. This custom suggests a possible phallic significance in a union of opposites and of fertility (Soustelle 1969: 142–44; Taggart 1983: 59). This idea is supported by pre-Hispanic images of chicahuaztli next to the primordial couple at the moment of procreation, the day of *1 Cipactli* (*Códice Borgia* 1963: pl. 9; see *Veinte himnos sacros* 1978: 144–45). However, the identification of this artifact becomes less clear if we analyze other documents of the sixteenth century. For instance, in book 1 of the *Florentine Codex*, deities as dissimilar as Chalchiuhtlicue, Huitzilopochtli, Tzapotlatenan, Opochtli, Xiuhtecuhtli, and Omacatl hold scepters with these characteristics, although with slight variations.[132] To this long list can be added certain pictographic and sculptural depictions of Mictlantecuhtli, Quetzalcoatl, and Xochiquetzal,

Figure 116:
Serpent scepter from the Templo Mayor and its pictographic portrayals (*Códice Borbónico* 1979: pls. 7, 25). (Drawing by José Luis García.)

as well as divinities of earth, rain, and maize (Neumann 1976). Nevertheless, several scholars agree that the chicahuaztli is the chief attribute of Xipe Totec. No other god appears so often with this staff (Heyden 1986; Neumann 1976), and there are very few depictions of this god that lack this particular fertility scepter (Fig. 118).[133]

The connection between Xipe Totec and the chicahuaztli in the offerings of Complex A is corroborated by the repeated presence of an obsidian plaque with its two ends split like a bifid tongue or a swallow's tail. Although the members of the Templo Mayor Project called them *nose-plugs*, we do not know their real purpose. We find the double swallow tail in nearly all the known images of Xipe Totec, typically adorning the copilli, the ears, the nose, the arms, the maxtlatl, or the chicahuaztli of this deity (*Códice Borgia* 1963: pls. 25, 49, 61; *Códice Tudela* 1980: fol. 12r; *Tonalámatl de Aubin* 1981: pl. 14; *Codex Magliabechiano* 1983: fol. 90r; *Códice Vaticano Latino 3738* 1964–1967: pls. 10, 12; Durán 1984: vol. 1, 96, pl. 15, 243, pl. 37).

Two ceramic artifacts generically called *cosmic symbols* shared with the divine paraphernalia the central zone of the offerings. They are the three-dimensional images of a spiral and of the glyph ollin. The latter, often found leaning against the spiral, is a partial representation of the *malinalli* ("twisted herb"), which is why it is also associated with the glyph atl-tlachinolli (Fig. 119) (Heyden 1988: 75–76). It appears in indigenous cosmovision as a symbol of hierogamy, of the helical intertwining of hot masculine fluids with cold feminine ones that twist inside the cosmic trees. According to Ulrich Kohler (1979), the ollin, a section of the malinalli, represents the movement and, by extension, the annual path of the sun around the earth. Following this logic, it is probable that with the spiral, the Mexica wished to reproduce a whirlpool, that is, a liminal zone through

Figure 117:
Oxomoco and Cipactonal
(*Códice Borbónico* 1979:
pl. 21).(Drawing by José
Luis García.)

which the divine fluids are distributed over the face of the earth. Or perhaps the whirlpool represents the twisting of forces (Fig. 120).

The piercing-cutting artifacts form another important symbolic cluster in the center of the Complex A deposits. The flint knives (*tecpatl*) are given a monstrous anthropomorphic character by the appliquéd eyes and teeth. Strangely, these knives were placed perpendicularly along the longitudinal axis of the deposit, with the eyes and teeth oriented in the opposite direction from the image of Xiuhtecuhtli and Tlaloc. Because of these particular features, it is clear that the knives were never used in actual sacrifices. It is more likely they were the personified symbols of the sacrificial instrument (*Die Azteken und ihre Vorläufer* 1986: vol. 2, 280; Nicholson and Quiñones Keber 1983: 40).[134] Regarding this, it should be recalled that the anthropomorphic knives are linked to Mictlantecuhtli, Huitzilopochtli, and Tlaltecuhtli (Nagao 1985b: 45, 63–64), as well as with Itztapaltotec (a deity associated with Xipe) (*Códice Telleriano-Remensis* 1964–1967: pl. 32; *Códice Vaticano Latino*

Figure 118:
Chicahuaztli of the
Templo Mayor and its
pictographic portrayals
(*Códice Borbónico* 1979:
pls. 20, 27). (Drawing by
José Luis García.)

3738 1964–1967: pl. 53; *Códice Borbónico* 1979: pl. 20; *Tonalámatl de Aubin* 1981: pl. 20) and to the rite of decapitation (Broda 1987a: 85, n. 93).

Other undecorated flint sacrificial knives (*ixcuac*) were found near the remains of the beheaded.[135] Their position and the lack of decoration suggest that these knives were used to kill the individuals buried in those offerings.

There were also many instruments of ritual mortification: prismatic blades of green obsidian and bloodletters made with the long bones of birds and mammals (Aguirre 2002). Although there are no signs of use on the blades, they could have been used to cut soft body parts (Rees Holland 1989). Several excavation records agree that the bloodletters lay in a circle before the images of Xiuhtecuhtli and Tlaloc, unmistakable evidence of the original existence of a zacatapayolli. In addition, abundant quail bone remains and a ball of copal were found in association with the gifts of blood.[136]

Human skulls are the most impressive elements of the fifth level. The presence of skulls with mandibles and the first cervical vertebrae attached is enough to indicate death by decapitation. As a rule, the skulls were placed in the center and at the head of the offerings. Unfortunately, little is yet known about the age, sex, ethnic origin, and possible pathology of the dead. Up to this time, only five young adult females from offering 1, deposited in front of the Coyolxauhqui monolith, have been studied (Peña 1978). It is relevant that the fifty skulls found in the 118 offerings were all located on the principal axes of Stage IVb and that forty-one belonged to the offerings of Complex A.[137]

The sixth and last level was found in five of the eleven offerings of Complex A. Ceramic incense burners were placed directly on top of the flagstones that covered the boxes of sillares. In

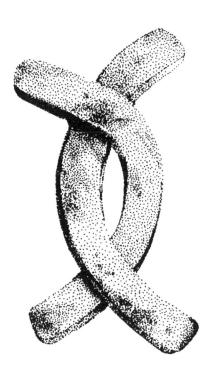

Figure 119:
Ceramic and
pictographic portrayals
of the glyph ollin.
(Drawing by José
Luis García.)

all cases, these objects were found severely fragmented, which makes us believe that they were ritually "killed" (Fig. 107).

In summary, the contextual evidence shows that the offerings of Complex A were buried coetaneously with the consecration ceremony of the Templo Mayor's Stage IVb. Apparently, these eleven deposits represent scale models of the three cosmic levels: the aquatic and deepest;[138] the intermediate terrestrial surface (*tlalticpac*); and the upper level, presided over by the gods of fire and of water, in which symbols of an opposite and complementary character stand out, as does the insignia of Xipe Totec and the skulls of the beheaded (cf. Matos Moctezuma 1988c: 88).

If each offering constitutes a discursive unit, then the different objects that compose it can be said to have functions similar to those of grammatical cases. Following this idea, the priest would be the tacit subject because his presence during the ceremony leaves no material trace. The images— the gods—would be the beneficiaries of the action expressed in the offering, and the representations of paraphernalia would denote the characteristics appropriate to each divinity. The copal, bloodletter, the quail, and human head perhaps served as the object of the gift itself, that is, the gifts that made communication possible between humans and the deity. Finally, the greater part of the animal material would indicate the circumstance, that is, it would create the appropriate time-space scenario (a section of the universe, a moment of the creation) so that the god might find a place and benefit from the offering. In this way the priests would make certain beings assimilable, placing them in the indicated places and at the exact time in order for the gods to benefit from them; otherwise, the god would not find the offering. If this is correct, the offering would be

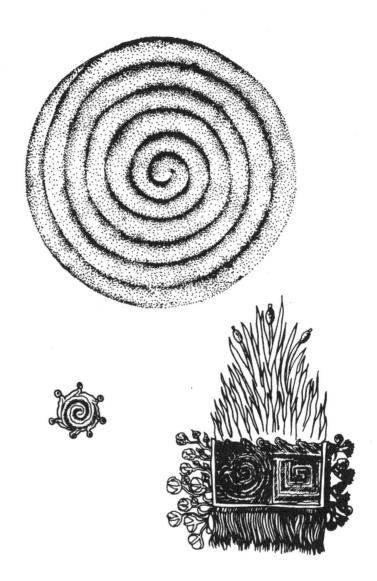

Figure 120:
Ceramic spiral and pictographic portrayals of red and blue whirlpools (*Historia tolteca-chichimeca* 1976: fols. 16v, 32v). (Drawing by José Luis García.)

a kind of image or statue (*ixiptla, toptli*), a container that could be filled with a divine force (see López Austin 1990b: 191–94; Townsend 1979: 33–34) that would permit the joining of god and gift.

SACRIFICE BY BEHEADING AND THE CONSECRATION OF CONSTRUCTIONS

The presence of decapitated humans in these offerings is one of the central keys to understanding the meaning of Complex A and of identifying the ritual ceremonies in which the gifts were made. As is well known, the religious custom of separating the head from the body goes back to the remotest eras of Mesoamerica and continued in Durango and Sinaloa until well into the seventeenth century (Moser 1973: 7).[139] Generally, the peoples of ancient Mexico associated the human head with tonalli, maize, and the sun (Durán 1984: vol. 1, 138; Heyden 1986; López Austin 1988c: 205–28, 1990b: 362–63), and they practiced ritual beheading in ceremonies that generally

Figure 121:
Pictographic portrayals of the burial of decapitated heads on hills and temples: (a) *Códice Borgia* 1963: pl. 6; (b) *Códice Cospi* 1964–1967: pl. 4; (c) *Códice Borgia* 1963: pl. 4; (d) *Códice Vaticanus* 3738 1964–1967: pl. 4; (e) *Códice Borgia* 1963: pl. 48 (Moser 1973: 33). (Drawing by José Luis García.)

emphasized binary oppositions: the ball game, sowing and harvesting rites, the sacrifice of prisoners of war to renew the tzompantli, and the consecration of temples (Moser 1973: 28–48; Nájera 1987: 170–81).

There have been many archaeological discoveries of skulls with the first vertebrae attached. They have been located at the corners of numerous cultural structures, which range from the middle pre-Classic to the late post-Classic periods and extend from Uaxactún, in the Mayan area, to Tzintzuntzan, in the heart of the Tarascan territory.[140]

The excavation data are fully corroborated by Mixtec and Maya pictographs, where it is easy to find depictions of decapitated heads at the top of or inside temples (Fig. 121) (*Códice Dresde* 1988: 34a; Seler 1963: pls. 4, 6; *Códice Cospi* 1964–1967: pl. 4; *Códice Vaticano Latino 3738* 1964–1967: pl. 4). This kind of image is also found in codices from the High Central Plateau. In folio 41r of the *Historia tolteca-chichimeca* (1976), there is a drawing of an unfinished pyramid that rests directly on a human head. The brief gloss in Nahuatl shows clearly the purpose of the sacrifice. "Year III acatl. On that date the Totomiuaque fed the earth with Mocatzin, the Huexotzinca; because of that

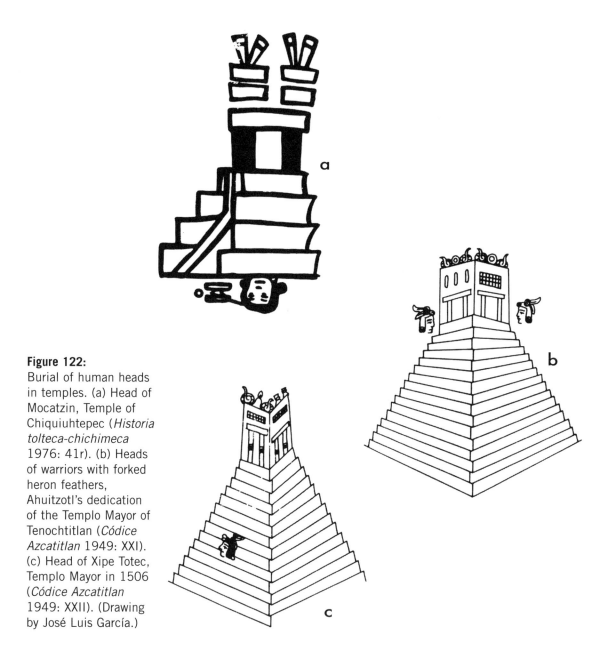

Figure 122:
Burial of human heads
in temples. (a) Head of
Mocatzin, Temple of
Chiquiuhtepec (*Historia
tolteca-chichimeca*
1976: 41r). (b) Heads
of warriors with forked
heron feathers,
Ahuitzotl's dedication
of the Templo Mayor of
Tenochtitlan (*Códice
Azcatitlan* 1949: XXI).
(c) Head of Xipe Totec,
Templo Mayor in 1506
(*Códice Azcatitlan*
1949: XXII). (Drawing
by José Luis García.)

they enlarged the *tetelli* ['stone pyramid'] of their *tlacatecolotl* ['owl man,' that is, 'evil magician']
in Chiquiuhtepec, Chiauhtla" (Fig. 122).

Paul Kirchhoff, Lina Güemes, and Luis Reyes García (*Historia tolteca-chichimeca* 1976: 213–14,
n. 2) maintained that the head buried on the occasion of the building's expansion was that of
Mocatzin, a noble with the title of *tlacatecpanecatl* ("courtier"), beheaded by the Totomiuaque in
order "to feed their earth."

In his *Monarquía Indiana*, Torquemada (1969: vol. 2, 167–68) commented that pre-
Hispanic people "spent a great deal in sacrifices and offerings" to consecrate their temples. The

ceremonies were known as *teichaliliztli* ("inauguration"). At the start of the sixteenth century, the Nahua and the Maya believed that a recently completed structure received a "soul" with the sacrifice and burial of a human body under its base. They also thought that the burial of heads not only supplied the energy necessary to expel negative forces from the site of the new construction but also provided the force required for its safety and functioning (González Torres 1975: 240; Nájera 1987: 36, 198–99).

As for the Mexica, the custom of consecrating temples with human sacrifices goes back to the time of their migration. According to the *Anales de Tlatelolco* (1948: 39–40; cf. *Códice Aubin* 1979: 93–94; *Historia de los mexicanos por sus pinturas* 1965: 54), the Mexica erected a new "seat of stone" for Huitzilopochtli's image when they settled in Tizaapan, a place located on Colhua territory. The leaders of the Colhua were guests at the festival for the dedication of the temple and took advantage of the occasion by ridiculing their hosts—burying at the "seat" an offering of excrement, trash, dust, spindles, and cotton. The Mexica immediately replaced these items with a reed, a thorn for self-sacrifice, and an *ahuehuetl* ("Mexican bald cypress," *Taxodium mucronatum*) that would serve "as its heart."[141]

Some time afterward, after having defeated the Xochimilca, the Mexica raised an earthen pyramid in the same place. Once again, they invited the Colhua nobles to the consecration, but only one of them, Coxcoxtli, attended. "When Coxcoxtli arrived, at that moment they were sacrificing the Xochimilca. They were placed in the center. Afterward they lowered the amaranth dough [an image of the god], brought down the *xiuhcoatl* and after that, the Xochimilca were taken to the sacrificial stone and killed. Immediately following that, they celebrated with a festival. They had not done anything similar anywhere since their arrival" (*Anales de Tlatelolco* 1948: 40).

A similar ritual took place when the Mexica founded their city on the island of Tenochtitlan in the year 2 *Calli*. At that time, the new arrivals built a "sod altar" that was consecrated with the death of the Colhua lord Ticomecatl Chichicuahuitl, whom "they placed inside the altar as if it were its heart" (*Códice Aubin* 1979: 95; *Anales de Tlatelolco* 1948: 43–44; *Historia de los mexicanos por sus pinturas* 1965: 56–57).

Fortunately, the burial of human heads in the offerings of the Templo Mayor was recorded in the written sources of the sixteenth century. Several chronicles stated that the Tenochca beheaded prisoners of war and offered their heads at their dedication of expansions of the Huey Teocalli or when the *temalacatl* ("gladiatorial sacrificial stone") began to function. These ceremonies were held only at a specific time of the solar year, during the month of Tlacaxipehualiztli.

Sahagún (1988: vol. 1, 110–11; see also Graulich 1982) probably best described the Tlacaxipehualiztli festival. Like his contemporaries, he placed special emphasis on the description of the gladiatory sacrifice, the *tlahuahuanaliztli* (Fig. 123). He said that once the prisoner was wounded ("striped") on the temalacatl by one of his opponents, the priest named Yohuallahuan approached to open his chest and take out his heart. "After knifing and killing the captives, all those present, priests and nobles and owners of slaves, began to dance in celebration around the stone where the captives had died. And the owners of the prisoners in the celebration, dancing and singing, *carried the heads of the dead in their right hands, clutching them by their hair. They called this celebration motzontecomaitotia*" (emphasis L.L.L.).[142]

Sahagún never mentioned what was finally done with the heads, but this information, so crucial for our purpose, did appear in other sixteenth-century documents. Alvarado Tezozómoc

Figure 123:
Gladiatorial sacrifice in
Tlacaxipehualiztli (*Códice
Tudela* 1980: pl. 12r).
(Drawing by José
Luis García.)

(1944: 119), for example, gave several clues in his description of the consecration of the temalacatl
and of the new addition to the Templo Mayor at the time of Motecuhzoma Ilhuicamina. He stated
that a considerable number of Huaxtec were sacrificed in honor of Xipe Totec during the ceremony.
"There the priests flayed the miserable bodies, and there they placed and dressed them. *The heads
were fastened to the walls of the temple of Huitzilopochtli.* When the Spanish came to this New Spain,
before the Mexican rebellion, eight soldiers climbed to the top of the cu and counted on the walls
sixty-two thousand skulls of people defeated in wars and sacrificed" (emphasis L.L.L.).

    Apparently, there was some confusion in the second part of this account, which stated
that the temples of the Huey Teocalli were filled with skulls—at least, the archaeological explorations of Stage II of the Templo Mayor did not find any evidence to verify this statement. It is

very probable that Alvarado Tezozómoc confused two different phenomena: the heads buried "in the walls" of the temple during Tlacaxipehualiztli and the innumerable skulls skewered on the tzompantli.

There is another explicit notation that leaves no doubt about this issue. It was written by Alva Ixtlilxóchitl (1975: vol. 2, 157) and referred to the expansion festivities of 1487, the most luxurious known. During the month of Tlacaxipehualiztli in that year, Zapotec, Tlapanec, Huexotzinca, and Atlixca prisoners of war were taken to the techcatl. "All of them were sacrificed before the statue of that demon, *and their heads were placed in some cavities intentionally made in the walls of the templo mayor*." It should be mentioned that Alvarado Tezozómoc (1944: 333) gave an equally clear description of the burial of heads in 1487.[143]

The rite of decapitation was associated with ceremonies other than the consecration of large edifices of the state cult. For instance, Nahua farmers of the sixteenth century performed similar rites to consecrate their houses. Pedro Ponce de León (1965: 129–30) noted that the celebration for homes was called *calchalia* (see Las Casas 1967: vol. 2, 223).[144] At the beginning of the ceremony, the dwellers placed "some small idol or stones of an attractive color, and a little tobacco" at each of the four corners (Pedro Ponce de León 1965: 129–30). The next day, they started a new fire in the center of the house and cut off the head of a hen, sprinkling its blood on the four corners, the four walls, the hearth, and the threshold of the building.

Durán (1984: vol. 1, 77–78) differed from Ponce de León. The Dominican said that the future dwellers repeated the moment of primordial genesis, pouring pulque and taking a lighted ember to each of the four posts. The ceremony was called *calmamalihua*, alluding to the helical movement of the malinalli in which the hot forces, represented by fire, and the cold ones, symbolized by pulque, are entwined (López Austin 1990b: 317).

Something of this thousand-year-old custom has survived to our times. Indeed, twentieth-century ethnography reveals a surprising cultural continuity between native societies and the endurance of the old Mesoamerican traditions. Like their pre-Hispanic ancestors, the Nahua, the Tzotzil, the Tzeltal, and the Huastec imitate the structure of the universe every time they build a dwelling (Galinier 1987: 104; Ichon 1973: 293–94, 297; Vogt 1983: 95–96). In fact, these groups believe that the different parts of the cosmos correspond not only to parts of the house but also to those of the human body, the maize plant, the temple, the people themselves, and the cornfield (López Austin 1990b: 226–27).

Today many consecration ceremonies follow patterns that surely originated in pre-Hispanic Mexico. As a rule, modern Indians bury the heads of sheep, hens, or turkeys in the foundation of their houses and communal buildings. They also offer gifts with complementary meanings: pulque and fire, pine leaves and red geraniums, or chicken broth and cane alcohol (*aguardiente*).

The natives of Tzinacapan, Puebla, build rectangular houses, oriented longitudinally from east to west. They believe that the four posts, the hearth, the altar, and the threshold of the door are the most important places in the structure and that each one of them belongs to a saint. Before living in the house, they must carry out a ceremony in which they bury offerings at each of the seven places mentioned. Strangely, while they are burying offerings at each of the four posts, they perform five repetitions on five separate occasions of the Lord's Prayer, directed to Tonal (the sun), and five Hail Marys, dedicated to the earth mother (Lok 1987).

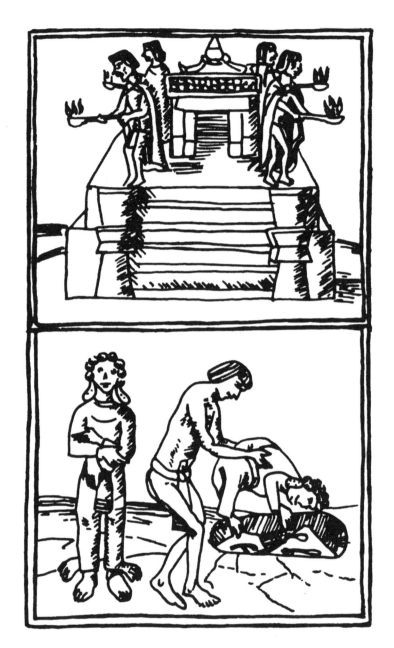

Figure 124:
Tlacaxipehualiztli (*Códice Florentino* 1979: bk. 2, fol. 26r). (Drawing by José Luis García.)

  The Otomi of the Northern Sierra of Puebla place a small tree in the center of the dwelling during the dedication rite. At its foot, they deposit food as an offering and invoke the "spirit of the woods." Jacques Galinier (1987: 105) believed this tree symbolizes the *axis mundi*.

  The Huastec consecrate a house before occupying it, imploring the earth not to make it fall down or cause its future inhabitants to fall ill. First, they offer alcohol and sprinkle the blood of recently sacrificed animals. Next, they "plant" a chicken under the threshold or, if they can afford it, one at each corner of the house. The same ceremony is done in dedications of the buildings used by local authorities—the prison, the church, and the priory (Ichon 1973: 244, 293–294).

The consecration practiced by the Tzotzil has two important moments (Guiteras 1965: 30; Vogt 1983: 84–89, 93–94). The *hol chuk* is performed when the walls are finished and the beams for the roof are in place. In this ritual, the workers hang a rope from the roof with which they tie four chickens by their feet (one for each corner). Then they cut off the birds' heads and bury them in the center of the floor. Finally, they "feed" the corners and the roof with chicken broth and cane alcohol. Once the work is completed, they celebrate the *ch'ul kantela* to compensate the Lord of the Earth and to convene the ancestral gods to give the house a soul. As in the preceding ceremony, they swing a rope from the top of the construction, to which they tie chickens that represent the new residents. The heads of these animals are partially placed in a cavity dug in the center of the floor. When everything is ready, a shaman cuts off the heads of the animals and lets their blood flow into the hole. As soon as they are completely drained, the heads and feathers are buried. Immediately afterward, the shaman takes a black rooster—a substitute for the owner of the house—twists its neck and buries it in the same place. Then the cavity is covered with dirt, and just above it is placed a cross decorated with pine branches and red geraniums. At that instant, all the celebrants begin a procession that moves past the four corners of the building, where they "plant" these pine seedlings and red geraniums and sprinkle chicken broth and cane alcohol. The walls and the beams of the roof are also sprinkled. At the close of the ceremony, the owners dress themselves in recently laundered and incensed clothing.

The Tzeltal celebrate two rituals very much like those of the Tzotzil. The first one is directed to the spirit of the posts—a mestizo (*ladino*) child—when the wooden structure is finished. The purpose of the ceremony is to introduce the occupants of the house to the spirit, to create a harmonious ambiance, and to protect the house against evil. With this in mind, they place an arch of branches and flowers, candles, liquor, cigarettes, palm crosses, and water in front of the central post. Then the future occupants sit down in front of the arch, and two *curanderos* (one for each half of the town) begin to officiate. Among other things, they burn candles and incense to make contact with the spirit, brush the participants with the branches, and drink liquor. Then the curanderos mix gunpowder with water and circulate a rattle among the guests. At the end of the ceremony, a palm cross is placed at each of the posts. The second Tzeltal ceremony is dedicated to the solar spirit of the house. Before beginning it, the central posts are adorned with arches made of branches and flowers. Then a lamb is hung from the central post, and its throat is cut. When all the blood has drained into a square hole dug in the center of the house, the animal is beheaded, and its head, which is considered to be the guardian of the house, is buried. Finally, the dwellers are served springwater with herbs, and a piece of clothing from each member of the family is incensed over the incense burner in the central part of the house (Nash 1975: 13–19).

TLACAXIPEHUALIZTLI AND THE CONSECRATION CEREMONIES OF THE TEMPLO MAYOR

After this brief review of the decapitation rites associated with the consecration of temples and houses, I will return to Tenochtitlan. I have identified Tlacaxipehualiztli as the ceremony in which the Mexica decapitated prisoners of war in order to consecrate their principal pyramid. In the following pages, I will analyze the historical records referring to the preparations and the consecration fiestas of the Templo Mayor (Fig. 124).

In Mexica society, religion has been so intertwined with state power that, even today, it is easy to detect the political connotations of ritual ceremonies. These connotations are particularly clear in the month of Tlacaxipehualiztli. Sources derived from the so-called *Crónica X* recorded how the consecration of the Huey Teocalli or of the temalacatl legitimized political expansion. The following pattern emerges:

1. Near completion of the expansion work, an expedition was organized for the conquest of some independent *tlatocayotl* ("principality"). Any pretext whatsoever justified these military campaigns: the assassination of merchants serving as Mexica agents, resistance to paying tribute to be used in the service of Huitzilopochtli, refusal to cooperate in building a new stage of the construction, not attending the dedication ceremony of the Templo Mayor, and others.

2. After the triumphant return of the Mexica armies, the prisoners of war (called "offerings to the gods") were forced to pay homage to the image of Huitzilopochtli and later to the tlatoani "who was considered to be the *alter ego* of the god." After that, it was only necessary to wait for the month of Tlacaxipehualiztli.

3. When the date of the dedication arrived, the rulers of allied domains, as well as those hostile to the Triple Alliance, were invited. Nonattendance was considered a clear sign of rebellion and sufficient reason for conquest. As an example, there is the *cassus belli* incited by Tlacaelel during Axayacatl's mandate, inviting the enemy nobles of Nonohualco, Cempoala, and Quiahuiztlan. "And the motive for this, Tlacaelel said, is to invite these people to see if they obey us and come at our call, because, if not, we will have reason to make war on them and to destroy them, and that is my intention. If they come, we will understand they are at our service and we will honor them" (Durán 1984: vol. 2, 276).

If they attended, the enemies had to come incognito to avoid any kind of attack by the townspeople.

> And so, before dawn, the lords and rulers of those cities came, changing the dress they were accustomed to wear. They dressed in the Mexican costume, and to further disguise their arrival, they made them carry flowers, branches and reeds with which they kept busy, as if they were people going to place branches and adorn the temple and the royal houses. And they were told not to answer people who greeted them, because of the difference in their language, telling them they [the hosts] would answer for all of them (Durán 1984: vol. 2, 338).

Of course, the allied lords were obliged to bring tributes and slaves to the solemnities.

4. During the festivals, special care was taken to intimidate the invited enemies by sacrificing prisoners taken from their homeland. At the end of the ceremonies, the heads of the slain were buried at the corners of the Templo Mayor, and gifts were distributed among the participants as a sign of subordination to the Tenochcan tlatoani.[145] When the guests departed, it was the custom to deliver an intimidating speech. For instance, after the consecration of the sacrificial stone, Axayacatl told the lords of Nonohualco, Cempoala, and Quiahuiztlan: "Be happy that you have seen and enjoyed the festival and solemnity of our god, and that you have seen the city of Mexico where he is honored. What I beg of you is to remain quiet and that you be calm and peaceful, because while you do so, you will enjoy our friendship and our favors. Thus you may go in peace and return happily to your homeland" (Durán 1984: vol. 2, 279). This way, the invited dignitaries returned to their land convinced that cooperation was the best answer to the threat of Mexica expansion.

It is very significant that the inaugural ceremonies of the Huey Teocalli and the temalacatl followed the pattern described, beginning with the rule of Motecuhzoma Ilhuicamina (Alvarado Tezozómoc 1944: 144), that is, at the beginning of the expansionist policy of the Tenochcan state. It was also at this time that Tlacaxipehualiztli was designated one of the four months when tribute payments were due. In fact, the first order for an expansion goes back to the era of the first Motecuhzoma (1440–1469) (Alvarado Tezozómoc 1944: 79–85; Durán 1984: vol. 2, 133–43). At that time, the shoreline cities of Texcoco, Xochimilco, Colhuacan, Cuitlahuac, Mizquic, Coyohuacan, Azcapotzalco, and Tlacopan agreed to contribute to the work of renovation by providing lime, *tlacuahuactetl* ("heavy stone"), tezontle, and manual labor. However, the inhabitants of Chalco never delivered the tezontle that was asked of them. This failure incited the Mexica to begin a military campaign against the Chalca, which, in the end, was victorious. It is reported that all the prisoners of war were sacrificed at the Cu de Huichilobos.

Around 1455 another addition was made to the Huey Teocalli,[146] and a temalacatl was carved with scenes from the conquest of Azcapotzalco (Alvarado Tezozómoc 1944: 114–21; Durán 1984: vol. 2, 185–95). For two years the neighboring towns brought huge quantities of quarried stone to the island. A short time before the work was completed, the Mexica army attacked the Huaxtec of Cuextlan and Tuxpan, taking many prisoners for the consecration of their temple. When Tlacaxipehualiztli arrived, the leaders of Texcoco, Tlacopan, Chalco, Xochimilco, Morelos, Couixco, Matlatzinco, and Mazahuacan, as well as "the neighboring people," journeyed to Tenochtitlan to attend the consecration of the building and the tlahuahuanaliztli, or gladiatory sacrifice.

Years later Motecuhzoma Ilhuicamina's troops conquered the Mixtec domain of Coixtlahuaca. When they heard about the victory, the tlatoani and Tlacaelel ordered "a likeness of the sun"—a new cuauhxicalli where the Mixtec prisoners would meet their death—to be carved (Alvarado Tezozómoc 1944: 132–41; Durán 1984: vol. 2, 185–93). "And they ordered that around it, as a border or patterned edge, they should paint all the wars they had till then, for which the sun had given them victory with his favor and help.... They engraved on it the victorious wars they had fought in Tepeaca, Tochpan, the Huasteca, Cuetlaxtlan, and Coixtlahuac, all elegantly carved" (Durán 1984: vol. 2, 191).

The inauguration of the stone took place at the solar festival of *nauhollin*, and the governors of Texcoco, Tlacopan, Chalco, Xochimilco, Culhuacan, Cuitlahuac, and Morelos attended. Durán (1984: vol. 2, 194) attributed to this era the spread of consecration rituals in which prisoners of war were sacrificed. "When the festival was over, the nobles from the cities returned to their provinces and kingdoms and, wishing to imitate the Mexica, they began to make and construct temples and to sacrifice men in the same fashion and style."

Near death, Motecuhzoma arranged for the construction of a new enlargement of the Templo Mayor (Alvarado Tezozómoc 1944: 153–66; Durán 1984: vol. 2, 225–33). Each of the allied states was assigned a specific task: the Texcoca were in charge of work on the principal facade; the Tlacopaneca, the rear facade; the Chalca, the southern side. The Xochimilca would work on the opposite side, the Mazahua would bring sand, and the towns from the hot lands would bring lime.[147]

> Motecuhzoma, seeing how fast his temple was being constructed, ordered all the nobles of the land, in order for his gods to be more honored and revered, to gather in all the cities a great number of precious stones, green jades, the ones they call *chalchihuites*, and beryls, blood stones, emeralds, rubies and cornelians. In short [to gather] every kind of rich stone and precious jewel and treasure, to throw those precious stones and rich jewels into the fill at each new *braza* of the building's growth. And so, giving tribute proportionately, each city came with the jewels and precious stones to cast into the layer, each in its turn (Durán 1984: vol. 2, 228).

At that time, a party of Mexica merchants was killed in Mitla, a deed that infuriated Motecuhzoma and determined him to make war against Oaxaca. But the military campaign had to be postponed until the Templo Mayor was finished. Moreover, a mistaken calculation prevented the Huey Teocalli from being consecrated immediately after the triumphal return of the army. The techcatl and the images of the *ilhuicatzitzique* ("supporters of the sky"), the *petlacontzitzique* ("canopy supports"), and the *tzitzimime* ("evil deities") had not been completed. Tlacaelel, in a conciliatory mood, urged his brother to sacrifice the prisoners from Oaxaca immediately and stated that when everything was ready, they would do the consecration with prisoners captured on the other side of the Sierra Nevada.[148]

After Motecuhzoma's death, Axayacatl (1469–1481), who ordered a cuauhxicalli and a temalacatl to be sculpted, came to power (Alvarado Tezozómoc 1944: 202–22; Durán 1984: vol. 2, 275–79). It was said that two huge stones were brought from Coyohuacan by the people of Azcapotzalco, Tlacopan, Coyohuacan, Culhuacan, Cuitlahuac, Chalco, Mizquic, Texcoco, and Huatitlan. As was the custom, the carvers decorated the edge of the temalacatl, on this occasion "recording in the work the history of the gods, principally Huitzilopochtli's" (Alvarado Tezozómoc 1944: 202). When the monoliths were finished, the armies of the Excan Tlatoloyan, under the command of Axayacatl, went to attack Matlatzinco. In the middle of the battle, the Tenochcan tlatoani succeeded in capturing a prisoner himself. Upon their return to Mexico, festivities were held (the tlahuahuanaliztli?) to dedicate the various monuments of Tlatelolco, a city recently conquered by the Tenochca.

And after Tlacaelel, the Cihuacoatl, had greeted him and he had rested, the next day he said to king Axayaca [sic], "Lord and son, it is an honor and a glory of kings to make sacrifice, and so with this your slave, won in a just war, you will make a sacrifice and an offering, that is, let us dedicate the market, temple and Cu of Tlatelolco in the name of *Huitzilopochtli*, our good lord and god, since for that purpose you left the Cu of the market of Tlatelulco." Axayaca [sic] was very pleased with this and he summoned *Petlacalcatl*, his chief steward and said to him, "Bring my arms and the tiger and eagle insignia, and my golden club with razor blades." This done, they dressed the prisoner, Axayaca's slave (Alvarado Tezozómoc 1944: 215).

At the celebration of Tlacaxipehualiztli, they performed the "striping" of the new temalacatl for the sacred site of Tenochtitlan, having invited for the occasion the tlatoque of the enemy domains of Nonohualco, Cempoala, and Quiahuiztlan. The consecration of the cuauhxicalli was arranged later. Texcoco, Tlacopan, and the other provinces were in charge of the construction of the platform that would support the monolith. After the work was concluded, the armed forces of the Triple Alliance tried unsuccessfully to subjugate the peoples of Michoacán, thereby causing a delay in the consecration of the cuauhxicalli (Alvarado Tezozómoc 1944; 222–35; Durán 1984: vol. 2, 279–85). In a second attempt, this time against Tliliuhquitepec, the Mexica were successful. Axayacatl invited the lords of Huexotzinco, Cholula, Tlaxcala, and Metztitlan (allies of the losers) to witness the death of 760 prisoners on the "eagle bowl" (Alvarado Tezozómoc 1944: 236–37; Durán 1984: vol. 2, 290–94).

In 1487 it was Ahuitzotl's turn to consecrate the expansion begun by Tizoc four years before (Fig. 125).[149] The war against the Huastec of Cuextlan produced a considerable group of prisoners for the ceremony, and the Huey Teocalli was finished as planned. The techcatl and the divine images[150] were taken up to the temple by the people of Acolhuacan, Tlalhuacpan, Tlacopan, and other nearby communities. All the temples, schools, and sleeping quarters in the city were also plastered and painted, and clusters of reeds and flowers were used to decorate streets and buildings. Meanwhile, the priests ordered sacrificial knives, ceramic incense burners, and devices of precious feathers, designed expressly for the occasion, to be made. The *calpixque* ("stewards"), for their part, collected tributes of food, animals, jewels, mantles, wood, and fuel.

> All these were turned over to the royal treasurer, or chief steward, so that he could divide them according to the orders he had received, especially to provide all that the priests requested for the cult of the gods and the present ceremony; second, to the officials of the silversmiths, the lapidaries, and feather worker,.... so they might solemnize the great festival for the renovation and completion of the temple (Durán 1984: vol. 2, 341).

When everything was ready, Ahuitzotl's emissaries left Tenochtitlan to invite the enemy lords of Tlaxcala, Huexotzinco, Cholula, Tecoac, Zacatlan, Yopitzinco, Metztitlan, and Michoacán. They also invited the nobles of the provinces of the Triple Alliance, who were forced to contribute prisoners for the holocaust.[151] Finally, they required the inhabitants of surrounding towns to attend under penalty of death.

Figure 125:
Expansion of the Templo Mayor during the reigns of Tizoc and Ahuitzotl (*Códice Telleriano-Remensis* 1964–1967: pl. XVIII and XIX). (Drawing by José Luis García.)

The ceremony began the first day of Tlacaxipehualiztli. At the top of the Templo Mayor, Ahuitzotl, assisted by five priests,[152] began to sacrifice the first group of prisoners, who were lined up along the Itztapalapa highway. In the cuauhxicalli, Tlacaelel and five helpers took out the hearts of the captives in a line going toward the Texcoco landing.[153] Nezahualpilli, lord of Acolhuacan, and five priests (two of whom personified Mixcuahuac and Yohualahua) were in the Yopico, slaying the prisoners lined up along the Calzada de Tepeyacac. Totoquihuatzin, huey tlatoani of the Tepanec, and his five assistants (two of whom were costumed as Coatlicue and Ometecuhtli) were in the Huitznahua Ayauhcaltitlan with a line of humans along the Tlacopan road. Sacrifices were held simultaneously at sixteen other places in the city.[154] Ministers and the faithful used the blood to anoint the supports, thresholds, and walls of the temples, as well as the rooms and the lips of the sacred images.

The *Chronicle X* sources stated that this massive slaughter caused the death of 80,400 in just four days.[155] When the sacrifices were over, Ahuitzotl divided gifts among the participants, said farewell to the enemy lords (who had watched the spectacle hidden on top of the Cihuatecpan), and then ordered the renewal of the tzompantli and the burial of some of the heads in the Templo Mayor.

The Mexica considered the absence of the lords of Teloloapan from this ceremony to be a rebellion, and Ahuitzotl and his hosts began a conquest, not only of Teloloapan but also of Alauiztla and Oztoman. Reports say that the prisoners taken there were sacrificed in the next Tlacaxipehualiztli festival.

The conquests of the Mixtec of Zozolan and Yanhuitlan date from the time of Motecuhzoma Xocoyotzin (1502–1520) (Alvarado Tezozómoc 1944: 447–51; Durán 1984: vol. 2, 436–37). We know that more than one thousand prisoners were sacrificed during the month of Tlacaxipehualiztli and that the guests came from the Huasteca, Huexotzinco, Cholula, Atlixco, Tlaxcala, Tliliuhquitepec, Meztitlan, Michoacán, and Yopitzinco.

Also during the reign of the second Motecuhzoma, the Coateocalli (temple "contained with that of Huitzilopochtli") was consecrated with captives from the rebellious province of Teutepec.[156] As usual the leaders of the allied provinces attended,[157] as did many enemy rulers.[158]

Shortly before the arrival of the Spaniards, Motecuhzoma Xocoyotzin ordered the carving of a temalacatl "for the Flaying Festival" (Alvarado Tezozómoc 1944: 494–99; Durán 1984: vol. 2, 489–90). The Tenochcan stone carvers went to Aculco, in the Chalco province, to get an adequate stone. But, even with the help of people from the many provinces,[159] it was impossible for them to move the monolith to Tenochtitlan. The stone fell into the lake as it was going across the Xoloco bridge, an event that was taken to be a bad omen.

This long enumeration of consecration ceremonies ends with the intention of Motecuhzoma Xocoyotzin to once more enlarge the Templo Mayor, a desire that was never carried out. "It seems proper to me that Huitzilopochtli's house should be solid gold, and that the interior should be chalchihuites and rich quetzal feathers" (*Anales de Cuauhtitlan* 1975: 61).

It should be remembered that taking and sacrificing prisoners of war to consecrate religious buildings was not practiced by the Mexica alone. Other contemporaneous societies of the High Central Plateau justified their campaigns of expansion in the same way, as recorded in the historical sources of the sixteenth century. For example, the *Anales de Cuauhtitlan* stated that "the nobles of Cuauhtitlan took prisoners that were converted into the heart of the temple" (see González Torres 1985: 242). We also know that when the new expansion to the Templo Mayor of Texcoco was completed in the year *1 Acatl*, Nezahualcoyotl asked for Motecuhzoma Ilhuicamina's consent to conquer the Tzompanca, the Xillotzinca, and the Citlaltepeca for the purpose of securing captives for the dedication ceremony (*Anales de Cuauhtitlan* 1975: 54). Years later, in 1481, Nezahualpilli subjugated the domains of Ahuilizapan, Tototlan, and Oztoticpac; the captives were fed the sacrificial stone at the dedication of the expansion of the Texcocan Huey Teocalli (Alva Ixtlilxóchitl 1975: vol. 2, 148–51). Finally, there is the case of the Cuauhnahuaca, who in 1490 consecrated their temple by slaying forty captives sent by Ahuitzotl especially for the occasion (*Anales de Cuauhtitlan* 1975: 58).

In summary, the Mexica state emerged as an advocate of temple construction beginning in 1440. The period between Motecuhzoma Ilhuicamina's ascent to power and the Spanish Conquest was a time of euphoric building of religious structures that corresponded to the growth of the political-military apparatus and Mexica power (Cerrillo M. de Cáceres et al. 1984: 50–51). A careful reading of Durán and Tezozómoc shows this interesting parallel: the Templo Mayor of Tenochtitlan grew at the same rate as the empire. In this way, the successive expansions of the Huey Teocalli glorified military expansion and served as an ideological justification for imperialist policy. Each addition symbolized, celebrated, and sanctified the obtaining of new tributaries within the sphere of Mexica dominion. If the armies of the Triple Alliance were not successful in conquering an independent domain, as happened in the case of Axayacatl's failed expedition to Michoacán, the consecration was postponed until a conquest was achieved. Thus political and economic interests were interrelated with their religious beliefs. This explains why there were so many expansions to the Templo Mayor in a relatively short time (Broda 1985; León-Portilla 1987; D. Carrasco 1981). In other words, there is a direct relationship between the growth of the empire and the expansion of the principal religious structure in the capital.

THE RELIGIOUS SIGNIFICANCE OF TLACAXIPEHUALIZTLI AND THE TEMPLO MAYOR

Strange as it may seem, after analyzing the historical information of the sixteenth century about consecration ceremonies, it would seem that Tlacaxipehualiztli was the principal festivity at the Templo Mayor. The same conclusion emerges from a review of some important archaeological data. First, the offerings of Complex A attest to the great importance of that twenty-day period. It is suggestive that the eleven offerings involved (characterized by the presence of images of Xiuhtecuhtli and Tlaloc, emblems of Xipe Totec, and the skulls of decapitated humans) make up the richest group of gifts recovered from the ruins of the building.

A second key piece of information comes from Batres's most important finding (1902; Peñafiel 1910: 11–12) in the final building stage of the Huey Teocalli—discovery Number V, found on October 16, 1900. Among the many objects found there, an image of Xiuhtecuhtli, a stone Tlaloc water jar, two sculptures of Ehecatl, and two polychrome ceramic vases stand out. One of the vases was decorated with a painting of the heads of three beheaded warriors, and the other had motifs alluding to the sun: the quincunx, the ollin, and the *xicalcoliuhqui* ("stepped fret design").

Manuel Gamio, who discovered the Templo Mayor, successfully explored the southwest corner of one of the most recent expansions to the building. In his laconic reports, we find that he recovered from the rubble an urn "made with slabs" that contained human skulls. Although Gamio (1917, 1921) did not elaborate in his report, it is quite possible that those skulls belonged to people slain in a decapitation ritual.

The discovery made on July 16, 1990, during the work of fixing the foundation of the ancient building of the Marqués del Apartado (which adjoins the Templo Mayor) should be noted.[160] There archaeologist Elsa Hernández Pons rescued an offering that contained a human skull with cervical vertebrae and six rectangular stone plaques. Bas-reliefs of severed arms and legs decorated four of the slabs, and engraved on the other two was the glyph of Tlacaxipehualiztli, the copilli topped by ribbons with split ends (Anon. 1990: 17, 30; Hernández Pons 1997). These resemble the tlacaxipehualiztli, chicahuaztli, and war emblems that were carved on the staircases of the principal facade in the double temple of Tenayuca (Caso 1928: pls. 1–5).

The last archaeological fact I will mention is the spatial orientation of the Templo Mayor. In Chapter 4, I noted that the specific direction of the architectural axes of the Mesoamerican building expressed the order of time and that, according to Tichy (1981), "the festival of a god was set in the solar year by the orientation of his temple." If we accept this, the precise calculation of the east-west deviation of a religious building would contribute to the chronological identification of its main festival. Today we have reliable means of measuring the orientation of the different building stages of the Templo Mayor. Ponce de León's averaged calculation showed that the sun rose each year perpendicularly in front of the facade of the Huey Teocalli on March 4 and October 10.[161] March 4 corresponds exactly to the beginning of the twenty-day period of Tlacaxipehualiztli, if we accept the date given by Sahagún and add the ten days of the Gregorian correction.[162] However, there is still disagreement about the correlation of the Mexica and Christian calendars. Several scholars accept Sahagún's dates as valid, but others challenge them (see Tena 1987: 87–88).

At any rate, a fragment from Motolinía's works confirms the tie between the building's orientation and Xipe Totec's festival. In his *Memoriales*, the Franciscan affirmed that the sun arose precisely between the chapels of Huitzilopochtli and Tlaloc during Tlacaxipehualiztli. "This fiesta was held when the Sun was in the middle of *Uichilobos*, which was the equinox, and because it was a little off-center, *Mutizuma* [sic] wanted to tear it down and straighten it" (Benavente 1971: 51).

Much of today's unexplained data would make sense if Tlacaxipehualiztli were one of the three main festivals of the Templo Mayor. If this were so, the festivities of the southern half of the building, corresponding to the cult of Huitzilopochtli, would have been held during Panquetzalizt li, the twenty days near the winter solstice. Complementarily, the solemnities for the northern half, corresponding to Tlaloc, would have been celebrated on Etzalcualiztli, the twenty days nearest the summer solstice. However, a third festival, dedicated to all of the Huey Teocalli would seem necessary. I propose that this festival took place on Tlacaxipehualiztli, the period corresponding to the spring equinox—the point of equilibrium between day and night, the dividing line between the months of the dry and rainy seasons (see Aguilera 1988, 1990). I believe this hypothesis would help solve questions such as (1) why the Mexica celebrated the sacrifice of Tlacaxipehualiztli from the time of migration;[163] (2) why this twenty-day period was the only one celebrated simultaneously in all the districts of Tenochtitlan (Durán 1984: vol. 1, 95–96); (3) why the Hucy Teocalli was dedicated only in this twenty-day period; (4) why the priests personified "all the gods" during the celebration;[164] (5) why in the *Primeros Memoriales*'s (1905: 39, fol. 269r) portrayal of the Sacred Precinct the two gods of highest rank are Huitzilopochtli and Xipe Totec (Fig. 19); (6) why the ceremony of Tlacaxipehualiztli was so widespread at the time of the Spaniards' arrival (Nicholson 1972b; Broda 1970; Graulich 1982); (7) why the calendar of some Mesoamerican people began with Tlacaxipehualiztli (González Torres 1975: 71); and (8) why in the historical sources of the sixteenth century this is the most frequently mentioned period and why its description takes up so much space (Couch 1985: 41; Broda 1970).

Durán (1984: vol. 1, 95–96), writing about the enormous relevance of the cult of Xipe Totec and the festivities of the Tlacaxipehualiztli, said

[Xipe Totec] was not a regional idol, celebrated here and there. It was a universal festival throughout the land, and everyone pays homage to him as a universal god. Therefore they had a special temple built for him with all possible honor and elegance, honored and feared him to the highest degree. In this festival they killed more men than in any other, since it was so universally celebrated. Even in the poorest towns and districts they sacrificed men on that day.... Forty days before the festival day they dressed an Indian like the idol.... They did this in each district...and so in the celebration they could dress an Indian slave to represent that idol, just as they did in the principal temple, something they did not do in any other fiesta of the year.

Torquemada (1969: vol. 2, 217; see Graulich 1982), describing the festivals of this month in Tlaxcala, stated, "The Tlaxcalans called this month *Coaylhuitl*, which means, general festival, because at that time they have great festivals and dances for the Lords and Rulers, as well as for the Common people, in the Temples and in the public Plazas."

In the light of the data from the explorations of the Templo Mayor Project, it would be advisable in the future to reconsider the total symbolic meaning of Tlacaxipehualiztli and therefore the attributes of Xipe Totec. Unfortunately, ever since Seler (1899) proposed for the first time, in 1899, that the flaying of victims in the Tlacaxipehualiztli alluded to the renovation of vegetation in the spring, that idea has dominated the field and has been uncritically accepted everywhere. Today many investigators seem to agree that Tlacaxipehualiztli was a vast communal exercise to propitiate fertility. However, as Nicholson (1972b) noted, Seler's hypothesis is only a conclusion based on Western logic, with absolutely no historical data to support it. As a matter of fact, the practice of flaying victims is associated with other deities—such as Tlazolteotl, Ixcuina, Teteoinnan-Toci, and Chicomecoatl-Xilonen—who have little or nothing to do with the renewal of spring. Nicholson (1972b) suggested taking other hypotheses (for example, obtaining trophies of war) into account in analyzing this festival.[165]

Gertrude Kurath and Samuel Martí (1964: 68–70, 76–77) developed an alternative proposal, similar to the one given here about the dual character of the offerings of Complex A and of the Templo Mayor itself. They discovered that most of the rituals described in Tlacaxipehualiztli had a consistent binary nature. In their opinion, the rituals represented the conflict between winter and summer, the sky and the earth, and light and darkness and symbolized rebirth after death. They pointed out the binary oppositions throughout the twenty-day period: the conflict between the eagle and jaguar warriors against the captives; the row of priests facing a line of prisoners and a row of warriors facing another line of prisoners; the skirmishes between *xipeme* ("captives who had personified Xipe") and *tototectin* ("sacrificed prisoners given the name of Totec"), two partial aspects of the god; the dances of the Tenochca warriors with the Tlatelolca military in two double columns; and the dance of two kinds of warriors (conscripts and veterans) with two kinds of women (mothers and prostitutes). To this can be added the dual offering of pulque and quail's blood made by the prisoner in the temalacatl (López Austin 1967: 16, 19).

In addition to this, there was constant allusion during the festivities of Tlacaxipehualiztli to the malinalli, the divine symbol of the union of contraries. On the first day of Tlacaxipehualiztli, the people of Tenochtitlan made some tortillas in a twisted form called *cocolli* (from *col*, meaning "twisted") that might well represent the *malinalli*.[166] "From these tortillas they made garlands and danced girded with them. All day they offered a great quantity of them" (Durán 1984: vol. 1, 243).

On the other hand, Sahagún's informants also said that when the tlahuahuanaliztli, or gladiatorial sacrifice, ended, one group of warriors dressed in the skins of xipeme and another group clad in the skins of the tototecti pretended to do battle. First, they aroused themselves by piercing their navels.

> Then the *xipeme* run. After them, pursuing them, goes a *Totec* named "Nocturnal drinker." He pursues them, fighting them, and [with him] go all the *tototectin.*
>
> At once they followed them. They continue to jab them; warring with them; they catch them; they seize them with their hands; they carry them by their legs. *And they come spinning, gyrating;*[167] they hit them with pine bludgeons, making them fight (López Austin 1967: 23–24; emphasis L.L.L.).

During this conflict, as the passage emphasizes, the two groups simulated the gyration of the malinalli; xipeme and tototectin gyrated in a way similar to the helical intertwining of the atl-tlachinolli, that is, the opposing fluids that symbolize war. The contest ended with the capture of the members of one of the two bands, who were beaten with chicahuaztli and taken to the Yopico.

The dual nature of the Tlacaxipehualiztli observed by Kurath and Martí is, to a certain extent, confirmed by the interpretations of A. Garibay. The learned Mexican translated the word *xipe* as "he who has a virile member." From this etymology he derived the phallic nature of Xipe Totec and the hierogamic nature of the Tlacaxipehualiztli (*Veinte himnos sacros de los nahuas* 1978: 177–80). Garibay suggested that the sacrifice by shooting arrows (*tlacacaliztli*) and the flayings conducted during that month referred to the cohabitation of the sun and earth that produced maize.[168] From this point of view, the tlacacaliztli reenacts the primogenital sexual union. This hypothesis was based on a passage from the *Anales de Cuauhtitlan*, which told how the *ixcuiname* sacrificed a group of Huastec prisoners. Upon arriving in Tula, the sorcerers addressed their captives in this way:

> We were going to Tula. Through you we will have sex with the earth; through you we will have a celebration. Until now we have not shot men to death with arrows. We are going to begin; we are going to shoot you. When the captives heard this they began to weep. That was when they began to shoot men with arrows.
>
> 9-Reed: On this date the Ixcuinname arrived in Tula. They had sex with the earth through their prisoners. They shot arrows through two of them. And the "husbands" of these diabolical witches were the captive Huastec. It was then the *tlacacaliztli* began (*Veinte himnos sacros de los nahuas* 1978: 144–45).[169]

Garibay (*Veinte himnos sacros de los nahuas* 1978: 144–45) also argued that the chicahuaztli (the chief insignia of Xipe Totec) symbolized simultaneously the solar ray that penetrates the earth and fertilizes it, the stick used to dig the earth and put in the seed, and the penis.

Figure 126:
Xipe Totec (*Códice
Borbónico* 1979: pl. 14).
(Drawing by José
Luis García.)

In a very interesting work, Graulich (1982) concluded that the Tlacaxipehualiztli was
directly related to war (union of opposites) and to the birth of the sun. After a detailed analysis
of the structure, the personages, and the sequence of the ceremony, he is convinced that the
tlahuahuanaliztli was a reenactment of the myth of the origin of the Fifth Sun in Teotihuacan
and of the first war: the massacre of four hundred *mimixcoah* ("cloud serpents") ordered by
Tonatiuh (Leyenda de los Soles 1975: 121–23; Sahagún 1988: vol. 2, 479–82). This proposal is very
relevant to our problem if we recall that gladiatorial sacrifice was the principal rite of the consecration ceremonies of the Templo Mayor. As I stated in Chapter 3, in many societies the dedication of religious buildings followed certain rituals that repeated the primordial act of creating
the universe, performed for the purpose of assuring its reality and its endurance. In this sense,
the act of building had to be similar to the cosmogonic action: to create a temple meant to re-
create time and the universe. With this in mind, it could be said that the consecration of the Templo
Mayor in Tlacaxipehualiztli re-created the primogenital moment in which, after the world had

Figure 127:
Xipe Totec (*Códice Borgia*
1963: pl. 49). (Drawing
by José Luis García.)

been engendered and destroyed four times, the gods met in Teotihuacan to undertake the fifth and definitive creation.[170]

In addition to defining the meaning of Tlacaxipehualiztli, the functions of Xipe Totec should be considered in the light of new and deeper investigations (Figs. 126–128). It is paradoxical that we know definitely so little about the attributes of a deity so transcendental in the cosmovision of Mesoamerican people.[171] In spite of Seler's belief, Xipe Totec had a strong, warlike character. The *Códice Vaticano Latino 3738* (1964–1967: 30, pl. 10) clearly illustrated this. "Of this [god] it is said that he was created in war, and because of that, they painted him with war insignia, a lance, a banner and a shield. They held him in great veneration. Moreover, they said that he was the first to open a road to the sky, because they had the false belief, among others, that only he who died in battle would go to heaven, as we have said before."

Perhaps because of this belief, the Mexica tlatoque dressed themselves as Xipe Totec during the military contests. On those occasions, each wore the skin of a flayed victim, a headdress of tlauhquechol, a shirt called tlauhquecholehuatl ("tlauhquechol skin"), a short skirt called *zapocueitl quetzalli*, and pendants with split ends; each also carried a drum, a shield, and the Xipe Totec's chicahuaztli (Alvarado Tezozómoc 1944: 402, 422, 511; see Nicholson 1959, 1972a; González Torres 1975: 139). In a parallel fashion, the *halach uinich* ("hereditary Maya ruler") used a shield with the face of the god Q, his Mayan equivalent (Heyden 1986).[172] To this may be added the bellicose representations of Axayacatl, Ahuitzotl, and Motecuhzoma Xocoyotzin, clad in this costume, on the cliffs of Chapultepec (Alvarado Tezozómoc 1944: 237, 389, 499; Nicholson 1959),[173] and in important pictographs (Fig. 129).[174]

As Graulich (1982) maintained and as the analyses of the offerings and the meaning of the Templo Mayor verify, Xipe Totec was a deity in whom opposite forces (the complementary forces of sky and earth) joined and fought. In other words, there is a very close tie between the

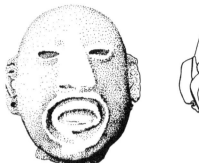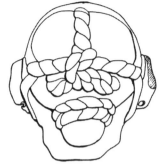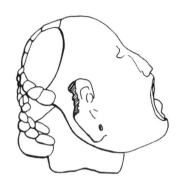

Figure 128: Sculpture of Xipe Totec found in the rubble of the Templo Mayor. (Drawing by Amelia Malagamba.)

Xipe Totec cult and war, an activity the Mexica equated metaphorically with the atl-tlachinolli,[175] and hierogamy. It is clear that this deity was associated with fertility and the birth of maize, both phenomena resulting from the sexual union of sky and earth.

Before leaving this topic, I wish to recall what many investigators have repeated to the point of exhaustion: practically all aspects of Mexica society were suffused by binary taxonomy. The various kinds of bipolar oppositions were omnipresent in indigenous concepts and fomented a holistic dual classification that was almost obsessive. This peculiar way of dividing the world takes us first to the cosmogonic myths and the concept of a double path of the forces-times-destinies on the surface of the earth. It also occurs in the distribution of governmental duties. One has only to recall the complementary functions of the *tlatoani* and the *cihuacoatl*, the *tlacatecatl* and the *tlacochcalcatl*, the *hueicalpixqui* and the *petlacalcatl*, the *Quetzalcoatl Totec tlamacazqui* and the *Quetzalcoatl Tlaloc tlamacazqui*, and, in Cholula, the *tlaquiach* and the *tlalchiac* (Zantwijk 1963). The binary taxonomy is found in many ceremonies, for instance, that of harvest[176] and of baptism.[177] It also occurs in the Tlacaxipehualiztli rites and their material remains: the offerings at Complex A dedicated to Xiuhtecuhtli and Tlaloc.

On an even larger scale, it is found in the dual structure of the Templo Mayor, a monument supposedly erected above two caves from which the *tleatl-atlatlayan* ("water of fire, place of the burning water") and the *matlalatl-tozpalatl* ("blue water–yellow water") issued (Alvarado Tezozómoc 1949: 63) or, according to another source, above a double stream of thick blue and red fluids (Durán 1984: vol. 2, 48). The structure of the Huey Teocalli was, in turn, projected onto the organization of the capital of the empire, a capital divided into two antagonistic twin cities. Torquemada (1969: vol. 1, 79–80) wrote that the origin of these disputes goes back to the time of the migration. He said that, at that time, Huitzilopochtli gave a sacred bundle to each of the two opposing factions of the Mexica. One of them contained a precious stone "that shone with the very clear signs of an Emerald," while the other contained two fire sticks. The desire to possess the precious stone resulted in fierce quarrels between the two bands. Those who were afterward called the Tlatelolca were able to keep it. Many years later, in 1337, the Tlatelolca decided to separate and to settle on a nearby island. The divided settlement reproduced the dual character of the Templo Mayor and the offerings to the God of Fire and to the God of Rain in Complex

Figure 129: Portrait of Axayacatl dressed as Xipe Totec, now at the Handschriftensammlung Österreichische National Bibliothek in Vienna.

A: Mexico-Tenochtitlan, the owners of the fire-generating sticks, remained in the south, and Mexico-Tlatelolco, owners of the greenstone symbolizing water, was established to the north. Correlatively, the Tenochca used the eagle as their symbol, while the Tlatelolca adopted the jaguar (*Codice Azcatitlan* 1949: XIV).

THE TEMPLO MAYOR AS A MODEL OF THE COSMOS

In Chapter 5, I did not deal with the meaning of the four base bodies of the Templo Mayor pyramid. I did mention that the Mesoamericans considered the structures actual microcosms and that the number of bodies built reproduced the levels of the universe they were meant to emulate. In the specific case of the Huey Teocalli, we can count four celestial levels, if we take into account only the sum of the bodies, or five, if we count the temple level. Although it is hard to reach a definite solution to the problem, I will give two tentative proposals that agree with my analysis of the offerings of Complex A.[178]

The first one derives from the possible military significance of the building. This is based on Seler's (1960b: 29) interpretation of plate 1 of the *Códice Vaticano Latino 3738*. The German researcher, using a translation of the glosses that accompanied the images on the plate, concluded that the fourth sky was inhabited by Huixtocihuatl or Chalchiuhtlicue and that the fifth was the region of fire. Seler called the union of both levels the region of atl-tlachinolli, or of war; from that he inferred that the *teoyaomiqui* ("slain warriors") and the *mocihuaquetzque* ("women goddesses") dwelt on those celestial levels. The chief problem with this hypothesis is that two other sources attribute different characteristics to the fourth and fifth levels (*Historia de los mexicanos por sus pinturas* 1965: 69; *Histoire du Mechique* 1965: 103).

The second proposal asserts that the base bodies of the pyramid allude to the four levels of the lower sky (a region in which man coexisted with plants, animals, astral bodies, clouds, rain, and wind) and that the temples referred to the fifth level (the door of access to the nine upper levels). In the opinion of López Austin (1988c: vol. 1, 53–58), the gloss *Ylhuicatl mamaluacoca*, which accompanied the fifth level, should be translated as "sky where the gyrating is." He believed that this was the place where divine influences acquired the impetus to gyrate down, an impetus usually shown as the malinalli (López Austin 1988c: vol. 1, 209–10). Regarding this celestial level and the introduction of the original tonalli (in the human being), López Austin (1988c: vol. 1, 209–10) commented:

> It was established before that the *tonalli* could be breathed into a yet unborn human being on one of the higher levels. It is possible that the irradiation may have surged forth precisely on the lowest of the nine true celestial levels, the fifth in the general count of thirteen. It is logical to suppose that on the plane separating the true heaven and the lower one, a place may have existed from which the forces of the gods from the upper levels emanated.

The illustration of the fifth sky in this codex is a rectangle in which four arrows pointing downward are inserted into four of the five circles or chalchihuites (*Códice Vaticano Latino*

3738 1964–1967: pl. 1). Like Garibay, we can conclude that we are again encountering a hierogamic image: on one hand, the arrow was the symbol of the celestial phallus that penetrated the earth; on the other hand, the chalchihuitl (literally "the [stone] that has been perforated") symbolized the earth's surface, of a feminine and aquatic nature. In the *Códice Vindobonensis* (1964–1967: pl. 16), this opposition can be seen in the trunk of the cosmic cruciform tree that emerges from the head of a decapitated man. The left half of the tree is adorned with chalchihuites and the right with descending arrows.

According to the second proposal, the level of the Huitzilopochtli and Tlaloc temples could be related to the fifth cosmic level: "sky where the gyrating is," a place where celestial fire and the aquatic torrent from the underworld mix in a helix that will later erupt over the face of the earth, creating (under the sign of cosmic war) time, change, and destiny. In brief, the Huey Teocalli would be the synthesis of the oppositions and complements of the universe.

Epilogue

T he most significant discovery of offerings in the history of Mexica archaeology came about at a moment of fleeting economic bonanza and political opportunity, through the efforts of the interdisciplinary team that made up the Templo Mayor Project. The unusual circumstances that prevailed between 1978 and 1982 made possible a painstaking exploration and a detailed recording of archaeological contexts. Thanks to those conditions, we were able to excavate 110 offerings under the same criteria and to systematize an unusual amount of information. Since then we have a comprehensive vision that offers us a new perspective on how oblation was conducted in the building with the greatest religious and political significance in Tenochtitlan—the Templo Mayor.

In the first part of the investigation, it was possible to detect the contextual regularities of 118 offerings, using visual analysis and descriptive statistics. Distinct patterns were identified that followed criteria of time (era of the offering), space (location within the building), container (type and dimensions of the receptacle), content (richness and variety of the gifts), and internal distribution (placement of the objects). By studying these, we could perceive that the various patterns of giving were tied to the different meanings and functions of the offerings.

Moreover, a study of the contexts proved that the offerings were laid out in an intentional order that obeyed a specific code of communication. To a certain degree, the contexts of the Templo Mayor are analogous to the syntax of ritual ceremonies and to that of verbal language. In this respect, we could speak of the "innate language" of the offerings, which shows similarities to the basic principles of writing, not only expressed in signs and symbols but also having grammatical (or contextual) rules. It is apparent that the social significance of any offering depended upon the intrinsic characteristics of its objects, their organization, and the spatial connections with larger analytical units. The symbols of the offerings like those in the codices, the ones painted or carved on the walls, and upon stone monuments, belong to codes whose references go far beyond the area of aesthetic emotion. These symbols include the taxonomic, structural bases of the cosmos and were produced by people who based their actions on a belief in a universal harmony and projection.

In the second part of the investigation, numerical taxonomy was used to detect more subtle patterns. Computer analysis gave us twenty complexes of offerings, with homogeneous contents, that frequently shared the same internal distribution of objects and a correlative spatial location. Moreover, it was concluded that sixteen offerings could not be assigned to groups.

Later, some complexes of offerings were compared to other products of the same cosmovision, such as mythology, pictographic portrayals, and sculptural depictions, that had the same fundamental meaning. Archaeological materials and their contexts, pre-Hispanic pictographs, the first relations written by conquerors and missionaries, texts set down in Latin script by indigenous chroniclers, and ethnographic descriptions of native people today are only part of the evidence that sheds light on the meaning of the offerings.

Perhaps one of the most relevant conclusions is that the diversity of meanings of the offerings is much greater than was formerly assumed. I believe that the burial of gifts in cult structures can no longer be seen as the product of a single purpose. The great variety in quantity, quality, and arrangement of the materials leads to the conclusion that, in the past, there were many reasons for oblation. It is evident that the offering of gifts to the supernatural was performed in very different rituals. The offerings were buried in the Templo Mayor and in neighboring temples in both regular and unusual celebrations: during the construction or enlargement of an architectural structure; at the festival for its consecration; at the dedication of a religious monument; at times of economic and social crises; at the main celebrations of the xiuhpohualli; at certain rites of social promotion; at the funeral rites of personages of high rank, and so forth.

Many questions are still unanswered. The general significance of most of the complexes found through numerical taxonomy has yet to be elucidated. There should also be deeper analyses to determine the reasons for the differences in quantity, quality, and distribution of objects belonging to offerings in the same complex.

Fortunately, we now have a database that will continue to be enriched with new discoveries (several offerings still remain unexplored) and that will make possible even more ambitious investigations. Among other things, we can predict that future discoveries will produce evidence that the communicative system of the offerings had a greater power of expression than is currently believed. It is clear that there is a long way to go before reaching a complete understanding of the code of offerings. Practically everything is yet to be done.

Relationship of Offerings to Corresponding Complexes

			Page
97.	Offering C	Complex Q (Appendix 2)	302
98.	Offering D	Complex Q (Appendix 2)	302
99.	Offering E	Complex T (Appendix 2)	311
100.	Offering F	Subcomplex J1 (Appendix 2)	282
101.	Offering G	Complex R (Appendix 2)	304
102.	Offering H	Unique offering (Appendix 3)	321
103.	Offering I	Complex S (Appendix 2)	309
104.	Offering J	Complex F (Appendix 2)	264
105.	Offering K	Complex H (Appendix 2)	274
106.	Offering L	Unique offering (Appendix 3)	325
107.	Offering M	Complex Q (Appendix 2)	302
108.	Offering N	Complex H (Appendix 2)	275
109.	Offering Ñ	Complex S (Appendix 2)	308
110.	Offering O	Complex R (Appendix 2)	304
111.	Offering P	Complex J (Appendix 2)	281
112.	Offering Q	Complex T (Appendix 2)	312
113.	Chamber 2	Complex B (Appendix 2)	244
114.	Chamber 3	Complex B (Appendix 2)	246
115.	Burial 1	Unique offering (Appendix 3)	333
116.	Offering B1 (1948)	Complex H (Appendix 2)	276
117.	Offering B2 (1948)	Complex K (Appendix 2)	289
118.	Offering CA (1966)	Complex C (Appendix 2)	251

Description of the Offerings Complexes

COMPLEX A

Offerings: 13, 17, 11, 20, 6, 1, 23, 60, 7, 61, and 88.

Number of offerings in complex: 11.

Dendrogram

Split: 37 unshared presences/absences, coefficient of similarity = 0.21.

Subgroups: 11–20 (9 *upas* [total number of unshared presences/absences]), 7–61 (10 upas), 11–20–6 (16 upas), 7–61–88 (18 upas), 13–17 (20 upas), 23–60 (21 upas), 23–60–7–61–88 (27 upas), 13–17–11–20–6 (28 upas), 13–17–11–20–6–1 (30 upas).

Relationships: It is related to the 19 remaining complexes and with their 16 unique offerings by 47 upas (0.00 coefficient of similarity).

Comments: Complex A is the last one to be formed. However, the offerings that constitute it are quite similar to each other. It can be divided into two subcomplexes: 13–17–11–20–6–1 and 23–60–7–61–88.

Frequency of presences by object type complex

Percentage of the total possible presences in each of the object type complexes: A (97.96%), B (90.90%), C (81.81%), D (31.81%), E (9.09%), F (50%), G (15.15%), H (34.09%), I (9.87%), J (95.45%), K (86.3%), L (77.27%), M (64.03%).

Most common object type complexes

Complexes A, J, B, and K.

Quantity and diversity of objects

Average number of elements: 165.5.

Range of the number of elements: 49–249.

Average number of object types: 36.

Range of the number of object types: 28–40.

Time and space locations of the offerings

Building: Templo Mayor (all),[1] Huitzilopochtli (6, 1, 60, 7), Tlaloc (23, 61, 88), Huitzilopochtli-Tlaloc (13, 17, 11, 20).

Building stage: IVb (all).

Approximate date: 1469–1481.

Vertical location: floor (17, 60, 7, 61, 88), platform (13, 11, 20, 6, 1, 23).

Horizontal location: Principal axis: N center (61), S center (7), E (17, 20, 88), W (13, 11, 6, 1, 23), SE (60).

General characteristics of the offerings

Container: sillares box (13, 17, 1, 23, 60, 7, 61, 88), fill below floor (11, 20, 6).

Primary orientation of objects: N (61), S (60, 7), E (88), W (13, 17, 11, 20, 6, 1, 23).

Number of excavation levels: 1 (60), 2 (17), 3 (20, 7), 4 (11, 6, 1, 23), 6 (61), 7 (88, 13).

Number of proposed levels: 5 (17, 11, 20, 6, 60), 6 (13, 23, 7, 61, 88).

Maximum internal dimensions of the offerings (cm)

Offering	N-S axis	E-W axis	Z axis[2]
13	130	150	40
17	95	170	55
11	125	90	
20	155	125	
6	65	65	
1	102	94	102
23	93	143	105
60	165	125	?
7	150	110	95
61	147	85	80
88	120	180	80

Distribution of objects (levels, axes, and groupings)

The 11 offerings of Complex A are all located on the principal axes of Stage IVb. Of these, 8 offerings were deposited in boxes with sides of tezontle sillares (hewn stone slabs) and flagstone floors; 6 of these were also covered with flagstones. The 3 remaining offerings were placed in building fill, under the stucco floor corresponding to the platform of the building.

Offerings 7 and 61 were the simplest in regard to the object types contained. Offerings 6, 11, and 20 were the richest and most varied. In contrast to the others, they were placed in the building fill and had greenstone anthropomorphic sculptures. The 6 vertical levels can be detected in the vertical placement of the objects.

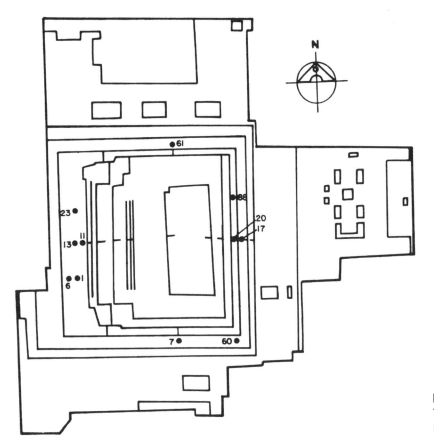

Figure 130:
The location of offerings
in Complex A

Level 1: In all the offerings of this complex, except 60, the deepest level was composed of very fine gray sand; offering 7 also had fine black sand. The sand formed a homogeneous layer with a maximum depth of 4 cm. Occasionally, the sand contained marine material (fine gravel, fish remains, fish, shells, conch shells, and sea urchins).

Level 2: This level was made up of a layer of small conch shells (*Strombus* sp.) and conch shells. The layer was homogeneous in offerings 88, 61, 7, 23, 1, 20, and 11, although greater quantities of material could be seen. On the other hand, in offerings 13, 17, 6, and 60, this level was scanty and did not form a continuous layer. The second level also contained greenstone beads, copper bells, and sea urchins. Anthropomorphic copal figures were also found in offerings 6 and 20. Sand dollars and crab claws were found in offering 1.

Level 3: The third level was characterized by marine remains of larger size than those of the second level: *Strombus* and *Xancus* conch shells, brain, lace, and deer antler corals. Offerings 17, 23, 11, 88, 61, and 7 had very fragmented lace coral distributed along their longitudinal axes. Offerings 17, 23, 88, and 7 also had deer antler coral placed, respectively, in 1, 2, 3, and 4 corners of the deposit. Offerings 17, 88, and 7 included, respectively, 6, 4, and 3 brain corals. Offerings 88, 61, 7, and 23 had

2 *Strombus* conch shells, each placed longitudinally at opposite ends of the box (except offering 61) and following the primary orientation of the deposit (except offering 23). Offerings 88, 61, 7, 23, 6, 17, and 20 contained, respectively, 9, 10, 12, 8, 5, 5, and 4 *Xancus* conch shells with the same orientation as the offering (except offering 23).

Level 4: This level was filled by parts of the skins of various animals (alligators, fish, felines), by turtle shells, and by nose cartilages of sawfish (*Pristis pectinatus*). All these "skins" probably formed a uniform layer that physically and visually separated levels 3 and 5. The alligator (cranium and dorsal scales) is the most prominent animal at this level. Its remains were always located longitudinally inside the deposit. The cranium was aligned in the same direction as the deity sculptures of the fifth level but was placed at the other end. Remains of 1 alligator were found in offerings 17 (mandible), 60 (skin scales and phalanges), and 61 (teeth, skin scales, and phalanges). The remains of 2 specimens (2 crania and skin scales) were found in offerings 23, 88, and 7 (this one also contained phalanges).

Sawfish nose cartilages were placed longitudinally, with the point aiming toward the deities of the fifth level. Offerings 60, 7, and 11 had 1 cartilage, and offerings 17, 20, 88, and 6 had 2.

Turtle shells were abundant in the offerings of Complex A. No skeletons of these animals were found, nor were any percussion instruments that would indicate a musical function for the carapaces. The turtle shells were placed randomly up or down in the offerings: 7 (40 mud turtles, *Kinosternon* sp., and 33 pond sliders, *Chrysemis scripta*), 61 (7 mud turtles and 15 pond sliders), 88 (1 mud turtle), 23 (13 mud turtles and 14 pond sliders), 6 (7 pond sliders), 20 (remains of 1 mud turtle and 8 pond sliders), 11 (1 mud turtle and 10 pond sliders), and 17 (2 mud turtles and 3 pond sliders).

Fish remains were also numerous. Scales predominated, which showed that the whole animal was not buried. They were found in the following offerings: 1 (remains of a smooth hound shark, *Mustelus* sp., 23 fish from the Atherinidae family, 2 from the Balistidae family, 4 from the Chaetodontidae, 1 from Dasyatidae, an unknown number from the Goodeidae family, 3 from the Labridae, 1 from the Serranidae, 3 from the Scaridae, 1 from the Scombridae, 6 from the Scorpaenidae, and 7 from the suborder Synentognathi); 6 (31 red snapper, 26 spotfin hogfish, *Bodianus* sp., 2 grunts, *Haemulon* sp., 2 ballyhoo, *Hemirhamphus* sp., 2 grouper, *Hemanthias* sp., 1 croaker, *Micropogon undulatus*, 1 toad fish, *Batrachoides* sp.); 7 (2 ballyhoo, 1 toad fish, 1 croaker, and remains of needle fish, *Tylosurus acus*, red snapper, spotfin hogfish, grunt, and yellow fin mojarra, *Gerres cinereus*); 13 (35 ballyhoo, 5 needlefish, 1 scorpion fish, Scorpaenidae fam., and remains from the Elasmobranchs fam.); 17 (17 needlefish, 5 ballyhoo, 1 shark, and remains from the Teleost class); 20 (dental plate of a stingray); 23 (1 toad fish and remains of spotfin hogfish, lemon shark, *Negapion brevirostris*, cutlass fish, *Trichiurus lepturus*, barracuda, trigger fish, *Balistes carolinensis*, fugu fish, *Sphoeroides* sp., and porcupine fish); 60 (10 porcupine fish, *Diodon hystrix*, 4 shark, 2 needlefish, 1 yellow fin mojarra, 1 ballyhoo, 1 trunk fish, *Lactophrys* sp., 1 striped searobin, *Prionotus cf. evolans*, and remains of tiger shark, *Galeocerdo cuvieri*, parrot fish, *Sparisoma* sp. and puffer fish, *Lagocephalus laevigatus*); 61 (9 needlefish, 7 red snapper, 1 from the Elasmobranchs family, and remains of sea urchin, amber jack, *Caranx hippos*, trumpet fish, *Fistularia* sp., shark, yellow fin mojarra, spotfin hogfish, trigger fish, and parrot fish); and 88 (1 sea urchin, 1 striped searobin, 1 shark, 1 yellow fin mojarra, and 1 ballyhoo).

Other animal remains were less abundant. Apparently, with the passage of time, some skeletal remains from the fifth level collapsed onto the fourth level. In offering 1 were found the skeleton of a coyote (?) oriented toward the west with a sacrificial knife in its jaws, 1 complete golden eagle, 26 complete falcons, the bones of 2 turkeys, and 1 bird feather. From offering 6 came a complete golden eagle skeleton, claws of 1 feline, bones of an Old World mouse (intrusion), and 2 birds (*Corvidae* and *Tyrannidae* sp.). Offering 7 had 1 boa maxilla, 5 serpent teeth, 15 rattlesnake, and 2 fer-de-lance (*Bothrops* sp.) mandibles, as well as 2 instruments made from pelican bones. Offering 11 had feline claws, several bird bones (*Tyrannidae* sp.), and the metatarsal of a sheep (intrusion). Offering 13 contained snake bones, 1 instrument made from the bone of a golden eagle, and remains of the crania and vertebrae of 17 rattlesnakes (skins located in the eastern half). Offering 17 had bone remains (mostly crania) of 8 rattlesnakes, 4 snake mandibles, bones of 1 golden eagle, and the humerus of a toucan. Offering 20 contained the mandible of a Mexican meadow mouse (*Microtus mexicanus*), the tarsus of a falcon (*Falco* sp.), and the tarsus of a flycatcher. Offering 23 held 4 toad skeletons, the cranium of a boa, remains of 1 snake and 5 rattlesnakes, the cranium and claws of 1 mountain lion (the skin covered the remains of an alligator), the skeleton of a white heron (on top of the mountain lion), and the remains of a rabbit. Offering 60 had the cranial remains of a rabbit, the radius of a mountain lion, the calcaneum of a bobcat (*Lynx rufus*), and the vertebral columns of 3 serpents. Offering 61 had the mandibles and other bones of 18 rattlesnakes.

Other objects that showed up on this level were a wooden feline claw (offering 13) and wild grass remains (offering 61).

Level 5: Undoubtedly, the fifth level was the richest of the complex. Basically, it contained images of gods and of sacred paraphernalia and piercing-cutting instruments.

The divine images were situated at the head of or in the center of each offering, as if presiding. The Xiuhtecuhtli sculptures (images with two protuberances on the head)[3] and the water jars with the face of Tlaloc were always together and oriented in the same direction as the offering.

Offerings 13, 11, 20, 23, 60, 7, 61, and 88 had 1 image of each god; offerings 1, 17, and 6 had 2 Tlaloc water jars and 2 Xiuhtecuhtli sculptures. Usually, 1 image was beside the other. However, in offerings 88 and 20, the Xiuhtecuhtli sculpture is back to back with the Tlaloc jar. There seemed to be no fixed rule for the relative positioning of the images. In offerings 88, 61, 7, and 1, Xiuhtecuhtli was to the east of Tlaloc; in offerings 60 and 20, Tlaloc was to the east of Xiuhtecuhtli; in offerings 6, 13, and 11, Xiuhtecuhtli was to the north of Tlaloc; and in offerings 23 and 17, Tlaloc was to the north of Xiuhtecuhtli. Offering 6 had an additional image of a pulque god.[4]

The anthropomorphic sculptures were placed in the center, parallel to the longitudinal axis of the offering. We found them in offerings 6 (6 complete figures and 7 greenstone masks), 88 (2 copal figures), 11 (5 full-body figures, 6 masks, and 6 penates in greenstone), and 20 (7 complete figures, 8 masks, 6 penates of greenstone, and 2 copal figures).

Personified knives numbering respectively 8, 10, 4, 4, 4, (?), 1, and 1 came from offerings 13, 17, 11, 20, 6, 1, 23, and 60. In almost every case, they were placed in the center, perpendicular to the longitudinal axis of the offering, with the eye and mouth pointing in the opposite direction from the images of Tlaloc and Xiuhtecuhtli.

Ceramic jars with the image of a fertility deity also belonged to this level. They all had copal inside. One jar was found in offering 11, and 2 were found in offerings 23, 88, 61, and 7. In the latter, the jars were found in the center of the deposit, 1 at each end of the transversal axis with the same orientation as the images of the gods. Skull-masks with shell and pyrite inserts in the eye sockets were found in the offerings: 13 (2 skull-masks), 17 (2), 11 (3), 20 (3), 6 (2), and 1 (1 with holes drilled into the temples). Some skull-masks had a flint sacrificial knife in their mouths. In general, they were placed in the middle of the offering; they faced either in the same or opposite direction as the deity.

This level was also characterized by the abundance of representations of sacred paraphernalia. A serpent scepter and a deerhead scepter were found in offerings 17, 1, and 11, and offering 20 had 2 serpent scepters and 1 deerhead scepter. These scepters were located in the middle of the offering and oriented in the same direction as the deity images. The chicahuaztli and the split-end noseplug (?), which are characteristic of Xipe Totec, were placed and oriented in the same way as the scepters. Offerings 17, 13, 1, 11, 20, 23, 7, and 61 had 1 chicahuaztli, and offering 88 had 2. Offerings 17, 13, 11, and 20 contained 1 noseplug, and offering 13 had 3.

Ceramic spirals and ollin representations were closely associated and in the center of the offering. The ollin always rested against the spiral. A single ollin was found in offerings 7, 61, and 23, and 2 were in offering 88. One spiral was found in offerings 61, 88, and 23, and offering 7 had 2.

Miniature braziers were generally found in the center of the offerings in Complex A or very close to the image of Xiuhtecuhtli. Offerings 17, 11, and 1 also had stone brazier sculptures decorated with a bow knot. Ceramic braziers with canes were found in offerings 17, 11, 6, 1, 7, 61, and 88.

The offerings of Complex A had numerous decapitated skulls. In fact, sacrificial skulls were buried in those offerings situated on the principal axes of the front and back facades corresponding to stage IVb—that is, in offerings 6 (3 decapitated skulls), 11 (5), 13 (6), 17 (5), 20 (9), 23 (2), 60 (5), 88 (1), and 1 (5). As a rule, they were placed in the center or at the head of the offering, and if there were more than 5 heads, they were placed close to each other in no specific order.

Piercing-cutting instruments were placed exactly in the center of the offering and oriented in the same direction as the Tlaloc and Xiuhtecuhtli images. Flint sacrificial knives were deposited in offerings 61 (1 knife), 60 (9), 11 (1), 13 (1), 17 (1), 6 (5), 23 (3), 1 (17), and 7 (1). Sixteen greenstone blanks were found in offering 1. Obsidian projectile points were grouped in clusters of 2, 3, 4, 5, and 6 and were found as follows in the offerings: 88 (19 points), 61 (11), 7 (17), 17 (13), 13 (13), 23 (26), 20 (38), 11 (32), and 6 (?). One prismatic obsidian blade was found in offerings 61, 13, 20, and 88. Bone bloodletters were also usually found, invariably located in the center of the offering and laid out in a circle. These artifacts were found in offerings 17 (18 awls), 13 (5), 7 (7), 60 (14), 88 (4), 61 (3), 23 (4), and 1 (21).

Sacrificed quail were in nearly all the offerings—that is: 6 (1 montezuma quail, *Cyrtonix montezumae*); 7 (4 scaled quail, *Caliplepla squamata*); 11 (1 montezuma quail); 13 (6 common bobwhite, *Colinus virginianus*, 3 scaled quail, and remains of a montezuma quail); 17 (12 scaled quails, 1 bobwhite, and 1 montezuma quail); 23 (92 scaled quails, 2 common bobwhite, and 1 montezuma quail); 60 (18 montezuma quail); 61 (4 montezuma quail); and 88 (1 montezuma quail).

A ball of copal was placed directly in front of the images of Xiuhtecuhtli and Tlaloc. This was found in offerings 6, 1, 88, 61, 7 (2 balls), 60, 17, and 13. Behind these images or in the center of the deposit were found oyohualli and perforated shell disks. Oyohualli were found in offerings 23 (2 oyohualli), 20 (2), 88 (1), 61 (1), 7 (1), 60 (2), 13 (1), and 11 (1); perforated shell disks were found in 23 (4 disks), 6 (2), 20 (5), 61 (3), 7 (2), 60 (7), 17 (4), 13 (7), and 11 (2).

Greenstone beads were irregularly distributed in level 5 of offerings 13 (3 beads), 17 (?), 88 (7), 61 (5), 60 (4), 11, 20, 23 (9), 6, and 1.

Obsidian earplugs were found in offerings 13 (1 earplug), 17 (4), 60 (5), 20 (2), 11 (2), 1 (7), and 6 (2). They were accompanied by obsidian scepters with a globular end in offerings 17 (2 scepters), 20 (3), and 11 (1).

Coral was placed beside the deity images in offerings 23, 88 (on both sides), 7 (on the right side), and 61 (on the left side).

Several white stone miniature atlatl were found in offerings: 13 (8 atlatl), 11 (3), 20, and 6. All the offerings contained traces of wood.

Other less common objects found in 1 or 2 of the offerings of the complex were: shell ear- and noseplugs; curved obsidian knives, obsidian snakes, and snake heads; copper bells; greenstone scrapers and miniature mallets; and ceramic models of cradles and receptacles.

Level 6: Ceramic incense burners were placed on the flagstones covering some offerings in Complex A. All were in fragments. A single incense burner was found in offerings 23, 88, 7, and 61, and the remains of at least 6 were found in offering 13.

COMPLEX B

Offerings: Chamber 2 (C2) and Chamber 3 (C3).
Number of offerings in complex: 2.
Dendrogram

Split: 30 unshared presences/absences, coefficient of similarity = 0.36.

Subgroups: none.

Relationships: It is tied to Complexes C, D, E, F, G, H, I, J, K, L, M, N, O, P, Q, R, S, and T, with Burial 1 and with the offerings 41, 78, 54, H, 64, L, 85, 45, 82, 16, 38, 71, 76, 30, and 9 by 38 upas (0.19 coefficient of similarity).

Frequency of presences by object type complex

Percentage of the total possible presences in each of the object type complexes: A (100%), B (100%), C (50%), D (0%), E (75%), F (100%), G (0%), H (75%), I (17.24%), J (0%), K (100%), L (75%), M (19.56%).

Most common object type complexes

Complexes A, B, F, K, E, H, and L.

Quantity and diversity of objects

Average number of elements: 309.

Range of the number of elements: 254–364.

Average number of object types: 32.

Range of the number of object types: 29–35.

Time and space locations of the offerings
  Building: Tlaloc (both).
  Building stage: IVa (C3), IVb (C2).
  Approximate date: 1469–1481.
  Vertical location: platform (both).
  Horizontal location: W (C2), NW (C3).
General characteristics of the offerings
  Container: sillares box (both).
  Primary orientation of objects: W (both).
  Number of excavation levels: 8 (C3), 11 (C2).
  Number of proposed levels: 2 (C3), 3 (C2).

Maximum internal dimensions of the offerings (cm)

Offering	N-S axis	E-W axis	Z axis
Chamber 2	108	130	86
Antechamber 2	68	164	86
Chamber 3	112	109	135

Distribution of objects (levels, axes, and groupings)
Chambers 2 and 3 will be described separately because they are very different in regard to the quantity and the distribution of the objects placed in them.

Chamber 2

Chamber 2 is spatially symmetrical to offering 5. The top and floor of the box were made with flagstones, and the sides were made with quarry stone sillares covered with plaster on the inside. To the west of the box in Chamber 2, an antechamber or entrance passage was found. The antechamber was filled with tezontle pieces, earth, and a few mica fragments. The construction of this antechamber is logical if we take into account the fact that the stairway of the building was built directly over the chamber. During the consecration ceremony, the only way to deposit the offering in the chamber was through the antechamber on the west side. As soon as the offering was deposited, the antechamber was filled in again, replacing the floor of the platform.

Chamber 2 is characterized by its complexity and enormous abundance. In spite of the fact that, during the archaeological work, the deposit was divided into 11 excavation levels, the materials were actually distributed in only 3. Sculptures and anthropomorphic masks of greenstone and marine material predominated.

Level 1: The first level of the offering was marked by the abundance of objects related to the aquatic world of Mexica cosmovision. Greenstone pieces and marine material are dominant. Apparently, the donors did not attempt to place all the objects in an orderly manner but just tried to create a uniform layer. This level had 298 complete shells and 757 fragments; 39 shell plaques and 10 fragments; 13 shell circles; 3,997 conch shells and 22 fragments; 12 fragments of chiton plaques; 39 sawfish

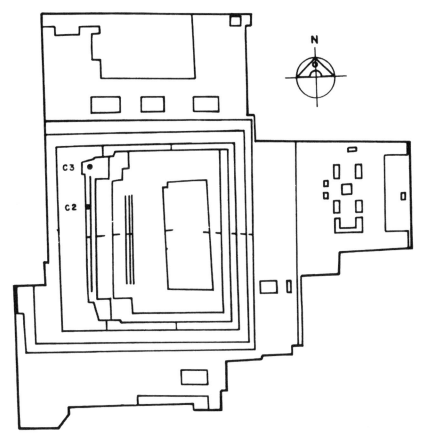

Figure 131:
The location of offerings
in Complex B

nose teeth; 2 bones and 2 teeth of unidentified animals; 32 round pebbles; 42 fragments of unworked greenstone; 716 fragments of carved greenstone; 2,178 complete greenstone beads and 192 fragments; 1 breastplate and 4 fragments; 8 pendants; 25 earplugs and 326 fragments; 7 anthropomorphic copal figures; 1 small greenstone vessel; 1 ceramic tripod vessel; 5 Xipe Totec noseplugs (?) with split ends; and 1 zoomorphic sculpture.

Level 2: At this level were found greenstone anthropomorphic sculptures from the Mezcala region (98 complete figures and 56 masks), 57 large conch shells, 1 Mixtec-type penate, 18 small conch shells, 38 shells, 224 chiton plaques, numerous coral fragments, 60 greenstone beads, 1 group of images of aquatic animals (composed of shell plaques, and greenstone beads), 1 earplug, 1 box with cover, 1 necklace of gold beads and remains of charcoal and copal. Most of the greenstone sculptures were decorated with red, blue, ocher, white, and black paint; often, the decoration portrayed the facial traits of Tlaloc (headdress, rings around the eyes, and noseplug). Some sculptures had a glyph drawn on their back side and painted black or, in some cases, ocher or red and ocher (Ahuja 1982b).

As a rule, the objects at the second level were distributed in an orderly fashion and formed 3 great strips. The eastern strip was characterized by complete anthropomorphic figures. These figures were placed in an upright position, leaning against each other, in several rows. All of the sculptures are oriented toward the west. Along the eastern wall were also found some shells and conch shells. The central strip was composed of anthropomorphic masks resting against each other and oriented to the west. At the exact center of this strip was placed a necklace made of gold beads, as well as a compound of zoomorphic figures (frogs, turtles, fish, serpents) made of shell and greenstone. On the western strip, shells, conch shells, and corals predominated.

Level 3: The third level consists of pieces that stand out because of their larger size, although they were placed on the same layer as those of the second level. These materials formed an axis in an E-W direction and were oriented toward the west. A puma's skeleton covered the eastern half of the deposit. The skeleton still retained traces of red pigment and had a greenstone bead in its mouth. In the center of the imaginary axis and of the offering were found 2 sculptures presiding over the deposit and upon which the puma's head probably lay. The sculpture farthest to the east was a masculine, anthropomorphic image with 2 protuberances on its head shaped like turtle shells. It is similar to the sculptures I have identified as Xiuhtecuhtli, although it also has certain features that perhaps make it a representation of the God of Fire in the underworld.[5] A little farther to the west is a greenstone, seated image of Tlaloc. Finally, to the extreme west of the box, there is a ceramic water jar with sides decorated with charcoal. On one side, it has an anthropomorphic relief of a complete figure representing Chalchiuhtlicue. The water jar was intentionally placed as if it were pouring liquid, its mouth oriented toward the west. Inside were found 1 bivalve, 1 anthropomorphic head, 1 flat greenstone head, and charcoal remains.

It should also be mentioned that the remains of 2 montezuma quail were found in the stone and earth filling that covered the deposit.

Chamber 3

This is a real chamber, or room, with walls of quarry stone sillares and with a floor and roof made of huge flagstones. The inside of Chamber 3 was covered with a thick coat of plaster, and its walls were adorned with paintings barely perceptible today. On the south wall, there are still traces of a design of 2 thigh bones painted black.

In pre-Hispanic times, one entered the chamber through a circular opening at the northwest corner of the floor of offering 48. The access was covered with a tezontle disk 61 cm in diameter and 8 cm thick. Just below the circular opening, there is a stone imbedded in the western wall and protruding 15 cm, which served as a step. The presence of this step and the removable discoidal cover leads to the conclusion that this chamber was entered more than once for the purpose of depositing gifts. In contrast to the other offerings, which were definitely sealed off after the placement of gifts, it is probable that Chamber 3 was used as a receptacle for gifts at various ritual ceremonies. We can detect 5 different vertical placement levels. Objects made of greenstone and images of the gods Xiuhtecuhtli and Tlaloc predominated in this chamber.

Level 1: The deepest level is characterized by marine fauna and stone artifacts. All the objects formed a homogeneous layer and lacked a clearly perceived order and orientation. The marine material is found in the western half of the deposit (especially in the southwest corner). There were 948 conch shells, 266 shells, the remains of branch and lace coral, sea urchins, the bones of 1 parrot fish (*Sparisoma* sp.), and 2 sand dollars. We also recovered 26 olive shells (*Oliva* sp.), which formed part of a necklace and were placed in the center of the offering.

The stone objects did not show any apparent order either. Scattered in an irregular way throughout the level were 201 beads (most of them in the southeast corner), 8 zoomorphic sculptures (2 representations of conch shells), 1 plant sculpture, and 21 irregular greenstone fragments. One travertine flagstone was placed to the east of the offering. The upper side had a bas-relief depicting the god Tlaltecuhtli.

The other objects taken from this level were: 19 copper bells and 1 bone bloodletter.

Level 2: The second level was composed chiefly of sculptures of divinities, musical instruments, ceramic containers, masks, and anthropomorphic figures.

Most of the divine images were concentrated on the eastern side of the chamber and oriented to the west. Among the divine images, several stood out. There was 1 travertine seated sculpture with a yacametztli, which was placed in the center of the box. To the west of the deposit were found 1 basalt Xiuhtecuhtli and 1 Tlaloc ceramic water jar (on its side and with its mouth toward the west) at the southwest corner. Between the two images, 2 cajetes had been deposited, containing earth and copal and covered with 2 other inverted cajetes. To the north of the basalt sculpture of Xiuhtecuhtli was placed 1 flint, turquoise, and pyrite mosaic image of Xiuhcoatl oriented E-W. Next to the eastern side was the skeleton of 1 puma placed in a face-downward, crouching position. It had a flint sacrificial knife in its mouth and another knife near its tail. The animal was placed in an E-W direction, with its head toward the east and its tail to the west. Over the skeleton were found remnants of textiles in a very poor state of preservation. Slightly to the north of the skeleton there was a necklace of shell plaques. Two large water jars, each 60 cm in height, were placed in the northeast and southwest corners of the chamber, flanking the puma skeleton. Both jars were polychrome with portrayals of Chicomecoatl on the western side and Tlaloc on the eastern side. The necks of the jars were covered with a Mezcala-style anthropomorphic mask made of greenstone. The northeast jar also had a ceramic cover. The objects they had inside are described later. Five standing copal figures, oriented to the west, flanked the jars: 3 on the southeast and 2 on the northwest.

The musical instruments, the anthropomorphic sculptures, marine materials, and other objects were concentrated in the western half of the chamber and oriented toward the west. The musical instruments were distributed along the length of the west wall: 10 flutes and 1 ceramic flute fragment at the center of the wall, oriented E-W; 7 basalt representations of teponaztli surrounded the flutes (3 to the northwest, 2 in the center, and 2 to the southwest), oriented in a N-S direction; and 4 basalt chicahuaztli along the western wall and oriented to the south.

Most of the anthropomorphic sculptures (5 heads, 65 masks, and 36 complete figures) were in the Mezcala style. Some sculptures were polychrome and had glyphs in the back side (Olmedo and González 1986). All were placed on the western half of the chamber, generally oriented to the west.

Identified among the marine materials were: 18 mother-of-pearl shells (2 with a greenstone bead inside and 2 with an incised spiral) distributed on the western half; 1 *Spondylus* shell to the west; and 5 *Xancus* conch shells (4 in the northwest corner and 1 in the center) with the apex toward the east. Also found on the western side were 8 greenstone pendants, 1 fragment of a Teotihuacan-style greenstone bowl, and remains of copal, wood, and textiles.

NE Jar: The northeastern polychrome jar is from Texcoco. It had 5 internal placement levels. Greenstone sculptures and their fragments predominate.

Level 1: 28 beads, 6 anthropomorphic figures, 1 small head, 1 miniature metate, 2 earplugs, 2 fragments of earplugs, 1 miniature vessel, 1 carved plaque, 2 circular stones, 9 pendants and pieces of greenstone, 1 perforated shark's tooth, and 3 small conch shells.

Level 2: 143 beads, 21 anthropomorphic figures (oriented to the west), 8 fragments of anthropomorphic figures, 3 masks (oriented to the west), 2 fragments of a mask, 1 small head, 6 earplugs, 22 plaques, 5 round stones, 1 cylinder, 3 disks, 14 pendants and pieces of greenstone, 5 small conch shells, and 2 shells.

Level 3: 13 beads, 1 earplug, 1 plaque, 3 cylinders, 5 semispherical stones and pieces of greenstone, and 1 conch shell.

Level 4: 43 beads, 21 fragments of beads, 3 anthropomorphic figures, 11 earplugs, 21 earplug fragments, 1 pendant, 4 trapezoidal stones, 2 plaques and fragments of greenstone, and 3 small conch shells.

Level 5: 232 beads, 1 small head, 1 mask, 1 earplug, 4 plaques, 1 sphere, 3 disks and 5 pendants, and 2 small conch shells.

SE Jar: The southeast Texcocan polychrome jar contained approximately 3,000 greenstone beads.

COMPLEX C

Offerings: 22, 58, 24, 15, 62, 70, and CA.
Number of offerings in complex: 7.
Dendrogram
Split: 28 unshared presences/absences, coefficient of similarity = 0.40.
Subgroups: 22–28 (11 upas), 15–62 (12 upas), 22–58–24 (17 upas), 70–CA (17 upas), 15–62–70–CA (22 upas).
Relationships: It is tied to all the complexes, with the exception of the Complexes A and B and offerings 41, 78, 54, and H by 33 upas (0.30 coefficient of similarity).
Frequency of presences by object type complex
Percentage of the total possible presences in each of the object type complexes: A (90.47%), B (71.42%), C (71.42%), D (42.85%), E (21.42%), F (28.57%), G (9.52%), H (21.42%), I (3.44%), J (35.71%), K (67.85%), L (64.28%), M (33.11%).

Most common object type complexes
Complexes A, B, C, K, and L.
Quantity and diversity of objects
Average number of elements: 76.42.
Range of the number of elements: 44–126.
Average number of object types: 22.42.
Range of the number of object types: 19–25.
Time and space locations of the offerings
Building: Templo Mayor (all): Huitzilopochtli (15, 62, 70, CA), Tlaloc (22, 58, 24).
Building stage: IVb (22, 58, 24, 15, 62, CA), VI (70).
Approximate date: 1469–1481 and 1486–1502.
Vertical location: floor (15, 62, 70), platform (22, 58, 24, CA).
Horizontal location: S center (62, 70), E (15), W (24), NE (22), NW (58), SW (CA).
Comments: Offering 70 is the only one that does not fit in context.
General characteristics of the offerings
Container: sillares box (70), fill below floor (22, 58, 24, 15, 62, CA).
Primary orientation of objects: N (22), S (58, 62, CA), E (15), W (24, 70).
Number of excavation levels: 2 (62), 3 (58, 15, CA), 4 (22, 24), 7 (70).
Number of proposed levels: 3 (15, CA), 4 (62, 70), 5 (22, 58), 6 (24).

Maximum internal dimensions of the offerings (cm)

Offering	N-S axis	E-W axis	Z axis
22	90	110	
58	100	80	
24	80	110	
15	100	90	
62	100	350	
70	38	65	25
CA	100	100	

Distribution of objects (levels, axes, and groupings)
Although this complex was homogeneous in regard to its location in space and the quality of its contents, it varied a great deal in the placement of objects. Because of their diversity in quantity and in object placements, offerings 24, 70, and CA will be described individually. In contrast, there was great similarity in the location of objects in offerings 22 and 58 (Subcomplex C_1), as well as in offerings 15 and 62 (Subcomplex C_2): thus they will be discussed in pairs.

Offering 24

This offering was found under the stucco floor of Stage IVb. It was deposited on a layer of loose earth and covered with several flagstones. It had 6 vertical levels and a very complex stratigraphy in comparison to that of the other offerings in the complex.

Level 1: The deepest level contained small marine objects and greenstone beads, placed in an orderly way. We found conch shells, shells, sea urchins, 1 shell pendant, and several greenstone beads.

Level 2: The second level also had marine material, although larger in size. In the center of the deposit were 2 *Xancus* conch shells, 8 mother-of-pearl shells, fragments of branch coral, remains of wood, and 4 turtle shells (pond sliders). Eight greenstone beads were found inside 1 of the mother-of-pearl shells. At the eastern end, located from north to south with orientation to the south, were found: 1 deerhead scepter, 1 chicahuaztli, 2 serpent scepters, and 1 Xipe Totec noseplug (?) with cloven ends.

Level 3: The third level had 2 nose cartilages of sawfish. They were placed one above the other and oriented from east to west. Several greenstone beads were associated with them.

Level 4: The skeleton of 1 puma was placed directly above the 2 nose cartilages. It was crouching, face down, with the cranium toward the west and the tail toward the east.

Level 5: In the center, just above the puma's skeleton on the fourth level, there was another sawfish nose cartilage, oriented E-W. In the northeast corner of the deposit was a skull-mask of an infant. Twelve copper bells, which probably formed a necklace, were found with its jawbone. In the northwest corner, there was the skull of an adult with 1 sacrificial knife in its mouth and 1 knife next to the mandible. The skull was oriented to the west. At the south end of the offering, we found 1 necklace of shell plaques, the bone remains of a white heron, 1 greenstone earplug, and 2 flint sacrificial knives (both oriented to the west).

Level 6: On the last level, we discovered 1 basalt sculpture of Xiuhtecuhtli and 1 ceramic Tlaloc water jar. They flanked the nose cartilage to the east and west, respectively. Both images faced the west.

Offering 70

Offering 70 was quite different from the other offerings of Complex C in its spatial location and in the quantity and placement of its objects. It was deposited in a box with sides of tezontle sillares and a flagstone cover. Four distinct levels were detected.

Level 1: There were small conch shells and sea urchins all over the surface of the first level. To the extreme west, we found 4 bone bloodletters, the points aimed to the west, and 1 shell pendant.

Level 2: The second level had a uniform layer consisting of 20 sacrificial knives and 3 personified knives. All were oriented to the west and associated with small shells, conch shells, lace coral, and copper bells. In the center of the offering were 7 perforated shell disks, and at the southern end were 7 obsidian projectile points.

Level 3: To the west of the box and on top of the sacrificial knives lay several images of gods turned toward the west. There was 1 sculpture of Xiuhtecuhtli and 1 of Tlaloc, both of tezontle, as well as

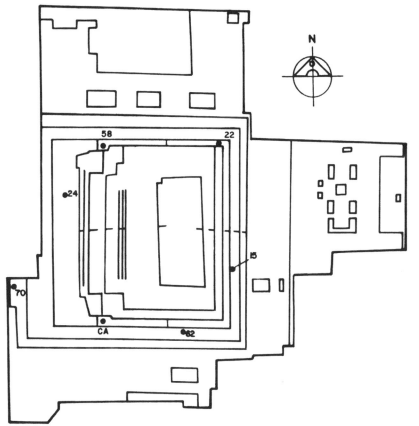

Figure 132:
The location of offerings
in Complex C

3 anthropomorphic copal figures. Other associated objects were 1 perforated shell disk and several copper bells.

Level 4: Over the divine images was another level of knives and the remains of bones. A total of 13 sacrificial knives were oriented to the west, and 1 personified knife was placed in a N-S direction. One complete skeleton of a golden eagle and the remains of another (skull, claws, and wing bones) were associated with the knives and turned toward the west. No clear anatomical relationship was seen, although it is possible the wings were spread out because the remains were found at the ends of the box. Next to the bone remains were 9 olive shells, 4 West Indian Top shells, small conch shells, corals, copper bells, 12 obsidian projectile points, 1 greenstone earplug, and the effigy of 1 travertine atlatl. All the material at this level was mixed up because it had been disturbed by a deep telephone line.

Offering CA

In general, the placement of objects of offering CA is similar to that of Complex A and offering 24. There are no sketches of the different levels, making its description difficult. The following

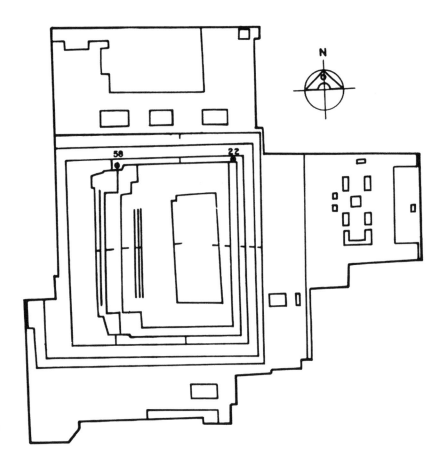

Figure 133:
The location of offerings
in Subcomplex C_1

things were observed in the photographs taken. At the deepest level, there were small shells, mother-of-pearl shells, conch shells, and copper bells lying on a gravel layer. Slightly above lay a sawfish nose cartilage, which was oriented to the N-S. Finally, on the upper level, there was 1 basalt sculpture of Xiuhtecuhtli and 1 ceramic Tlaloc water jar, presiding over the offering. These were placed at the northern end and oriented to the south. Numerous objects were placed in front of them, almost always turned in a N-S direction: masks and Mezcala-style anthropomorphic figures, earplugs, Mixtec greenstone penates; 3 human skulls of decapitated individuals (with their first vertical vertebrae); 2 skull-masks, 1 personified knife (in a transversal position), and 1 tezontle sculpture of Tlaloc.

SUBCOMPLEX C_1

Offerings: 22 and 58.
Number of offerings in complex: 2.
Dendrogram
   Split: 11 unshared presences/absences, coefficient of similarity = 0.77.
   Relationships: It is tied to offering 24 by 17 upas (0.64 coefficient of similarity).

Frequency of presences by object type complexes

Percentage of the total possible presences in each of the object type complexes: A (100%), B (100%), C (50%), D (50%), E (50%), F (25%), G (0%), H (16.66%), I (7.75%), J (25%), K (25%), L (25%), M (41.30%).

Most common object type complexes

Complexes A, B, C, D, E, and M.

Quantity and diversity of objects

Average number of objects: 64.

Range of the number of elements: 52–76.

Average number of object types: 24.5.

Range of the number of object types: 24–25.

Time and space locations of the offerings

Building: Tlaloc (both).

Building Stage: IVb (both).

Approximate date: 1469–1481.

Vertical location: platform (both).

Horizontal location: NE (22), NW (58).

General characteristics of the offerings

Container: fill under floor (both).

Primary orientation of objects: N (22), S (58).

Number of excavation levels: 3 (58), 4 (22).

Number of proposed levels: 5 (both).

Maximum internal dimensions of the offerings (cm)

Offering	N-S axis	E-W axis
22	90	110
58	100	80

Distribution of objects (levels, axes, and groupings)

Offerings 22 and 58 were deposited in a cavity dug in the floor of the Stage IVb platform. Five different levels of objects were deposited on a layer of loose soil.

Level 1: It was composed of well-defined concentrations of marine material and beads (small shells, conch shells, sand, sea urchins, and greenstone beads). Placed in the center of this level in a longitudinal position were 1 deerhead scepter, 1 chicahuaztli, 2 serpent scepters, 1 Xipe Totec split-end noseplug (?), and 1 perforated obsidian circle.

Level 2: Marine objects also predominated at the second level: 1 *Xancus* conch shell and 10 mother-of-pearl shells were placed indiscriminately, with the smooth surface either up or down. These objects were located in offering 22 to the east of the nose cartilage of the third level and in offering 58 to the west of the nose cartilage on level 3. The remains of coral and Elasmobranchs vertebrae were also found in offering 22.

Level 3: A longitudinally oriented sawfish nose cartilage was placed in the center of the deposit. Several turtle shells (pond sliders) were associated with the cartilage: 6 in offering 22 and 5 in offering 58. The turtle shells were found to the north of the nose cartilage in offering 22 and to the east of the cartilage in offering 58. A cluster of greenstone beads was also found at this level.

Level 4: The fourth level was more complicated. The principal object was a skull-mask with a necklace of olive shells and copper bells. It was placed at the eastern end of the offering and faced east; in offering 58, the mask was placed at the northern end and oriented to the north. One human skull with a knife in its mouth was placed close to the skull-mask and was turned in the opposite direction. At this level, we also found 1 effigy jar containing copal; it was to the north in offering 22 (oriented to the north) and to the south (oriented east) in offering 59. One representation of a ceramic deforming cradle was placed to the south in offering 22 and to the northeast in offering 58. The cradle in offering 58 was in the form of a conch shell. There were also 4 greenstone beads and 1 obsidian prismatic blade in offering 22, and in offering 58, there were 2 greenstone beads, 1 wooden deerhead scepter, one shell oyohualli, wooden remains, and the jawbones of a fish.

Level 5: On the last level were found a quail's bones, mixed with tezontle stones. Also found in offering 22 were potsherds, copal, and charcoal.

SUBCOMPLEX C$_2$

Offerings: 15 and 62.
Number of offerings in complex: 2.
Dendrogram
    Split: 12 unshared presences/absences, coefficient of similarity = 0.74.
    Relationships: It is tied to offerings 70 and CA by 22 upas (0.53 coefficient of similarity).
Frequency of presences by object type complex
    Percentage of the total possible presences in each of the object type complexes: A (66.66%), B (100%), C (66.66%), D (50%), E (0%), F (0%), G (33.33%), H (25%), I (0%), J (75%), K (100%), L (50%), M (26.08%).
Most common object type complexes
    Complexes B, K, J, A, and C.
Quantity and diversity of objects
    Average number of elements: 53.5.
    Range of the number of elements: 44–63.
    Average number of object types: 21.
    Range of the number of object types: 21–21.
Time and space locations of the offerings
    Building: Huitzilopochtli (both).
    Building stage: IVb (both).

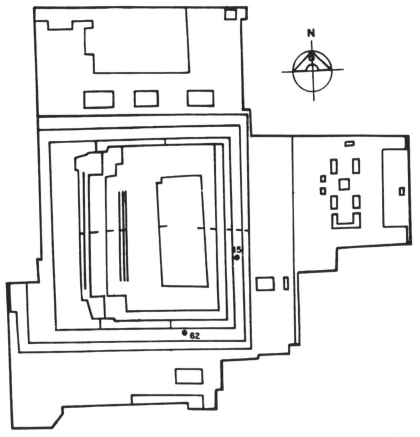

Figure 134:
The location of offerings
in Subcomplex C$_2$

Approximate date: 1469–1481.

Vertical location: floor (both).

Horizontal location: S (62), E (15).

General characteristics of the offerings

Container: fill under the floor (both).

Primary orientation of objects: S (62), E (15).

Number of excavation levels: 2 (62), 3 (15).

Number of proposed levels: 3 (15), 4 (62).

Maximum internal dimensions of the offerings (cm)

Offering	N-S axis	E-W axis
15	100	90
62	100	350

Distribution of objects (levels, axes, and groupings)

Offerings 15 and 62 were found in the fill under the floor. The objects were placed directly on tezontle stones and covered with flagstones. Because of this they had become jumbled and deteriorated. There were 4 poorly defined vertical levels in which marine fauna predominated.

Level 1: At the floor of the offering, a small, crude representation of Xiuhtecuhtli was found, oriented to the west in offering 15 and to the south in offering 62. Over this basalt sculpture were placed shells, conch shells, corals, remains of copal, and chitons (only in offering 62) haphazardly placed. There were also 62 copper bells in offering 62 and 15 shell disks and 2 obsidian earplugs in offering 15.

Level 2: On the second level, we found 2 Mixtec greenstone penates, with Tlaloc attributes. Both were oriented longitudinally in the opposite direction from the Xiuhtecuhtli sculpture (to the east in offering 15 and to the north in offering 62). One of the penates in offering 15 held ears of corn in his hands. Accompanying these images were 1 anthropomorphic copal figure (oriented longitudinally) and 2 flint sacrificial knives (1 placed longitudinally and 1 crosswise). There were also numerous marine remains, especially of fish: 5 needlefish, 3 yellow fin mojarra, 2 spotfin hogfish, 1 shark, 1 elasmobranch, 1 teleost, 1 grouper (*Hemanthias* sp.), and 1 barracuda, as well as the remains of sea urchins and coral in offering 15; 12 ballyhoo, 3 spotfin hogfish, 2 grouper, 1 elasmobranch, 1 shark, 1 parrot fish, and 1 trunkfish, as well as the remains of coral in offering 62.

Level 3: In the center of the deposit on level 3, 2 skull-masks were found (1 adult and 1 infant) in a bad state of preservation. Associated with them were olive shells, 1 bone bloodletter (offering 15), and 1 obsidian prismatic blade (offering 62). In offering 15, there was 1 tezontle Tlaloc mask and 1 penate, and in offering 62, there was 1 tezontle Tlaloc effigy. Animal remains predominated at this level: olive shells, brain coral (4 in offering 15 and 6 in offering 62), pond sliders (1 shell in offering 15 and several plaques in offering 62), alligator (1 jawbone and 1 dermal plate in offering 15 and 1 skull and several dermal plates in offering 62), 1 intrusive sheep tooth (offering 15), and intrusive pocket gopher bones (offering 62). Other objects recorded are shell disks (1 in each offering), obsidian disks (1 in offering 15 and 2 in offering 62), 1 obsidian projectile point (offering 15), copal remains (offering 15), and 2 greenstone beads (offering 62).

Level 4: In offering 62, we observed a fourth level, consisting of the remains of a ceramic censer and 2 montezuma quail.

COMPLEX D

Offerings: 3 and 5 (also called Chamber 1).
Number of offerings in complex: 2.
Dendrogram
   Split: 12 unshared presences/absences, coefficient of similarity = 0.74.
   Subgroups: none.
   Relationships: It is tied to Complex E by 24 upas (0.49 coefficient of similarity).
Frequency of presences by object type complex
   Percentage of total possible presences in each of the object type complexes: A (100%), B (100%),

C (83.33%), D (0%), E (0%), F (75%), G (50%), H (0%), I (2.58%), J (75%), K (25%), L (50%), M (17.39%).

Most common object type complexes

Complexes A, B, C, E, and J.

Quantity and diversity of objects

Average number of objects: 135.5.

Range of the number of elements: 119–152.

Average number of object types: 18.5.

Range of the number of object types: 17–20.

Time and space locations of the objects

Building: Huitzilopochtli (both).

Building stage: IVb (both).

Approximate date: 1469–1481.

Vertical location: platform (both).

Horizontal location: W (both).

Comments: They are very similar in their contexts.

General characteristics of the offerings

Container: sillares box (both).

Primary orientation of objects: W (5), undetermined (3).

Number of excavation levels: 1 (both).

Number of proposed levels: 1 (5), 3 (3).

Comments: They are very much alike in their general characteristics.

Maximum internal dimensions of the offerings (cm)

Offering	N-S axis	E-W axis	Z axis
3	60 (diameter)	60 (diameter)	80
5 (Chamber 1)	150	200	125
5 (antechamber)	80	225	

Distribution of objects (levels, axes, and groupings)

In spite of the fact that the offerings in this complex are similar in regard to their spatial location, they are quite different in the internal distribution of gifts. They will be described separately.

Offering 3

This offering was deposited inside a cylindrical, tezontle sillares box. It was covered with two quarry stone sillares and, immediately afterward, by the floor of the platform of Stage IVb. The objects underwent an intense heat, to the degree that some obsidian objects are deformed. All the material was jumbled. The vague reports by García Cook and Arana (1978: 51–53) and the information from Carramiñana (1988) allow us to reconstruct 3 levels for the placement of objects.

Level 1: The first level contained copper bells and copal remains.

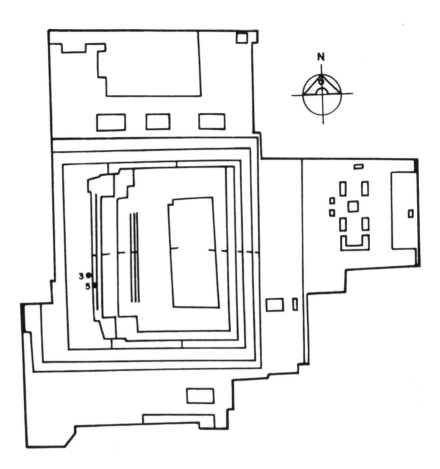

Figure 135:
The location of offerings
in Complex D

Level 2: The next level had abundant remains of carbon and ashes. Also recovered (without recording their original position) was an undetermined number of gold, silver, and copper bells; 1 shell carved in the form of an eagle head; remains of human bones; fragments of coral, sponges, and sea urchins; bones of 2 turkeys, 1 opossum, 1 stingray, 2 fish (1 from the Diodontidae family and 1 from the order Tetraodontiformes), and 19 rattlesnakes (from 3 different species), as well as the teeth and skull of 1 alligator.

Level 3: The highest level had 9 unburned complete American kestrel (*Falco sparverius*) skeletons.

Offering 5

Offering 5 is also known as Chamber 1. It is positioned in space symmetrically to Chamber 2. The floor of the box was made with quarry stone sillares, the walls with tezontle sillares, and the top with huge flagstones. The offering had only 1 deposition level. Greenstone sculptures predominated (García Cook and Arana 1978:58–66).

Level 1: The most important object in the offering was located in the center of the chamber and oriented to the west. It was a monolith of greenstone, 132 cm x 40 cm x 15 cm, portraying the goddess Mayahuel (López Austin 1979). Liquid copal had been poured around the large sculpture and then covered with yellow clay. Numerous objects were distributed around the monolith: greenstone sculptures (irregular fragments, beads, 1 earplug, fragments of earplugs, 2 disks with deities in bas-relief, and 12 Mezcala-style anthropomorphic sculptures), obsidian sculptures (disks, mortars and grinders, images of rattlesnakes, projectile points), pieces of metal (clay beads covered with gold, golden disks, 1 copper bracelet, 1 copper needle, pyrite cubes, and hematite), calcareous objects (conch shells, shells, chitons, coral, shell pectorals, and disks), organic remains (wood and copal), and other stone objects (flint projectile points, flint sacrificial knives, and basalt and andesite mallets).

COMPLEX E

Offerings: 34, 39, 44, 74, 29, 10, 37, and 14.
Number of Offerings in Complex: 8.
Dendrogram
    Split: 17 unshared presences/absences, coefficient of similarity = 0.64.
    Subgroups: 44–74 (2 upas), 44–74–29 (3 upas), 44–74–29–10 (5 upas), 44–74–29–10–37 (7 upas), 34–39 (11 upas), 44–74–29–10–37–14 (11 upas).
    Relationships: It is tied to Complex D by 24 upas (0.49 coefficient of similarity).
Frequency of presences by object type complex
    Percentage of the total possible of presences in each of the object type complexes: A (4.16%), B (12.5%), C (20.83%), D (12.5%), E (6.25%), F (12.5%), G (79.16%), H (3.12%), I (4.31%), J (6.25%), K (0%), L (12.5%), M (2.71%).
Most common object type complexes
    Complexes G, C, B, D, F, and L.
Quantity and diversity of objects
    Average number of elements: 19.25.
    Range of the number of elements: 3–78.
    Average number of object types: 7.5.
    Range of the number of object types: 3–15.
Time and space locations of the offerings
    Building: Huitzilopochtli (34, 39, 44, 29, 10, 37, 14), I (74).
    Building stage: II (34, 39, 44, 37), III (29), IVb (10, 14), VI (74).
    Approximate date: 1375–1440, 1469–1481, and 1486–1502.
    Vertical location: platform (74, 10, 14), main body (29), temple (34, 39, 44, 37).
    Horizontal location: center (34, 39, 44, 37), S (29), W (10, 14), SE (74).
General characteristics of the offerings
    Container: stone urn (29), fill under floor (34, 39, 44, 74, 10, 37, 14).
    Primary orientation of objects: W (34, 39, 44, 29, 10, 37, 14), undetermined (74).
    Number of excavation levels: 1 (44, 74, 29, 10), 2 (34, 14), 3 (37), 4 (39).
    Number of proposed levels: 1 (44, 74, 29, 10, 37, 14), 2 (34, 39).

Maximum internal dimensions of the offerings (cm)

Offering	N-S axis	E-W axis	Z axis
34	100	80	
39	23	35	
44	20	20	
74	20	20	
29	35	45	17
10	55	55	
37	20	20	
14	85	85	

Distribution of objects (levels, axes, and groupings)

The offerings of Complex E can be divided into 2 groups in accordance with the distribution of gifts inside. The first group consists of offerings 44, 74, 29, 10, 37, and 14; the second, of offerings 34 and 39. Each group will be described separately.

Group 1

The location of the 6 offerings of the first group varies: offerings 10, 14, 37, and 74 were placed among the earth and stones after breaking through the stucco floor and making a cavity in the building fill. Afterward, they were covered with earth and protected with a flagstone. Offering 44 was similarly placed but on the inside of a bench. Offering 29 was placed in the building fill of Stage III. The objects of these offerings were found primarily in one level.

Level 1: The common feature of these 6 offerings was the presence of urns containing incinerated remains and, in some cases, artifacts. All were oriented to the west. The urns differed from each other: 1 plumbate ceramic vessel, in the form of a dog and with a cajete as a cover (offering 44); 1 orange ceramic jar (offering 74); 1 basalt urn with a cover (offering 29); 1 orange ceramic vase with straight sides and a circular base, with a bas-relief portraying deities, and with a circular ceramic lid (offerings 10 and 14); and 1 orange ceramic tripod cajete decorated with blue pigment (offering 37). Only the urns in offerings 44 and 74 did not contain artifacts associated with the incinerated remains. Most of the objects found in offerings 29, 10, 37, and 14 are beads: 1 greenstone bead in offering 29; 2 greenstone, 4 gold, and 30 turquoise beads in offering 37; 1 greenstone bead, 14 obsidian beads in the shape of a duckhead, and 2 helicoidal obsidian beads in offering 14. Piercing-cutting instruments were next in abundance: 1 bone bloodletter in offering 29; 1 obsidian prismatic blade and 1 flint projectile point in offering 37; and 1 bone bloodletter and 1 obsidian projectile point in offering 14. Offering 10 had 1 greenstone zoomorphic sculpture; it is the fragmented depiction of a serpent crossing a rectangular frame.

Group 2

This group is made up of offerings 34 and 39. Both were placed inside the building fill under the floor of the Huitzilopochtli Temple. The two offerings are similar in content and location. It is

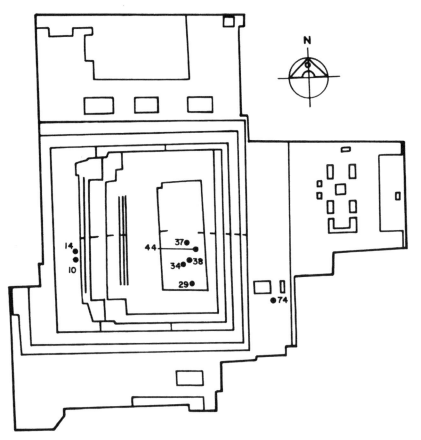

Figure 136:
The location of offerings
in Complex E

interesting that they have a relative position analogous to that of offerings 10 and 14. Two deposition levels for objects can be distinguished.

Level 1: Objects were placed on the first level in no apparent order. Some objects predominate, and stone beads were the most abundant: 2 spherical beads, 2 helicoidal beads, and 36 beads in various forms carved from greenstone in offering 34; 4 plant-shaped beads, 10 helicoidal beads (grouped in 2 clusters of 5 elements), 23 beads with different shapes carved from greenstone, 7 rock crystal beads, and 6 beads of white stone in offering 39. Other stone objects were: 2 greenstone earplugs, 1 perforated obsidian disk, 1 small head and 1 greenstone anthropomorphic mask, 1 duckhead sculpture, and 1 flint sacrificial blade in offering 34; 17 obsidian earplugs, 3 greenstone earplugs, 6 obsidian perforated disks, and 2 greenstone plaques with anthropomorphic carvings in offering 39. There were also metal artifacts: 2 copper bells and 1 miniature metallic vessel in offering 34; 1 pyrite disk in offering 39. Finally, in offering 34, there was a mass of copal to the west of the funerary urn.

Level 2: In the center of the second level, there was a stone urn, apparently representing the god Mictlantecuhtli, oriented to the west. The container of offering 34 and its cover were carved from obsidian. The container of offering 39 is of travertine with an obsidian cover. Inside the urn in offering 34 were found incinerated remains, 1 gold bell with the glyph ollin and 1 silver anthropomorphic mask, apparently portraying a monkey. The urn in offering 39 had incinerated remains, 1 gold bell, and 2 greenstone disks, perforated in the center.

COMPLEX F

Offerings: 18, 19, 89, 69, 49, 50, J, 84, and 48.
Number of offerings in complex: 9.
Dendrogram
    Split: 18 unshared presences/absences, coefficient of similarity = 0.62.
    Subgroups: 18–19 (2 upas), 18–19–89 (5 upas), 18–19–89–69 (8 upas), 49–50–J (10 upas), 18–19–89–69–49–50–J (13 upas), 18–19–89–69–49–50–J–84 (16 upas).
    Relationships: It is tied to Complexes G, H, I, and J and with offerings 64 and L by 20 upas (0.57 coefficient of similarity).
Frequency of presences by object type complex
    Percentage of the total possible presences in each of the object type complexes: A (62.96%), B (88.88%), C (18.51%), D (38.88%), E (0%), F (16.66%), G (0%), H (11.11%), I (2.10%), J (5.55%), K (41.66%), L (5.55%), M (7.24%).
Most common object type complexes
    Complexes B, A, K, and D.
Quantity and diversity of objects
    Average number of elements: 35.55.
    Range of the number of elements: 11–157.
    Average number of object types: 9.77.
    Range of the number of object types: 9–14.
Time and space locations of the offerings
    Building: Tlaloc (69, 49, 50, 84, 48), Huitzilopochtli-Tlaloc (18, 19), C (J), outside patio (89).
    Building stage: IVa (18, 19, 48), IVb (69), VI (89), VII (49, 50, J, 84).
    Approximate date: 1440–1520.
    Vertical location: floor (89, 69, 49, 50), platform (18, 19, 84, 48), stairway (J).
    Horizontal location: N center (84, 69), E (89, 49, 50, J), W (18, 19), NW (48).
    Comments: The majority of offerings were deposited in the Tlaloc Temple.
General characteristics of the offerings
    Container: stone urn (18, 19), sillares box (89, 84, 48), fill below the floor (69), fill (49, 50, J).
    Primary orientation of objects: N (69, 48), S (18, 19), W (89, 49, 50, J, 84).
    Number of excavation levels: 1 (18, 19, 49, 50), 3 (89, J, 84), 4 (69), 5 (48).
    Number of proposed levels: 1 (69), 2 (49, 50), 3 (18, 19, J), 4 (89, 84), 5 (48).
    Comments: The number of shared traits is equal to the number of unshared traits in this complex.

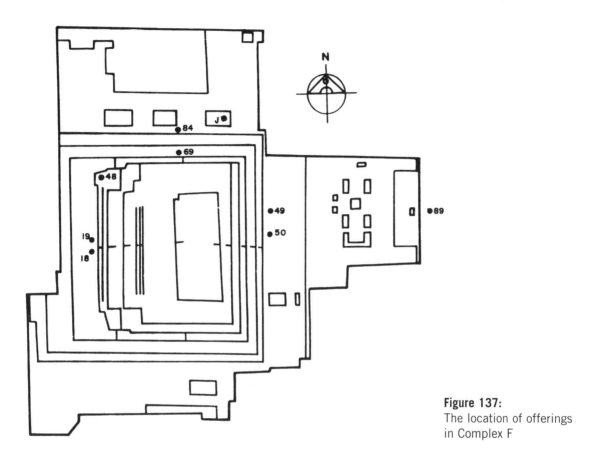

Figure 137:
The location of offerings
in Complex F

Maximum internal dimensions of the offerings (cm)

Offering	N-S axis	E-W axis	Z axis
18	52	47	40
19	45	38	50
89	?	?	?
69	40	135	
49	45	45	
50	45	45	
1/8	35	40	
84	47	37	
48	180	120	

Distribution of the objects (levels, axes, and groupings)

Offerings 89, 69, J, 84, and 48 will be described individually because of their diversity both in quantity and placement of objects. Offerings 18 and 19 (Subcomplex F_1) and offerings 49 and 50 (Subcomplex F_2) will be described in two later sections because they are very similar.

Offering 89

This offering was deposited inside a tezontle sillares box of unknown size. Unfortunately, the entire deposit was found completely submerged under the water table level and thus was not completely recorded. The box was oriented to the E-W, the same direction as the majority of the objects taken from it. Apparently, they were superimposed upon each other at 4 vertical levels.

Level 1: Three sea shells were found at the deepest level.

Level 2: At the second level, 18 tezontle sculptures representing teponaztli were removed.

Level 3: On the third level, there were objects decorated with blue pigment: 13 tezontle sculptures, some of their fragments, and 12 ceramic flutes.

Level 4: Placed in the center of the highest level was a ceramic Tlaloc water jar, decorated with red, white, and blue pigment. It was oriented to the west. The jar contained greenstone beads and plates. There were also remains of copal, wood, and bone, all in a very poor state of preservation.

Offering 69

This offering was placed inside the building fill. Its objects were arranged on a thin layer of tezontle stones (each one approximately 5 cm thick) and were protected by flagstones. The objects were distributed on a single level in no perceivable order. They were very mixed up, although a N-S orientation predominated.

Level 1: One penate, 1 greenstone flute, and 1 copal figure were placed in the center of the first level and were oriented to the north. The bone remains of an unidentified animal and 2 penates (oriented E-W) were found at the eastern end of the deposit. To the west, at the opposite end of the deposit, were found 1 ball of copal and miniature images in white stone of 1 chicahuaztli, 1 huehuetl, and 1 flute. Other objects found were: 1 mother-of-pearl shell, small conch shells, 18 olive shells, fragments of shell, 1 greenstone bead, remains of copal, 1 anthropomorphic ceramic fragment, and 2 potsherds.

Offering J

The offering was deposited in the building fill and was covered with stone, earth, and mortar. It was placed at the level of the first stair step of Building C. There were 3 levels, in which marine material and sacrificial knives predominated.

Level 1: One penate, an image of 1 omichicahuaztli, and 1 greenstone cylindrical bar were placed at the center of the first level, oriented to the west. At the eastern and western ends of the deposit were found remains of lace coral, and at the southeast corner, there was a layer of small calcareous stones. In the southwest corner, there was a concentration of sand with the remains of wood and fish bones.

Level 2: Five flint knives were on the second level, placed in a parallel position in a N-S direction and oriented to the west.

Level 3: Very deteriorated wooden remains lay on top of the objects described earlier.

Offering 84

This offering was placed in a box with tezontle sillar sides and flagstone floor and cover. The box was made in the fill of Stage VII. There were 4 object deposition levels.

Level 1: Marine objects uniformly distributed and without any evident orientation predominated. We found small shells, small conch shells, 14 large conch shells, 16 large shells, and 7 sea urchins, as well as net and deer antler corals (these were concentrated at the north end).

Level 2: The second level was a layer of gray, clayish mud and charcoal of variable thickness.

Level 3: Three anthropomorphic copal figures dominated this level. They took up almost all the surface of the deposit and were oriented to the west. Over the figures were found 20 serpent scepters (13 of flint and 7 of obsidian). Under the figures were another 3 scepters (2 obsidian and 1 flint). All the scepters were oriented in an E-W direction. Associated with the heads of the figures (at the eastern end) were the claws and large bones of a golden eagle, and at the foot of the figures (western end), there was the complete skeleton of a rattlesnake. Also to the east of the deposit was found a ceramic flute with the portrayal of Xochipilli's head at its far end.

Level 4: The upper level had only a homogeneous layer of wood in a bad state of preservation.

Offering 48

This offering was placed on a small altar located in the northwestern part of the Tlaloc Temple. A box made of quarry stone sillares with a flagstone floor was erected there. The inside was plastered. Offering 48 contained objects at 5 vertical levels. Bone remains predominated: the bones of at least 42 children between the ages of 2 and 7 (22 male, 6 female, and 10 of undetermined sex). Thirty-two children had cranial deformation (27 with horizontal-lambdoidal deformation and 5 with tabula-erect deformation), and 21 had bone pathologies due to nutritional deficits. Apparently, the children had their throats cut (Román Berrelleza 1986).

Level 1: The deepest level was covered with a homogeneous layer of sand averaging 1 cm in depth.

Level 2: The second level is characterized by children's skeletons laid down on their backs in a bent position and without any definite orientation. Many anatomical relationships were seen. Two children had circular wooden breastplates with applications of turtle shell and turquoise mosaic. Others had necklaces composed of small greenstone beads around their cervical vertebrae. They also had 1 greenstone bead in their mouths. Altogether, 241 beads were found in this offering.

Level 3: There were more bone remains of children at this level, showing traces of blue pigment.

Level 4: Over the skeletons were placed the remains of copal and wood, the bone remains of birds, prismatic obsidian blades, crafted sea shells, pumpkins, and small conch shells. The remains of these objects were found in a very bad state of preservation, and they were distributed irregularly over all the surface of the fourth level.

Level 5: Eleven tezontle sculptures representing water jars with a Tlaloc face formed the fifth level. The sculptures were plastered and decorated with white, blue, red, and black pigment. Ten jars were concentrated in the southern half of the box. All were lying on their sides, simulating the pouring of water: 6 with the face of Tlaloc upward and 5 downward. They were placed in an E-W direction (3 oriented to the west and 8 to the east).

SUBCOMPLEX F₁

Offerings: 18 and 19.
Number of offerings in complex: 2.
Dendrogram
　　Split: 2 unshared presences/absences, coefficient of similarity = 0.96.
　　Relationships: It is tied to offering 89 by 5 upas (0.89 coefficient of similarity).
Frequency of presences by object type complex
　　Percentage of the total possible presences in each of the object type complexes: A (83.33%), B (100%), C (0%), D (100%), E (0%), F (50%), G (0%), H (0%), I (0%), J (0%), K (25%), L (0%), M (0%).
Most common object type complexes
　　Complexes B, D, A, and F.
Quantity and diversity of objects
　　Average number of elements: 14.
　　Range of the number of elements: 14–14.
　　Average number of object types: 7.5.
　　Range of the number of object types: 7–8.
Time and space locations of the offerings
　　Building: Huitzilopochtli-Tlaloc (both); nearer to Huitzilopochtli (18), nearer to Tlaloc (19).
　　Building stage: IVa (both).
　　Approximate date: about 1469.

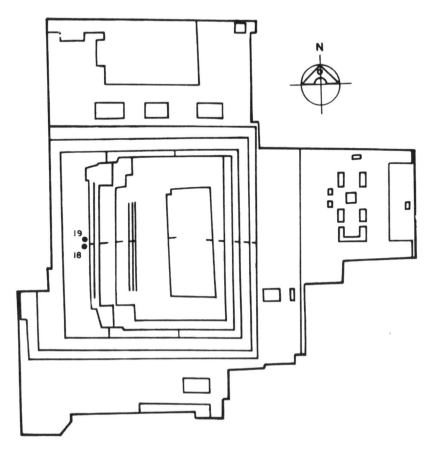

Figure 138:
The location of offerings
in Subcomplex F_1

Vertical location: platform (both).
Horizontal location: W (both).

General characteristics of the offerings
Container: stone urn (both).
Primary orientation of objects: S (both).
Number of excavation levels: 1 (both).
Number of proposed levels: 3 (both).
Comments: Their characteristics are generally quite similar.

Maximum internal dimensions of the offerings (cm)

Offering	N-S axis	E-W axis	Z axis
18	52	57	40
19	45	38	30

Distribution of objects (levels, axes, and groupings)
The objects of offerings 18 and 19 were placed inside boxes with covers (2 pieces) made of plastered basalt. Both boxes were placed under the floor of the platform of Stage IVa, separated by about

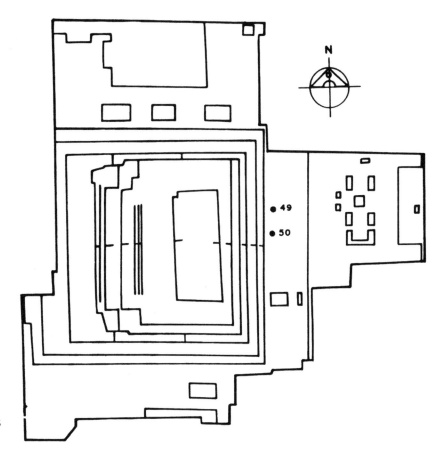

Figure 139:
The location of offerings
in Subcomplex F$_2$

40 cm. They were oriented in accord with the cardinal directions. In their quality, quantity, and the distribution of objects, these offerings are practically identical. A description of the placement of objects at the 3 levels follows.

Level 1: The first level contained objects related to the aquatic world: small conch shells (1,041 in offering 18 and 1,118 in 19), greenstone beads (173 in offering 18 and 109 in offering 19), 1 shell (offering 18), and 1 seed (offering 19).

Level 2: The second level was made up of 13 greenstone Mezcala-style anthropomorphic sculptures. All were decorated with blue, black, red, white, and ocher pigments. They portrayed the facial features of the god Tlaloc (headdress, rings around the eyes, and mustache). Eleven sculptures were male, and 2 were female. The sculptures in offering 18 were smaller (10–15 cm) than those in offering 19 (15–30 cm). In both offerings, the sculptures were placed in a vertical position, resting against the northern side of the box, in 2 rows and oriented to the south. Two irregular masses of copal were placed before them.

Level 3: One prismatic obsidian blade and fragments of ceramics were found outside the urns.

SUBCOMPLEX F$_2$

Offerings: 49 and 50.

Number of offerings in complex: 2.

Dendrogram

Split: 4 unshared presences/absences, coefficient of similarity = 0.91.

Relationships: It is tied to offering J by 10 upas (0.79 coefficient of similarity).

Frequency of presences by object type complex

Percentage of the total possible presences in each of the object type complexes: A (50%), B (100%), C (0%), D (0%), E (0%), F (0%), G (0%), H (25%), I (1.72%), J (0%), K (25%), L (0%), M (10.86%).

Most common object type complexes

Complexes B, A, H, and K.

Quantity and diversity of objects

Average number of elements: 12.5.

Range of the number of elements: 12–13.

Average number of object types: 10.

Range of the number of object types: 9–11.

Time and space locations of the offerings

Building: Tlaloc (both).

Building stage: VII (both).

Approximate date: 1502–1520.

Vertical location: floor (both).

Horizontal location: E (both).

Comments: They are very similar in their context. They are symmetrical to offerings 52 and 57 (Complex G), which are located in the Huitzilopochtli Temple and perhaps were dedicated to the patron god of the Mexica.

General characteristics of the offerings

Container: fill (both).

Primary orientation of objects: W (both).

Number of excavation levels: 1 (both).

Number of proposed levels: 2 (both).

Maximum internal dimensions of the offerings (cm)

Offering	N-S axis	E-W axis
49	45	45
50	45	45

Distribution of objects (levels, axes, and groupings)

The 2 offerings of this subcomplex were placed on a thin layer of earth in the building fill. They are practically identical in quality, quantity, and distribution. Both have 2 levels that show objects related to the aquatic world of Mexica cosmovision.

Level 1: A homogeneous layer of sand with blue-green pigment, 1 cm thick, is found at the first level. Remains of copal, porcupine fish bones, and small conch shells (124 in offering 49 and 123 in offering 50) were mixed with the sand. Remains of serpent bones were found in offering 50.

Level 2: All the objects at the second level were arranged longitudinally in an E-W direction, oriented to the west. The only exception was a greenstone flute in offering 49. In the center of both offerings, there was a greenstone flute that divided the remaining objects into 2 zones. To the south of the flute was placed a Mixtec penate, and to the north was 1 copal anthropomorphic figure. Eleven flint serpent scepters flanked these objects: 3 scepters to the south of the penate; 4 scepters to the north of the copal figure; 2 scepters to the northeast; and 2 scepters to the southeast of the greenstone flute.

COMPLEX G

Offerings: 52 and 57.
Number of offerings in complex: 2.
Dendrogram
 Split: 9 unshared presences/absences, coefficient of similarity = 0.81.
 Subgroups: none.
 Relationships: It is tied to Complexes H, I, and J and with offerings 64 and L by 19 upas (0.60 coefficient of similarity).
Frequency of presences by object type complex
 Percentage of the total possible presences in each of the object type complexes: A (0%), B (50%), C (66.66%), D (0%), E (0%), F (25%), G (16.66%), H (0%), I (0%), J (50%), K (50%), L (50%), M (13.04%).
Most common object type complexes
 Complexes C, B, K, and L.
Quantity and diversity of objects
 Average number of elements: 62.
 Range of the number of elements: 58–66.
 Average number of object types: 10.5.
 Range of the number of object types: 9–12.
Time and space locations of the offerings
 Building: Huitzilopochtli (both).
 Building stage: VII (both).
 Approximate date: 1502–1520.
 Vertical location: floor (both).
 Horizontal location: E (both).
 Comments: Offerings 52 and 57 have quite similar contexts. They are symmetrical to offerings 49 and 50 (Subcomplex F_2) in the Tlaloc Temple, which were perhaps dedicated to the God of Rain.

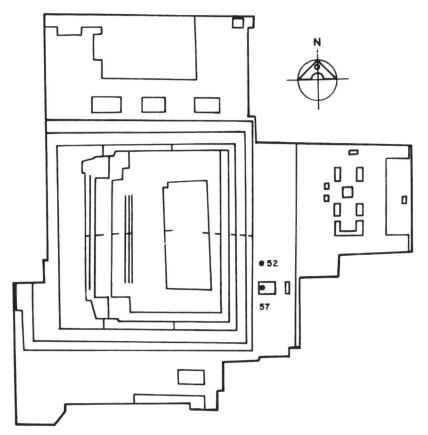

Figure 140:
The location of offerings
in Complex G

General characteristics of the offerings
> Container: fill (both).
> Primary orientation of offerings: E (52), W (57).
> Number of excavation levels: 2 (both).
> Number of proposed levels: 3 (both).

Maximum internal dimensions of the offerings (cm)

Offering	N-S axis	E-W axis
52	65	80
57	100	80

Distribution of objects (levels, axes, and groupings)

The offerings of this complex have a high degree of internal similarity. They were placed on a thin layer of earth inside the building fill. Three very different object placement levels can be detected.

Level 1: The first layer consists of a layer of sand 1 cm thick.

Level 2: The second level contains several different objects. In the center of the offering, an anthropomorphic copal figure stands out. In offering 52, it was oriented to the east, and in 57 in the opposite direction. In the latter offering, the copal figure was partly dovetailed onto the sawfish nose cartilage. Also found on the second level were perforated shell disks (9 in offering 52 and 4 in 57), obsidian earplugs (2 in each offering), curved flint knives (1 in the center of offering 52 and 2 at the eastern and western ends of 57), and the remains of olive shells.

Offering 52 differed from 57 in that it had the bone remains of a porcupine fish and 3 obsidian scepters with a globular end at the western end. Offering 57 contained 1 shell pendant, sea urchin remains, and 1 ehecacozcatl made of shell and red-colored earth.

Level 3: The third and last level was characterized by personified knives. Most of them were oriented longitudinally from east to west, although some of them were placed crosswise. In offering 52, 52 knives (25 oriented to the east and 27 to the south) were removed, and in offering 57, we obtained 40 (32 oriented to the west and 8 to the south). Also recorded were lace coral and rusted heaps of copper bells.

COMPLEX H

Offerings: 87, 27, K, 68, N, and B1.
Number of offerings in complex: 6.
Dendrogram
 Split: 12 unshared presences/absences, coefficient of similarity = 0.74.
 Subgroups: 87–27 (5 upas), 68–N (6 upas), 87–27–K (10 upas), 87–27–K–68–N (11 upas).
 Relationships: It is tied to Complexes I and J and with offerings 64 and L by 16 upas (0.66 coefficient of similarity).
 Comments: Offering 77 was eliminated from this complex, although it appears on the dendrogram between offerings 27 and K. It is not comparable because it was altered, and it was included in Complex Q, which groups these kinds of offerings.
Frequency of presences by object type complex
 Percentage of the total possible presences in each of the object type complexes: A (83.33%), B (100%), C (61.11%), D (58.33%), E (8.33%), F (8.33%), G (0%), H (12.5%), I (0.57%), J (8.33%), K (12.5%), L (8.33%), M (7.97%).
Most common object type complexes
 Complexes B, A, C, and D.
Quantity and diversity of objects
 Average number of elements: 55.66.
 Range of the number of elements: 17–116.
 Average number of object types: 10.33.
 Range of the number of object types: 8–14.
Time and space locations of the offerings
 Building: Huitzilopochtli (87, B1), A (K), B (N), J (27), I (68).
 Building stage: V (27, N, B1), VI (87, K), VII (68).

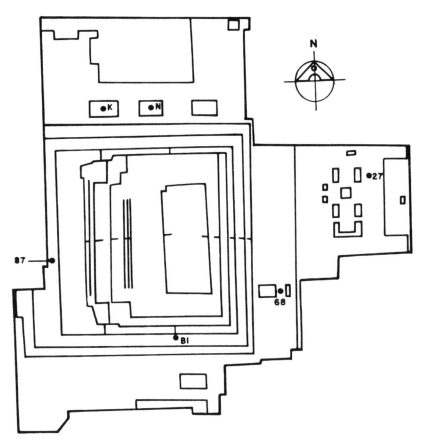

Figure 141:
The location of offerings
in Complex H

Approximate date: 1481–1520.

Vertical location: platform (B1, 87, 27, 68), temple (K, N).

Horizontal location: center (N), S center (B1), E (K), W (87, 68), NE (27).

Comments: All the offerings in this complex are different in context.

General characteristics of the offerings

Container: fill (87, 27, B1, N), sillares box (K), filling under floor (68).

Primary orientation of objects: S (87, B1), W (K, 68, N), E (27).

Number of excavation levels: 1 (87, 27, B1), 3 (68), 4 (K), 7 (N).

Number of proposed levels: 1 (87, 27, B1), 3 (68), 4 (K), 5 (N).

Maximum internal dimensions of the offerings (cm)

Offering	N-S axis	E-W axis	Z axis
87	40	30	
27	105	120	
K	43	92	48
68	40	74	
N	65	75	
B1	75	40	

Distribution of objects (levels, axes, and groupings)
The 6 offerings that make up this complex are very different in their internal distribution of objects. They will be described separately.

Offering 87

This offering was found in the building fill of stones and earth at Stage VI, directly under the modern cement pavement. The objects were deposited on a layer of fresh mortar and covered with it. As a consequence, at the time of their discovery, almost all the objects were firmly bound to the mortar and in some cases, shattered. They showed no apparent order but were stacked in a haphazard way. There seemed to be only 1 level of objects, most of them marine material and greenstone beads.

Level 1: The objects nearest the surface were 3 flint sacrificial knives with traces of red, blue, and black pigment. They were found very fragmented. Associated with them were 51 small conch shells, 1 *Strombus* conch shell, 50 small shells, 1 mother-of-pearl shell, chiton plaques, 91 copper bells (with no signs of rust), wood remains (perhaps the beads of a necklace), 569 greenstone beads (spherical, discoidal, tubular, irregular, and with traces of blue coloring), 4 pendants of gold sheets, 2 Mezcala-style anthropomorphic greenstone figures (the head and left leg were missing from 1), and remains of copal.

Offering 27

It was found in the tezontle and earth building fill, over a layer of loose earth. There was 1 level, containing primarily objects of marine origin.

Level 1: A flint serpent scepter had been placed in the center of the offering. To the east, there were 2 flint sacrificial knives, both oriented to the east. Other objects were dispersed in no particular order: 336 small shells, 100 small perforated shells, 12 olive shells, 2 small conch shells, 1 greenstone bead, 8 potsherds, 1 ramus of a puma's mandible, 19 copper bells, and copal remains.

Offering K

Offering K was deposited in a box with tezontle sillares sides and covered with stucco, and it had a floor and cover of flagstones. The offering belonged to Stage VIa and apparently was superficially stirred during Stage VII. The last levels had been altered by the intrusion of a well. This was the reason that many objects were displaced and broken. It is probable that there were 4 different levels originally.

Level 1: At the deepest level, there was the complete skeleton of a young puma. It was placed in a crouched position with its head down and oriented east and its tail oriented to the west.

Level 2: The second level is dominated by marine objects: numerous shells and small conch shells; 9 olive shells (on the puma's abdomen); 27 greenstone beads; remains of wood and copal; 2 projectile points; 2 prismatic blades and 5 obsidian scepters with a globular end; 56 copper bells; sand; and several potsherds.

Level 3: This level was very mixed up, and many of the objects had been broken in pre-Hispanic times. A total of 40 flint knives formed a uniform layer, primarily oriented in an E-W direction. The bones of a golden eagle were associated with the knives.

Level 4: All the objects found outside the box are thought to belong to the highest level. There were greenstone beads, small conch shells, olive shells, and potsherds with no order.

Offering 68

This offering was located under the floor of the platform of Building I. It has 3 well-defined levels where sacrificial knives and bone remains predominate.

Level 1: The first level was composed of 41 flint sacrificial knives placed in 2 clusters: 26 to the east (13 oriented to the east and 13 to the west), and 15 to the west (7 oriented to the east and 8 to the west). At the third level, we also found 2 groups of obsidian projectile points flanking the skeleton. Four of them pointed to the north and 3 to the south. There were also some copal remains and 1 obsidian prismatic blade.

Level 2: In it was a snake's skeleton with the skull missing. It was placed longitudinally from east to west.

Level 3: The complete skeleton of a wolf lay at this level, in a crouching position, head downward, with the cranium to the west and its tail to the east. At the level of the abdomen, the animal had 11 olive shells. Small conch shells were spread over all the surface of this level.

Offering N

Offering N was found under the box of Offering H. Its objects were deposited on a layer of earth that, in turn, rested upon the building fill of Building B. Five levels could be detected, dominated by marine material, copal, and sacrificial knives.

Level 1: At the center of the deepest level were placed 6 flint sacrificial knives, facing west. One obsidian projectile point was associated with the knives. The eastern half of the offering was taken up by several lace corals, which formed a homogeneous layer. At the opposite end, to the west, lay an anthropomorphic figure of copal oriented to the west.

Level 2: The center of the second level contained 1 greenstone anthropomorphic mask (oriented to the west), 1 greenstone pendant, and several small shells and conch shells.

Level 3: The next level had mother-of-pearl shells. Six shells were found in a circle, with the inner side turned upward. In the center of the circle, there was 1 complete mother-of-pearl shell (bivalve), which had inside 97 greenstone beads, 2 small sacrificial knives, and 1 conch shell.

Level 4: Marine objects predominated at this level. In the center was 1 Teotihuacan-style anthropomorphic mask, facing west. Around the mask was an arrangement of small shells, 6 small conch shells, 35 olive shells, and 1 greenstone bead.

Level 5: The last level was composed of sacrificial knives and copal objects of different shapes. In the western half of the offering were 21 flint sacrificial knives (19 facing east, 1 to the west, and 1 to the north). Next to the knives were 9 olive shells. On the southern half, the deposit was characterized by the presence of 10 semitubular bars of copal (35 cm x 5 cm) aligned in an E-W direction and placed in parallel from north to south. Clusters of copal balls were placed at the ends of this level: 5 balls to the north (aligned in an E-W direction), 5 to the south (aligned in an E-W direction), 3 to the east (aligned in a N-S direction), and 3 to the west (aligned N-S). Other flat, irregular fragments of copal were found at this level. Remains of quail and 2 serpents were scattered about the offering.

Offering B1

This offering was found in 1948 inside the building fill of Stage V. It had 1 level for placing objects.

Level 1: One infant skull-mask with a flint knife in its mouth had been placed at the center of the offering, facing west. There were traces of copal dust on the frontal bone of the mask, 2 obsidian projectile points were above its palatine arch, and 1 prismatic blade was over its mandible. To the north of the cranium mask, there was 1 madrepore coral, and at the other end, to the south, was 1 small sculpture of Xiuhtecuhtli, facing the north. Two greenstone vessels were also recorded (1 to the east and 1 to the northeast), as well as remains of copal, 5 small shells, 1 potsherd, and 7 flint sacrificial knives (6 oriented to the south and 1 to the east).

COMPLEX I

Offerings: 21, 56, and 31.
Number of offerings in complex: 3.
Dendrogram
    Split: 7 unshared presences/absences, coefficient of similarity = 0.85.
    Subgroups: 21–26 (3 upas).
    Relationships: It is tied to Complex J by 12 upas (0.74 coefficient of similarity).

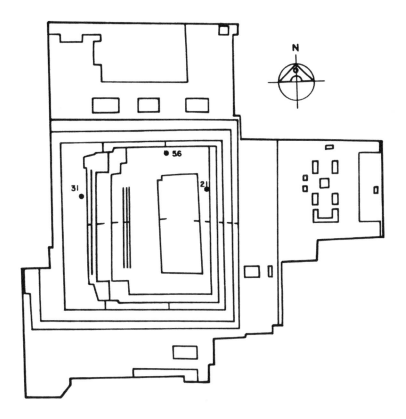

Figure 142:
The location of offerings
in Complex I

Frequency of presences by object type complex

Percentage of the total possible presences in each of the object type complexes: A (77.8%), B (66.66%), C (44.4%), D (0%), E (0%), F (16.7%), G (0%), H (0%), I (0.6%), J (100%), K (33.33%), L (0%), M (5.8%).

Most common object type complexes

Complexes J, A, B, and C.

Quantity and diversity of objects

Average number of elements: 51.3.

Range of the number of elements: 11–131.

Average number of object types: 9.7.

Range of the number of object types: 8–12.

Time and space locations of the offerings

Building: Tlaloc (all).

Building stage: IV (21, 56), IVa (31).

Approximate date: 1440–1469.

Vertical location: platform (31), main body (21, 56).

Horizontal location: N (56), E (21), W (31).

General characteristics of the offerings

Container: sillares box (all).

Primary orientation of objects: S (56), E (31), W (21).

Number of excavation levels: 1 (56), 3 (21, 31).

Number of proposed levels: 2 (all).

Comments: The offerings in the complex were oriented in an opposite direction to their general placement inside the building.

Maximum internal dimensions of the offerings (cm)

Offering	N-S axis	E-W axis	Z axis
21	90	70	70
56	90	65	70
31	42	40	65

Comments: The sizes of offerings 21 and 56 are about the same.

Distribution of objects (levels, axes, and groupings)

The offerings of this complex were deposited in tezontle sillar boxes with flagstone floors. Offering 31 had a flagstone covering. The 3 boxes were made inside architectural structures: 21 in the main body of Stage III but intruding from Stage IV; 56 in the fill of the body of Stage IV; and 31 in the floor of Stage IVa. In spite of the fact that the box of offering 21 was built over the main body of Stage III, it belonged to Stage IV, as shown by its enormous likeness to offering 56 and its covering made from the building fill of Stage IV.

Offerings 21 and 56 were almost identical in their contents and in the distribution of their objects, and 31 also resembles them. The 3 offerings had 2 levels for the placement of objects, principally water jars with the effigy of Tlaloc, greenstone objects, and objects deriving from the coasts.

Level 1: The chief materials at the first level were the remains of terrestrial and marine fauna and sacrificial knives. The first level of offerings 21 and 56 was relatively devoid of objects. Most of them were placed in front of a Tlaloc water jar, which had been deposited on the next level. At the western end of offering 21 were found the skeletons of 3 quail and 1 sawfish nose cartilage; at the extreme south of offering 56, there were 3 montezuma quail, 1 scaled quail, the skull of 1 rattlesnake, and 1 sawfish nose cartilage. The beak cartilages were of young animals and were oriented according to the longitudinal axis of the offering, pointing to the Tlaloc water jar.

Other objects had been placed in the center of the offering, precisely below the Tlaloc water jar. There was 1 sawfish nose cartilage and 1 flint sacrificial knife (oriented to the east) in offering 21; 1 sacrificial knife (oriented to the south) was in offering 56. The knife was placed in accord with the longitudinal axis of the offering.

The first level of offering 31 was much richer in materials. Forming a homogeneous layer were 358 shells, 79 conch shells, 1 greenstone bead, unidentified bone remains, and fragments of branch coral. The animal remains came from different species; among them, mother-of-pearl shells and 3 *Strombus* conch shells oriented toward the east stood out. There was also the sawfish nose cartilage oriented in an E-W direction.

Level 2: The most important object in each offering was a jar with a modeled (offerings 21 and 56) or engraved (offering 31) Tlaloc face. The jar was polychrome, with blue, black, and white as the

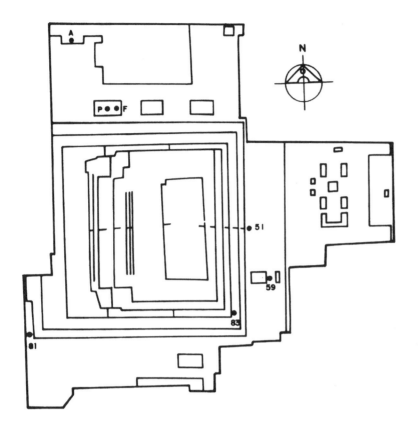

Figure 143:
The location of offerings in Complex J

predominant colors. The jar in offering 31 was on its side, the mouth turned to the west, similar to the containers of Complex N, in Chamber 2, and to offering 48. Inside each Tlaloc jar, several objects were found. The jars in offerings 21 and 56 had the same contents: 4 mother-of-pearl shells and 4 greenstone beads. In offering 31, the jar contained 3 Mezcala-style anthropomorphic sculptures. In both offerings 21 and 56, the Tlaloc jar was flanked by 2 copal balls.

COMPLEX J

Offerings: 83, F, 51, 59, A, P, and 81.
Number of offerings in complex: 7.
Dendrogram
> Split: 10 unshared presences/absences, coefficient of similarity = 0.79.
> Subgroups: 83–F (4 upas), 51–59 (4 upas), A–P (5 upas), 51–59–A–P (6 upas), 51–59–A–P–81 (9 upas).
> Relationships: It is tied to Complex I by 12 upas (0.74 coefficient of similarity).

Frequency of presences by object type complex
> Percentage of the total possible presences in each of the object type complexes: A (52.38%), B (42.85%), C (90.47%), D (0%), E (0%), F (0%), G (0%), H (0%), I (0.24%), J (14.28%), K (53.57%), L (0%), M (4.34%).

Most common object type complexes

Complexes C, K, A, and B.

Quantity and diversity of objects

Average number of elements: 42.14.

Range of the number of elements: 16–75.

Average number of object types: 8.28.

Range of the number of object types: 6–12.

Time and space locations of the offerings

Building: Huitzilopochtli (83, 81), Huitzilopochtli-Tlaloc (51), A (P, F), I (59), E (A).

Building stage: IVb (83), V (P), VII (F, 51, 59, A, 81).

Approximate date: 1469–1486 and 1502–1520.

Vertical location: floor (83), platform (51, 59, 81), stairway (F, A), temple (P).

Horizontal location: center (P), E (F, 51, 59), S center (A), SE (83), SW (81).

General characteristics of the offerings

Container: fill (F, 51, 59, A), sillares box (P, 81), fill under floor (83).

Primary orientation of objects: S (A), E (P), W (83, F, 51, 59, 81).

Number of excavation levels: 1 (51), 2 (83, 59, A), 3 (F), 5 (P, 81).

Number of proposed levels: 1 (51, 59, A), 2 (F), 3 (83, 81), 6 (P).

Maximum internal dimensions of the offerings (cm)

Offering	N-S axis	E-W axis	Z axis
83	75	90	
F	55	75	
51	85	75	
59	75	90	
A	72	72	
P	47	50	73
81	32	50	38

Distribution of objects (levels, axes, and groupings)

Offerings A, P, and 81 will be described separately because of their diversity in quantity and the placement of objects. On the other hand, offerings 88 and F (Subcomplex J_1) and offerings 51 and 59 (Subcomplex J_2) are very similar and will be described together.

Offering A

It was found in the building fill at the height of the sixth step of the north stairway. It was covered with a layer of tezontle and mortar. It had 1 level in which marine material and sacrificial knives painted with red and blue pigment predominated.

Level 1: This level had wood debris scattered over its entire surface. Thirteen flint sacrificial knives, sprinkled with red pigment and oriented to the south, were found in the center of the offering.

Some of the knives were partially buried under a layer of lace coral located in the northern half of the deposit. To the north was found 1 cluster of 21 olive shells, and another with 22 elements was to the south. Also found were 3 clusters, each having 5 copper bells, associated with the sacrificial knives. In the southern half of the deposit were grouped other marine objects: 1 *Xancus* conch shell (with its apex to the south), 12 small shells, 12 small conch shells, 1 mother-of-pearl shell, and the bone remains of porcupine fish and parrot fish.

Offering P

Because of its contents, this offering was closely related to Complex A. The offering box was located 40 cm under offering K. The sides, floor, and cover were made of flagstones. Six levels could be detected within.

Level 1: It contained 3 complete, anatomically undisturbed skeletons of golden eagles (the claws toward the west and the skulls to the east).

Level 2: A large number of marine remains were deposited throughout this offering. Most of them were concentrated at this level, perhaps because they were shifted by gravity. A total of 1,423 small conch shells were recorded, as well as 60 olive shells (necklace), small shells, lace coral, and the bone remains of fish.

Level 3: This level was composed of 17 copal anthropomorphic figures in an upright position but leaning on each other, all oriented to the east. They portrayed seated individuals with their hands on their knees. Some of them had copper bells at their feet. There were 1,134 small conch shells and 73 olive shells scattered among these figures.

Level 4: Presiding over this level was 1 sculpture of Xiuhtecuhtli and 1 container with a Tlaloc face made of black stone. Both images were leaning against the western wall (Tlaloc in the northwest corner) and oriented to the east.

Level 5: Five face-down mother-of-pearl shells partially covered the copal figures. At the eastern end, there was wood debris.

Level 6: Outside the offering box and partially resting against the western wall were 7 flint sacrificial knives, turned toward the east.

Offering 81

The objects were deposited in a box with tezontle sillares sides and a flagstone floor. During the excavation, we observed 3 different vertical levels.

Level 1: The deepest level consisted of a very thin layer of sand covering the southern half of the offering. To the north, we noticed an area with red and blue pigment.

Level 2: The second level was made up chiefly of flint sacrificial knives and marine material. Twenty-five knives formed a homogeneous layer covering the surface. They were oriented to the east. We found 2 concentrations of olive shells: 30 to the east and 30 more at the center. There were also 2 clusters of copper bells: 13 to the east and 13 to the west. Other objects were 1 *Xancus* conch shell at the northeast corner (with its apex to the west), 1 small shell, and the remains of sea urchins and 1 golden eagle (cranium to the east and claws to the west).

Level 3: A sculpture of Xiuhtecuhtli presided over this level. It was leaning against the western wall, looking toward the east. There were 5 copper bells above it. Just as in offering P, Xiuhtecuhtli's image was to the west, and the eagle's skull was to the east. Over the objects on level 2, there were remains of wood panels.

SUBCOMPLEX J$_1$

Offerings: 83 and F.
Number of offerings in complex: 2.
Dendrogram
  Split: 4 unshared presences/absences, coefficient of similarity = 0.91.
  Relationships: It is tied to offerings 51, 59, A, P, and 81 by 10 upas (0.79 coefficient of similarity).
Frequency of presences by object type complex
  Percentage of the total possible presences in each of the object type complexes: A (50%), B (100%), C (75%), D (0%), E (0%), F (0%), G (0%), H (0%), I (0%), J (0%), K (75%), L (0%), M (2.17%).
Most common object type complexes
  Complexes B, C, K, and A.
Quantity and diversity of objects
  Average number of elements: 22.5.
  Range of the number of elements: 16–29.
  Average number of object types: 8.
  Range of the number of object types: 8–8.
Time and space locations of the offerings
  Building: Huitzilopochtli (83), A (F).
  Building stage: IVb (83), VII (F).
  Approximate date: 1469–1481 and 1502–1520.
  Vertical location: floor (83), stairway (F).
  Horizontal location: E (F), SE (83).
  Comments: Contextually, offering 83 is very similar to the offerings of Complex A.
General characteristics of the offerings
  Container: fill under floor (83), fill (F).
  Primary orientation of objects: W (both).
  Number of excavation levels: 2 (83), 3 (F).

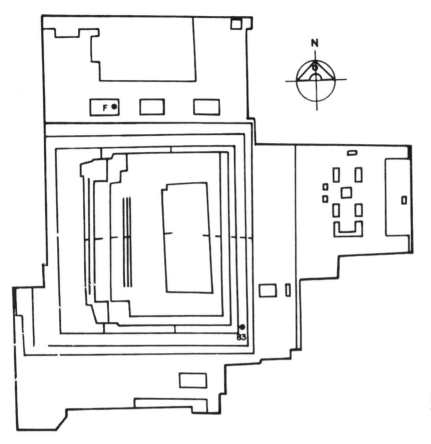

Figure 144:
The location of offerings in Subcomplex J$_1$

Number of proposed levels: 2 (F), 3 (83).

Maximum internal dimensions of the offerings (cm)

Offering	N-S axis	E-W axis
83	75	90
F	55	75

Distribution of objects (levels, axes, and groupings)

These offerings were laid on a layer of earth inside the building fill and covered with large flagstones. There were 3 levels for placing objects in offering 83; F had only 2. The principal objects are sculptures of Tlaloc and Xiuhtecuhtli, which is why this complex is closely associated with the offerings of Complex A.

Level 1: This level is composed of a homogeneous layer of flint sacrificial knives, copal, conch shells, and other objects. In offering 83 we found 14 knives, 13 of them oriented to the west and 1 to the north. All of them had the remains of wood stuck to 1 of their sides. On some knives, there were traces of red coloring. Offering F had 45 knives, 25 oriented to the west and 20 to the east. Two had traces of red paint, and 1 had traces of copal; another showed traces of the application of flint (personified knife). Conch shells were also numerous. In offering 83, there were 9 olive shells pointed to the north and 12 to the south; in F, there were 24 olive shells in the eastern half and 14 of different species scattered around. We also found small fragments of copal: 2 in the center of offering 83 and 1 on the south of offering F. Both had different objects: 1 anthropomorphic bead and 2 spherical greenstone beads in offering 83; 8 projectile points (4 obsidian at the bottom and 4 flint ones higher up), 55 spherical copper bells and 18 elongated ones (in the center of E), and 1 curved obsidian blade (to the west and oriented to the east) in offering F.

Level 2: Three images of gods presided over this level: 1 black tezontle Tlaloc jar, 1 red tezontle Xiuhtecuhtli, and 1 copal anthropomorphic figure. In offering 83, they were placed in the northern half (Tlaloc a little more to the west than Xiuhtecuhtli) and oriented to the west. The copal figure was unintentionally removed during the excavation of the fill, but apparently it was placed to the north. In offering F, these images were placed in the center (Tlaloc's image a little more to the north, Xiuhtecuhtli in the center, and the copal figure a little more to the south) and oriented to the west.

Level 3: Offering 83 had a third level, consisting of 5 large pieces of badly preserved, red-colored wood.

SUBCOMPLEX J₂

Offerings: 51 and 59.
Number of offerings in complex: 2.
Dendrogram
    Split: 4 unshared presences/absences, coefficient of similarity = 0.91.
    Relationships: It is tied to offerings A and P by 6 upas (0.87 coefficient of similarity).
Frequency of presences by object type complex
    Percentage of the total possible presences in each of the object type complexes: A (33.33%), B (0%), C (100%), D (0%), E (0%), F (0%), G (0%), H (0%), I (0%), J (0%), K (37.5%), L (0%), M (4.34%).
Most common object type complexes
    Complexes C, K, and A.
Quantity and diversity of objects
    Average number of elements: 43.5.
    Range of the number of elements: 16–71.
    Comments: The average and the range do not correspond to the facts because all the knives in offering 51 were recorded with a single element number.
    Average number of object types: 6.5.
    Range of the number of object types: 7.
Time and space locations of the offerings
    Building: Huitzilopochtli-Tlaloc (51), I (59).

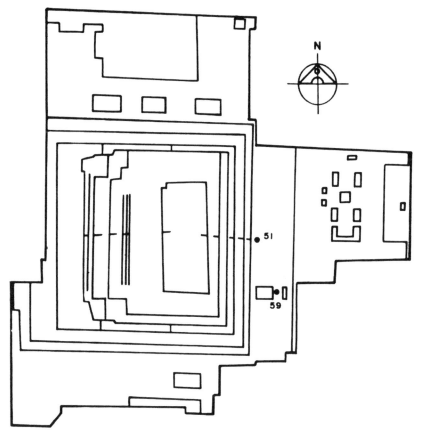

Figure 145:
The location of offerings
in Subcomplex J_2

Building stage: VII (both).

Approximate date: 1502–1520.

Vertical location: platform (both).

Horizontal location: E (both).

Comments: Both offerings are very similar in context.

Offering 59 had a contextual relationship with offerings 57 and 65. Offering 51 is between two
  pairs of offerings: 49–59 (Subcomplex F_2) and 52–57 (Complex G).

General characteristics of the offerings

Container: fill (both).

Primary orientation of objects: W (both).

Number of excavation levels: 1 (51), 2 (59).

Number of proposed levels: 1 (both).

Maximum internal dimensions of the offerings (cm)

Offering	N-S axis	E-W axis
51	85	75
59	75	90

Distribution of objects (levels, axes, and groupings)
The offerings of this subcomplex were very similar in their internal arrangements. There was 1 level of objects placed inside the building fill.

Level 1: The predominating material consisted of flint sacrificial knives. Offering 51 had 53 knives, 48 of them oriented westward and 5 to the east. Offering 59 had 54 knives, 50 turned to the west and 4 to the east. The latter were decorated with red, green, black, or white paint or a combination of two or more of them. In both offerings, we found fragments of deteriorated wood aligned longitudinally from north to south. To the east, we found 2 corals (1 branch and 1 lace) oriented to the north and 100 copper bells. There were also necklaces of olive shells: 30 in the northwest corner of offering 51 and 35 in the southwest corner of offering 59. In offering 51, there were 2 sculptures of Xiuhtecuhtli (1 to the north and 1 to the south) oriented toward the west and the jawbones of 7 rattlesnakes. Offering 59 included the skull of 1 eagle (southwest corner), serpent vertebrae with red and blue pigment (northwest corner), and the bone remains of 1 needlefish.

COMPLEX K

Offerings: 86, B, 53, and B2.
Number of offerings in complex: 4.
Dendrogram
    Split: 11 unshared presences/absences, coefficient of similarity = 0.77.
    Subgroups: 86–B (4 upas), 86–B–53 (5 upas).
    Relationships: It is tied to offering 85 by 16 upas (0.66 coefficient of similarity).
    Comments: According to the dendrogram, offering B2 is very different from the 3 others.
Frequency of presences by object type complex
    Percentage of the total possible presences in each of the object type complexes: A (58.33%), B (50%), C (50%), D (0%), E (12.5%), F (0%), G (0%), H (0%), I (0.43%), J (0%), K (12.5%), L (75%), M (10.86%).
Most common object type complexes
    Complexes L, A, B, and C.
Quantity and diversity of objects
    Average number of elements: 26.
    Range of the number of elements: 6–61.
    Average number of object types: 8.75.
    Range of the number of object types: 5–12.
Time and space locations of the offerings
    Building: Huitzilopochtli (B2), Tlaloc (86, 53), E (B).
    Building stage: IVb (53), V (86, B2), VII (B).
    Approximate date: 1469–1486 and 1502–1520.
    Vertical location: floor (53), platform (B2, 86), stairway (B).

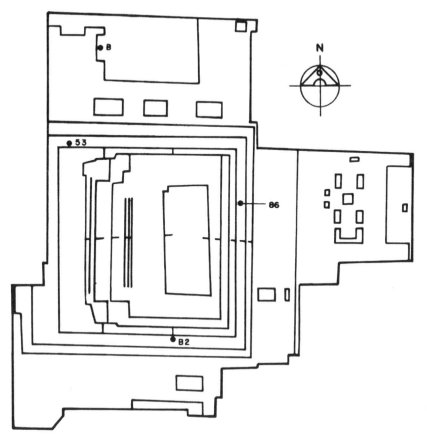

Figure 146:
The location of offerings in Complex K

Horizontal location: S center (B2), E (86), W (B), NW (53).
Comments: These offerings are very different in context.

General characteristics of the offerings

Container: fill (86, B, B2), fill under floor (53).
Primary orientation of objects: S (53, B2), E (86), W (B).
Number of excavation levels: 1 (86, B, B2), 2 (B).
Number of proposed levels: 1 (B2), 2 (86, 53), 3 (B).

Maximum internal dimensions of the offerings (cm)

Offering	N-S axis	E-W axis
86	33	4
B	65	85
53	55	30
B2	?	?

Distribution of objects (levels, axes, and groupings)

The offerings of Complex K share the presence of sacrificial knives, disks, and shell oyohualli. However, the internal distribution of these offerings differs greatly. Therefore, they are described separately.

Offering 86

The objects of the offering were found inside the earth and rock fill of Stage V. It is easy to detect 2 different levels for placing objects.

Level 1: The deepest level was covered by a very thin layer of sand, not over 1 cm thick.

Level 2: The second level is characterized by 2 flint sacrificial knives oriented to the east and 5 randomly placed greenstone beads. In the center of the deposit, between the knives, were placed 1 perforated disk and 2 shell oyohualli.

Offering B

It was found in the building fill, on a thick layer of mortar that, at the same time, rested against the third step of stairway E. The offering had 3 levels.

Level 1: This level had a thin layer of very deteriorated wood.

Level 2: It was composed of 32 flint sacrificial knives that formed a homogeneous layer: 30 had copal applications on the bottom end, 1 had a flint appliqué in the form of a tooth, and 1 had traces of red paint. Twenty-nine were oriented to the west and 3 to the east. Associated with them were 2 greenstone beads, the bone remains of a serpent, 2 shell disks, and 2 oyohualli. At each corner (NE, NW, SE, and SW), there was 1 mortar and 1 curved obsidian blade.

Level 3: On the third level, there were 4 anthropomorphic copal figures, 2 large and 2 small. The large figures were placed in the center of the offering (1 facing east and 1 west). The small figures were at the eastern end, oriented to the west. At the western end of the offering, there were 4 mother-of-pearl shells, 3 small conch shells, fragments of shells, and 1 *Xancus* conch shell (with the apex pointed east).

Offering 53

It was found 64 cm under the stucco floor of Stage IVb. The offering was placed in the fill and covered with a rectangular block of mortar. Two placement levels and 1 annex were detected (1 m to the north of the offering).

Level 1: The first level was composed of a layer of earth mixed with spherical seeds 2 mm in diameter.

Level 2: At this level, there were 2 copal anthropomorphic figures, oriented to the south: 1 on the northwest corner and 1 on the southwest. Five greenstone beads were associated with the figure on the northwest corner. A flint knife oriented to the south lay partly under the figure at the southeastern corner.

Annex: Directly on top of the building fill, there was 1 disk and 2 shell oyohualli.

Offering B2

It was located in the building fill of Stage V. In the center of the offering was placed a skull-mask belonging to a child (about 5 years old). A necklace of 10 olive shells was associated with the skull-mask. Other objects recovered were fragments of copal, several conch shells, 1 shell, 1 circular object of travertine, 1 bar of copal, 1 *Strombus* conch shell, 1 obsidian projectile point, copper bells, 1 mother-of-pearl shell, thorns, 3 jadeite tripod vessels decorated with red paint, 5 flint sacrificial knives decorated with red paint, 2 disks, and 2 shell oyohualli disks.

COMPLEX L

Offerings: 8, 92, and 12.
Number of offerings in complex: 3.
Dendrogram
    Split: 7 unshared presences/absences, coefficient of similarity = 0.85.
    Subgroups: 8–92 (6 upas).
    Relationships: It is tied to Complexes M, N, O, P, Q, R, and S, with Burial 1, and with offerings 16, 38, 71, 76, and 30 by 11 upas (0.77 coefficient of similarity).
Frequency of presences by object type complex
    Percentage of the total possible presences in each of the object type complexes: A (22.22%), B (33.33%), C (33.33%), D (33.33%), E (16.66%), F (16.66%), G (0%), H (0%), I (1.14%), J (83.33%), K (0%), L (0%), M (4.34%).
Most common object type complexes
    Complexes J, B, C, and D.
Quantity and diversity of objects
    Average number of elements: 17.66.
    Range of the number of elements: 7–25.
    Average number of object types: 6.66.
    Range of the number of object types: 5–8.
Time and space locations of the offerings
    Building: Huitzilopochtli (all).
    Building stage: IV (8), IVa (92), IVb (12).
    Approximate date: 1440–1481.
    Vertical location: floor (12), platform (92), main body (8).
    Horizontal location: E (8, 12), W (92).
    Comments: Although offering 8 was found in the main body of Stage III, it was deposited when Stage IV was being built. This is shown by the fill that was reused to cover this offering, as well as that of 21, both forming part of the building system of Stage IV. The boxes were probably built into the body of Stage III during an enlargement, or the boxes of former

offerings may have been used. This would explain why offering 21, even though it was located at Stage III, was identical to offering 56 built in the filling at Stage IV (see Complex I). As a result, the link that Graulich (1977) indicated between offering 8 and glyph 4 Acatl at Stage III does not exist.

General characteristics of the offerings

Container: sillares box (8), fill under floor (92, 12).

Primary orientation of objects: W (all).

Number of excavation levels: 1 (8, 12), 2 (92), 1 (12), 2 (8, 92).

Maximum internal dimensions of the offerings (cm)

Offering	N-S axis	E-W axis	Z axis
8	100	74	71
92	60	100	
12	33	26	

Distribution of objects (levels, axes, and groupings)

The 3 offerings that make up this complex are very different in their temporal placement and the internal distribution of objects. The common denominators were sacrificial knives and quail remains, as well as their location in the Huitzilopochtli Temple. The 3 offerings will be described separately.

Offering 8

The objects in this offering were placed in a box with tezontle sillares sides and a floor of quarry stone sillares. The box was made on the landing of the first body of Stage III. The offering was not sealed with a lid but was covered with the tezontle and earth of the next stage, which intruded almost to the floor. It was possible to detect 2 vertical object levels.

Level 1: Nine flint sacrificial knives were found at the center of the offering. Three were oriented to the east and 6 to the west. Six conch shells were associated with them. At the eastern end, there were 2 clusters of an unidentified white material.

Level 2: At this level, there were skeletons of 5 montezuma quail, bone remains of fish, 2 skulls and remains of rattlesnake skin, and the jawbone of an American mouse (probably an intrusion). At the center of the offering were traces of burned soil and 4 Aztec-type potsherds mixed in the fill that covered the offering.

Offering 92

Offering 92 was found in the building fill of Stage IVa, precisely under the stucco floor located at the foot of the Coyolxauhqui II sculpture. It had been placed on a layer of earth and tezontle stone. The offering had 2 levels.

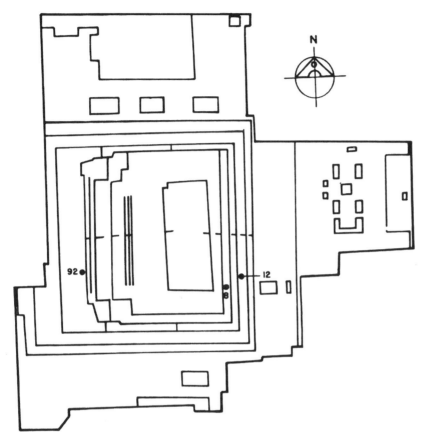

Figure 147:
The location of offerings
in Complex L

Level 1: At this level, there was a sawfish nose cartilage oriented in an E-W direction, 1 obsidian prismatic blade, and 180 greenstone beads forming a necklace.

Level 2: In the center of the upper level were 10 flint sacrificial knives. Seven were oriented to the east and 1 to the west. Also found were 40 olive shells, 265 carbonate beads painted blue, 1 ball of copal, and the skeletons of 12 quail.

Offering 12

It was found on the layer of tezontle and earth that covered Stage IV, under the flagstone floor of Stage IVb. It had only 1 level. This offering can be related to those of Complex A by their spatial location and the presence of 3 Tlaloc jars and a brazier with a bow knot.

Level 1: At the center, there were 3 small greenstone Tlaloc jars, 2 copper bells, 1 greenstone anthropomorphic Mezcala-style figure, and 1 basalt brazier adorned with a bow knot. All the objects were oriented to the west. Also recorded were 1 flint sacrificial knife (oriented to the south), quail and fish bones, and 3 teeth from the sawfish nose cartilage.

COMPLEX M

Offerings: 33 and 40.

Number of offerings in complex: 2.

Dendrogram

Split: 3 unshared presences/absences, coefficient of similarity = 0.94.

Subgroups: none.

Relationships: It is tied to offerings 2, 16, and 38 by 6 upas (0.87 coefficient of similarity).

Frequency of presences by object type complex

Percentage of the total possible presences in each of the object type complexes: A (33.33%), B (100%), C (0%), D (25%), E (0%), F (0%), G (0%), H (0%), I (2.58%), J (50%), K (0%), L (0%), M (0%).

Most common object type complexes

Complexes B, A, and J.

Quantity and diversity of objects

Average number of elements: 9.5.

Range of the number of elements: 5–14.

Average number of object types: 5.

Range of the number of object types: 5–5.

Time and space locations of the offerings

Building: Huitzilopochtli (33), Tlaloc (40).

Building stage: II (both).

Approximate date: 1375–1427.

Vertical location: temple (both).

Horizontal location: center (both).

Comments: Both offerings are placed symmetrically in space.

General characteristics of the offerings

Container: sillares box (33), fill under floor (40).

Primary orientation of objects: W (both).

Number of excavation levels: 1 (40), 2 (33).

Number of proposed levels: 3 (both).

Maximum internal dimensions of the offerings (cm)

Offering	N-S axis	E-W axis	Z axis
33	22	22	20
40	60	80	

Distribution of objects (levels, axes, and groupings)

Offerings 33 and 40 were quite different in their distribution of objects, although both are similar in the quality of their contents and their spatial distribution. They will be described separately.

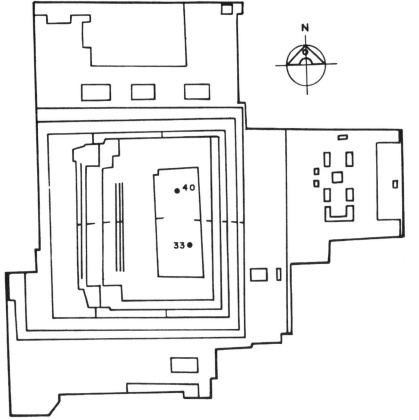

Figure 148:
The location of offerings
in Complex M

Offering 33

This offering was deposited in an irregularly shaped box with walls of tezontle sillares and a tezontle and earth floor. The cover was the stucco floor of Stage II. Three levels were detected, and polished stone objects were the most prominent.

Level 1: The first level consisted of a thin homogeneous layer of charcoal.

Level 2: Found here were the bone remains of 2 spotted quail and 1 bird of the *Tyrannidae* genus. The remains were scattered in a haphazard fashion and showed no anatomical relationships. We also found 2 amorphous masses of copal at the northern and western ends of the box. Finally, at the southeastern corner, there were 3 stone beads and a greenstone *chimalli* ("shield") representation.

Level 3: The last level was made up of greenstone beads. In the center, there was a tubular greenstone bead and, over it, 1 helicoidal bead. Both were oriented in an E-W direction. There was also a spherical greenstone bead at each corner of the box (NE, NW, SE, and SW).

Offering 40

It was deposited in a cavity made in the earth and stone fill and covered with a quarry stone sillar. There were 3 levels, where objects of polished stone predominated.

Level 1: There was a 20-cm-deep charcoal layer at the bottom of the deposit.

Level 2: A ball of copal was at the center of the offering, and at the western end, there were 2 clusters of 3 greenstone beads, remains of rubber, and quail bones.

Level 3: A few potsherds were placed at the highest level.

COMPLEX N

Offerings: 28, 43, 26, 25, 35, and 47.
Number of offerings in complex: 6.
Dendrogram
    Split: 1 unshared presences/absences, coefficient of similarity = 0.98.
    Subgroups: 28–43–26–25 (0 upas), 35–47 (0 upas).
    Relationships: It is tied to Complexes O, P, Q, and R, with Burial 1, and with offerings 71, 76, and 30 by 5 upas (0.89 coefficient of similarity).
Frequency of presences by object type complex
    Percentage of the total possible presences in each of the object type complexes: A (33.33%), B (33.33%), C (0%), D (0%), E (100%), F (0%), G (0%), H (0%), I (0%), J (0%), K (0%), L (0%), M (0%).
Most common object type complexes
    Complexes E, A, and B.
Quantity and diversity of objects
    Average number of elements: 3.3.
    Range of the number of elements: 3–4.
    Average number of object types: 3.3.
    Range of the number of object types: 3–4.
Time and space locations of the offerings
    Building: Tlaloc (all).
    Building stage: III (all).
    Approximate date: 1427–1440.
    Vertical location: main body (all).
    Horizontal location: E (43, 26, 25, 47), N (28), NE (35).
General characteristics of the offerings
    Container: fill (all).
    Primary orientation of objects: N (28, 26, 25, 35), W (43, 47).

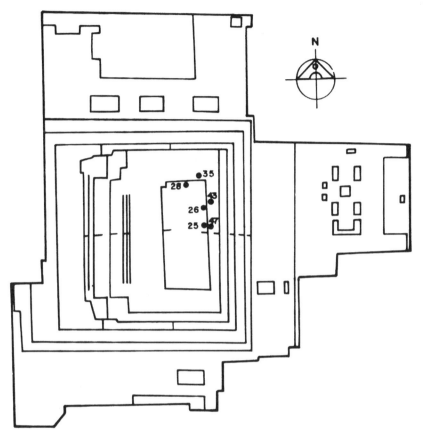

Figure 149:
The location of offerings in Complex N

Number of excavation levels: 1 (all).
Number of proposed levels: 1 (all).

Maximum internal dimensions of the offerings (cm)

Offering	N-S axis	E-W axis
28	30	30
43	30	30
26	30	30
25	30	30
35	30	30
47	30	30

Distribution of objects (levels, axes, and groupings)
The offerings of this complex were deposited while the construction of Stage III was under way. Offerings 25, 26, and 35 were placed on a layer of earth and stone and covered with very fine soil. Offerings 43 and 47 were also protected with large flagstones. In every case, the wall of Stage II was the border for depositing gifts.

All the offerings were on 1 level, and their principal contents were ceramic containers and greenstone beads.

Level 1: This level was characterized by the presence of 1 jar and 1 small cajete, and both were orange ceramic monochrome with spots of blue. The jar in offering 28 also had traces of white and orange coloring, and the one in offering 35 had pairs of black stripes. The cajetes in offerings 25, 35, and 43 had a tripod support, and the others were on a flat base. The cajetes in offerings 26 and 28 retained traces of red paint, with white geometric designs.

In all the offerings, the jars had been intentionally placed on their sides. Jars in offerings 28, 26, 25, and 35 had their mouths to the north, and those of offerings 43 and 47 were turned to the west. Directly under the mouth of each jar was placed a cajete, seeming to receive the liquid poured from above. The only exception was the cajete in offering 25, placed in an upright position as a covering for the jar.

All the jars had greenstone beads inside: 3 tubular and 1 spherical in offering 25; 3 tubular, 1 spherical, and 1 plant-shaped in 26; and 3 spherical in 28.

Also recorded were charcoal remains under the jar in offering 26 and copal remains in offerings 35 and 47.

COMPLEX O

Offerings: 67, 75, and 63.
Number of offerings in complex: 3.
Dendrogram
  Split: 0 unshared presences/absences, coefficient of similarity = 1.
  Subgroups: none.
  Relationships: It is tired to offering 91 by 1 upas (0.98 coefficient of similarity).
Frequency of presences by object type complex
  Percentage of the total possible presences in each of the object type complexes: A (0%), B (100%), C (0%), D (0%), E (0%), F (0%), G (0%), H (0%), I (0%), J (0%), K (0%), L (0%), M (0%).
Most common object type complexes
  Complex B.
Quantity and diversity of objects
  Average number of elements: 1.
  Range of the number of elements: 1.
  Average number of object types: 1.
  Range of the number of object types: 1.
Time and space locations of the offerings
  Building: Tlaloc (all).
  Building stage: IVb.

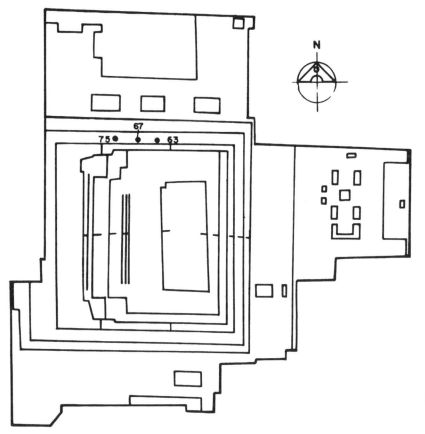

Figure 150:
The location of offerings
in Complex O

Approximate date: 1469–1481.

Vertical location: floor (all).

Horizontal location: NW (all).

Comments: It is very probable that 3 more similar offerings still exist, placed symmetrically
south of the Templo Mayor on the Huitzilopochtli side, below the floor of Stage IVb.

General characteristics of the offerings

Container: fill under the floor (all).

Primary orientation of objects: N (all).

Number of excavation levels: 1 (all).

Number of proposed levels: 1 (all).

Maximum internal dimensions of the offerings (cm)

Offering	N-S axis	E-W axis
67	60	60
75	60	60
63	60	60

Distribution of objects (levels, axes, and groupings)
The offerings of Complex O were deposited 160 cm deep under the flagstone floor of Stage IVb. They were placed inside the building fill, on a thin layer of compacted earth and surrounded by sillares to protect them. The offerings were copal cylinders placed on 1 level.

Level 1: This level has only 1 cylinder, approximately 30 cm in diameter and 30 cm in height. Each cylinder had a slight depression in the central part of its upper side. It was in a poor state of preservation.

COMPLEX P

Offerings: 72 and 73.
Number of offerings in complex: 2.
Dendrogram
　Split: 0 unshared presences/absences, coefficient of similarity = 1.
　Subgroups: none.
　Relationships: It is tied to Complexes Q and R and with offering 71 by 2 upas (0.96 coefficient of similarity).
Frequency of presences by object type complex
　Percentage of the total possible presences in each of the object type complexes: A (0%), B (0%), C (0%), D (0%), E (0%), F (0%), G (0%), H (0%), I (0%), J (0%), K (0%), L (0%), M (4.3%).
Most common object type complexes
　Complex M.
Quantity and diversity of objects
　Average number of elements: 1.
　Range of the number of elements: 1.
　Average number of object types: 1.
　Range of the number of object types: 1.
Time and space locations of the offerings
　Building: 1 (both).
　Building stage: VI (both).
　Approximate date: 1486–1502.
　Vertical location: floor (both).
　Horizontal location: E (both).
General characteristics of the offerings
　Container: fill (both).
　Primary orientation of objects: N (72), undetermined (73).
　Number of excavation levels: 1 (both).
　Number of proposed levels: 1 (both).

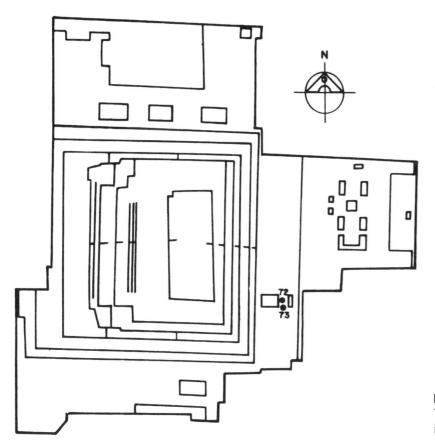

Figure 151:
The location of offerings
in Complex P

Maximum internal dimensions of the offerings (cm)

Offering	N-S axis	E-W axis	Z axis
72	87	60	18
73	20	20	5

Distribution of objects (levels, axes, and groupings)

The offerings of Complex P were deposited on a layer of earth inside the fill. There was 1 level of maguey thorns.

Level 1: There was an irregular cluster of maguey thorns; their length varied between 5 and 8 cm. They had no particular orientation, nor did their points converge toward 1 point. In offering 72, a few remains of maguey stalk skin accompanied the numerous thorns.

COMPLEX Q

Offerings: M, D, C, 90, 79, 55, 36, 32, 4, 2, 77, and 91.
Number of offerings in complex: 12.

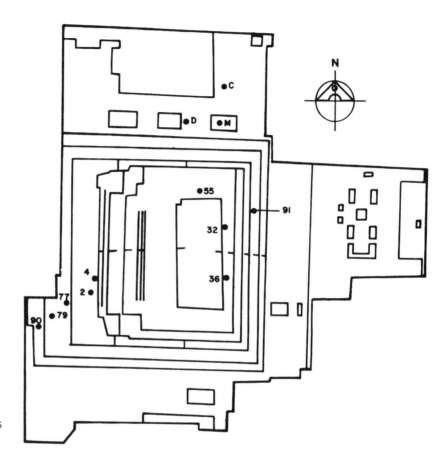

Figure 152:
The location of offerings
in Complex Q

Dendrogram

Split: Offerings M, D, C, 90, 79, 55, 36, 32, and 4 have 0 unshared presences/absences, coefficient of similarity = 1.

Subgroups: none.

Relationships: The offerings M, D, C, 90, 79, 55, 36, 32, and 4 are tied to Complexes P and R and with offering 71 by 2 upas (0.96 coefficient of similarity). Offering 2 is tied to offering 16 by 4 upas (0.91 coefficient of similarity). Offering 77 is tied to offerings 87 and 27, which belong in Complex H by 6 upas (0.87 coefficient of similarity). Offering 91 is tied to Complex O by 1 upas (0.98 coefficient of similarity).

Comments: Although they contain several elements, offerings 2, 77, and 91 were very altered when found. Therefore, they were incorporated into Complex Q and not into the complexes generated by the computer dendrogram.

Frequency of presences by object type complex

Percentage of total possible presences in each of the object type complexes: Offerings M, D, C, 90, 79, 55, 36, 32, and 4: A (0%), B (0%), C (0%), D (0%), E (0%), F (0%), G (0%), H (0%), I (0%), J (0%), K (0%), L (0%), M (0%). Offering 2: A (33.33%), B (0%), C (33.33%),

D (0%), E (0%), F (0%), G (33.33%), H (0%), I (0%), J (0%), K (0%), L (0%), M (0%). Offering 77: A (100%), B (0%), C (33.33%), D (50%), E (0%), F (0%), G (0%), H (0%), I (1.7%), J (0%), K (0%), L (0%), M (4.3%). Offering 91: A (33.33%), B (100%), C (0%), D (0%), E (0%), F (0%), G (0%), H (0%), I (0%), J (0%), K (0%), L (0%), M (0%).

Quantity and diversity of objects

Average number of elements: 0.

Range of the number of elements: 0.

Average number of object types: 0.

Range of the number of object types: 0.

Time and space locations of the offerings

Building: Huitzilopochtli (36, 90, 79, 4, 2, 77), Tlaloc (91, 55, 32), B (D), C (M), E (C).

Building stage: III (55, 36, 32), IVb (2, 4, 91), V (77), VI (79, 90), VII (M, D, C).

Approximate date: 1427–1440 and 1469–1520.

Vertical location: floor (D, 90), platform (79, 4, 2, 77), main body (C, 55, 36, 32), temple (M).

Horizontal location: center (M), N center (55), E (D, 36, 32, 91), W (C, 90, 79, 4, 2, 77).

General characteristics of the offerings

Container: sillares box (M, D, C, 90, 79, 55, 32, 4, 2, 77, 36), fill under floor (91).

Primary orientation of objects: undetermined (all).

Number of excavation levels: 0 (M, D, C, 90, 79, 55, 36, 32, 4), 1 (2, 77), 2 (91).

Number of proposed levels: 0 (M, D, C, 90, 79, 55, 36, 32, 4), 1 (77, 2), 2 (91).

Maximum internal dimensions of the offerings (cm)

Offering	N-S axis	E-W axis	Z axis
M	150	99	200
D	?	?	?
C	85	85	45
90	43	44	53
79	60	125	100
55	40	45	25
36	60	60	?
32	55	85	45
4	85	230	125
2	40	50	80
77	80	100	35
91	20	16	

Distribution of objects (levels, axes, and groupings)

All the offerings that were altered after deposition and those which, for sundry reasons, cannot be compared with offerings of other complexes have been placed in this complex. The 12 offerings that compose Complex Q can be divided into 3 groups.

Offerings With a Cultural Transformation

Included here are the offerings intentionally or unintentionally altered by humans. We observed that 2 offerings (79 and 90) had been disturbed, possibly in pre-Hispanic times. One offering (D) was destroyed during the colonial era, and 4 other offerings (M, C, 77, and 2) had undergone looting in the twentieth century.

Offering 79

This box had tezontle sides and a flagstone floor. When it was excavated, the eastern side and cover were missing. The staircase in which it was located was also partially destroyed. There were no objects inside. It should be mentioned that it was near the main drain line of 1900.

Offering 90

The walls of this offering were made with 4 flagstones in a vertical position and another for the floor. It lacked a cover. Inside, we found tezontle pieces, mortar, and sand. The archaeologist Isabel Gutiérrez believes the offering was extracted and then filled with mortar and rock when Stage VII of the building was under construction.

Offering D

The flagstone box was found to be partially destroyed. Inside were several pre-Hispanic and colonial potsherds.

Offering M

It is a box with tezontle sides and a floor of flagstones covered with plaster. A modern concrete foundation rested directly above the box. It was filled with tezontle stones and the remains of a ceramic brazier. Outside the box, we found 1 flagstone, shaped like a sacrificial knife (similar to those in offering 78, which is its symmetrical pair). There were impressions on the sediment of what could have been representations of musical instruments (see Olmedo 2002).

Offering C

This offering was inside a tezontle box with a flagstone cover and floor. A modern foundation of concrete had been built 10 cm above the box. The box had been partially destroyed, and inside, there were only stones and hard-packed earth.

Offering 77

This offering featured a box with tezontle sides and a flagstone floor. The western side had been destroyed by a telephone conduit. The offering was empty. Around it, there were isolated remnants of ceramics, bone, wood, conch shells, shells, and beveled turquoise, as well as 2 copper bells, 1 obsidian projectile point, and 2 greenstone beads. Fragments of plastic and cigarette packs were also found as intrusive material.

Offering 2

The box was made of tezontle; the cover and floor were quarry stone covered with plaster. According to García Cook and Arana (1978: 50), the southern wall was pried loose and the offering sacked in 1900, when the drain that crosses the archaeological zone was built.

Offerings Altered by Nature

In this group are all the offerings modified by an act of nature. Some offerings, in spite of not showing any evident alteration, had bone remains of mammals from both the Old and the New World, which probably came into them after their original placement. For example, the remains of a gopher were identified in offering 62, a mouse in offering 8, a Mexican meadow mouse in offering 20, a mouse and a rat in offering 6, and a sheep in offering 11. As to the severely damaged deposits, we found 1 offering (36) altered by rodents and 2 empty offerings (32 and 55) that probably contained organic material that had decayed to the point of leaving no trace of its past existence.

Offering 36

Only the hewn tezontle stone north wall and part of the eastern wall remained of this offering. It had been converted into a mouse burrow. Among the remains removed were a large rat bone, a mouse's jaw, 2 plastic combs, a plastic strip, a piece of automobile tire, tin foil, cockroach remains, glass vials, and 1 flint knife with remains of copal. This knife does not appear on the general listing because it was recorded as an independent element.

Offering 32

The box of this offering was intact. It had sides and a cover of quarry stone and a flagstone floor. Inside, there was a thin layer of sediment that probably came in through some hole. An analysis of the sediment showed no plant remains.

Offering 55

The sides and floor of this offering were tezontle sillares. A stone flagstone partially covered the box. Earth from the fill had infiltrated inside, and there were charcoal and ash remains. The walls showed sign of having been burned.

Atypical Offerings

Under this heading are the offerings that, for particular reasons, cannot be compared with the others. I refer to offering 4, which is really a passage that served as an antechamber to offering 5 and was mistakenly reported as a looted offering, and to offering 91, which was only partially excavated.

Offering 4

The north, east, and south sides were made of quarry stone sillares held together with mud. The western side is convex and was built of tezontle sillares. García Cook and Arana (1978: 55–56) commented about offering 4:

> We are convinced, by what we saw in exploring the inner nucleus of the cyst, that in Prehispanic times the cyst was excavated and prepared for placing some kind of offering. But when the stucco floor of the preceding period was broken, a floor with reliefs of the same type as those on the monolith [of Coyolxauhqui] was found. This is why no other offering was placed over these reliefs and why they [the Mexica] again covered them carefully and respectfully.

However, upon excavating the symmetrically corresponding area in the Tlaloc Temple, we detected an identical structure. We could see that it was not made to contain an offering but was an antechamber, or entrance passage, to Chamber 2. In the comparison, it was evident that the so-called offering 4 was not that but, in fact, was the entrance to offering 5 (also called Chamber 1). Just as in the case of offering 4, we found the access passage to Chamber 2 filled with dirt and tezontle. Building both antechambers was logical if we take into account that the antechambers were built first and that the stairway of the edifice was built over them at a later time. The only way to enter the chambers to deposit gifts during the consecration ceremonies was through an antechamber. Once the offerings had been deposited, the antechambers were refilled, making them the floor of the platform.

Offering 91

This offering was placed in the fill underneath the flagstone floor. Greenstone anthropomorphic sculptures, pendants, and beads, as well as copal fragments, were removed during the excavation. Unfortunately, the work of excavation remained unfinished because the time limit for excavation of the Templo Mayor Project came to an end. The deposit was sealed off in the hope that, at some future date, the work may be resumed.

COMPLEX R

Offerings: O and G.
Number of offerings in complex: 2.

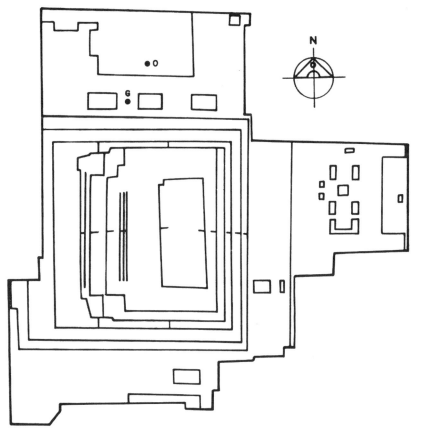

Figure 153:
The location of offerings in Complex R

Dendrogram

Split: 0 unshared presences/absences, coefficient of similarity = 1.

Subgroups: none.

Relationships: It is tied to Complexes P and Q and with offering 71 by 2 upas (0.96 coefficient of similarity).

Frequency of presences by object type complex

Percentage of the total possible presences in each of the object type complexes: A (0%), B (0%), C (0%), D (0%), E (0%), F (0%), G (0%), H (0%), I (1.72%), J (0%), K (0%), L (0%), M (0%).

Most common object type complexes

Complex I.

Quantity and diversity of objects

Average number of elements: 1.

Range of the number of elements: 1–1.

Average number of object types: 1.

Range of the number of object types: 1–1.

Time and space locations of the offerings

Building: North plaza (G), E (O).

Building stage: V (O), VI (G).

Approximate date: 1481–1502.

Vertical location: floor (G), temple (O).

Horizontal location: center (both).

General characteristics of the offerings

Container: fill under floor (G), sillares box (O).

Primary orientation of objects: undetermined (both).

Number of excavation levels: 1 (both).

Number of proposed levels: 1 (both).

Maximum internal dimensions of the offerings (cm)

Offering	N-S axis	E-W axis	Z axis
G	73 (diameter)	73 (diameter)	42
O	122	122	50

Distribution of objects (levels, axes, and groupings)

The box for offering O had a flagstone floor and sides of vertical quarry stone sillares. It was deposited under the stucco floor of Room 1 of Building E (the House of Eagles). Offering G was placed between Building A and B under the flagstone floor of the plaza. The floor of this offering was made with flagstones 42 cm under the surface. Both offerings had 1 level of ash mixed with clayey mud and small fragments of charcoal.

Level 1: In offering O, there was a layer of ash mixed with clayey mud between 2 and 15 cm thick. This layer was covered with approximately 10 cm of earth and, higher up, with tezontle stones. The offering was not sealed, perhaps because the receptacle was used daily to burn charcoal. Because of its position inside the precinct, there is no doubt that it was a *tlecuil* ("fire pit"). When Stage VI was built, it was covered with tezontle stones. Offering G had a 42-cm layer of ash mixed with clayey mud (approximately 0.175m^3).

COMPLEX S

Offerings: Ñ, 93, and I.

Number of offerings in complex: 3.

Dendrogram

Split: 4 unshared presences/absences, coefficient of similarity = 0.91.

Subgroups: Ñ–93 (3 upas).

Relationships: It is tied to Complexes N, O, P, Q, R, with Burial 1, and with offerings 71, 76, and 30 by 6 upas (0.87 coefficient of similarity).

Frequency of presences by object type complex

Percentage of the total possible presences in each of the object type complexes: A (0%), B (66.66%), C (55.55%), D (0%), E (0%), F (0%), G (0%), H (0%), I (0%), J (33.33%),

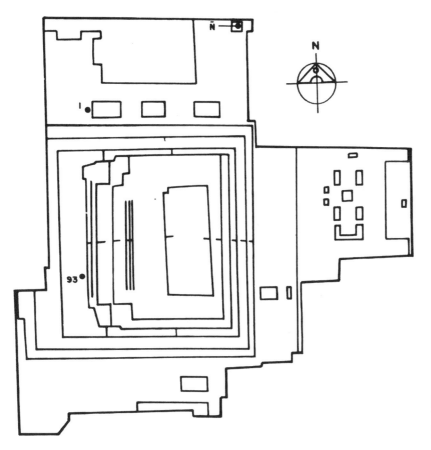

Figure 154:
The location of offerings in Complex S

K (0%), L (0%), M (4.34%).

Most common object type complexes

Complexes B, C, and J.

Quantity and diversity of objects

Average number of elements: 28.66.

Range of the number of elements: 4–67.

Average number of object types: 4.

Range of the number of object types: 4–4.

Time and space locations of the offerings

Building: Huitzilopochtli (93), A (I), D (Ñ).

Building stage: IVa (93), VII (I).

Approximate date: ca. 1469 and 1502–1520.

Vertical location: platform (93), stairway (Ñ, I).

Horizontal location: W (all).

General characteristics of the offerings

Container: fill (Ñ), sillares box (93, I).

Primary orientation of objects: E (Ñ, I), E-W (93).

Number of excavation levels: 1 (93), 2 (Ñ), 4 (I).
Number of proposed levels: 1 (93), 3 (Ñ), 5 (I).

Maximum internal dimensions of the offerings (cm)

Offering	N-S axis	E-W axis	Z axis
Ñ	40	35	
93	60	105	50
I	45	65	

Distribution of objects (levels, axes, and groupings)

Although the offerings in this complex have very similar contents, they are quite different in their spatial locations and the inner distribution of objects. Therefore, they will be described separately.

Offering Ñ

Offering Ñ is placed over a step of Stage VI in Building D, and it was covered by the building fill of the next stage. It is doubtless an offering for the enlargement of the building. Three levels for placing objects, mostly sacrificial knives, were observed. At the time of excavation, the offering was completely covered with water, one reason why several fragments of wood were well preserved.

Level 1: The objects of the deepest level were placed partly over the tread of the first step of Building D and partly over the building fill. This level had 9 flint knives, 7 oriented to the east and 2 to the south. At the southern and western ends, small bones of birds were found, including 2 small claws, possibly of an eagle. To the extreme west and in the center of the offering, there were remains of wood, among them a rod with an E-W orientation.

Level 2: It was made up of a layer of carbonates with polychrome designs (blue, red, and black). According to biologists in the Department of Prehistory, it is probably the decoration of a maguey leaf that had disintegrated with the passage of time.

Level 3: The last level was only an amorphous layer of mortar.

Offering 93

This offering was deposited inside a box with 6 rows of tezontle sillares and a flagstone floor and cover. It is very different from the other offerings of Complex S and Complex T. It has only 1 level.

Level 1: A sawfish nose cartilage placed in the center of the offering was the most important object. Its point was toward the east. To the north of the box, copal remains were discovered; in the northwest corner, the bone remains of quail were found; and in the southwest corner, 1 small Mezcala-style anthropomorphic sculpture oriented to the east was discovered.

Offering I

The objects in this offering were placed in a box with sides and floor of quarry stone sillares. The box, which had no cover, was built into the building fill above the platform of Stage VI of Building A. As in the case of Offering Ñ, it celebrated the enlargement of the building. The offering had 5 levels, with 62 sacrificial knives.

Level 1: On the first level, 5 flint sacrificial knives were found, oriented to the east. One of the knives had traces of black coloring. A few remains of quail bones seemed to be associated with these artifacts.

Level 2: Thirteen sacrificial knives were excavated here. Seven had black pigment, and 4 had copal adhesions. All were oriented to the east.

Level 3: There were 18 sacrificial knives distributed at this level. Five had black pigment, and 1 had copal stuck to it. All were oriented to the east, with the exception of 1 pointing in the opposite direction.

Level 4: This level consisted of 26 sacrificial knives, spatially divided into 2 groups, with 13 knives oriented to the east and the others to the west.

Level 5: The highest level contained a few fragments of charcoal.

COMPLEX T

Offerings: 42, 46, 66, E, Q, 94, 80, and 65.
Number of offerings in complex: 8.
Dendrogram
    Split: 7 unshared presences/absences, coefficient of similarity = 0.85.
    Subgroups: 46–66 (1 upas), Q–94 (1 upas), 46–66–E (3 upas), Q–94–80 (3 upas),
        46–66–E–Q–94–80 (4 upas), 42–46–66–E–Q–94–80 (6 upas).
    Relationships: It is tied to Complexes M, N, O, P, Q, R, and S, to Burial 1, and with offerings
        16, 38, 71, 76, and 30 by 8 upas (0.83 coefficient of similarity).
Frequency of presences by object type complex
    Percentage of the total possible presences in each of the object type complexes: A (25%),
        B (12.5%), C (33.33%), D (16.75%), E (6.25%), F (0%), G (0%), H (3.12%), I (0.86%),
        J (6.25%), K (3.12%), L (0%), M (1.08%).
Most common object type complexes
    Complexes C, A, and D.
Quantity and diversity of objects
    Average number of elements: 19.62.
    Range of the number of elements: 1–93.
    Average number of object types: 3.37.

Range of the number of object types: 1–5.

Time and space locations of the offerings

Building: Huitzilopochtli (46), Tlaloc (42, 94, 80), A (E), I (66, 65), E (14).

Building stage: II (42, 94), III (46), V (Q, 80), VI (65), VII (66, E).

Approximate date: 1375–1440 and 1481–1520.

Vertical location: floor (E), platform (66, 80, 65), main body (46), temple (42, Q, 94).

Horizontal location: center (42, Q, 94), E (46, E), W (66, 80, 65).

General characteristics of the offerings

Container: fill (46, 80), sillares box (Q), fill under floor (42, 66, Q, 94, 65).

Primary orientation of objects: S (80), E (66), W (42, 46, E, 94, 65), E-W (Q).

Number of excavation levels: 1 (46, 66, E, Q, 94, 80), 2 (42), 4 (65).

Number of proposed levels: 1 (all).

Maximum internal dimensions of the offerings (cm)

Offering	N-S axis	E-W axis	Z axis
42	45	65	
46	38	53	
66	25	32	
E	40	30	
Q	40	50	40
94	71	35	15
80	50	50	
65	50	35	

Distribution of objects (levels, axes, and groupings)

The offerings of Complex T are similar in the quality of their contents, but they are quite different as to their spatial location and distribution. All the offerings had only 1 level for placing objects. Offerings 66, E, and Q are the most alike in their internal distribution. They will be described separately.

Offering 42

This offering is on the northeast corner of the inside bench of the Tlaloc Temple. It is exactly under the layer of plaster that covers the bench.

The only level of offering 42 had 1 golden obsidian sacrificial knife. It was intentionally broken in the middle. The distal half was stuck in an upright position, with the point below. The proximal half was set leaning horizontally on the other half and aimed to the east. There were 5 black-on-orange, Aztec III potsherds, and 3 potsherds of cream-colored paste, with decorative bands, accompanying the knife.

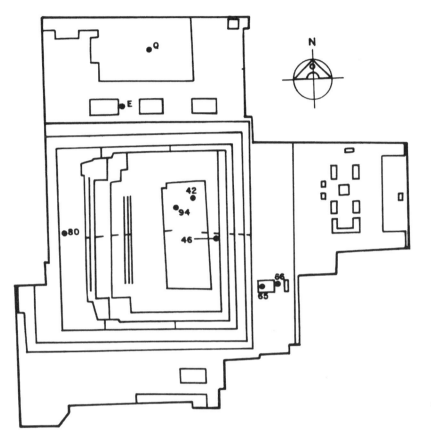

Figure 155:
The location of offerings
in Complex T

Offering 46

This offering was limited to 1 flint sacrificial knife placed on a layer of earth in the building fill. It was protected at the time of its placement by some irregular flagstones. The knife was oriented to the west.

Offering 66

Offering 66 was placed on a layer of mud 3 cm thick, which, in turn, rested on the northern platform of Building I. On its only level were distributed 7 flint sacrificial knives. Six of them were oriented to the east and 1 to the west. The knives were aligned in a N-S direction. After it had been deposited, the offering was covering with earth and tezontle stones.

Offering E

It was found in the fill next to the east stairway of Building A. The objects were deposited directly in the fill of soil and rocks. There were 8 flint sacrificial knives distributed in a N-S direction and oriented to the west. Next to them were a lace coral and 2 small conch shells.

Offering Q

It was placed inside the central bench of Room 2 of Building E (the House of Eagles). It was deposited in a tezontle sillares box with floor and lid of flagstones. Inside, there were bone remains of an eagle and a feline (with no additional relationships) and 1 greenstone bead. Six flint sacrificial knives were found with the bone remains. These artifacts were aligned in a N-S axis and oriented toward the west.

Offering 94

It was found inside a box made with irregular stones of the building fill. The inner surface was flat because the stones were covered with a thick layer of plaster. The sculpture of chacmool belonging to Stage II covered the box. A total of 52 small green obsidian knives were distributed uniformly in the floor of the box. However, it is possible to detect 2 areas of higher concentration (north and south). Some knives were partially superimposed. Thirty knives were oriented in a N-S direction, and the other 22 lay in an E-W position. Forty-one greenstone beads were associated with the knives, most of them in the center of the box.

Offering 80

It was in the tezontle fill placed over the platform of Stage IVb. The objects were on a layer of earth, covered with earth and stones. The offering consisted of 1 flint sacrificial knife oriented to the south, the remains of a shell, 1 conch shell, and 1 greenstone bead.

Offering 65

This offering was found on the platform of Building I, exactly in the middle of 4 standard-bearers. There were 18 flint sacrificial knives superimposed upon one another. Fifteen knives were oriented to the west, and the others were oriented to the east. To the north of this group, there was an amorphous mass of copal, 1 greenstone bead, remains of charcoal and clayey mud, and the jawbones and vertebrae of 2 rattlesnakes.

Description of Unique Offerings

OFFERING 41

Dendrogram

    Relationships: It is tied to offering 78 by 25 *upas* (total number of unshared presences/absences) (0.47 coefficient of similarity).

Frequency of presences by object type complex

    Percentage of the total possible presences in each of the object type complexes: A (100%), B (0%), C (0%), D (0%), E (50%), F (100%), G (0%), H (25%), I (13.79%), J (50%), K (50%), L (50%), M (13.04%).

Most common object type complexes

    Complexes A, F, E, K, and L.

Quantity and diversity of objects

    Number of elements: 196.

    Number of object types: 22.

Time and space locations of the offerings

    Building: Tlaloc.

    Building stage: IVb.

    Approximate date: 1469–1481.

    Vertical location: platform.

    Horizontal location: W center.

General characteristics of the offerings
　　Container: stone urn inside a sillares box.
　　Primary orientation of objects: W.
　　Number of excavation levels: 9.
　　Number of proposed levels: 4.

Maximum internal dimensions of the offerings (cm)

Offering	N-S axis	E-W axis	Z axis
sillares box	100	97	57
urn	55	45	35

Distribution of objects (levels, axes, and groupings)
The box of offering 41 had sides of tezontle sillares (hewn stone slabs) and a slab bottom and cover. Inside, there was a basalt urn and lid (outside dimension 67 x 56 x 48 cm). All sides of the urn were decorated with blue pigment of organic origin.

　　The four sides and the cover of the urn were carved: The cover represented a Tlaloc mask with its mouth toward the west and its forehead to the east. The north and south sides had a carving of a half-bent leg wearing a sandal and with some adornment on the calves. Thus the urn would portray the body of the deity resting in a seated position, while the lid would be the head. On the eastern wall of the urn there are 2 calendric glyphs: the upper glyph is *13 Rain* and the lower *13 Reed*. On the west wall there is a glyph, as yet unidentified; it could be another date, but that is not clear (González 1982).

Outside the Urn

In the 4 rectangular spaces between the box and the urn, we found numerous objects related to the aquatic world of the Mexica cosmovision: 421 conch shells, 63 sea shells, 1 mother-of-pearl shell, the remains of porcupine fish mandibles, 5 greenstone fragments (placed at the northeast, northwest, and southeast corners), and 1 ceramic water jar (at the eastern end).

Inside the Urn

The objects were placed at 4 distinct levels inside the urn. Carved replicas in greenstone and travertine of animals and of lacustrine instruments predominated.

Level 1: Numerous sculptures were homogeneously placed at this level. The most abundant were greenstone objects: 78 beads (among them 1 anthropomorphic and 1 zoomorphic bead), 18 zoomorphic depictions (7 birds, 4 fish, 1 dog, 1 conch shell, and 5 unidentified), 1 earplug, 1 small water jar, 4 breastplates (1 anthropomorphic, 1 zoomorphic, and 2 rectangular). Also recovered were 24 fish made from shell, 1 travertine fish, and 1 small conch shell. In the center of the urn and oriented in an E-W direction were miniature reproductions of 1 L-shaped staff, 1 canoe, 1 oar, and 1 rudder, carved in white stone. We also found 4 scepters shaped like a rattlesnake and oriented to the west:

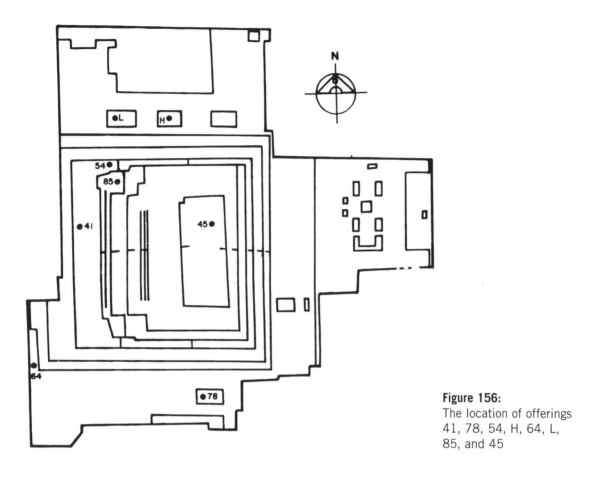

Figure 156:
The location of offerings
41, 78, 54, H, 64, L,
85, and 45

2 at the northern end and 2 at the southern end. At the western end, we found 1 tubular scepter aligned in an E-W direction. Finally, 3 Mezcala-style anthropomorphic greenstone sculptures were recorded, facing toward the west (located to the north, at the center, and to the south, respectively).

Level 2: The second level contained only objects of polished stone. Most numerous were greenstone objects: 21 evenly distributed beads, 13 zoomorphic sculptures aligned in an E-W direction (11 serpents, 1 lizard, and 1 unidentified), 2 Mezcala-style anthropomorphic sculptures at the northeast corner, and 1 Tlaloc head at the eastern end (oriented to the west). One travertine brazier with its cover was found in the center of the urn.

Level 3: In the center of the third level were miniature depictions of 1 canoe, 1 oar, 1 atlatl, and a trident (carved in travertine and decorated with red pigment), as well as 4 fish made from shell. In the southwest corner, there was 1 *Spondylus* shell with 2 greenstone beads inside.

Level 4: At the highest level, there were 4 Mezcala-style masks: 2 turned to the west, 1 to the north, and 1 to the south. Two *Strombus* conch shells with traces of blue pigment were found at the northeast and southeast corners. They were oriented toward the east.

OFFERINGS 78 AND 78-A

Dendrogram

Relationships: They are tied to offering 41 by 25 upas (0.47 coefficient of similarity).

Frequency of presences by object type complex

Percentage of the total possible presences in each of the object type complexes: A (100%), B (100%), C (66.66%), D (100%), E (0%), F (100%), G (33.33%), H (50%), I (13.79%), J (100%), K (25%), L (50%), M (17.39%).

Most common object type complexes

Complexes A, B, D, F, J, and C.

Quantity and diversity of objects

Number of elements: 235.

Number of object types: 28.

Time and space locations of the offerings

Building: F.

Building stage: VI.

Approximate date: 1486–1502.

Vertical location: temple.

Horizontal location: E.

General characteristics of the offerings

Container: sillares box.

Primary orientation of objects: E.

Number of excavation levels: 4.

Number of proposed levels: 3.

Maximum internal dimensions of the offerings (cm)

Offering	N-S axis	E-W axis	Z axis
78	157	97	150
78-A	26	24	23

Distribution of objects (levels, axes, and groupings)

Offering 78 was placed inside a box with thick tezontle sillares. The inside was finely plastered. The bottom was made of a thick layer of stucco (8-cm-thick) decorated with red pigment. The box did not have a slab lid, but it was covered from the surface down to approximately 1 m deep with loosely packed fill of earth and tezontle. Inside this layer of fill, there were many pieces of broken ("killed") ceramics and a red-colored carved slab, resembling an enormous sacrificial knife. Most of the objects were found under the earth and stone filling. Apparently, the placement was at 3 vertical levels, where marine material predominated, as well as greenstone beads and the replicas of musical instruments.

Level 1: The deepest level was characterized by the abundance of marine material. In the center of the offering, there was an area of sand containing 20 small shells and 26 small conch shells.

To the east were found bone remains of 1 porcupine fish, 1 trigger fish, and 1 trunkfish, as well as a few carbonized seeds that could not be identified.

Level 2: Two large slabs representing sacrificial knives occupied the second level. Just over them lay the greater part of the offering's objects. Both slabs were oriented to the west. The northernmost slab (with maximum dimensions of 77 cm x 36 cm x 3 cm) had flat, polished surfaces, with rounded edges and point. It was almond shaped, and the nearest end was flat. The slab to the south (maximum dimensions of 83 cm x 41 cm x 4 cm) had flaked edges and an angular point. It was also almond shaped. The 2 slabs had red, ocher, white, and black polychrome anthropomorphic designs on their surfaces. In the middle, there were drawings of 2 eyes, 1 nose, and 2 earplugs shaped like a hand, and there was an open mouth at the end of the slab.

Level 3: The highest level was made up of innumerable objects, lying on each other and concentrated at the center of the offering. Minor groupings of materials were found at the northeast and southwest corners, in the 2 triangular areas that bordered the knife-shaped slabs (to the east and west), and along the eastern and western sides. This level is characterized by stone miniatures and marine material. Almost all the objects were oriented longitudinally from east to west. No definite groupings of objects having the same characteristics were observed, nor were any imaginary distribution axes perceived—only simple irregular heaps.

At this level, there were many replicas of musical instruments: 9 greenstone and 3 basalt teponaztli; 9 huehuetl; 9 greenstone, 3 tezontle, and 1 ceramic flutes; 2 basalt and 1 ceramic rattles; 1 basalt turtle shell; 1 basalt omichicahuaztli; 1 ceramic tetl glyph; and 17 copper bells.

Other greenstone objects found were: 13 triangular pendants, 13 serpent scepters, 8 penates, 4 anthropomorphic masks, 4 Tlaloc masks, 1 representation of a serpent, 1 flat plaque, 3 full-body anthropomorphic figures, 3 earplugs, 5 cylinders, 5 irregular fragments, 386 spherical beads (some with red coloring), and 14 cylindrical beads. There were also sculptures in other kinds of stone: 21 flint sacrificial knives (in the center and to the east of the offering); 1 prismatic blade, 5 beads, and 1 earplug in obsidian; and 1 chicahuaztli, 6 scepters, 3 cylindrical objects, 1 eagle head, and 1 eagle's claw in basalt.

Ceramic objects were included in this level: 1 cylinder, 4 small faces, and several potsherds. The remains of flora and fauna we found were: copal fragments, 113 small conch shells, 2 *Strombus* conch shells, 12 olive shells (*Oliva* sp.), 172 small shells, 1 *Spondylus* shell, remains of a sea urchin, part of the skeleton of 1 golden eagle, 2 montezuma quail, and a few remnants of an armadillo shell.

OFFERING 78-A

This small box was found just under the floor of offering 78. The container, with tezontle walls and a bottom of quarry stone sillares, was filled with dense mortar and 4 potsherds.

OFFERING 54

Dendrogram

Relationships: It is tied to offering H by 27 upas (0.43 coefficient of similarity).

Frequency of presences by object type complex

Percentage of the total possible presences in each of the object type complexes: A (33.33%), B (100%), C (33.33%), D (100%), E (0%), F (0%), G (0%), H (0%), I (12.06%), J (0%), K (0%), L (0%), M (21.73%).

Most common object type complexes

Complexes B, D, A, and C.

Quantity and diversity of objects

Number of elements: 75.

Number of object types: 16.

Time and space locations of the offerings

Building: Tlaloc.

Building stage: V.

Approximate date: 1481–1486.

Vertical location: main body.

Horizontal location: NW.

General characteristics of the offerings

Container: sillares box.

Primary orientation of objects: E-W.

Number of excavation levels: 5.

Number of proposed levels: 5.

Maximum internal dimensions of the offerings (cm)

N-S axis	E-W axis	Z axis
93	133	100

Distribution of objects (levels, axes, and groupings)

Offering 54 was deposited in a stone slab box. The sides were tezontle sillares covered with a thin layer of plaster. Apparently, they had been exposed to fire because there are remains of soot and charcoal. The bottom of the box was 12-cm-thick tamped mortar. During colonial times, the box cover and the northern side were destroyed when a hole was dug to make a dump for ceramic debris.

Five levels of objects contained in a kaolin matrix (0.927 m³) from the vicinity of Pachuca, Hidalgo (analysis made by the Department of Prehistory laboratories), were found in the offering. In the central part of the deposit, there were clear signs of a gray stain and the remains of charcoal produced in the kaolin by fire. Once the offering had been excavated, the kaolin was sieved. Charcoal and copal remains, 6 potsherds, and 3 small bones were recovered. The objects described in the following text were discovered inside the matrix.

Level 1: The objects at the first level were placed inside the kaolin matrix, 2 cm above the bottom of the box. This level had the most objects. There were 14 textile strips (with an average size of 25 cm x 10 cm). The strips were placed longitudinally from east to west. Some had traces of red coloring; others had traces of black and ocher. At the western end of the box, 6 strips were placed in a row from north to south. Next to them, a little more to the east, there was another row (north to south), made up of 5 strips. Finally, at the eastern end, 1 row made up of 3 strips was found.

Several objects had been placed above the textiles of the second row. There was 1 wooden serpent scepter over the first strip coming from the north, another over the second, and 1 more over the fifth. Over the third strip lay 1 small nose cartilage of a sawfish. These objects were perhaps once joined by a cord and oriented in an E-W direction.

At the western end of the box, traces of a bird feather were found, as well as a vegetable fiber engraved on the kaolin. In the southeast corner, there were a few bark remains.

Level 2: The objects at the second level were found in a matrix of kaolin 4 cm above the floor. Almost all the objects at this level were placed at the western end of the box. Thirteen copal balls, charcoal remains, and 2 greenstone beads were irregularly distributed at the western half of the offering. There were also 4 ceramic flutes with their mouths turned to the north—2 in the northwest corner and 2 in the southwest. At the western end, there were 3 ceramic objects: 1 brazier, 1 cane or brazier stirrer, and 1 spiral disk. In the southwestern corner, next to a pair of flutes, there were miniature ceramic replicas of 1 canoe and 1 cluster of implements (atlatl, trident, and oar), oriented N-S. In the center, there were 2 bracelets with 8 greenstone beads each. One bean and 1 corn seed were in the southeast corner.

Level 3: In the kaolin deposit, some 30 cm above the floor, the trace of an oval-shaped leaf was still visible. In the center, there was 1 obsidian prismatic blade.

Level 4: Sixty cm above the floor, there were 2 potsherds, numerous small pieces of tezontle (about 2 cm in size), and a few unidentified bone remains. At the western end, an area (about 10 cm x 2 cm x 13 cm) of sea sand was found.

Level 5: In the center of the box 65 cm above the floor, we found 8 greenstone beads and 1 potsherd, as well as a layer of red paint and copal resin approximately 1 mm thick.

OFFERING H

Dendrogram
Relationships: It is tied to the complexes by 27 upas (0.43 coefficient of similarity).
Frequency of presences by object type complex
Percentage of the total possible presences in each of the object type complexes: A (100%), B (100%), C (33.33%), D (50%), E (0%), F (0%), G (0%), H (50%), I (17.24%), J (0%), K (50%), L (50%), M (26.08%).

Most common object type complexes
  Complexes A, B, H, K, and L.

Quantity and diversity of objects
  Number of elements: 150.
  Number of object types: 27.

Time and space locations of the offerings
  Building: B.
  Building stage: VIb.
  Approximate date: 1486–1502.
  Vertical location: temple.
  Horizontal location: center.
  Comments: Offering H is spatially associated with offering Ñ.

General characteristics of the offerings
  Container: sillares box.
  Primary orientation of objects: W.
  Number of excavation levels: 6.
  Number of proposed levels: 5.

Maximum internal dimensions of the offerings (cm)

N-S axis	E-W axis	Z axis
52	84	57

Distribution of objects (levels, axes, and groupings)

Offering H was deposited in a box with sides made of 3 rows of tezontle sillares. The bottom and the lid were made with large slabs. The objects offered were placed at 5 vertical, well-defined levels. This offering was marked by the great diversity of its objects (López Luján and Polaco 1991).

Level 1: The first level consisted chiefly of marine remains and objects related to the aquatic world of Mexica cosmovision. Many objects were found distributed in a homogeneous way and without a specific orientation: 54 small shells, 182 small conch shells, 4 greenstone beads, 30 obsidian projectile points (in clusters with 10, 8, 8, and 4 elements), and 10 West Indian Top (*Cittarium pica*) shells (in clusters with 3, 3, 2, and 1 elements). One West Indian Top shell contained 5 white stone beads. Also at this level, there were greenstone miniatures representing 18 teponaztli and 9 tlalpanhuehuetl, oriented in a N-S direction. Four small areas of marine sand with chiton plaques were placed, respectively, at the center, north, south, and west of the offering. We also found 2 lace corals at the eastern and western ends of the offering, facing south.

In the center of the deposit, there was a greenstone representation of a conch shell, 1 necklace made of 120 greenstone beads (oriented E-W), and 1 copal ball.

At the eastern end, we found 5 greenstone anthropomorphic sculptures placed in a N-S direction and oriented to the west: 4 were full-body representations (2 of them penates with Tlaloc's face), and the other was an anthropomorphic mask. In the same area, we found 1 greenstone miniature representing a rattle.

At the western end of the box, there were 4 shell disks perforated in the center, 2 conch shells (also with holes in the middle), 3 zoomorphic greenstone sculptures (2 frogs and 1 turtle), and 1 very large conch shell (*Hexaplex brassica*).

Level 2: The next level was a uniform layer of flint sacrificial knives. There was a total of 40, of which 32 were decorated with geometric designs done with black, white, blue, red, or ocher pigment. The knives were grouped in 3 poorly defined clusters—13 objects at the eastern end, 18 in the center, and 9 at the western end. All the knives were oriented to the west, with the exception of one placed at the center of the offering and oriented to the north.

Level 3: Two quadruped skeletons in perfect anatomical correspondence occupied this level: a jaguar in the northern half and a wolf in the southern half. They were 2 young animals placed in a crouching position, facing down with their heads to the west.

Level 4: This level contained chiefly Mexica ceramic objects. At the eastern end, we found 1 Tlaloc water jar, oriented to the west. Its cover was 1 spiral-shaped disk. Inside, there were 30 small conch shells, 3 small shells, 120 greenstone beads, and charcoal remains. At the opposite end, at the west of the box, there was a small brazier, placed on a cane or brazier stirrer, and 1 spiral-shaped disk.

To the north were placed ceramic representations of 1 chicahuaztli, 1 serpent scepter, and 1 conch shell, all oriented to the west. To the south, we also found an identical set of 3 objects, also oriented to the west.

In the 4 corners of the box, there were ceramic representations of musical instruments: 1 flute in the northeast corner and 1 in the northwest (oriented E-W), as well as 1 teponaztli in the southeast corner and 1 in the southwest (the first oriented E-W, the other N-S).

In the center of the box, we found 1 lace coral, 1 necklace made of 40 olive shells (oriented longitudinally N-S), 3 greenstone beads, and 4 obsidian projectile points (oriented to the east).

Finally, in both the northeast and southeast corners, we found 2 clusters with 4 flint projectile points each.

Level 5: The last level of offering H was placed outside the box, along the western wall. The most impressive item on this level was a skeleton of a young wolf placed in a crouching position, facing down with its skull oriented toward the west. There were also 5 sacrificial knives, 4 of them placed at the height of the animal's abdomen and 1 in its jaws. The 5 knives were oriented to the east. A few potsherds were associated with the objects at this level.

OFFERING 64

Dendrogram
Relationships: It is tied to offering L by 12 upas (0.74 coefficient of similarity).
Frequency of presences by object type complex
Percentage of the total possible presences in each of the object type complexes: A (100%),

B (100%), C (33.33%), D (0%), E (0%), F (0%), G (0%), H (0%), I (1.72%), J (0%), K (25%), L (50%), M (17.39%).

Most common object type complexes

Complexes A, B, L, and C.

Quantity and diversity of objects

Number of elements: 64.

Number of object types: 12.

Time and space locations of the offerings

Building: Huitzilopochtli.

Building stage: VII.

Approximate date: 1502–1520.

Vertical location: platform.

Horizontal location: SW.

General characteristics of the offerings

Container: fill.

Primary orientation of objects: W.

Number of excavation levels: 2.

Number of proposed levels: 2.

Maximum internal dimensions of the offerings (cm)

N-S axis	E-W axis
100	140

Distribution of objects (levels, axes, and groupings)

Offering 64 was deposited on a bed of earth and afterward covered with building fill. It had 2 levels for placing objects.

Level 1: The first level is mostly marine material. Among the objects distributed homogeneously throughout the level, we found 15 greenstone beads and 47 obsidian projectile points (grouped in units of 1, 2, 3, and 4 objects). In the center of the deposit, there was a shell disk. At the northern end, 1 lace coral oriented to the north and 1 *Spondylus* shell with the inner side facing upward were found. At the other end, to the south, there was 1 poorly preserved sawfish nose cartilage. The teeth of the same cartilage and 3 amorphous masses of copal were placed in 3 areas corresponding to the center, northwest, and southwest of the offering. The anatomically unrelated bone remains of a jaguar were placed irregularly in the eastern half of the deposit. A total of 20 copper bells were at the corners of the offering (NE, NW, SE, and SW). Sea shells and small conch shells were found mostly in the center and to the east.

Level 2: On the second and last level 3 skull-masks, each with a flint sacrificial knife in the mouth, stood out. These differed from the other skull-masks in that they lacked shell and pyrite inserts in the eye sockets. They were placed in the center, northwest, and southwest of the offering, respectively, and facing west. Twenty-nine olive shells made up the 3 necklaces associated with the mandibles of the skull-masks. There were 13 conch shells next to the northwest mask, 13 conch shells beside the southwest mask, and 6 conch shells used as a necklace for the central mask. Aside from the 3 sacrificial knives mentioned previously, we located 20 more, spread homogeneously throughout the level. Four of them, each with a copal ball on the proximal end, were at the corners of the deposit. Those at the northeast and southeast corners were oriented to the west. Those at the northwest and southwest corners were oriented to the east. Of the 20 sacrificial knives, 12 were oriented to the east, 6 to the west, 1 to the north, and 1 to the south. Finally, in the center and in each corner of the offering (NE, NW, SE, and SW), there were 2 mud turtles, for a total of 10.

OFFERING L

Dendrogram

Relationships: It is tied to offering 64 by 12 upas (0.74 coefficient of similarity).

Frequency of presences by object type complex

Percentage of the total possible presences in each of the object type complexes: A (66.66%), B (0%), C (100%), D (0%), E (0%), F (0%), G (0%), H (0%), I (0%), J (50%), K (100%), L (0%), M (21.73%).

Most common object type complexes

Complexes C, K, A, and J.

Quantity and diversity of objects

Number of elements: 77.

Number of object types: 15.

Time and space locations of the offerings

Building: A.

Building stage: VII.

Approximate date: 1502–1520.

Vertical location: stairway.

Horizontal location: W.

General characteristics of the offerings

Container: fill.

Primary orientation of objects: W.

Number of excavation levels: 7.

Number of proposed levels: 5.

Maximum internal dimensions of the offerings (cm)

N-S axis	E-W axis
75	65

Distribution of objects (levels, axes, and groupings)

Offering L was located in the building fill at the height of the fourth step of Building A. Four different levels for placing objects were recorded in which images of the gods Tlaloc and Xiuhtecuhtli predominated, tying this offering to those of Complex A.

Level 1: There was a headless serpent skeleton on the first level. It measured 100 cm and was placed in the shape of a U, with the two ends facing south. To the west of the skeleton, there were 6 obsidian projectile points.

Level 2: Directly over these bone remains were placed 21 flint sacrificial knives. Sixteen were oriented to the west and 5 to the east. Groups of 1, 2, 3, 4, 5, and 6 copper bells, making a total 76, were found at the proximal end. At this level, there were also 2 thorns for self-sacrifice, 2 obsidian mortars (in the center), bone remains of puffer fish, fragments of turtle shell, and copal.

Level 3: On the third level, marine objects were placed: 4 small conch shells, 2 *Strombus* conch shells (1 to the north and 1 to the southwest), 6 small shells, 1 mother-of-pearl shell (to the west), and 2 areas of fragmented lace coral (north and south).

Level 4: At the fourth level, there were images of 3 deities: 1 small black stone Xiuhtecuhtli, 1 black stone Tlaloc water jar with traces of blue coloring, and 1 copal anthropomorphic figure. The 3 images were located to the east of the offering, aligned in a N-S direction (Xiuhtecuhtli to the north, Tlaloc in the center, and the copal figure to the south). They were resting against the building's stairway and oriented to the west.

Level 5: Part of the offering was covered with a convex layer of mortar resembling a cave. There were openings at the eastern and western ends. Stuck inside there were many fragments of lace coral and the bone remains of quail and 1 snake.

OFFERING 85

Dendrogram
  Relationships: It is tied to Complex K by 16 upas (0.66 coefficient of similarity).
Frequency of presences by object type complex
  Percentage of the total possible presences in each of the object type complexes: A (100%), B (0%), C (0%), D (0%), E (50%), F (50%), G (0%), H (0%), I (6.89%), J (50%), K (0%), L (100%), M (0%).
Most common object type complexes
  Complexes A, L, F, and J.
Quantity and diversity of objects
  Number of elements: 98.
  Number of object types: 12.
Time and space locations of the offerings
  Building: Tlaloc.
  Building stage: IVa.
  Approximate date: ca. 1469.
  Vertical location: platform.

Horizontal location: NW.

Comments: Spatially, it is related to offering 48 and Chamber 3.

General characteristics of the offerings

Container: fill.

Primary orientation of objects: W.

Number of excavation levels: 7.

Number of proposed levels: 3.

Maximum internal dimensions of the offerings (cm)

N-S axis	E-W axis
75	72

Distribution of objects (levels, axes, and groupings)

Offering 85 was deposited in an irregular cavity dug under Chamber 3. Three deposition levels are easily seen. The objects were not superimposed on each other, and the levels were separated from each other by a layer of earth. However, it should be pointed out that some objects were placed uniformly in all levels: 142 olive shells, 107 small conch shells, 16 small sea shells, 137 white stone beads, 257 greenstone beads, 83 purple stone beads, 706 black stone beads, and 3 irregular fragments of greenstone. In general, the objects were associated with the aquatic world of Mexica cosmovision and directly related to those of Chamber 3 and offering 48.

Level 1: The first level had very diverse materials. At the center were 2 orange ceramic jars, engraved after being fired and painted blue. One of them contained 7 beads and 1 irregular piece of greenstone. The other one had 7 beads and an irregular piece of greenstone, 1 black stone bead and plaque, 1 bead in the shape of a bird, and 1 shell plaque. Around the jars, there were 3 greenstone anthropomorphic figures (oriented to the north), irregular jet fragments, fish bones, 4 greenstone breastplates, 2 white stone polishers, 1 engraved feline fang, 8 seashell plaques, and 4 *Xancus* conch shells (oriented to the west).

Level 2: This level consisted solely of 28 mother-of-pearl shells evenly distributed over the surface.

Level 3: A few remains of charcoal were taken from the highest level.

OFFERING 45

Dendrogram

Relationships: It was tied to offering 82 by 11 upas (0.83 coefficient of similarity).

Frequency of presences by object type complex

Percentage of the total possible presences in each of the object type complexes: A (0%), B (100%), C (0%), D (0%), E (0%), F (100%), G (0%), H (0%), I (5.17%), J (0%), K (0%), L (0%), M (0%).

Most common object type complexes

Complexes B, F, and I.

Quantity and diversity of objects

Number of elements: 68.

Number of object types: 6.

Time and space locations of the offerings

Building: Tlaloc.

Building stage: II.

Approximate date: 1325–1427.

Vertical location: temple.

Horizontal location: center.

General characteristics of the offerings

Container: sillares box.

Primary orientation of objects: W.

Number of excavation levels: 2.

Number of proposed levels: 2.

Maximum internal dimensions of the offerings (cm)

N-S axis	E-W axis	Z axis
30	39	28

Distribution of objects (levels, axes, and groupings)

This offering was deposited in a box with sides, cover, and bottom of tezontle sillares, covered with a thin layer of plaster. The box mostly had objects of polished stone and remains of charcoal and copal distributed at 2 distinct levels.

Level 1: Greenstone beads, distributed in an irregular way, predominated at the first level: 46 spherical beads, 11 tubular, 2 anthropomorphic, 2 zoomorphic, and 1 plant-shaped. There were also 1 earplug and a cluster of obsidian prismatic blades, as well as 2 small greenstone sheets. In the center, we found a greenstone anthropomorphic figure, oriented toward the west.

Level 2: The second level had a few remains of copal and charcoal.

OFFERING 82

Dendrogram

Relationships: It was tied to offering 45 by 11 upas (0.83 coefficient of similarity).

Comments: Offerings 82 and 45 only have the presence of 1 necklace of greenstone beads in common.

Frequency of presences by object type complex

Percentage of the total possible presences in each of the object type complexes: A (0%), B (00%),

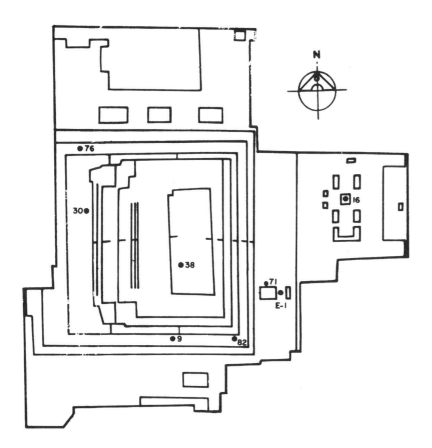

Figure 157:
The location of offerings 82, 16, 38, 71, 76, 30, and 9 and of Burial 1

C (0%), D (0%), E (0%), F (50%), G (0%), H (25%), I (5.17%), J (0%), K (0%), L (50%), M (8.69%).

Most common object type complexes

Complexes F, L, and H.

Quantity and diversity of objects

Number of elements: 11.

Number of object types: 8.

Time and space locations of the offerings

Building: Huitzilopochtli.

Building stage: IVb.

Approximate date: 1469–1481.

Vertical location: floor.

Horizontal location: SE.

General characteristics of the offerings

Container: fill under floor.

Primary orientation of objects: S.

Number of excavation levels: 5.
Number of proposed levels: 4.

Maximum internal dimensions of the offerings (cm)

N-S axis	E-W axis
55	40

Distribution of objects (levels, axes, and groupings)

This offering was found inside the rocks and earth building fill, 100 cm below the slab floor of Stage IVb. The offering had 4 deposition levels, among which anthropomorphic masks stood out.

Level 1: At the deepest level, there was 1 travertine Mexica-style anthropomorphic mask, oriented to the south.

Level 2: This level had small greenstone objects: 12 tubular and 26 spherical beads (perhaps a necklace), 3 miniature axes, 3 miniature mallets, 1 representation of a duck, 1 earplug, 1 labret, and 1 engraved plaque.

Level 3: One greenstone Teotihuacan-style mask was found at this level. It was oriented to the south. Two circular greenstone earspools were associated with it. It is possible that the objects found at this level were part of the trappings of this mask.

Level 4: A human skull with its first cervical vertebrae, which shows that it was decapitated, was found above the objects just described. The skull was placed in a left parietal position, with the face toward the east.

OFFERINGS 16 AND 16-A

Dendrogram

Relationships: They were tied to offering 91 by 4 upas (0.91 coefficient of similarity).
Comments: Offerings 16 and 91 cannot be compared because the latter was only partially excavated.

Frequency of presences by object type complex

Percentage of the total possible presences in each of the object type complexes: A (33.33%), B (50%), C (0%), D (0%), E (0%), F (0%), G (0%), H (0%), I (0%), J (0%), K (25%), L (0%), M (0%).

Most common object type complexes

Complexes B, A, and K.

Quantity and diversity of objects

Number of elements: 13.
Number of object types: 3.

Time and space locations of the offerings

Building: L.

Building stage: VI.
Approximate date: 1486–1502.
Vertical location: floor.
Horizontal location: W.

General characteristics of the offerings

Container: sillares box.
Primary orientation of objects: W.
Number of excavation levels: 1.
Number of proposed levels: 1.

Maximum internal dimensions of the offerings (cm)

Offering	N-S axis	E-W axis	Z axis
16	45	40	40
16-A	30	25	28

Distribution of objects (levels, axes, and groupings)

Offerings 16 and 16-A were found at the foot of the west side of Building L. The offering annex (see following text) was located at the base of Building L but at the eastern end. Offering 16 was deposited in a box of quarry stone sillares. The sides (arranged in 3 rows), the bottom, and the cover were made of the same kind of material. Offering 16-A had been placed in a similar but smaller box. This box was placed along the east wall of offering 16. Both had 1 deposition level.

Offering 16

Level 1: In this offering, we found only a sculpture of Xiuhtecuhtli, greenstone beads, and 1 obsidian prismatic blade. The offering was presided over by an andesite image of the god Xiuhtecuhtli. It was at the western end of the box, oriented to the west. We also found 5 greenstone beads placed in the center and at each of the corners of the box (NE, NW, SE, and SW). The bead placed in the center was larger than the 4 others. Also in the center was 1 small obsidian prismatic blade.

Offering 16-A

This offering consisted of only 5 greenstone beads arranged similarly (center, NE, NW, SE, and SW) to those of offering 16. They differed in that the central bead was smaller than the other 4.

Offering annex

For some reason unknown to me, no number was given to the offering found on the eastern side of Building L, under the stucco floor. It was a polychrome Tlaloc vessel, containing 24 greenstone beads. This deposit was protected on its upper side by a stone slab (Contreras and Luna 1982). Unfortunately, this offering could not be included in the numerical taxonomy.

OFFERING 38

Dendrogram

Relationships: It is tied to offerings 2 and 16 and to Complex M by 6 upas (0.87 coefficient of similarity).

Frequency of presences by object type complex

Percentage of the total possible presences in each of the object type complexes: A (33.33%), B (0%), C (33.33%), D (0%), E (0%), F (0%), G (0%), H (0%), I (3.44%), J (50%), K (0%), L (0%), M (0%).

Most common object type complexes

Complexes J, A, and B.

Quantity and diversity of objects

Number of elements: 13.

Number of object types: 5.

Time and space locations of the offerings

Building: Huitzilopochtli.

Building stage: II.

Approximate date: 1375–1427.

Vertical location: temple.

Horizontal location: center.

General characteristics of the offerings

Container: sillares box.

Primary orientation of objects: W.

Number of excavation levels: 3.

Number of proposed levels: 1.

Maximum internal dimensions of the offerings (cm)

N-S axis	E-W axis	Z axis
35	18	35

Distribution of objects (levels, axes, and groupings)

Offering 38 was placed inside a box whose sides (5 rows) and bottom were formed with tezontle sillares. The techcatl, or sacrificial stone, of Stage II acted as a cover for the objects deposited inside. This offering had 1 level, where flint sacrificial knives predominated.

Level 1: A total of 5 flint sacrificial knives, showing no particular placement pattern, took up practically all this level. Four small white stone knives were oriented toward the west, and 1 brown one was oriented to the north. The knives surrounded stone and bone remains, primarily greenstone objects: 9 amorphous fragments, 1 tubular bead (oriented north and south), and 2 spherical beads. The incomplete bone remains of 2 different species of small falcons, 2 of montezuma quail, and 1 common bobwhite were also found.

BURIAL 1

Dendrogram
> Relationships: It is tied to Complexes O, P, Q, and R and with offerings 71 and 76 by 3 upas (0.94 coefficient of similarity).

Frequency of presences by object type complex
> Percentage of the total possible presences in each of the object type complexes: A (0%), B (0%), C (0%), D (0%), E (50%), F (0%), G (0%), H (0%), I (1.72%), J (0%), K (0%), L (0%), M (0%).

Most common object type complexes
> Complexes E and I.

Quantity and diversity of objects
> Number of elements: 2.
> Number of object types: 2.

Time and space locations of the offerings
> Building: I.
> Building stage: VI.
> Approximate date: 1486–1502.
> Vertical location: floor.
> Horizontal location: E.

General characteristics of the offerings
> Container: fill.
> Primary orientation of objects: N.
> Number of excavation levels: 1.
> Number of proposed levels: 1.

Maximum internal dimensions of the offerings (cm)

N-S axis	E-W axis
56	56

Distribution of objects (levels, axes, and groupings)

Burial 1 was deposited next to the east wall of Building I. It was found inside the building fill, made up of a very compact layer of earth. There was 1 human skeleton on its single level.

Level 1: The skeleton was of an adult female. It was a primary, direct burial. The individual was in a seated position and oriented to the north. The skeleton was well preserved, and there were no signs of the cause of death. An Aztec ceramic plate placed before the corpse served as a burial offering.

OFFERING 71

Dendrogram

Relationships: It is tied to Complexes P, Q, and R by 2 upas (0.96 coefficient of similarity).

Frequency of presences by object type complex

Percentage of the total possible presences in each of the object type complexes: A (0%), B (0%), C (0%), D (0%), E (50%), F (0%), G (0%), H (0%), I (0%), J (0%), K (0%), L (0%), M (0%).

Most common object type complexes

Complex E.

Quantity and diversity of objects

Number of elements: 10.

Number of object types: 1.

Time and space locations of the offerings

Building: I.

Building stage: VI.

Approximate date: 1486–1502.

Vertical location: floor.

Horizontal location: N center.

General characteristics of the offerings

Container: fill.

Primary orientation of objects: undetermined.

Number of excavation levels: 1.

Number of proposed levels: 1.

Maximum internal dimensions of the offerings (cm)

N-S axis	E-W axis
30	40

Distribution of objects (levels, axes, and groupings)

The objects were placed on a layer of earth and covered with the building fill of Stage VI. The objects were ceramic containers offered on a single level.

Level 1: The offering is only 10 cajetes. Nine were made with an orange paste and had a tripod support. The other was a Red Texcoco type. They were superimposed in no particular order. Some were face up, some face down, and others in an upright position. Five bowls were very fragmented.

OFFERING 76

Dendrogram

Relationships: It is tied to Complexes O, P, Q, and R, with Burial 1, and with offering 71 by 3 upas (0.94 coefficient of similarity).

Comments: It is connected to offerings that have no elements or that only have 1 object type.

Frequency of presences by object type complex

Percentage of the total possible presences in each of the object type complexes: A (0%), B (0%), C (50%), D (0%), E (0%), F (0%), G (0%), H (0%), I (1.7%), J (0%), K (0%), L (0%), M (0%).

Most common object type complexes

Complex I.

Quantity and diversity of objects

Number of elements: 5.

Number of object types: 2.

Time and space locations of the offerings

Building: Tlaloc.

Building stage: IVb.

Approximate date: 1469–1481.

Vertical location: floor.

Horizontal location: NW.

Comments: This offering of incense burners had a spatial location similar to the copal offerings of Complex O.

General characteristics of the offerings

Container: fill.

Primary orientation of objects: N.

Number of excavation levels: 1.

Number of proposed levels: 1.

Maximum internal dimensions of the offerings (cm)

N-S axis	E-W axis
100	90

Distribution of objects (levels, axes, and groupings)

Offering 76 was deposited inside the building fill, 87 cm below the slab floor of Stage IVb. The objects were placed on a nucleus of tezontle stone and earth. By its content and spatial location, it is associated with the cylindrical offering of copal in Complex O.

Level 1: The offering is composed of 4 orange ceramic incense burners, decorated with white, blue, and black pigment. Because of the pressure they underwent, the incense burners were fragmented and deformed. In spite of this, we saw that they were oriented longitudinally from north to south. Associated with these artifacts was 1 small grey obsidian flake.

OFFERING 30

Dendrogram

Relationships: It is tied to Complexes N, O, P, Q, and R, with Burial 1, and with offerings 71 and 76 by 5 upas (0.89 coefficient of similarity).

Comments: It is tied to offerings that have no objects or few object types.

Frequency of presences by object type complex

Percentage of the total possible presences in each of the object type complexes: A (33.33%), B (100%), C (1.72%), D (0%), E (0%), F (0%), G (0%), H (0%), I (0%), J (0%), K (0%), L (0%), M (4.34%).

Most common object type complexes

Complexes B and A.

Quantity and diversity of objects

Number of elements: 16.

Number of object types: 4.

Time and space locations of the offerings

Building: Tlaloc.

Building stage: IVa.

Approximate date: ca. 1469.

Vertical location: platform.

Horizontal location: W.

General characteristics of the offerings

Container: sillares box.

Primary orientation of objects: W.

Number of excavation levels: 1.

Number of proposed levels: 1.

Maximum internal dimensions of the offerings (cm)

N-S axis	E-W axis	Z axis
30	100	23

Distribution of objects (levels, axes, and groupings)

The objects of this offering were deposited in a box with sides, bottom, and cover of quarry stone sillares. All the material, placed on 1 level, was related to the aquatic world of Mesoamerican cosmovision.

Level 1: The greater part of the surface of this level was taken up by the skeletal remains of a small alligator. The remains were jumbled. It is probable that the burial of this skeleton was secondary because the skull is at the western end and the jawbone is in the opposite direction. Nine small spherical beads and 1 large one were placed in the offering in an irregular manner. We also found 4 concentrations of rubber positioned longitudinally in the box, as well as some copal remains.

OFFERING 9

Dendrogram

Relationships: It is tied to Complexes K, L, M, N, O, P, Q, R, S, with Burial 1, and with offerings 85, 45, 82, 16, 38, 71, 76, and 30 by 21 upas (0.68 coefficient of similarity).

Frequency of presences by object type complex

Percentage of the total possible presences in each of the object type complexes: A (66.66%), B (100%), C (33.33%), D (0%), E (0%), F (100%), G (0%), H (25%), I (5.17%), J (0%), K (75%), L (0%), M (17.39%).

Most common object type complexes

Complexes B, K, and A.

Quantity and diversity of objects

Number of elements: 58.

Number of object types: 17.

Time and space locations of the offerings

Building: Huitzilopochtli.

Building stage: IVb.

Approximate date: 1469–1481.

Vertical location: floor.

Horizontal location: S center.

General characteristics of the offerings

Container: fill.

Primary orientation of objects: S.

Number of excavation levels: 2.

Number of proposed levels: 1.

Maximum internal dimensions of the offerings (cm)

Offering	N-S axis	E-W axis
9	55	65
annex	55	80

Distribution of objects (levels, axes, and groupings)

Offering 9 was found in the building fill of earth and stones that covered Stage IV, 130 cm under the slab floor of Stage IVb. There were 27 elements placed on a single level and an "annex" located 65 cm to the north of the offering.

Level 1: The objects in this offering were in great disorder. In the center, there was a Mezcala-style anthropomorphic sculpture, wearing a conical headdress. It was oriented toward the north and was flanked by 2 Mixtec penates—1 to the east of the sculpture with a northern orientation and 1 to the south with a southern orientation. In the center, we also found 1 anthropomorphic copal figure (oriented to the east) and 2 miniature Mezcala-style sculptures. To the south, we found a miniature travertine sculpture—an atlatl. Elsewhere, scattered about the area, were 9 conch shells, 58 shells, 6 greenstone beads, deer antler coral fragments, 3 obsidian beads, 1 miniature greenstone hatchet, and copal remains.

Annex

In the annex, there was 1 very deteriorated jaguar skeleton that showed some anatomical organization (ribs, vertebrae, and lower extremities).

Plan, Matrices, and Dendrograms

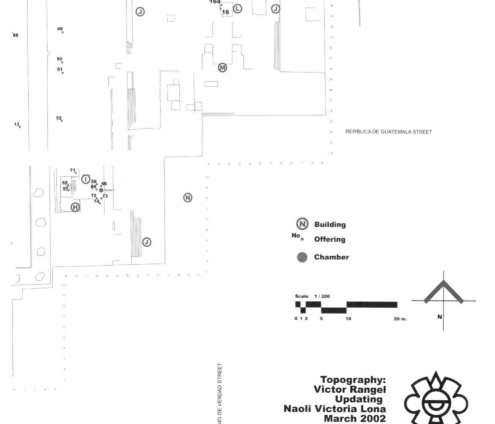

JUSTO SIERRA STREET

Templo Mayor archeaological zone

REPÚBLICA DE GUATEMALA STREET

PRIMO DE VERDAD STREET

Ⓝ **Building**

No. **Offering**

⬤ **Chamber**

Scale 1 / 200

0 1 2   5   10   20 m.

N

**Topography:
Victor Rangel
Updating
Naoli Victoria Lona
March 2002**

NO. OFRENDA		1	2	3	4	5	6	7	8	9	10	11	12	13	14	15	16	17	18	19	20	21	22	23	24	25
Ubicación gral.																										
CALA		T'	S'	R'	S'	Q'	T'U'D'		E	F'	S'R'S'	I	S'T'R'S'H			A,B,H		S'	S'	G	E	F	S'	T'	B	B
CUADRO		24	23	25	24	24	24	13	23	13	25	29	25	29	26	26	35	29	29	29	29	35	44	34	34	30
EDIFICIO		1	1	1	1	1	1	1	1	1	3	1	3	1	1	11	3	3	3	3	2		2	2	2	
ETAPA		5	5	5	5	5	5	3	5	5	5	5	5	7	5	4	4	5	5	5	5		5	5	5	2
UB. VERTICAL		2	2	2	2	2	2	1	3	1	2	2	1	2	2	1	1	1	2	2	2		3	2	2	3
UB. HORIZONTAL		5	5	5	5	5	3	4	3	5	5	4	4	5	4	3	4	5	4	4	10		5	5	4	
Caract. ofrenda																										
DIMENSION N-S		102	40	60	85	150	65	150	100	55	55	125	33	130	85	100	45	95	52	45	155	90	90	93	80	30
DIMENSION E-W		94	50	60	230	200	65	110	74	65	55	90	26	150	85	90	40	170	47	38	125	70	110	143	110	30
DIMENSION Z		102	80	80	125	125		95	71					40			40	55	40	30		70		105		
ORIENTACION		4	6	6	6	4		2	4	2		4		4	4	3	4		3		4		4	1	4	
NIVEL EXCAVADO		4	1	1	0	1	3	1	2	1	4	1		7	2	3	1	2	1	1	3	3	4	4	4	1
NIVEL PROPUESTO		6	1	3	0	1	5	6	2	1	1	5		6	3	3		5	3	3	5	2	5	6	6	1
CONTINENTE		3	3	3	3	3	4	3	3	1	4	4		3	4	4	3	3	2	2	4	3	4	3	4	1
RANGO ELEMENTOS		4	1	3	1	4	4	3	1	2	1	4	1	5	1	1	1	5	1	1	4	1	2	5	2	1
No. ELEMENTOS		173	3	119	0	152	152	121	21	58	4	195	7	226	23	44	13	114	14	14	172	12	76	249	58	3
	SUMA	42	3	20	0	17	37	29	5	17	5	42	8	40	10	21	3	41	8	7	45	12	25	39	25	3

Tipo de objeto		1	2	3	4	5	6	7	8	9	10	11	12	13	14	15	16	17	18	19	20	21	22	23	24	25
1 XIUHTECUHTLI	2						1	1				1			1		1	1	1						1	1
2 TONACATECUHTLI	1	1																								
3 MICTLANTECUHTLI	0							1																		
4 TLATECUHTLI	1																									
5 TEZCATLIPOCA	0														1											
6 EHECATL	0									1	1	1								1						
7 TLALOC	2	1					1	1			1		1		1		1	1	1	1	1			1	1	
8 CHALCHIUHTLICUE	0	1					1				1		1		1		1			1		1		1		
9 MASCARA-CRANEO	0						1				1						1			1						
10 MAS.ANTROPOMORFA	2						1				1															
11 FIG.ANTROPOMORFA	2			1		1			1		1	1														
12 PENATE	1						1			1				1												
13 TECPATL	0	1					1				1		1				1			1						
14 DEIDAD OLLA	1					1																	1	1		
15 DEIDAD COPAL	0	1					1				1		1		1											
16 XIUHCOATL	0	1									1		1		1											
17 CETRO VENADO	0	1									1		1				1					1		1		
18 CETRO SERPENTIFORME	1	1									1		1				1					1		1		
19 CHICAHUAZTLI	2	1						1			1		1				1					1		1		
20 CROTALO-CABEZA	0	1		1		1	1				1		1				1									
21 MORTERO o MANO	0	1		1	1	1					1		1				1					1				
22 REP. CUNA	0																									
23 BRASERO c/ MOÑO	0	1									1		1												1	
24 NARIGUERA XIPE	1										1						1							1		
25 OYOHUALLI	0						1				1		1				1					1	1	1		
26 CIRCULO CONCHA	1	1			1	1	1				1		1		1		1			1		1	1	1		
27 CIRCULO OBSIDIANA	0	1		1	1	1					1		1	1												
28 EPCOLOLLI	0						1				1		1				1						1			
29 ARENA	0						1	1			1						1			1			1			
30 HULE	0	1																								
31 CUENTA P.V.	3	1	1	1		1	1				1		1			1	1	1	1	1	1	1	1	1		
32 P.V.FRAGMENTADA	2																									
33 ALABASTRO	1																									
34 TURQUESA	1																									
35 AZABACHE	0																									
36 JAGUAR	0									1														1		1
37 PUMA	2						1																	1	1	
38 LINCE	0													1												
39 LOBO	0	1									1															
40 ARMADILLO	0																							1		
41 CONEJO	0																							1		
42 AGUILA	1	1					1			1			1				1							1		
43 HALCON	0						1																			
44 CUERVO	0																1									
45 TUCAN	0																							1	1	
46 GARZA	0																									
47 PELICANO	0							1																		
48 GUAJOLOTE	0									1																
49 COCODRILO	0	1		1			1	1						1			1									
50 SERPIENTE	0							1					1		1		1			1	1	1	1			
51 TORTUGA	0						1	1					1		1		1					1	1			
52 SAPO	0														1		1						1			
53 TIBURON	1						1						1		1		1			1	1	1	1	1		
54 PEZ SIERRA	1						1	1					1		1		1			1	1	1	1	1		
55 PESCADO	0	1		1			1	1	1			1	1	1		1	1			1	1	1	1	1		
56 CARACOL	1	1		1	1	1	1	1		1		1	1		1		1			1	1	1	1	1		
57 CONCHA	3	1		1	1	1	1	1		1		1	1		1		1			1	1	1	1	1		
58 CRUSTACEO	0	1																								
59 CUITON	1	1		1													1									
60 ERIZO	0	1					1					1			1		1			1		1	1			
61 CORAL	3	1		1			1					1			1		1			1	1	1	1	1		
62 REP. FELINO	0														1											
63 REP. AVE	0															1										
64 REP. SERPIENTE	1									1																
65 REP. TORTUGA	1																									
66 REP. PEZ	2																									
67 REP. CARACOL	0																									
68 REP. FITOMORFA	0																							1		
69 MALINALLI	0						1							1										1		
70 CUENTA HELICOIDE	0																							1		
71 ESPIRAL	0						1						1	1	1		1							1		
72 PUNZON	1	1					1																	1		
73 MANTA RAYA	0												1	1		1		1	1	1	1		1			
74 NAVAJILLA	0																									
75 NUCLEO	0																									
76 CUCHILLO	3	1		1		1	1	1			1	1	1		1		1			1			1	1		
77 RASPADOR	0	1											1				1									
78 CRANEO DECAPITADO	0	1					1						1				1									
79 NIÑO DEGOLLADO	0																									
80 CODORNIZ	0	1		1			1	1	1			1	1			1							1			
81 SAHUMADOR	1							1					1										1			
82 TEPALCATE	0						1	1					1													
83 BRASERO	0	1					1	1					1				1						1			
84 OLLA	2																									
85 CAJETE	1																									
86 CARBON	0			1									1									1	1			
87 COPAL	2	1		1									1									1	1	1	1	
88 SEMILLA	0	1																								
89 INST. MUSICAL	1								1																	
90 CANOA	0																									
91 ATLATL	0												1								1					
92 HACHA o MAZO	0	1		1			1			1			1				1			1			1			
93 PUNTA PROYECTIL	0			1			1	1		1			1		1		1			1						
94 COLLAR ORO	0																									
95 COLLAR TURQUESA	0																									
96 COLLAR CRISTAL	0																1									
97 COLLAR P.V.	0																								1	
98 PECTORAL Y PEND	2												1							1		1	1	1		
99 OREJERA o NARIGUERA	2	1		1			1	1		1			1				1			1		1	1	1		
100 CASCABEL	2	1	1	1		1	1			1			1		1		1			1		1	1	1		
101 TEXTIL	0																									
102 PLUMA	0	1																								
103 RELIQUIA	0												1									1				
104 INCINERADO	0		1	1						1			1													
105 NO INCINERADO	0																									
106 URNA	0									1																
107 CUENTA EN BOCA	1																				1	1			1	1
108 MADERA	2	1		1									1		1		1			1		1	1	1		
109 MOSAICO TURQUESA	1	1					1						1				1									

25	26	27	28	29	30	31	32	33	34	35	36	37	38	39	40	41	42	43	44	45	46	47	48	49	50	51	52	53	54	55	56
B	D	B'	A'	R'S'S'	C	D	A'	A'	C	C	D	A	C'D'A'	C'	U'V'A		C	A	A'B'C		C	D	Q'	M	M	M	M	U'	Q'	B'	D'	M
30	34	40	37	21	34	34	34	25	25	38	23	28	25	26	33	34	36	34	27	33	29	29	40	33	30	29	26	44	43	39	42
2	2	9	2	1	2	2	2	2	1	2	1	1	1	1	2	2	2	2	1	2	1	2	2	2	2	3	1	2	2	2	2
2	2	6	2	4	4			1	2	2	1	1	1	1	5	1	2	1	1	2	2	5	8	8	8	5	6	2	3		
3	3	2	3	3	2	2		5	5	3	3	5	5	5	5	2	5	3	5	5	3	3	2	1	1	2	1	1	3	3	3
4	4	10	2	3	5	5		1	6	4	1	1	1	1	5	1	4	1	1	1	4	4	4	4	11	4	4	11	11	2	2

30	30	105	30	35	30	42	55	22	100	30	60	20	35	23	60	100	45	30	20	30	38	30	180	45	45	85	65	55	93	40	90	1
30	30	120	30	45	100	40	65	22	80	30	60	20	18	35	80	97	65	30	20	39	53	30	120	45	45	75	80	30	133	45	65	
		17	23	65	45		?			35			57			28			50						100	25	70					
1	1	3	1	4	4	3	6	4	4	1	6	4	4	4	4	4	4	2	1	4	4	4	4	3	2	5	6	2				
1	1	1	1	4	4	3	0	2	2	1	0	3	3	4	1	9	2	1	2	1	1	5	1	4	4	1	2	1	5	0	1
1	1	1	1	1	1	2	0	3	2	1	0	1	1	2	3	4	1	1	1	2	1	5	2	2	1	3	2	5	0	2	
1	1	1	1	2	3	3	3	3	4	1	3	4	3	4	4	3	4	1	4	3	1	1	3	1	1	1	1	4	3	3	3
1	1	1	1	1	1	3	1	1	1	1	1	1	2	1	4	1	1	1	2	1	1	4	1	1	1	1	2	1	2	1	1
3	3	17	3	17	16	131	0	14	13	4	0	13	13	78	5	196	4	3	3	68	1	4	157	13	12	16	58	6	75	0	11

3	3	9	3	4	4	9	0	5	14	4	0	6	5	15	5	22	4	3	3	6	2	4	12	9	11	6	12	7	17	0	8

```
 57  58  59  60  61  62  63  64  65  66  67  68  69  70  71  72  73  74  75  76  77  78  79  80  81  82  83  84  85  86  87  8

    Ñ'O'O  G   D'E'B'C'I'   D"  M   O  P K'  O   E'F'E"   N   O   P   P   N  T'U'X'  C   Z'  V'  D"  M   M   F'  Q'  I   Z'  H
 19  43  19  13  44  13  44  10  19  19  44  19  44  23  20  18  18  17  44  44  24   4  18  29  10  14  13  49  40  33  26   3
 13   2  10   1   2   1   2   1  10  10   2  10   2   1  10  10  10  10   2   2   1   8   1   2   1   1   1   2   2   2   1
  8   5   8   5   5   5   8   7   8   5   8   5   7   7   7   7   5   5   6   7   6   8   5   5   8   4   6   7
  1   2   2   1   1   1   1   2   2   2   1   2   1   1   1   1   2   1   1   2   5   2   2   2   1   1   2   2   2   2
  5  11   4  12   2   3   7  13   5   4   7   4   2   5   2  12  12   4   7  11   5   1   5  13  12  12   2  11   4   5

 00 100  75 165 147 100  60 100  50  25  60  40  40  38  30  87  20  20  60 100  80 157  60  50  32  55  75  47  75  33  40  12
 80  80  90 125  85 350  60 140  35  32  60  74 135  65  40  60  20  20  60  90 100  97 125  50  50  40  90  37  72  45  30  18
              ?          80                      25      18   5               35 150 100      38          35               8
  4   2   4   2   1   2   1   4   4   3   1   4   1   4   6   1   6   6   1   1   6   3   6   2   4   2   4   4   3   2
  2   3   2   1   6   2   1   2   4   1   1   3   4   7   1   1   1   1   1   4   0   1   5   5   2   3   7   1   1
  3   5   1   5   6   4   1   2   1   1   3   1   4   1   1   1   1   3   0   1   3   4   3   4   3   2   1
  1   4   1   3   3   4   4   1   4   4   4   4   3   1   1   1   4   1   3   3   3   1   3   4   4   3   1   1   1
  2   2   2   2   1   2   1   2   1   1   2   1   3   1   1   1   1   1   5   1   1   2   1   1   1   2   1   1
 66  52  71  77  49  63   1  64  25   7   1  62  26 126  11   1   1   3   1   5  11 235   0   3  75  11  29  20  98   6  18  18

  9  24   7  30  28  21   1  13   5   1   1   8  11  19   1   1   1   3   1   2   7  29   0   4   9   8   8  14  12   6  10   3
```

```
      8  89  90  91  92  93  94 C2  C3  A   B   C   D   E   F   G   H   I   J   K   L   M   N   Ñ   O   P   Q  E1  B1  B2  CA

     MUS  B  B'H  S'  S'  C'  Q'  Q'  U'  Q'  B   E'  L'  M'N'K'  G'  Q'  C   Ñ'O'Q  C   G'  H   H'I'H'O'H'  O   D'  E'  Ñ'
  4  MUS 17  33  24  24  33  34  40  62  60  57  51  51  51  51  51  50  51  50  50  50  51  66  57  50  61  18  13  13  15
  2   12  1   2   1   1   2   2   2  14  14   5   4   4  15   5   4   6   4   4   6   5   7  14   4  14  10   1   1   1
  5    7  7   5   4   4   1   5   4   8   8   8   8   8   7   7   8   8   7   8   8   6   8   6   6   6   7   6   6   5
  1    1  1   1   2   2   5   2   2   4  '4'  3   1   1   4   1   5   4   4   5   4   5   5   4   5   5   5   1   2   2   2
  4    4  5   4   5   5   1   5  11   3   5   5   4   4   4   1   4   5   4   4   5   1   5   1   1   1   4   3   3  13

  0    ?  43  20  60  60  71 116 112  72  65  85   ?      40  55  73  52 110  35  43  75 150  65  40 122  47  40  56  75   ? 100
  0    ?  44  16 100 105  35 156 109  72  85  85   ?      30  75  73  84 120  40  92  65  99  75  35 122  50  50  56  40   ? 100
  0    ?  53         50  15  94 135          45   ?           42  57  25      48          200      50  43  40
  3    4  6   6   4   5   4   4   4   2   4   6   6   4   4   6   4   3   4   4   6   4   3   6   3   5   1   2   2   2
  7    3  0   2   2   1   1  11   8   2   2   0   0   1   3   1   4   3   4   7   0   4   3   4   7   0   7   2   1   1
  6    4  0   2   2   1   1   3   2   1   3   0   0   1   2   1   5   5   3   4   5   0   5   3   1   6   1   1   1   3
  3    3  3   4   4   3   4   3   3   1   1   1   3   3   4   1   4   3   3   1   3   1   3   1   1   3   3   3   1   4
  4    2  1   1   1   2   7   6   1   2   1   2   1   1   1   1   3   1   3   1   3   1   1   2   1   1   1   1   3
  5   53  0  12  25   4  93 364 254  35  61   0   0  11  16   1 150  67  11 116  77   0 102  15   1  53   8   2  19  31 116

  7    7  0   2   7   4   2  29  35   9  10   0   0   3   8   1  27   4   9  14  15   0  12   4   1  12   5   2   9  12  22
  1                        1   1                             1                             1               1               1
                               1
                               1

  1    1                  1   1                  1       1       1       1                     1                                 1
                               1
  1    1                  1   1                                                        1                                     1  1  1
                               1                         1                                             1                            1
  1                      1                                   1                         1
  1                      1   1       1           1               1       1       1                                              1
  1    1                  1   1                          1
                                 1                                   1   1
                                                                                                                                1
  1                      1                       1                                                                          1
  1                      1           1                       1                                                          1  1
                                                                     1   1   1                                              1
  1            1          1   1   1   1           1               1       1               1                   1               1
                         1   1
                         1
                         1
                             1   1                               1
                                                                     1
  1                              1                       1                   1           1     1  1
  1    1                              1                       1                           1   1  1
  1            1   1          1                  1                           1           1                       1  1  1
  1    1          1           1   1   1   1           1   1       1   1   1   1       1   1           1  1       1  1  1
  1                          1                                   1               1                         1
  1                          1   1   1               1               1       1       1               1               1
                         1
                             1
                             1   1                   1
                             1                       1
  1                                                          1
  1                                                  1                       1
  1                          1                               1                               1
  1            1                  1                      1       1               1     1
                 1       1               1   1   1       1   1   1   1       1   1           1  1       1  1  1
  1                                                                  1                                         1
  1            1   1                  1                      1   1  1
  1                                                          1   1
  1                                                          1                               1  1
                         1   1                                               1
  1    1          1   1   1   1   1       1                   1   1       1           1           1  1
  1       1                       1                          1
  1                                              1                   1
  1                          1           1   1  1                       1                   1  1
       1                                  1           1
  1                          1   1           1                   1
  1            1             1   1                           1
  1                          1   1       1                   1   1                   1               1  1
                                                                                        1
  1    1                  1       1   1                               1   1   1   1       1     5
                             1
```

No. OFRENDA

	13	17	11	2(	6	1	23	60	/	61	88	C2	C3	41	78	54	H	22	58	24	15	62	70	CA
Ubicacion gral.																								
SALA	S'T'H	S'	G	T'U'T'	S'	G	D'	D'E'	H	Q'	Q'	U'V'C	Q'	G'	E	F	Ñ'O'T'	H	B'C'E"	Ñ'	R			
CUADRO	29	29	29	24	24	34	13	13	44	34	34	40	34	4	43	51	44	43	34	26	13	23	15	
EDIFICIO	3	3	3	1	1	2	1	2	2	2	2	8	2	5	2	2	2	1	1	1				
ETAPA	5	5	5	4	5	5	5	5	5	4	5	7	6	7	5	5	5	7	5					
UB. VERTICAL	2	1	2	2	2	1	1	1	1	2	2	5	3	5	2	2	1	1	2					
UB. HORIZONTAL	5	4	5	4	5	5	5	12	3	2	4	5	11	5	1	11	1	10	11	5	4	3	5	13
Caract. ofrenda																								
DIMENSION N-S	130	95	125	155	65	102	93	165	150	147	120	116	112	100	157	93	52	90	100	80	100	100	38	100
DIMENSION E-W	150	170	90	125	65	94	143	125	110	85	180	156	109	97	97	133	84	110	80	110	90	350	65	100
DIMENSION Z	40	55				102	105	?		95	80	80	94	135	57	150	100	57					25	
ORIENTACION	4	4	4	4	4	4	2	4	1	3	3	4	4	3	5	4	1	2	4	3	2	4	2	
NIVEL EXCAVADO	7	2	4	3	4	4	6	1	3	6	7	11	8	9	4	5	6	4	3	2	7	3		
NIVEL PROPUESTO	6	5	5	5	6	6	5	6	6	6	3	2	4	3	5	5	5	6	4	1				
CONTINENTE	3	3	4	3	3	3	3	3	3	3	3	3	3	3	4	4	4	4	4	1				
RANGO ELEMENTOS	5	5	4	4	4	4	4	5	2	3	1	4	7	6	4	5	2	3	2	1	2	3	3	
No. ELEMENTOS	226	114	195	172	152	173	249	77	121	49	185	364	254	196	235	75	150	76	52	58	44	63	126	116

Tipo de objeto	SUMA	40	41	42	45	37	42	39	30	29	28	37	29	35	22	29	17	27	25	24	25	21	21	19	22
56 CARACOL	58	1	1	1	1	1	1	1	1			1	1	1	1			1	1	1	1	1		1	1
57 CONCHA	50	1	1	1	1	1	1	1	1			1	1	1	1	1		1	1	1	1		1	1	1
31 CUENTA P.V.	57	1	1	1	1	1	1	1	1			1	1	1	1			1	1	1	1	1		1	1
87 COPAL	61	1	1	1	1	1	1	1	1			1	1	1	1	1		1	1	1	1		1	1	
100 CASCABEL	38	1	1	1	1	1		1				1			1			1	1	1		1		1	
108 MADERA	39	1	1	1	1	1						1			1			1		1				1	
76 CUCHILLO	57	1	1	1	1	1	1	1				1			1			1		1	1	1		1	1
74 NAVAJILLA	21	1			1							1						1	1		1			1	1
82 TEPALCATE	22	1							1			1	1		1			1	1		1			1	1
84 OLLA	18											1	1	1	1			1	1		1				
85 CAJETE	11													1										1	
11 FIG.ANTROPOMORFA	19			1	1							1	1	1	1			1							1
99 OREJERA o NARIGUERA	22	1	1	1	1	1						1	1	1	1			1							1
104 INCINERADO	10																								
106 URNA	8													1											
27 CIRCULO OBSIDIANA	14		1	1	1	1							1			1					1	1			
10 MAS.ANTROPOMORFA	12			1	1							1	1			1					1	1			
37 PUMA	9			1	1		1	1				1	1			1									
12 PENATE	14			1	1							1				1			1			1	1		1
14 DEIDAD OLLA	8						1	1	1	1		1													
69 MALINALLI	5						1		1	1		1													
71 ESPIRAL	6						1		1	1		1			1	1									
32 P.V.FRAGMENTADA	7											1	1	1		1									
63 REP. AVE	4											1	1			1									
103 RELIQUIA	6			1	1				1				1	1											1
23 BRASERO c/ MOÑO	5		1	1	1		1																		
3 MICTLANTECUHTLI	4			1	1	1																			
70 CUENTA HELICOIDE	4																								
68 REP. FITOMORFA	5											1		1		1									
36 JAGUAR	3											1	1												
64 REP. SERPIENTE	4			1	1																				
6 EHECATL	4			1	1																				
17 CETRO VENADO	7		1	1	1		1											1	1	1					
24 NARIGUERA XIPE	10	1	1	1	1		1					1		1				1	1	1					
39 LOBO	4			1			1											1							
59 QUITON	5						1					1						1							
16 XIUHCOATL	4	1			1		1													1					
77 RASPADOR	3	1	1				1																		
4 TLATECUHTLI	1												1												
34 TURQUESA	1												1												
2 TONACATECUHTLI	2						1						1												
66 REP. PEZ	3											1	1												
38 LINCE	1									1															
75 NUCLEO	2									1															
41 CONEJO	3							1	1																
65 REP. TORTUGA	3													1	1		1								
67 REP. CARACOL	3												1	1		1									
30 HULE	2														1	1									
90 CANOA	2														1	1									
88 SEMILLA	5							1					1		1	1									
102 PLUMA	2							1								1									
101 TEXTIL	3		1										1		1										
33 ALABASTRO	2												1												
35 AZABACHE	1									1															
47 PELICANO	1								1																
58 CRUSTACEO	3							1	1																
22 REP. CUNA	3			1															1	1					
52 SAPO	1								1																
73 MANTA RAYA	1								1																
46 GARZA	2																					1			
48 GUAJOLOTE	1																								
79 NIÑO DEGOLLADO	1																								
96 COLLAR CRISTAL	1																								
105 NO INCINERADO	1																								
62 REP. FELINO	1	1																							
45 TUCAN	1		1																						
44 CUERVO	1					1																			
40 ARMADILLO	1														1										
5 TEZCATLIPOCA	1																								
95 COLLAR TURQUESA	2				1																				
43 HALCON	2				1																				
8 CHALCHIUHTLICUE	1												1												
107 CUENTA EN BOCA	3												1												
94 COLLAR ORO	3												1												
81 SAHUMADOR	7	1						1	1	1		1	1												
97 COLLAR P.V.	8							1																	
89 INST. MUSICAL	11											1		1	1	1		1							
86 CARBON	16	1										1						1	1	1	1				
55 PESCADO	28	1	1	1	1		1	1	1	1	1	1		1	1			1		1	1	1			
80 CODORNIZ	31	1	1	1	1	1	1	1	1	1	1	1	1	1	1		1			1	1	1			
1 XIUHTECUHTLI	26	1	1	1	1	1	1	1	1	1	1	1	1		1			1			1	1	1		
7 TLALOC	36	1	1	1	1	1	1	1	1	1	1	1	1	1	1		1			1	1	1	1	1	
15 DEIDAD COPAL	24	1		1	1	1	1		1			1	1	1	1					1	1	1			
61 CORAL	39	1	1	1	1	1		1	1	1	1	1	1	1	1			1	1	1	1	1	1	1	
26 CIRCULO CONCHA	27	1	1	1	1	1	1	1	1	1	1	1	1		1				1	1	1	1	1	1	
98 PECTORAL Y PEND	23	1	1	1	1		1					1	1		1			1	1	1	1	1		1	
9 MASCARA-CRANEO	15	1	1	1	1	1												1	1	1	1		1		
51 TORTUGA	16									1	1	1	:	:				1	1	1	1	1			
54 PEZ SIERRA	23	1	1	1	1		1	1				1	1		1		1			1	1	1			
18 CETRO SERPENTIFORME	17	1	1	1	1	1	1	1				1	1			1	1	1							
19 CHICAHUAZTLI	19	1	1	1			1	1				1	1			1	1	1			1				
67 ERIZO	18			1	1		1	1	1	1		1	1			1		1			1				
25 ARENA	20			1	1		1	1	1	1		1	1			1		1					1		
25 OYOHUALLI	14	1		1	1		1		1			1	1			1			1						
50 SERPIENTE	15		1				1	1	1	1		1										1	1		
49 COCODRILO	12		1		1	1	1	1	1	1												1	1		
53 TIBURON	11	1	1				1	1	1			1							1			1	1		
72 PUNZON	19	1	1				1	1	1	1		1							1			1	1		
83 BRASERO	11			1	1		1	1	1				1		1										
91 ATLATL	9	1	1	1	1		1	1					1		1										
42 AGUILA	15	1	1		1	1	1	1				1											1		
28 EPCOLOLLI	6			1																				1	
92 HACHA o MAZO	7	1	1				1		1															1	
20 CROTALO-CABEZA	8	1	1				1		1															1	
109 MOSAICO TURQUESA	9	1	1	1	1	1	1		1			1													
21 MORTERO o MANO	13	1	1	1	1	1	1		1									1		1			1	1	
29 TECPATL	14	1	1	1	1	1																			
78 CRANEO DECAPITADO	15	1	1	1	1	1	1		1					1			1	1	1			1			
93 PUNTA PROYECTIL	25	1	1	1	1	1	1	1	1	1	1	1						1			1			1	

```
  3   5  34  39  44  74  29  10  37  14  18  19  89  69  49  50  J   84  48  52  57  87  27  77  K   68  N   B1  64  L   21  56  3

'   Q'  A'  A'  A   P   A'  S'R'A   R'S'S'  S'  MUS E'F'M  M   C   F'  Q'  M   M   Z'  D   X'  Ñ'O'O   G'  D'  D"  Q   E   D'  S'
25  24  25  26  27  17  21  25  28  26  29  29  MUS 44  33  30  51  49  40  26  19  26  40  24  50  19  51  13  10  50  35  42  3
 1   1   1   1   1  10   1   1   1   1   1   3   3  12   2   2   2   6   2   2   1  13   1   9   1   4  10   5   1   1   4   2   2
 5   5   1   1   1   7   2   5   1   5   4   4   7   5   8   8   8   5   8   8   7   6   6   7   8   6   6   8   8   3   3
 2   2   5   5   5   2   3   2   5   2   2   2   1   1   1   4   2   2   1   2   2   5   2   5   2   2   4   3   3
 5   5   1   1   1   4   3   5   1   5   5   5   4   2   4   4   4   2  11   4   5   5  10   5   4   4   1   3  13   5   4   2

60 150 100  23  20  20  35  55  26  85  52  45   ?  40  45  45  35  47 180  65 100  40 105  80  43  40  65  75 100  75  90  90  4
60 200  80  35  20  20  45  55  20  85  47  38   ? 135  45  45  40  37 120  80  80  30 120 100  92  74  75  40 140  65  70  65  4
80 125          17              40  30   ?              35  50                  35  48                      70  70  6
 6   4   4   4   4   6   4   4   4   4   2   2       4   1   4   4   4   1   3   4   2   3   6   4   4   2   4   4   4   2
 1   1   2   4   1   1   1   1   3   2   1   1   3   4   1   1   3   3   5   2   2   1   1   1   4   3   5   1   2   5   2   2
 3   3   4   4   1   2   4   4   2   2   3   4   1   1   1   3   3   4   5   3   3   1   1   1   3   4   1   1   1   3   3
 3   4   1   2   1   1   1   1   1   1   1   2   1   1   1   1   1   2   2   1   1   1   3   2   3   1   2   2   1   1
19 152  13  78   3   3  17   4  13  23  14  14  53  26  13  12  11  20 157  58  66  18  17  11 116  62 102  19  64  77  12  11 13

20  17  14  15   3   3   4   5   6  10   8   7   7  11   9  11   9  14  12  12   9  10   9   7  14   8  12   9  13  15  12  8
```

```
        1  83  F     51  59  A   P     81  86  B     53  B2  85  45  82   8  92  12   2  16  33  40  38  28  43  26  25  35  47  67  75  63

        M   M'N'M   O   U'  H'O'D"  I   Q'  U'  E'  Q'  A'B'M  E   S'  I   S'  A,B,A'  C'  C'D'B'  C   B   B   C   CD K'  N   I'  H
        4  13  51  29  19  62  50  10  33  60  44  13  40  33  14  23  24  25  23  35  25  33  25  37  34  34  30  38  29  44  44  44
        2   1   4   3  10  14   4   1   2  14   2   1   2   2   1   1   1   1  11   1   2   1   2  *2   2   2   2   2   2   2   2   2
        4   5   8   8   8   8   6   8   6   8   5   6   4   1   5   3   4   5   5   7   1   1   1   2   2   2   2   2   5   5   5
        2   1   4   2   2   4   5   2   2   4   1   2   2   5   1   3   2   1   2   1   5   1   5   5   3   3   3   3   3   1   1   1
        5  12   4   4   4   3   1  13   4   5  11   3  11   1  12   4   5   4   5   3   1   1   2   4   4   4   6   4   7   7   7

        2  75  55  85  75  72  47  32  33  65  55   ?  75  30  55 100  60  33  40  45  22  60  35  30  30  30  30  30  30  60  60  60
        0  90  75  75  90  72  50  50  45  85  30   ?  72  39  40  74 100  26  50  40  22  80  18  30  30  30  30  30  30  60  60  60
        5                  43  38              28          71          80  40  20          35
        3   4   4   4   4   2   3   4   3   4   2   4   4   2   4   4   6   4   4   4   1   4   1   1   1   4   1   1   1
        3   2   3   1   2   2   5   5   1   2   1   1   7   2   5   1   2   1   1   2   1   3   1   1   1   1   1   1   1
        2   3   2   1   1   1   6   3   2   3   2   1   3   3   1   3   1   1   1   1   3   4   3   1   1   1   1   1   1
        3   4   1   1   1   1   3   3   1   1   4   1   1   2   4   3   4   3   3   4   3   1   1   1   1   1   1   4   4   4
        3   1   1   1   2   1   2   2   1   2   1   1   2   2   1   1   1   1   1   1   1   1   1   1   1   1   1   1   1
        1  29  16  16  71  35  53  75   6  61   6  31  98  68  11  21  25   7   3  13  14   5  13   3   3   3   3   4   4   1   1   1

        9   8   8   6   7   9  12   9   6  10   7  12  12   6   8   5   7   8   3   3   5   5   5   3   3   3   3   4   4   1   1   1

        1   1   1   1   1   1   1   1   1       1       1   1                   1   1
        1   1               1   1       1       1   1
        1   1                       1   1   1   1       1                   1   1   1   1   1   1   1   1   1   1
                1   1   1   1   1   1           1   1       1                   1   1           1   1   1   1   1   1
                    1   1   1   1   1                   1                   1   1
                1   1   1   1   1   1   1   1   1   1   1           1   1   1       1           1
                                    1   1       1                       1                   1   1   1   1   1   1
                                                                        1                   1   1   1   1   1   1
        1                                       1   1                   1
                                                    1   1
                                                    1
                                        1
```

```
    91  72  73  M   D   C       90  79  55  36  32   4  G   O      71 E1      76  30 Ñ      93 I      42  46  66 E   Q      94  80  65   9

        O   P   C  E'   B       B' B'Z'  B'  C   D   C   D  S'      K' H'I'N   O  T'U'R'S'H  S' Q'      A   C   O  P  L'  H'  C'  V'   M  F'
    33  18  18  50  51  57  17  18  39  23  34  24  51  57  20  18  44  34  66  24  50  36  29  19  51  61  33  29  19  13
     2  10  10   6   5  14   1   1   2   1   2   1  15  14  10  10   2   2   7   1   4   2   1  10   4  14   2   2  10   1
     5   7   7   8   8   8   7   7   2   2   2   5   7   6   7   7   5   4   8   4   8   1   2   8   8   6   1   6   7   5
     1   1   1   5   1   3   1   2   3   3   3   2   1   5   1   1   2   4   2   4   5   3   2   1   5   5   5   2   2   1
     4  12  12   1   4   5   5   5   2   4   4   5   1   1   2   4  11   5   5   5   5   1   4   4   4   1   1   5   5   3

    20  87  20 150   ?      85  43  60  40  60  55  85  73 122  30  56 100  30  40  60 110  45  38  25  40  40  71  50  50  55
    16  60  20  99   ?      85  44 125  45  60  85 230  73 122  40  56  90 100  35 105 120  65  53  32  30  50  35  50  35  65
        18   5 200   ?      45  53 100  25   ?      45 125  42  50              23          50  25              40  15
     6   1   6   6   6   6   6   6   6   6   6   6   6   6   1   1   4   3   5   3   4   4   3   4   5   4   2   4   2
     2   1   1   0   0   0   0   0   0   0   0   0   1   1   1   1   1   1   2   1   4   2   1   1   1   1   1   1   4   2
     2   1   1   0   0   0   0   0   0   0   0   0   1   1   1   1   1   1   3   1   5   1   1   1   1   1   1   1   4   1
     4   1   1   3   3   3   3   3   3   3   3   4   1   1   1   1   1   3   1   3   3   4   1   4   4   3   4   1   4   1
     1   1   1   1   1   1   1   1   1   1   1   1   1   1   1   1   1   1   1   1   1   2   1   1   1   1   2   1   1   2
    12   1   1   0   0   0   0   0   0   0   0   0   1   1  11   2   5  16  15   4  67   4   1   7  11   8  93   3  25  58

     2   1   1   0   0   0   0   0   0   0   0   0   0   1   1   1   2   2   4   4   4   4   4   2   1   3   5   2   4   5  17
                                                                                                            1
                                                                                                                1       1
     1                                                                   1                               1   1   1
     1                                                                   1               1       1                       1
                                                                            1       1   1   1   1   1   1   1   1   1
                                                                    1                           1
                                                                                                1
                                         1   1                       1                   1
                                                                                                            1
                                                                                                            1
```

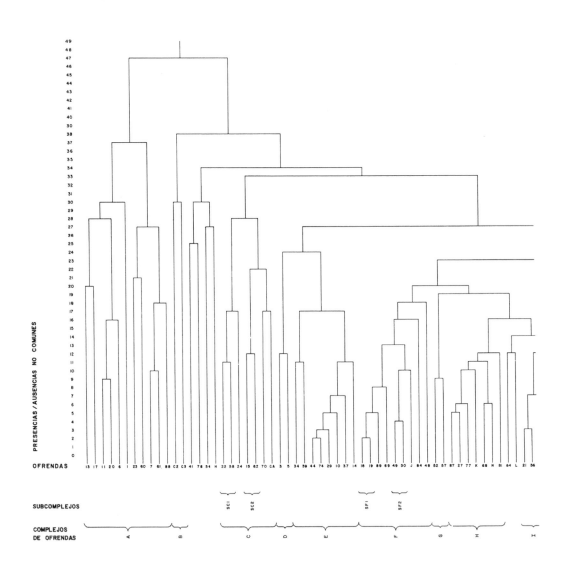

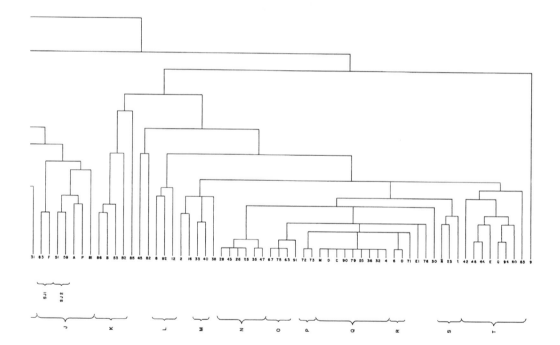

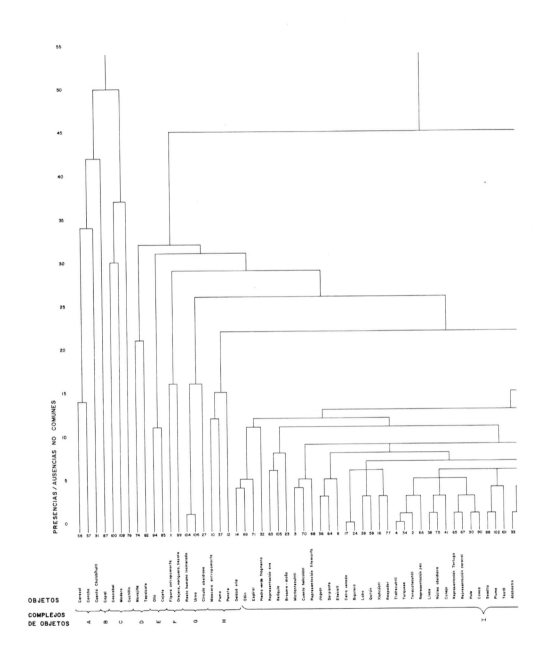

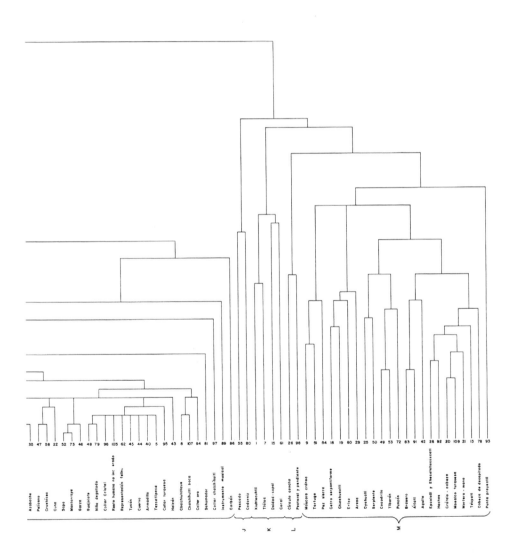

Notes

CHAPTER 1

1. These practices were not unknown before the arrival of the Spanish in the New World. Various Mesoamerican peoples frequently obtained "antiquities" from the ruins of abandoned cities. See López Luján (1989b: 17–19, 62–65, 2001b) concerning the exploration of ancient tombs and offerings in pre-Columbian Mexico.

2. I want to make clear that I do not deny the great value of previous works referring to the Mexica offerings. I only point out their limitations and urge investigators to be cautious in using them.

3. The results were published in *Tlatelolco a través de los tiempos* (vols. 1–10, supplements to the *Memorias de la Academia Mexicana de la Historia*, 1944–1947).

4. Espejo (1945) distinguished between offerings with a ceremonial function deposited for that purpose in the body of the architectural structures (type 2) and those of a mortuary character (type 1).

5. Speaking of conservation in situ, Espejo (1945: 16) said that the wooden objects were preserved by applying an acetone solution of celluloid or liquid paraffin in alcohol.

6. The report was sent to Eduardo Noguera, the director of the department, on January 5, 1949. Presently, it is found in volume 42 of the papers of the Archives of the Consejo de Arqueología in Mexico City.

7. Doris Heyden (1972) speaks of a verbal communication by Eduardo Contreras: "A great number of maguey thorns arranged in a circle without other objects have been found. Contreras found thorns associated with the burial of children. On one occasion a blue-green *petate* (reed mat) was found with an offering of maguey thorns on top" (see also Gonzáles Rul 1979, 1988).

8. Another interesting find was published by González Rul (1963).

9. Raúl M. Arana, Angel García Cook, Santiago Analco, Francisco Hinojosa, Guillermo Ahuja, and Francisco González Rul participated in the excavation of offerings. Alejandro Nishimura and Esperanza Teixier were in charge of in situ conservation.

CHAPTER 2

1. In 1977 the INAH planned the Museum of Tenochtitlan project, which "had as its purpose excavating at the site of the Templo Mayor and establishing a museum about what had once been the ancient Mexica city" (Matos Moctezuma 1978). Because of circumstances that will be described later, the project was never carried out.

2. This short text by López Portillo reveals a great deal about ties existing between Mexican archaeology and political power.

3. The coordinators of this section have been José Arroyo (1978), Yolanda Santaella (1978–1981), María Luisa Franco Brizuela (1981–1982), and Bertha Peña Tenorio (1983–1991).

4. The coordinators have been Francisco Hinojosa (1978), Juan Alberto Román Berrelleza (1978–1982), Guillermo Ahuja (1983–1990), and Adrián Velázquez (1990–1991).

5. Víctor Baca, Francisco Ahuja, Salvador Guil'liem, Don Patterson, and Germán Zúñiga have been involved in this group.

6. This group was made up of Amelia Malagamba, Don Patterson, Víctor Rangel, and Alberto Zúñiga.

7. Guillermo Ahuja (1982) was in charge of analyzing pre-Hispanic ceramics. Gonzalo López Cervantes (1982) studied the colonial ceramics.

8. It was headed by Mariano López.

9. So far, twenty-five professional theses have been presented, and more than 350 works related to the findings of the Templo Mayor Project have been published. A preliminary bibliography of these works was done by Mónica Ros Torres (in Matos Moctezuma 1989: 163–66). Nelly Gutiérrez Solana (1989) organized much of the information contained in those publications in a topical index and a bibliography.

10. These were the big parking area of the Secretaría de Hacienda y Crédito Público along the north side of Guatemala Street, the lot on the opposite side of the street, and the vacant space at Justo Sierra #13 (Matos Moctezuma 1982c).

11. These were located on Justo Sierra #11 and 15; Guatemala #42, 51, and 58; and Argentina #3, 5, 7, and 11.

12. These were at Argentina #1 and 3.

13. These were at Guatemala #48–50 and 49.

14. For a detailed description of the extent of the excavation month by month, see Matos Moctezuma (1982a), Contreras and Luna (1982), and I. Gutiérrez (1982).

15. Using the same criteria as Eduardo Matos Moctezuma did, depending on the circumstances, an "element" number was given to each archaeological object (of natural or cultural origin) or to each group of objects of the same type that constituted a unit per se. For example, under these criteria, several greenstone beads forming a necklace, a homogenous bed composed of many small conch shells, or the bones of a puffer fish were given a single element number. Therefore, the number of elements does not always correspond to the number of individual objects.

16. These roofs were built to protect the large monolithic sculptures and the mural paintings that remained in situ. They were iron structures that supported sheets of aluminum

painted with gray, noncorrosive paint. Gray plastic curtains hung from the sides (Franco Brizuela 1986: 126–27).

17. In spite of the measures taken to protect the architectural structures (cleaning, consolidation, waterproofing, and so on), at present they are deteriorating rapidly. The chief factors are: (1) atmospheric pollution by great quantities of ozone, sulphur dioxide, carbon monoxide, lead, and nitrogen dioxide; (2) the high level of humidity in the subsoil; (3) solar radiation; (4) temperature fluctuations; (5) earth tremors; and (6) abrasion, deposition, and chemical processes of oxidation-reduction caused by the dust. It is paradoxical that these factors, in a brief length of time, have caused more damage than centuries of burial underground.

18. The following persons—including both students and degreed archaeologists—participated: Guillermo Ahuja Ormaechea, Mariana Arguimbau, Ludtwig Beutelspacher Baigts, Antonieta Castrejón Rubio, Eduardo Contreras, Mercedes Gómez Mont, Carlos Javier González,* Teresa Gracia Franco, Mónica Guerrero Pérez, Salvador Guil'liem Arroyo,* Isabel Gutiérrez Sansano, María de los Angeles Heredia, Elsa Hernández Pons, Francisco Hinojosa, Françoise Laffite, Daniel Levine, Leonardo López Luján,* Pilar Luna Erreguerena, Bertina Olmedo Vera, Rosa de la Peña Virchez, Juan Alberto Román Berrelleza,* Luis Sisniega, Cecilia Urueta Flores, and Diana Wagner. (People who still are part of the Templo Mayor Project are marked by an asterisk.)

19. Among others, the following workers participated: Maximiliano Acevedo Aguilar, Tomás Cruz Ruiz, Felipe García Romero, Andrés Juárez, Raymundo Juárez, Erasmo Hernández Cruz, Fidel Ledezma, Tomás López Gómez, Encarnación Novoa González, Telésforo Pérez García, Jesús Ruiz Cruz, Tomás Ruiz Ruiz, Roberto Ruiz, and Andrés Santiago Pérez.

20. The first offering excavated in the project was given the number 6, due to the fact that the Archaeological Salvage Department had previously explored five offerings associated with the Coyolxauhqui monolith. See Chapter 1.

21. The Archaeological Salvage Department and the Templo Mayor Project recovered 115 offerings. A total of 20 offerings were found in 1978 (1–20); 20 in 1979 (21–39 and Chamber 2); 22 in 1980 (40–59 and A-B); 42 in 1981 (60–86, C–Ñ, Chamber 3, and Burial 1); 8 in 1982 (87–91 and O–Q); 2 in 1987 (92–93) and 1 in 1989 (94). Many more offerings have been discovered since 1991 (see López Luján 2005).

22. For a detailed description of excavations and the recording of offerings, see Román Berrelleza (1986: 26–38). Wagner (1982) not only gave a detailed description of the technique of exploration and organized the information about the finds but also classified the first offerings discovered in the Templo Mayor Project, according to their "common characteristics."

23. The slate included the name of the project, the date of the photograph, the x and y coordinates of the location, the number of the offering, and the level excavated.

24. As Franco Brizuela (1986: 63, 74) pointed out, "The acid soils are found chiefly in humid areas. They are acid because the original stone contains more than 60% silica."

25. The cycle of capillary water follows three phases of physicochemical changes in the archaeological contexts: dissolution and hydrolysis; the migration of salts; and crystallization (Orea Magaña et al. 1990).

26. The following people worked on conservation and restoration of materials from the offerings: José Arroyo, Elvira Cásares, Charles Dabo, María Luisa Franco Brizuela, María Elena Franco, Mercedes Gómez Urquiza, Bárbara Hasbach Lugo, Emma E. Herrera, Alejandro León, Vida Mercado, Lucía de la Parra, Bertha Peña Tenorio, Doris Peña, Rocío Pérez González, Ezequiel Pérez Herrera, Eugenia Ritter, Yolanda Santaella, Regina Trespalacios, and María Pía Valenzuela.

27. The following materials were used: Primal AC-33 (acrylic copolymer emulsion polymethyl methacrylate/Rohm and Haas) in damp materials, organic objects, and pigments; Paraloid B72 (polymethyl methacrylate/Rohm and Haas) dissolved in xylene in dry materials, bone remains, ceramics, and marine objects; and Carbowax (polyethylene glycol E1000/Union Carbide) dissolved in ethyl alcohol for wood. Some stone objects were completely submerged in Wacker OH strengthening agent (ethyl-silicate-based adhesive/Wacker Chemie) dissolved in benzene or Mowilith 30 (polyvinyl acetate/Hoechst) dissolved in xylene.

28. This technique involves covering the object with cloth or paper to which an adhesive is applied. In our case, this was Mowilith DM4 and DMH1 in distilled water or Mowilith 50 in acetone (all these are polyvinyl acetates made by Hoechst).

29. Soluble salts were eliminated with compresses of paper pulp moistened with distilled water, and insoluble salts were removed with formic acid.

30. Fungus stains were eliminated with oxalic acid in areas without pigment and with peroxide in areas with pigment. These chemicals were applied in different concentrations (between 1% and 10%) with a brush or with cotton compresses.

31. Mowital B60H (polyvinyl butiral/Hoechst) dissolved in ethyl alcohol and ethyl acetate was used.

32. For this, Paraloid B72 (polymethyl methacrylate/Rohm and Haas), Primal AC-33 (acrylic copolymer emulsion polymethyl methacrylate/Rohm and Haas), or Wacker OH (ethyl-silicate-based adhesive/Wacker Chemie) was used. The original pigments were fixed with 2% nylon in ethanol.

33. Synthetic resins such as polyvinyl acetate (Mowilith 50 or Mowital B60H dissolved in ethyl alcohol and ethyl acetate) were used. Natural resins were used for very heavy stone objects.

34. A filler paste made from kaolin, calcium carbonate, ceramic fibers, polyvinyl acetate (Mowilith 30), and different solvents (acetone or ethyl acetate) were used.

35. Powdered pigment, acrylic paint, and natural soil with resin were used, without exactly duplicating the color. An effort was made to make the repair distinguishable at close quarters.

CHAPTER 3

1. Leeuw (1964: 379–80) gave examples of liminal locations for different cultures of the Old World.

CHAPTER 4

1. In general, these documents have drawings of the sanctuary accompanied by glyphs, glosses, or descriptions of its history or the ritual ceremonies that took place there. Some representations of the Templo Mayor at the dawn of the sixteenth century are found in: *Códice Aubin* (1979: 83); *Códice Azcatitlan* (1949: pl. 12); *Codex Magliabechiano* (1983: pl. 70r); *Códice Matritense* (1906: fig. 2); *Códice Telleriano-Remensis* (1964–1967: pls. 17, 19); *Códice Tudela* (1980: pls. 51r, 53r); *Códice Vaticano Latino 3738* (1964–1967: pls. 120, 121); and *Lienzo de Tlaxcalla* (n.d.: pl. 36).

    Among the most interesting indigenous accounts are: "Costumbres, fiestas, enterramientos" (1965); *Historia de los mexicanos por sus pinturas* (1965: 57, 62); Alva Ixtlilxóchitl (1975: vol. 1, 466–67, vol. 2, 157–58, 221, 228–31); Alvarado Tezozómoc (1944: 79–82, 114–18, 149, 156–59, 163, 202–4, 245–47, 298–300, 318, 330–34, 338, 388, 399, 410, 436, 494); *Anales de Tlatelolco* (1948); Chimalpahin (1965).

2. See Aguilar (1977: 80–81); Cortés (1967: 74); Díaz del Castillo (1982: 183–96, 273–279); Tapia (1963: 65–70).

3. Most outstanding are: Acosta (1962: 237–39); Durán (1984: vol. 1, 17–24, 38–39, 47–48, 62–64, 81–82, 96–100, 125–31, 143–49, fig. 4, vol. 2, 171–75, 188–93, 226–33, 275–79, 333, 341, 344–48, 395, 435–36, 439, 571, figs. 29 and 30); Mendieta (1945: vol. 1, 90–96); Benavente (1971: 37, 82–83, 210–11); Sahagún (1988: vol. 1, 181–92, vol. 2, 837, 847–48, 851–53); Torquemada (1969: vol. 2, 71–72, 144–56, 464); Tovar (1972: 57, 85–89, 96, 101, 109–10, fig. 20).

4. For these types of sources, see Boone (1987); Keen (1971: 49–309). See also Conquistador Anónimo (1986: 199–125, 149–51).

5. A Spanish version of the corresponding Nahuatl section of the *Códice Florentino* is given in López Austin (1965).

6. The model was made by Carmen de Antúnez and Manuel Calderón. The figures were cast in lead by Pedro Elías Ruso and Efrén Medina Miranda. For information about the Sacred Precinct, consult Marquina (1951: 180–204, 1960) and Serrato-Combe (2001).

7. The Templo Mayor of Texcoco can be added to the list of these archaeologically explored buildings. Its striking resemblance to the others is demonstrated by its representation on plate 112v of the *Codex Ixtlilxóchitl* (Fig. 13).

8. The mixture for the stucco was made of lime (calcium oxide) and sand. The type and size of the filler and the thickness of the plaster coat vary from place to place, from the whitewash on the walls to 40-cm-thick floors. The composition of stucco at the different construction stages is the following: (1) Stage II, a clay-sand aggregate of plagioclase, hornblende, and tezontle and clay aggregates cemented with calcium carbonate; (2) Stage IVb, a sand-mud aggregate of plagioclase, hypersthene, hornblende, hematite, and clay-tezontle aggregates cemented with calcium carbonate; (3) Stage VII, a gravel, sand, and clay-mud aggregate with calcium carbonate and clayey minerals (Franco Brizuela 1990: 32–34; López Luján, Torres, and Montúfar 2003).

9. This is crystallized calcium carbonate of various colors.

10. Thus, the number of additions detected is twelve. The Templo Mayor at Tlatelolco has the same number of building stages. However, it should be noted that at the Huey

Teocalli of Tenochtitlan, there were also small modifications or failed attempts at expansion, such as the strange staircase found on the Temple of Tlaloc at Stage II.

11. For more detail about this sculpture, see Matos Moctezuma (1991).

12. The interior paintings represent Maize Gods and shields; the exterior was painted using the tempera technique with black-and-white, concentric circles on alternating stripes of blue and black. Pigments were red (hematite), ocher (goethite), white (calcite), blue (palygorskite and sepiolite), black (charcoal), and gray (clay and carbonate of calcium). These colors were applied to the surface of walls of quicklime and sand, quicklime and clay, or sand and clay (López Luján 2005).

13. The bodies of six serpents have a nucleus of earth and tezontle stones, covered with stucco. The bodies of the other two serpents were simulated with large basalt stones. The heads have an average size of 120 cm x 80 cm x 70 cm. Four heads were carved in basalt, four in augitic basalt, and one in andesite. They are decorated with red, white, ocher, blue and/or black pigments (Franco Brizuela 1986: 50–56).

14. Four braziers were found in a good state of preservation, but only the bases of the others were detected. The braziers were made with a nucleus of tezontle and earth, covered with plaster. These sculptures consist of two inverted truncated cones placed one above the other. In some cases, there was a spherical body between the two cones. The braziers were decorated with volutes and knots or with an effigy of Tlaloc. Some have remains of red, ocher, blue, black, and white pigments (Franco Brizuela 1986: 56–59).

15. It has maximum dimensions of 325 cm x 295 cm x 30 cm. It was carved from an extrusive volcanic tuff known as pink traquiandesite. It has traces of polychrome paint, primarily ocher and red. A representation of the same goddess made of pieces of basalt covered with stucco, corresponding to Stage IVa, lies under this monumental sculpture (Franco Brizuela 1986: 46–47, 61).

16. Graulich (1987) warned that the analysis of written sources should be done cautiously, given the existence of great chronological contradictions. The date of the same historical event can vary enormously from one document to another, perhaps because of the use of different calendars.

17. Matos Moctezuma based this on a fragment on page 47 of the *Historia de los mexicanos por sus pinturas* (1965), which said, "On the second year of the populating of Mexico the Mexicans began the foundations of the great temple of Huitzilopochtli, *which kept growing because each lord who succeeded another built a strip as broad as the first one made by these people*, and so the Spanish found it to be very tall, very strong, and amazing to see" (emphasis L.L.L.). However, Matos Moctezuma (1981b: 17, 19) cautioned that some amplifications could have been done because of flooding or the settling of the subsoil.

18. Umberger (1987) tied this date to the glyph 8 *Calli* (perhaps A.D. 1461), which Gamio found carved on the marble floor located at the southwest corner of Stage IVb. From that evidence, she proposed that Stage IVb was constructed in 1461 or before and that the plate with the glyph 3 *Calli* was placed later.

19. As additional proof that the date 4 *Acatl* refers to the calendric name of Huehueteotl, Graulich (1987) pointed to its southern location (on the side of Huitzilopochtli, the sun)

and its proximity to offering 8, which contains burnt material. However, despite the fact that offering 8 was found in the nucleus of Stage III, it was deposited there when Stage IV was constructed. This is shown by the filling with which it was covered, which was part of the construction of Stage IV.

20. A flaw in Graulich's argument is that the glyph *1 Tecpatl* (Huitzilopochtli's calendric name) was not found at the Templo Mayor.

21. Ponce de León (1982: 31–32, n. 20) obtained two kinds of measurements in 1981. For example, in Stage II he measured the axis that passes through the upper part of the building, exactly between the two temples, as well as the lower axis that passes between the two central balustrades at the height of the placing of the foundation. The azimuthal values of these two axes are different, due to the current amount of settling.

22. Here I include only the most important solar recordings—those related to dawn, that is, to the east. Without a doubt, the most important solar phenomenon at the Templo Mayor was registered at sunrise. At dates very near to the equinoxes, the observer stood in front of the shrines of Huitzilopochtli and Tlaloc, that is, to the west (perhaps upon the very Templo Mayor, in the plaza, or on the Temple of Quetzalcoatl) to admire the sun rising behind the temple. This was mentioned in the following citation from Torquemada (1969: 51): "Tlacaxipeualistli . . . this festival occurred when the sun was in the middle of Uichilobos, at the equinox, and because it was a little off balance, Mutizuma wanted to tear it down and straighten it." There is an interesting discussion about the observer's position in regard to the Templo Mayor in Aveni and Gibbs (1976) and in Aveni, Calnek, and Hartung (1988).

23. *Tzompantli-altars* generally means "altars that are adorned with skulls and crossbones, but which possibly were not used for placing skulls" (Matos Moctezuma 1986a: 116). In the case of Building B, the characteristics of the offerings deposited inside (H and N) and their northerly position in relation to the Templo Mayor seem to indicate that they are related more to the death cult and to Mictlan than to human remains (Matos Moctezuma 1984b: 73) or burial of Xiuhmolpilli sculptures.

24. For more information about Buildings C and F, see López Luján (1989b: 37–42) and Olmedo (2002).

25. Regarding the "teotihuacanoid" building found on Guatemala Street, Gussinyer (1970b) said that, in spite of a certain resemblance, the system of construction is quite different from that of the Teotihuacan structures.

26. Like the Teotihuacan murals in Buildings C and F, the color red predominates (used chiefly as a background), although there is frequent use of blue, ocher, black, and white. The motifs painted on the walls of both buildings are rhythmically repeated in patterns along the length of the construction. Building C has concentric circles, conch shell cross sections, currents of water—motifs that resemble those of Teotihuacan. Building F has, on its talus, pairs of ribbons as a repeated motif. On its panel, there is a central representation of a quadruped flanked on each side by three anthropomorphic images in profile (López Luján 1989b: 40–42).

27. These sculptures measure approximately 190 cm high and are composed of four pieces that can be fitted together: the legs, the thighs-abdomen, the torso-arms, and the head

(López Luján 2005). Several interpretations of the meaning of these sculptures were published by Bonifaz Nuño (1990), Fuente (1990), and López Luján (2005).

28. In the middle of the twentieth century, several pits at least 4 m deep were sunk to determine the type of subsoil under a proposed parking structure. These pits were never refilled but rather were covered with slabs of reinforced cement. The platform and the small altars that lay below it had sustained irreparable damage in the construction of colonial buildings (Contreras and Luna 1982).

29. See the discussion of the significance of offerings 16 and 16-A in Chapter 8.

CHAPTER 5

1. Cristóbal del Castillo (1966: 92) used a variety of names for the island where the Mexica settled permanently after their long pilgrimage: *Aztecatl Metztli* and *Apan* ("in the lake of the water of the moon"), *Xochitlalpan* ("in the flowery land"), and *Tonacatlalpan* ("in the land of our sustenance").

2. On plate 5-III of the *Codex Selden 3135* (A.2), the portrayal of a spring that flows from a cavern can be seen, and on plate 22 of the *Codex Nuttall*, there is a drawing of a cave from which a fountain of water and a tree emerge at the same time.

3. There is evidence of the existence of springs in the center of the island of Tenochtitlan. As Fray Toribio de Benavente (1969: 146) noted: "Mexico: some interpret this to mean fountain or spring according to the etymology of the language; and to tell the truth, there are many springs on it and around it, so that the name does not seem to be far from the truth."

    Sahagún (1979: vol. 1, 183, 184, 186, 188) mentioned that there were four springs at the Sacred Precinct of Tenochtitlan: Tlilapan, "place of black water"; Tezcaapan, "place of the mirror water"; Coaapan, "serpent water"; and Tozpalatl, "yellow water."

    Torquemada (1969: vol. 2, 155) said that the spring named Tozpalatl and the others were stopped up when the Templo Mayor was built. However, it reappeared in 1582 in the Plazuela del Marqués, where it was covered again five years later. Apparently, Leopoldo Batres found one of these springs during his exploration of the rear of the Metropolitan Cathedral in 1900 (cited in Pasztory 1988; Calnek 1977). And more recently, Rubén Cabrera (1979) found traces of a spring under the Metropolitan Cathedral.

4. According to Heyden (1988: 58–59, 73–75), the names *Tleatl* and *Atlatlayan* refer to a single spring and metaphorically allude to war, one of the manifest destinies of the Mexica people. This researcher has also emphasized the ties between blue and yellow water and purification rites.

5. The Pyramid of the Sun was built over a large tunnel 100 m long, which ran in an east-west direction and ended in a chamber with four lobes. A stone drainage system in the cavern may indicate the past existence of a spring (Heyden 1975).

6. Manzanilla et al. (1989) detected possible subterranean hollows, which would pass under the Pyramid of the Moon, by using gravimetric, magnetometric, and electrical resistivity techniques.

7. A cave 10 m long containing seven tombs with rich funeral offerings was found under this structure (Carlson 1981).

8. According to Alvarado Tezozómoc (1949: 67), the place where the Mexica built the first *tlachcuitetelli* ("hillock for the ballgame") and the first *tlalmomoztli* ("earth shrine") was named Oztotempan, that is, "place on the edge of the cave."

9. In this connection, an image of plate 9-III of the *Codex Selden 3135* (A.2) is very interesting. It shows a temple built over a cave that is depicted as the mouth of the Earth Monster, from which two springs emerge. Plate 79b-c of the *Codex Nuttall* shows a pyramid with a cave at its top. Another noteworthy example is the mural of Tepantitla known as "the Tlalocan." The themes of the motifs represented there are very similar to the myth of the founding of Tenochtitlan. The central personage of the famous Teotihuacan painting combines iconographic elements related to the God of Fire and the Gods of Rain. The painting rests on a platform that covers a cave. Inside the cave are starfish, seeds, and jade beads, and from the cave flow two streams of water, creating colorful waves, one red and the other blue, as in Tenochtitlan. Behind the personage rise two great cosmic trees that intertwine in the form of a *malinalli* ("twisted grass") spiral topped with flowers and leaves (Winning 1987: vol. 1, 135–36; Heyden 1988: 59, 77–78).

10. There is an interesting fragment written by Torquemada (1969: vol. 2, 140) on this topic, in which he discussed some plans for urban distribution used in ancient Mexico:

   > The common practice in building temples in this land was this: first . . . whether the town was large or small, the most eminent and honored place in all the city was chosen. Then they made a great plaza, or square foundation. This plaza or square foundation was encircled by a wall one or two *estados* [1.96 m] in height. There were four doors to the patio, each one corresponding to one of the four parts of the sky, East, West, North and South. The four principal streets of the city and roads that came from other regions corresponded to these four doors. All these streets ran in this manner and so well leveled that they came straight to the patio without the slightest deviation . . . so that streets and roads went directly to the temple that they were building.

11. Matos Moctezuma (1986c: 65, 69) said that the Mesoamerican temples were superimposed upon each other instead of built on different sites because they always had to be at the fundamental center.

12. The kinds of opposition most common in Mesoamerica are: *contradictory* (p/not p), *opposite* (hot/cold), *complementary* (male/female), *associated* (sun/moon), *symmetrical* (right/left), and *asymmetrical* (head/feet). The most common oppositions in indigenous Mexican concepts are: mother/father, female/male, cold/hot, below/above, jaguar/eagle, 9/13, underworld/sky, wet/dry, darkness/light, weakness/strength, night/day, water/fire, death/life, wind/fire, ascending influence/descending influence, rainy season/dry season, cihuacoatl/tlatoani, obsidian/flint, north/south, and west/east (López Austin 1990b: 233–40; Graulich 1990).

13. It is interesting that the monolith known as the Teocalli de la Guerra Sagrada, which has been compared to the Templo Mayor, has several binary iconographic elements: for example,

representations of Tlaltecuhtli and the sun; images of Tlaloc and Xiuhtecuhtli; *cuauhxicallis* ("eagle vessels") with tiger stripes and eagle feathers; and *atl-tlachinolli* ("water, fire") glyphs emerging from an eagle's beak and from the mouths of four deities, with the dates 1 *Miquiztli* and 1 *Tecpatl*. A good description of this sculpture can be found in Pasztory (1983: 165–69).

14. Concerning the oppositions of the cardinal points, López Austin (1990b: 240) commented,

> Two cosmic oppositions of *above/below* are seen in ancient Nahua belief. Both divide the sky in halves, one with a *north/south* axis; the other with an *east/west* axis. The characteristics of the *above/below* dichotomy are selectively divided between the two. North and south remain respectively as *below/above*, with death toward the north and life toward the south, since the sun's course runs chiefly to the south. In the division of east and west, east is masculine and west is feminine; but it also implies division into what is little sexual and what is strongly sexual.

15. In several documents, the Templo Mayor is called Coatepetl (Alvarado Tezozómoc 1944: 300, 454; Sahagún 1979: bk. 2, fol. 108r; see Seler 1960b: vol. 4, 162). Images of Coatepec and of the Templo Mayor appear together on plate 6 of the *Códice Azcatitlan*. León-Portilla (1981: 79) said about this plate:

> Coatepec appears there close to Tula, where Huitzilopochtli was born. Many serpent heads emerge from the hill, and the Templo Mayor can be seen on top crowned by the god Huitzilopochtli. To the right, symbolizing the union of primordial Coatepec and the temple of Huitzilopochtli, there is another sanctuary, also with a serpent and a gloss in Nahuatl, *Cohuatepec xiuhcohuatl onca temoc*, "In Coatepec the serpent of fire came down."

16. Sahagún (1988), in his *Historia general*, mentioned the names of the parts of the temple that were most important in the ritual of Panquetzaliztli. The *coaxalpan* was between the steps and the lower patio (vol. 1, 152, 203); the *apetlac*, or *itlacuayan Huitzilopochtli*, was where the steps began (vol. 1, 145, vol. 2, 572–76), and the *tlacacohuan* was where the sacrifices were performed (vol. 1, 145).

17. Here she followed Pasztory (1975), Sullivan (1974), and Klein (1980), who, on the basis of multiple iconographic images of Tlaloc, discovered his ties to the earth, the underworld, the jaguar, caves, darkness, night, the night sun, food, wealth, and abundance.

18. For example, in Tlacaxipehualiztli, the skins of flayed victims were buried in a "chamber with movable stone" that was located under the stairway to the temple of Xipe Totec (Durán 1984: vol. 1, 102). In the month of Tepeilhuitl, two virgins were sacrificed and buried in a chamber inside the temple called Ayauhcalli (Broda 1971: 307). In Etzalcualiztli, two slaves who represented Tlaloc and Chalchiuhcueye were killed, and "they did not eat them, but threw them into a cave-like hollow which they had for that purpose" (Benavente 1971: 64). "Once a year, when the grain in their fields has sprouted one span's length," a festival was held in honor of Tlaloc. Two children were decapitated and their corpses deposited in a stone box (Benavente 1971: 66).

19. "There were also many offerings given [to the temple] and the lords gave a certain part of their tributes, and this was voluntary and they were put in with the rest [with what was obtained from lands belonging to the temple]" (Zorita 1942: 200).

20. "When the Mexicans arrived in the city of Mexico [after defeating the Tepeaca] they were very well received by all the city, with much rejoicing and festivities of the priests, who came out with braziers in their hands.... They greeted them and took them into the temple, where they made great offerings of the booty and the things that they brought from war" (Durán 1984: vol. 2, 153). See also *Códice Ramírez* (1944: 75), Durán (1984: vol. 2, 365–66), and Torquemada (1969: vol. 1, 157).

21. As the work of enlarging the Templo Mayor was in progress, "*Motecuzuma*, knowing that in *Guazacualco* there were many beautiful things of gold and other things, told *Tlacaellel* that it would be good if he would send for them to adorn the temple of their god *Huitzilopuchtli*, and by mutual agreement the two of them dispatched their messengers and couriers" (*Códice Ramírez* 1944: 180).

22. Nagao derived the significance of each type of offering by a comparison with iconographic representations and a study of historical sources. However, the identification of some cult images is debatable. Nagao never took into account the contextual information of the offerings, a fundamental key to their meaning: the quantity, location, and the association with other objects in the container and the relative position of each offering with respect to the other deposits and the architectural structures. It should be added that Nagao's conclusions in regard to the offerings excavated in the Templo Mayor Project were based on reports published before 1985, which represent a minimal percentage of the materials obtained. This was reflected in her conclusions.

23. Different proposals about the identification of these images are made in the analysis of offering 16 in Chapter 8.

CHAPTER 6

1. It should be noted that for the believer who made the offering, the gift might be retrievable.

2. For this, it is necessary to determine which areas of activity are contemporaneous. In regard to the different levels of spatial aggregation of entities, see Clarke (1977: 9–11).

3. The degree of distortion and transformation of contexts can be understood by studying the social and natural dynamics that took place in the medium where the offerings were deposited.

4. In other offerings where no modification of the original contents was observed, skeletal remains of animals that got in after the offerings had been laid down were identified: pocket gopher, mice (Old and New World), and rats. The bones of sheep were also found, possibly coming from a nearby colonial dump. See the description of Complex Q in Appendix 2.

5. Although we currently have few indications of the presence of perishable materials in the offerings, it is easy to infer their abundance through documental sources. In some deposits, we found traces of feathers, seeds, leaves, and textiles engraved in the matrix.

6. *Attribute* is "any logically irreducible character or property of a system, having two or more states (present/absent), acting as an independent variable and assumed by the observer to be of significance with reference to the frame of his study" (Clarke 1978: 489).

7. *Entity* is "an integrated ensemble of attributes forming a complex but coherent and unitary whole at a specific level of complexity" (Clarke 1978: 491).

8. In other words, a nominal multistate scale was developed. The numerical equivalent of each state serves only to simplify the analysis and lacks arithmetic value.

9. Information on the 110 offerings found in the Templo Mayor Project between 1978 and 1989 was obtained from three different registers: *Registro general de ofrendas del Templo Mayor* (5 manuscript volumes), *Catálogo general de la colección del Templo Mayor* (typescript), and *Tablas de distribución del material por etapa constructiva* (typescript). These registers were compared with the only two attempts to systematize information for the offerings—Wagner (1982) and González (in press).

10. See the upper part of the General Matrix of presences/absences.

11. Thanks to the use of spatial distribution maps, I found that many interdependent variables coincided in the spatial structure of the offerings. The offerings had: distributions that could be statistically simplified, quantitative and qualitative values, and significant statistical regularities (see Clarke 1977).

12. In the case of the Templo Mayor, the difference between the number of offerings in the northern and southern facades is due to the fact that the southern facade was not completely excavated at one end.

13. Several criteria were used in order to determine the orientation of the offerings in the pre-Hispanic era. When the offering was presided over by images placed in a vertical position, the orientation corresponded to the direction toward which they were "looking." If the divine images were in a horizontal position, they were hypothetically turned 90° until they were in a vertical position and reached the corresponding orientation; the same position was given to scepters, musical instruments, and so forth. In some offerings, not all the objects were directed toward the same cardinal direction. In these cases, I took the orientation of the majority of them (general tendency) or, in its absence, that of the principal objects (such as divine images, anthropomorphic masks, and skulls of decapitated humans). Apparently, the donors did not follow such criteria in offerings 28, 43, 26, 25, 35 and 47. These deposits contained jars set in a horizontal position that simulated the pouring of water into cajetes (see the description of Complex N in Chapter 8). Evidently, they took the direction in which the water was pouring as the orientation point. I base this on the presence of a similar jar in Chamber 2, with its mouth pointing in the same direction as the associated sculpted deities.

    In general, the longitudinal axis of the container was the same as that of the objects. There is an interesting fact about the personified knives: although they were perpendicular to the other objects, their eyes and mouths faced front.

14. We found offerings in all the expansions to the Templo Mayor (Stages II–VII). If Matos Moctezuma's chronology is correct, the offerings would be dated between A.D. 1375 and 1521.

15. It is assumed that the time between the placing of the offering and the construction just above it was very brief. The offering either preceded the ceremony consecrating the expansion or it was deposited by breaking through the floor when the new section was in use. The dating becomes complicated when the floors of previous stages were destroyed

in order to deposit the gifts. Nevertheless, through a careful analysis, it was possible to detect situations where intrusions occurred from more recent stages.

16. A true *sillar* can be defined as any stone used in construction that has been hewn on all sides and has a rectangular parallelepiped shape. The stones are regular in size.

17. Matos Moctezuma pointed out that products from societies outside Tenochcan control (such as the Tarasca and Maya) were not found among those recovered by the Templo Mayor Project.

18. The identification of the fauna recovered by the Salvage Department (offerings 1–5) can be found in Blanco (1978), Carramiñana (1988), and Villanueva (1987).

19. These studies are being done by the Paleozoology Laboratory of the Subdirección de Laboratorios y Apoyo a la Investigación of the INAH and the Chordate Laboratory of the Escuela Nacional de Ciencias Biológicas of the Instituto Politécnico Nacional. Biologist Oscar J. Polaco is coordinating the work of the team.

20. For arthropods, only crab claws (order Decapoda) and the exoskeleton of an unidentified species of crustacean (*Balanus* sp.) have appeared thus far. The only echinoderms recorded are the sea urchin (*Equinometra vanbrunti*) that lives among the coastal rocks of the Pacific Ocean and the sand dollar (*Mellita* sp.). Only small fragments of sponges, with spicules, that could belong to the genus *Haliclona* or *Callyspongia* have been recovered (Polaco 1982, 1986; Carramiñana 1988).

21. These are the soft corals *Alcyonum cf. dedalium*, *Gorgonia* sp., and *Gorgonia ventalina* and of the hard corals *Acropora cervicornis*, *Acropora palmata*, *Diploria strigosa* ("brain coral"), *Millepora alcicornis* ("fire coral"), and *Pocillopora damnicornis* (Polaco 1982; López Luján and Polaco 1991; Carramiñana 1988).

22. *Retinella indentata* is the only land snail. It occurs in the vicinity of Yautepec, Morelos (Polaco 1982).

23. Two freshwater mollusks—the shellfish *Physa osculans* and the conch shell *Helisoma cf. tenuis*—were found in offering 7. They live clinging to the roots of lilies in the lakes of the Basin of Mexico (Polaco 1982).

24. Only one polyplacophore has been identified—the sea cockroach or chiton (*Chiton marmoratus*) (López Luján and Polaco 1991; Carramiñana 1988).

25. The conch shell species identified thus far are: *Acmaea* sp., *Anachis floridana*, *Arca imbricata*, *Architectonica nobilis*, *Astraea olivecea*, *Astraea* sp., *Bittium larum*, *Bittium* sp., *Bulla occidentalis*, *Bulla* sp., *Busycon coarctatum*, *Busycon contrarium*, *Busycon spiratum*, *Cancellaria reticulata*, *Cittarium pica*, *Columbella mercatoria*, *Conus cf. granulatus*, *Conus* sp., *Conus spurius*, *Crepidula aculeata*, *Crepidula fornicata*, *Cymatium cf. pileare*, *Cymatium wiegmanni*, *Cypraea spurca*, *Cyprea nigropunctata*, *Charonia variegata*, *Diodora* sp., *Distorsio clathrata*, *Enaeta barnesii*, *Epitonium lamallosum*, *Fasciolaria tulipa*, *Hexaplex brassica*, *Latirus* sp., *Leucozonia nassa*, *Marginella* sp., *Melongena melongena*, *Modulus modulus*, *Murex (Hexaplex) erythrostomus*, *Murex (Hexaplex) nigritus*, *Murex florifer*, *Murex* sp., *Nassarius nanus*, *Nerita* scabricosta, Nerita sp., *Neritina reclivata*, *Opeatostoma pseudodon*, *Oliva sayana*, *Oliva* sp., *Olivella* sp., *Patella mexicana*, *Petaloconchus erectus*, *Petaloconchus* sp., *Phalium granulatum*, *Pleuroplaca gigantes*,

Polinices cf. *lacteus, Polinices duplicatus, Polinices hepaticus, Polinices* sp., *Purpura patula, Smaregdia viridis, Strombus alatus, Strombus gigas, Strombus gracilor, Strombus pugilis, Strombus reninus, Terebra salleana, Thais haemostoma, Thais rustica, Tonna galea, Tonna maculosa maculosa, Turbinella angulata, Vasum muricatum, Vermicularia* cf. *spirata* (Jiménez Badillo 1991; López Luján and Polaco 1991; Polaco 1982; Carramiñana 1988).

26. The bivalve species identified are: *Aequipecten muscosus, Anadara brasiliana, Anadara chemnitzii, Anadara floridana, Anadara notabilis, Anadara ovalis, Anadara transversa, Arca imbricata, Arca zebra, Arcopsis* sp., *Argopecten irradianas, Astrea* sp., *Barbatia* sp., *Chama congregata, Chama macerophylla, Chione cancellata, Chione* sp., *Codakia orbicularia, Corbula* sp., *Crassostrea virginica, Dinocardium robustum, Donax* sp., *Dosinia discus, Dosinia elegans, Equinochama arcinella, Glycymeris undata, Iphigenia basiliana, Isognomos radiatus, Laevicardium laevigatum laevigatum, Lyropecten nodosus, Macoma* cf *calcarea, Macrocallista maculata, Mercenaria mercenaria, Modiolus americanus, Noetia ponderosa, Ostrea* sp., *Pecten* sp., *Pholas campechiensis, Pinctada mazatlanica, Polymesoda caroliniana, Pseudochama radians, Rangia flexuosa, Semele* cf. *proficua, Spondylus americanus, Spondylus calcifer, Tagellus* sp., *Tellina* cf. *alternata, Tellina (Arcopagia) fausta, Trachycardium muricatum, Ventricolaria rugatina* (Jiménez Badillo 1991; López Luján and Polaco 1991; Polaco 1982; Carramiñana 1988).

27. See Jiménez Badillo (1991) for the sources of snails and conch shells and the forms of interchange in the late post-Classic period.

28. Particular body parts were found for 289 specimens: 73 mud turtles (*Kinosternon* sp.), 104 pond sliders (*Pseudemys scripta*), 2 boas (*Boa miniscula*), 15 snakes (*Colubridae* fam.), various rattlesnakes (*Crotalus* sp.), and 14 alligators (*Crocodylus moreletti* and *C. acutus*) (Alvarez and Ocaña 1991; Carramiñana 1988).

29. Some remains of the following were identified: 2 white herons (*Casmerodius albus*), 82 montezuma quail (*Cyrtonix montezumae*), 23 scaled quail (*Caliplepa squamata*), 11 common bobwhite (*Colinus virginianus*), 5 turkeys (*Meleagris gallopavo*), several golden eagles (*Aquila chrysaetos*), 1 kestrel (*Falconidae* fam.), 35 sparrow hawks (*Falco sparverius*), 1 falcon (*Falco* sp.), 1 toucan (*Ramphastus sulfuratus*), 6 flycatchers (*Tyrannidae* fam.), and 2 crows (?) or jays (?) (Alvarez and Ocaña 1991; Carramiñana 1988).

30. A bird feather in prime condition was found in offering 1 (Carramiñana 1988).

31. The skeletal parts of the following mammals were found: 1 armadillo (*Dasypus novemcinctus*, remains of the shell), 1 opossum (*Didelphis* sp.), 3 rabbits (*Syvilagus floridanus*), 1 gopher (*Pappogeomys merriami*), 1 mouse (*Reithrodontomys* sp.), 1 Mexican meadow mouse (*Microtus mexicanus*), remains of *Rattus rattus*, remains of *Mus musculus*, 2 wolves (*Canis lupus*), 1 coyote (*Canis latrans*), 3 felines (*Felis* sp.), 8 pumas (*Felis concolor*), 1 jaguar (*Felis onca*), 1 mountain lion (*Lynx rufus*), and 1 sheep (*Ovis aries*) (Alvarez and Ocaña 1991; Carramiñana 1988).

32. Díaz-Pardo and Teniente-Nivón (1991; Díaz-Pardo 1983) analyzed 1,314 skeletal remains belonging to 308 specimens of fish and elasmobranchs: 14 sharks (*Carcharhinus* sp.), 1 tiger shark (*Galeocerdo cuvieri*), 1 lemon shark (*Negaprion brevirostris*), 18 smalltooth sawfish (*Pristis pectinatus*, calcified fragments of frontal cartilage), 2 rays (*Dasyatis* sp.,

caudal spine and dental plate), 55 needlefish (*Tylosurus acus*), 61 half-beaks (*Hemirhanpus* sp.), 1 trumpet fish (*Fistularia* sp.), 6 barracuda (*Sphyraena barracuda*), 2 amberjack (*Caranx* sp.), 3 moon fish (*Selene* sp.), 15 red snapper (*Lutjanus* sp.), 3 grunts (*Conodon* sp.), 4 grunts (*Haemulon cf. plumieri*), 24 angelfish (*Pomacanthus cf. paru*), 26 spotfin hogfish (*Bodianus* sp.), 2 parrot fish (*Scarus guacamaia*), 4 parrot fish (*Sparisoma* sp.), 1 cutlass fish (*Trichiurus lepturus*), 1 scorpion fish (*Scorpaena plumieri*), 7 angelitos (*Prionotus cf. evolans*), 1 trigger fish (*Balistes carolinensis*), 4 trunkfish (*Lactophrys* sp.), 1 puffer fish (*Lagocephalus laevigatus*), 1 fugu fish (*Sphoeroides* sp.), 1 puffer fish (*Arothron* sp.), 30 porcupine fish (*Diodon* sp.), and 2 toad fish (*Batrachoides* sp.).

    Carramiñana (1988) identified the fish remains of offerings 1, 3, and 5 as 1 juvenile shark (*Carcharhinus* sp.) and specimens from the following families: 2 from Balistidae, 4 from Chaetodontidae, 2 from Dasyatidae, 2 from Diodontidae, 3 from Labridae, 1 from Serranidae, 4 from Scaridae (1 of them a parrot fish, *Scarus guacamaia*), 1 from Scombridae, 6 from Scorpaenidae, 1 from the order Tetraodontiformes, and 7 from the suborder Synentognathi.

33. Eleven groupers (*Epinephelus cf. analogus*) have been identified in the Templo Mayor offerings (Díaz-Pardo and Teniente-Nivón 1991).

34. I refer to the remains of Atherinidae (23 specimens of *Chirostoma* sp.) and of Goodeidae (an undetermined number of specimens of *Girardinichthys* [?] sp.) found in offering 1 (Carramiñana 1988).

35. Among the edible fish are two types of grunt, the amberjack, the red snapper, and the gray angelfish.

36. Traces of flowers were found by the archaeologists from the Department of Archaeological Salvage on the stone brazier of offering 1 (Francisco Hinojosa, pers. comm., March 1991).

37. Among the genera of wood identified were the pine (*Pinus* sp.), the cedar (*Cupressus* sp.), and the fir (*Abies* sp.). The wood sometimes had cultural modifications (Guil'liem Arroyo in press).

38. See the description of offering Complex A in Appendix 2.

39. See the description of offering 54 in Appendix 3.

40. See the description of the complex of funerary deposits (Complex E) in Chapter 8.

41. Children's skeletons were complete. Their ages range from six to twelve years old (Román Berrelleza 1986, 1987). See the description of offering 48 in Chapter 8.

42. Most adult skulls were masculine. The presence of the first cervical vertebrae indicate decapitation (Peña Gómez 1978; Román Berrelleza 1986, 1987).

43. Stone and ceramic images of Tlaloc predominate in the Templo Mayor. There are also sculptured figures of the deities we have identified as Xiuhtecuhtli, Tlaltecuhtli, Tonacatecuhtli, Mictlantecuhtli, and other fertility gods.

44. Among them are the scepters (*xiuhcoatl* ["turquoise serpent"], deerhead, serpentiform, *tlachieloni* ["that by which one sees"], rattlesnake, with a globular end), circular earplugs, representations of deforming cradles (Fig. 52), braziers with a bow, noseplugs (?) with split edges, the *oyohualli* ("oval rattle"), perforated circles of shells and obsidian, the *tzicolnacochtli* ("spiral ear ornaments"), and the *ehecacoxcatl* ("wind necklace").

45. I refer to the glyphs for ollin and the spiral or vortex.

46. Turtle shells were found, as well as sculptures of *huehuetl* ("upright drum"), *teponaztli* ("lateral log drum"), *chicahuaztli* ("rattle staff"), *omichicahuaztli* ("bone rattle staff") and *ayacachtli* ("wooden rattle") made from tezontle, basalt, or clay.

47. In a recent work, Rees Holland (1989) classified the carved stone of the offerings and the building fill of the Templo Mayor. He found 640 knives (25 different types), 194 projectile points (6 different types), 72 prismatic blades of green obsidian, 23 obsidian blanks, 11 xiuhcoatl, 5 serpentiform flint scepters, 3 "flint ladles," and 6 waste chips. These artifacts were carved from flint, obsidian, green silica, basalt, and rhyolite. In general, the carving technique was very specialized, and the minimal number of strokes needed to obtain the desired form were used.

48. Deposits that had no gifts due to decomposition, looting, or destruction were recorded as 0.

49. There is at least one offering—Chamber 3—in which objects were deposited on more than one occasion, as proven by the removable cover and the access stair.

50. In the corresponding figures, the altered levels of offerings that lack objects are labeled 0.

51. This is what happened with offering 48, for example (López Luján 1982). See also Chapter 8.

52. "Signa are those [indicators] in which the association is a cultural convention: *symbols* and *signs* contrast as subcategories of *signa*.... A *signum* is a *sign* when there is a previous intrinsic relationship between A and B because both belong to the same cultural context.... Correspondingly, a *signum* is a symbol when A represents B and there *is no* previous intrinsic relationship between A and B, that is, they belong to different cultural contexts" (Leach 1978: 18–20).

53. See Hodder (1988: 149–50) and Leach (1978: 16) for the simplicity of nonverbal language.

54. See Braudel (1974: 60–106) for a discussion of this theme.

CHAPTER 7

1. *To classify* can be defined as the action of "assigning entities to initially undefined classes in such a way that the members of the class are in some way related to each other" (Doran and Hodson 1975: 159).

2. According to Clarke (1978: 21), *regularities* can be defined as "systematically correlated attributes that give recognizable group identity to members of a given archaeological class or regularly follow membership in such a class, or sequence of classes."

3. A polythetic group is determined by the margin of variation between limits defined by attributes of which a high percentage are shared among the individual members of the group. There are several varieties of polythetic groups. Each variety depends on the number of attributes shared, the minimum and maximum number of attributes shared between any pair of entities, and the number of attributes in each entity (Clarke 1978: 36–37).

4. There are at least four requisites for correct classification: the entities belonging to a group must have similar attributes; the entities belonging to different groups must be

less alike than those of the same group; the groups must be correctly defined (the same results will be obtained if the procedure is repeated); and new entities should be easily assigned to an already established group (Orton 1988: 33). In order for a classification to be archaeologically useful, it must be: exhaustive (each entity must belong to a class); exclusive (no entity can belong to more than one class); defined in a precise manner (it should be possible to assign each entity to a class without hesitation); and natural (entities that are subjectively similar should belong to the same class) (Lock and Wilcock 1987: 38–39).

5. The basics were published in Sokal and Sneath (1963), but it is useful to look at a later edition of this seminal work (Sneath and Sokal 1973).

6. In numerical taxonomy the name *clusters* is typically used for groupings and *operational taxonomic units* applies to the entities. However, I will continue to use the customary names to avoid confusing the reader.

7. This is done so that the classifying system will be more stable because the elimination of a single attribute will not change the system (Anderberg 1973: 12; Sneath and Sokal 1973: 107).

8. Two entities are comparable only if their attributes have at least two alternative states (for example, presence/absence) (Clarke 1978: 157). The number of states for each attribute depends on our capacity for observing and understanding the structure of the attribute. In the case of two-state attributes, I only use the state of "presence" or of "absence." Multistate attributes will have alternative states in terms of percentages, frequencies, measures, and so forth.

9. Giving a different value to the attributes at the beginning influences directly the formation of the groups, and, consequently, the classification loses its objectivity (Sneath and Sokal 1973: 109–13).

10. Association coefficients show the concurrence of the states of attributes for each pair of entities. The best-known coefficients, Dice and Jaccard's, show common presences and absences.

11. This kind of coefficient shows differences spatially. The dissimilarity between two entities is represented as the distance between two points; the larger the calculated distance, the larger the dissimilarity coefficient. The best-known coefficients of this type are Minkowski, Manhattan, Euclidian, and metrical.

12. For the principles and application of each of these techniques, see Orton (1988: 50–67).

13. That is, they are agglomerative. Descriptions of the conglomerate and divisive methods can be found in Doran and Hodson (1975: 173–74) and Sneath and Sokal (1973: 202–5).

14. It is continuous because slight changes in the similarity matrix cause only slight changes in the dendrogram.

15. The results of applying numerical methods of grouping can also be represented on two-dimensional iconic models, such as shaded similarity matrices, skyline plots, Wroclaw diagrams, contour diagrams, linkage diagrams, and principal components ordination (Sneath and Sokal 1973: 259–75).

16. This program was written for PCs by the Mathematical Social Science Group of the School of Social Sciences at the University of California, Irvine.

17. If either the total of offerings or the total of object types is subtracted from this number of unshared states, one obtains the number of attributes with shared states.

18. *Frequency* was defined as the ratio of the number of times a "present" state occurred to the total possible number. Frequency was expressed in percentages. See Appendix 2 and the Dendrogram of Object Types.

19. The object complexes obtained were labeled with capital letters of the alphabet. The twenty complexes range from A to T. Six subcomplexes were obtained by dividing three complexes: C_1 and C_2, F_1 and F_2, and J_1 and J_2. See Appendix 2.

20. The offerings that did not form clusters were: 41, 78 (and 78-A), 54, J, H, 64, L, 85, 45, 82, 16 (and 16-A), 38, and Burials 1, 71, 76, 30, and 9. See Appendix 3.

21. The thirteen object type complexes were labeled with capital letters. They are: A (attributes 56, 57, 31), B (attribute 87), C (attributes 100, 108, 76), D (attributes 74, 82), E (attributes 84, 85), F (attributes 11, 99), G (attributes 104, 106, 27), H (attributes 10, 37, 12, 14), I (attributes 69, 71, 32, 63, 103, 23, 3, 70, 68, 36, 64, 6, 17, 24, 39, 59, 16, 77, 4, 34, 2, 66, 38, 75, 41, 65, 67, 30, 90, 88, 102, 101, 33, 35, 47, 58, 22, 52, 73, 46, 79, 96, 105, 62, 45, 44, 40, 5, 95, 43, 8, 107, 94, 81, 97, 89, 86), J (attributes 55, 80), K (attributes 1, 7, 15, 61), L (attributes 26, 98), and M (attributes 9, 51, 54, 18, 19, 60, 29, 25, 50, 49, 53, 72, 83, 91, 42, 28, 92, 20, 109, 21, 13, 78, 93). Complex I links infrequent object types, that is, those that are not present in more than 14 of the 118 offerings. On the other hand, the complexes at the ends (A, B, C, K, L, and M) link object types with high frequency indexes. See the Dendrogram of Object Types.

CHAPTER 8

1. Offering 16 is closely tied to two other deposits: 16-A and the "annex." Detailed information about this cluster of gifts can be found in Appendix 2.

2. See the Templo Mayor General Plan and a description of these constructions at the end of Chapter 4.

3. Numerous sculptures have been found in the immediate vicinity of the Templo Mayor: (1) in 1900 Batres (1902: 25–30) found one sculpture in deposit Number V, seven in Number VI, and one more in Number VII; (2) in 1937 Noguera (1968) found a sculpture in offering 2 at the Plaza of the Volador; (3) in 1948 Estrada Balmori (1979) recovered a similar image in the offering called B1; (4) Angulo (1966a) and Contreras (1979b) found a sculpture in the offering called CA; (5) in 1978 the Department of Salvage Archaeology found two sculptures in offering 1 (García Cook and Arana 1978: 39); and (6) between 1978 and 1989 members of the Templo Mayor Project found twenty-six sculptures in twenty-three offerings. Offerings 7, 11, 13, 15, 16, 20, 23, 24, 60, 61, 62, 70, 81, 83, 88, F, L, and P, as well as Chambers 2 and 3, contained only one image; offerings 6, 17, and 51 contained two (see the General Matrix). In addition, another sculpture of this type was found by Gussinyer (1970b) in offering 7 in Building L-3, located at the intersection of Pino

Suarez and Izazaga. In all, thirty-five of the forty-one sculptures with two protuberances on the head have been taken from the ruins of the Templo Mayor.

4. Some examples are: (1) piece number IV Ca 399 coll, C. Uhde at the Berlin Museum für Völkerkunde SMPK in Berlin; (2) piece number 62.03 at the American Museum of Natural History; (3) piece number 00.5.97 at the Metropolitan Museum of Art; (4) pieces number 5592 and 5738 at the Museum of the American Indian; and (5) piece number IVb 649 at the Basel Ethnographic Museum (cf. Nagao 1985a).

5. These images belong to Solis's Subgroup 12 and correspond to the male sculpture group.

6. The rectangular shape of the teeth must be emphasized. Some authors have not done so and instead of identifying them as human teeth, have mistakenly identified them as the pointed teeth of rain gods (Broda 1987a: 95).

7. The decoration of the image found by Gussinyer differs slightly from that seen in Templo Mayor images. Regarding this, Heyden (1970) said, "Almost all of the figure is painted blue, the color of water. *The original face was blue, except for the nose and a red circle around the mouth....* Over the original blue paint, some fine black lines have been painted above the eyelids, and *a broad black band on the lower part of the face....* The ears are white and the earplugs black on a background of red and blue.... The headdress has seven circles or *chalchihuitls* (precious jades) inside a white band; the *chalchihuitls*, are blue-black, and there are traces of red on the white background. The headdress is set off by two black cylindrical plumed protuberances. Around the wrists, there are more *chalchihuitls*, like bracelets" (emphasis L.L.L.).

8. As Nicholson and Quiñones Keber (1983: 87) pointed out, the turtle shells were erroneously identified as ears of corn by Nagao (1985b: 65–66) and by Pasztory (1983: 223).

9. A photograph can be seen in Bonifaz Nuño (1981: 129).

10. The unusual attributes of the sculpture in Chamber 2 are perhaps related to the symbolic context in which it was offered. It was found exactly below the skeleton of a puma and associated with materials related to the aquatic world of the Mesoamerican cosmovision: a seated sculpture of Tlaloc, shells, corals, a jar with the image of Chalchiuhtlicue, representations of fish, turtles, and frogs, and so on. Appendix 2 has a description of Complex B.

11. It belongs to Solís Olguín's (1985: 406) Subgroup 8, Variant 2: "figures arrayed with a headband of undulant bands, hook-shaped ear plugs and a half mask like a bird beak."

12. It belongs to Solís Olguín's (1985: 411) Subgroup 11: "figures arrayed with a five-pointed crest-like helmet, with two disks on the side of the head, one on the nape, from which smooth or braided strips hang."

13. One example is a piece from the Wetherell Collection of the British Museum in London with the catalog number 1849.6–29.2. See Pasztory (1983: pls. 197–198).

14. It belongs to Solís Olguín's (1985: 405) Subgroup 7, Variant 2: "figures wearing a headdress with points, a fantastic mask formed by rings around the eyes, braided nose and fangs."

15. An example is a sculpture in the Basel Ethnographic Museum with catalog number IVb 634, Slg. L. Vischer.

16. Nagao (1985a, 1985b: 63–66) wrote a summary of the different iconographic interpreta-tions of the images with the two protuberances on their heads. Her review did not include all the evidence for each of these hypotheses.

17. As I will show, Seler changed his mind two years later when he identified one of the figures rescued in the Calle de las Escalerillas as Xiuhtecuhtli-Huehueteotl.

18. They are the travertine sculpture found in Chamber 2 (Bonifaz Nuño 1981: 129) and piece number IVb 649 in the Basel Ethnographic Museum (Nicholson and Quiñones Keber 1983: 86–87).

19. Of the forty-one images found in the offerings, only one (in Chamber 2) is seated with her arms crossed over her knees. A direct analysis of the piece shows it is very unlikely that she is in a position to give birth.

20. As illustrated in Appendixes 2 and 3, as well as in the following pages, only one of the sculptures in question is buried in the stages related to the date *1 Tochtli* (1454), that is, Stages IV and IVa. Most come from offerings in Stage IVb, which is over the glyph *1 Tochtli* and which is numbered *3 Calli* (1469).

21. There are two sculptures that are closer to Ometeotl-Tonacatecuhtli than those with two protuberances on the head, that is, piece IV Ca 3201 C. Uhde at the Berlin Museum für Völkerkunde SMPK and one in offering 6 of the Templo Mayor Project (Fig. 71a) (Bonifaz Nuño 1981: 177). Both show a seated position, *maxtlatl* ("loincloth"), rectangular earplugs, a paper headdress, *xiuhuitzolli* ("royal crown"), and *yacametzli* ("moon-shaped nose plate"). The image of offering 6 has traces of black and red facial paint. Another similar sculpture was found in Chamber 3 (Matos Moctezuma 1988b: 24). It is in a sitting position and has rectangular earplugs, a paper headdress, yacametzli, and a diadem with a cord.

    In my judgment, these three sculptures are in a certain degree similar to the portrayal of Ometeotl-Tonacatecuhtli in the *Códice Vaticano Latino 3738*, plates 1 and 15. There the creator god is seen with rectangular earplugs, paper headdress, xiuhuitzolli, yacametzli, and red facial paint.

    However, as Nicholson and Quiñones Keber (1983: 91; see also Nicholson 1985b) indi-cated correctly, the attributes of the sculpture from offering 6 are usually associated with the gods of pulque. In accord with this interpretation, it should be remembered that offering 6 was found next to the monolith of Coyolxauhqui—the lunar goddess—and that Chamber 3 contained pulque jars.

22. Ometeotl-Tonacatecuhtli appears in only a few Mixtec codices and in the *Códice Vaticano Latino 3738*, the latter dating from the colonial period.

    Spranz (1982: 286–88) stated, "It is possible that this pair of gods [Tonacatecuhtli and Tonacacihuatl] have not been portrayed at all in pictographs, since the manuscripts do not provide an univocal iconography.... Tonacateuhtli-Tonacacihuatl [sic] are only listed by the interpreters as presiding over the first period of the tonalpohualli."

23. Seler (1903: 254) associated Xiuhtecuhtli to an image with two protuberances belonging to Batres's offering Number VII. Some time before, the Mexican anthropologist had related it to the so-called Indio Triste ("Sad Indian") (see also Tweedie 1901:211) to which Seler answered, "The face of the figure is also different from that of the 'Indio Triste', since it has wrinkles and

has the same teeth as the old *Ueueteotl*, the god of fire. The figure is the same as the ones portrayed in the sculptures of Teotihuacan, which have braziers on their heads. The two horn-shaped adornments of the crown of the head may represent the two pieces of wood, *ome quammalitli* ("two fire sticks"), that the god of fire used to decorate his headdress."

24. See the discussion of offering 16 and Complex A that follows (see also López Luján 2005).

25. There is an image of Xiuhtecuhtli wearing only a maxtlatl in Book 2 of the *Códice Florentino*.

26. Usually, the pre-Classic and the Classic period images of Huehueteotl, the "Old God," have signs of old age, such as wrinkles and missing teeth.

27. He is represented like this in: *Códice Telleriano-Remensis* (1964–1967: pl. 12); *Codex Magliabechiano* (1983: fol. 89r); and *Códice Vaticano Latino 3738* (1964–1967: pl. 72). In some cases, only the red pigment around the mouth is seen: *Códice Telleriano-Remensis* (1964–1967: pl. 32); *Códice Vaticano Latino 3738* (1964–1967: pls. 32 and 54); *Códice Tudela* (1980: fols. 54r and 103r). In others, there is one horizontal black strip covering the lower half of the face: *Códice Borbónico* (1979: pls. 9, 20, 23, and 37); *Códice Borgia* (Seler 1963: pls. 13, 14, and 69); *Códice Florentino* (1979: bk. 2); *Tonalámatl de Aubin* (1981: pls. 9 and 20); *Códice Fejérváry-Mayer* (1964–1967: pl. 1); and *Codex Magliabechiano* (1983: fol. 46r). Similar representations from other Mixtec codices can be seen in Spranz (1982: 365–67).

    With respect to the adornment of our images, Nagao (1985b: 67, 1985a) stated that "the blue face painting with an oval around the mouth does not correspond to any known deity," and "the meaning of the facial painting is up to now an unsolved problem."

28. There are several representations of Xiuhtecuhtli with ears painted in this color: *Códice Borbónico* (1979: pls. 9, 20, 23, and 37); *Tonalámatl de Aubin* (1981: pls. 9 and 20); *Códice Telleriano-Remensis* (1964–1967: pl. 12); and *Códice Vaticano Latino 3738* (1964–1967: pls. 32 and 72).

29. See *Códice Borbónico* (1979: pl. 9); *Códice Borgia* (Seler 1963: pl. 13); *Códice Telleriano-Remensis* (1964–1967: pl. 12); and *Códice Vaticano Latino 3738* (1964–1967: pls. 54 and 72).

30. See *Códice Borbónico* (1979: pls. 9, 20, 23, and 37); *Tonalámatl de Aubin* (1981: pls. 9 and 20); *Códice Borgia* (Seler 1963: pls. 14 and 69); *Códice Florentino* (1979: bk. 2); *Códice Tudela* (1980: fols. 54r and 103r); and *Codex Magliabechiano* (1983: fols. 46r and 89r). Similar representations from other Mixtec codices can be seen in Spranz (1982: 368).

    The Mexica *tlatoque* ("rulers") wear crowns (*xiuhuitzolli*) decorated with concentric circles in folios 51v and 54r of the *Primeros memoriales*.

31. Undulating elements are found on the diadem in: *Códice Borgia* (Seler 1963: pls. 14 and 69); *Tonalámatl de Aubin* (1981: pl. 9); and *Codex Magliabechiano* (1983: fol. 89r).

32. A clear image of a *xiuhtototl* in a crown is seen in: *Códice Borbónico* (1979: pls. 9, 20, 23, and 37); *Códice Borgia* (Seler 1963: pl. 13); and *Códice Fejérváry-Mayer* (1964–1967: pl. 1).

33. See *Códice Borbónico* (1979: pls. 9, 20, 23, and 37); *Códice Borgia* (Seler 1963: pls. 13, 14, and 69); *Códice Florentino* (1979: bk. 2); *Códice Tudela* (1980: fols. 54r and 103r); and *Codex Magliabechiano* (1983: fols. 4r and 89r). Similar images in other Mixtec codices are in Spranz (1982: 365–70). Also see Seler (1963: vol. 1, 95).

34. This also applies to the rectangular earplugs with a central pendant, typical of Tlaloc.

35. In some pictographs, the goddess Xochiquetzal (*Códice Fejérváry-Mayer* 1964–1967: pl. 35) and the *bacaboob*, or "sky bearers" (*Códice Dresde* 1988: pl. 37a), are shown with great tortoise shells on their backs. According to a secondary source, the turtle was related to the sun, and priests devoted to the cult of that astral body wore tortoise shells (Brambila Paz et al. 1980: 39).

36. It is very significant that, besides Xiuhtecuhtli, the only gods who appear crowned with xiuhuitzolli in two pictographs are Tonacatecuhtli and Mictlantecuhtli, that is, the divinities with whom the God of Fire is fused in the sky and in the underworld (see *Códice Vaticano Latino 3738* 1964–1967: pls. 1, 15, 32, 34, 54, and 72; *Códice Telleriano-Remensis* 1964–1967: pls. 12, 15, and 33).

37. Other authors that agree with this idea are Paso y Troncoso (1979: 243–46) and Spranz (1982: 364).

38. According to modern Maya, the bacaboob are found at the intersections of the cardinal directions. Modern Chorti, who live near Copán, use the quincunx as a symbol of the earth's surface. "They make it with four stones distributed on an altar: four of the corners correspond to the solstices and one in the middle represents the 'navel of the world'" (Villa Rojas 1985).

39. Matos Moctezuma (1988c: 93–94) had this to say about the reason why the Mexica gave offerings to this deity: "It seems that Xiuhtecuhtli was buried with the offerings at the Templo Mayor for very specific symbolic reasons related to the concepts of the heart and the center. Xiuhtecuhtli lived at the center of the earth symbolized by the Templo Mayor, and he was the Father of the Gods. It was said that he resided in the 'navel' of the world, the center and formation of all life." This theme will be dealt with in more detail in the last section of this chapter (see also López Luján 2005).

40. The sculptures come from offerings 1, 6, 7, 11, 13, 15, 16, 17, 20, 23, 24, 51, 60, 61, 62, 70, 81, 83, 88, F, L, P, CA, B1, and Chambers 2 and 3.

41. According to numerical taxonomy, the images of Tlaloc and the sculptures with the two protuberances on the head have a high coefficient of similarity contextually. This can be seen in the Dendrogram of Object Types, where the branches of the two deities come together at the level of seventeen unshared presences/absences.

    Only four of the deposits (15.4%) where the two-protuberance images were found had no effigies of Tlaloc: 16, 51, 81, and B1. However, these exceptional deposits show indirect links to the God of Rain. Offerings 16 and 51 are adjacent to two deposits (offerings "annex" and 50, respectively) dedicated exclusively to Tlaloc. And offerings B1 and 81 contain various objects in the aquatic world of Mesoamerican cosmovision: a shell, white coral, and two greenstone pulque vessels in offering B1 and marine sand, blue pigment, conch shells, shells, and sea urchins in offering 81.

42. Offering 48 joins the remaining eight offerings at the level of eighteen unshared presences/absences, that is, it has a low coefficient of similarity with other offerings in the complex (0.62). See the Dendrogram of Offerings.

43. On the bottom of the box corresponding to the top of the altar, a circular lid was found covering access to Chamber 3. Therefore, any future study of offering 48 should take into account

its symbolic relationship to Chamber 3 and to offering 85, which lies at an even deeper level. See the description of Chamber 3 in Appendix 2 and of offering 85 in Appendix 3.

44. The reader should be aware that the sketches of this offering correspond to five excavation levels. The first is the most superficial, and the last is the deepest. On the other hand, the text refers to the five levels of actual deposition. The first is the deepest, and the last is the one nearest the surface. The text reconstructs the sequence of the offerings and not that of the archaeological exploration.

45. Here I extend the linguistic concept of tropes to areas of semiotics, which are not strictly verbal but in which one sees equivalent phenomena.

46. See the discussion of the significance of recumbent jars in Complex N.

47. They included one two-year-old child, one three-year-old, thirteen four-year-olds, eleven five-year-olds, eleven six-year-olds, and five seven-year-olds (Román Berrelleza 1986: 76–97).

48. Only one femur shows a cut at the height of the diaphysis done with a dull blade (Román Berrelleza 1986: 131–35).

49. Some chroniclers referred to the sacrifice only on "hills": Benavente (1969: 35–36); Durán (1984: vol. 1, 83–86); and Pomar (1964–1968: 168–69). Others spoke of specific places. Sahagún (1988: vol. 2, 104–5) mentioned sacrifice on the hills that surround the Basin of Mexico (Cuauhtepetl, Yoaltecatl, Poyauhtla, and Cocotl) and the hills that rise from the Lake of Texcoco (Tepetzinco and Tepepulco). Durán (1984: vol. 1, 83–85) mentioned the practice of this kind of sacrifice on a rectangular structure called Tetzacualco, located at the top of Mount Tlaloc.

50. "I believe the new temple would have been completed quite a while before in anticipation of the corresponding ceremonies" (Umberger 1987).

51. See *Anales de Cuauhtitlan* (1975: 52); *Anales de Tlatelolco* (1948: 57); *Anales de Tula* (1979: 35, pl. 5); *Códice de Aubin* (1979: 69, 96); *Códice Vaticano Latino 3738* (1964–1967: pl. 109); *Códice Telleriano-Remensis* (1964–1967: pl. 7); and Chimalpahin (1965: 99–100, 200–1).

52. Sahagún (1988: vol. 1, 328–32) recorded an invocation to the tlaloque that shows desperation because of the lack of rain.

53. Martínez-Cortés (1970: 40; see also Victoria 2004) wrote about this resin as follows:

> The word copal comes from Nahuatl, derived from *copalli*, a term which, according to Hernández, the Mexica used to designate "any kind of gum." The name of the trees that produce this substance is formed with the word *copalli* to which are added other words ... to describe particular characteristics. The principal tree or the central one for the genus is the *copalquahuitl* and from it are derived names such as *xochicopalli* or flowery copal, the *tecopalquahuitl* or wild copal, etc.
>
> In Hernández we have found sixteen varieties of copal, all of which produce, spontaneously or after incisions, a white, transparent gum that "solidifies in broad slivers." Some trees produce white gum and others, a yellow gold-like one.
>
> The copal is a tree that belongs to the genus *Bursera*. We know that now forty species grow in Mexico, principally in hot, dry regions. Its resin or gum can not be dissolved in water, but it does dissolve in ether and other organic solvents.

54. Of the 118 offerings studied, 58 had objects made from copal (anthropomorphic figures, cylinders, bars, or amorphous remains) (Victoria 2002).

55. The provinces of Tlachco and Tepecuacuilco—situated in the present state of Guerrero—periodically gave copal as tribute to the Excan Tlatoloyan. The shipments were in the form of baskets of refined white copal, as well as balls of crude copal (*Códice Mendocino* 1964–1967: fols. 36r and 37r).

56. See Ramírez Acevedo (1989) for a detailed physical description of this type of artifact.

57. There was a frequency of 4.3% in object types in Complex M. See the Reordered General Matrix.

58. For a description of the characteristics and uses of the maguey, see O'Gorman (1963: 218) and López Luján (1983).

59. These objects show a frequency index of 1.72% in Complex I object types. See the Reordered General Matrix.

60. The bottom of the box was made of flagstones, and the sides from vertical quarry stone sillares. The inside dimensions of the stone container were 122 cm in a north-south direction, 122 cm to the east-west, and 50 cm in depth.

61. According to the field record, the stone box offering O was filled with a 10-cm-thick layer of dirt and, immediately afterward, with tezontle rocks. This was done at the beginning of the next expansion of Building E.

62. These attributes (jars and cajetes) have a 100% frequency index in offering Complex N (Fig. 56).

63. Some jars also had remnants of white, ocher, or black pigment. See the detailed description of Complex N in Appendix 2.

64. In two documents from the *Crónica X* tradition, three jars adorned the upper part of the Tlaloc temple at the Templo Mayor of Tenochtitlan (*Códice Ramírez* 1944: pl. 19; Durán 1984: vol. 2, pl. 30). The Templo Mayor of Tlatelolco is shown on pages 14 and 15 of the *Códice Cozcatzin* (1890). In this drawing, the figure of a human being presiding over the northern chapel can be seen, with his arm pointing toward two jars.

65. An image of Tlaloc holding a pitcher from which water pours is in the *Codex Magliabechiano* (1983: fol. 89r).

66. The Nahuatl description of the Etzacualiztli festival is in *Códice Matritense del Real Palacio* (1906: fols. 76r–83v), and in *Códice Florentino* (1979: bk. 2, fols. 37v–46r). The cited Spanish version is from López Austin (1985b: 235).

67. According to the *Diccionario de la Lengua Española*, a *barreño* is a large, rough, clay vessel, generally wider at the top than at the bottom, that, among other things, can be used to wash dishes.

68. For example, there were three greenstone beads in the water jar of offering 28, four beads in offering 25, and five beads in offering 26. The beads had different shapes; some were round, some were tubular, and one of them, in offering 26, was shaped like a plant.

69. "The *offerings* made to the gods were often symbols of what was desired from them. The greenstone beads represented drops of rain, for which they prayed to Tlaloc" (Krickeberg 1975: 152).

70. Molina (1944) translated the word *tepetlacalli* as "tomb or stone box."

71. This is box number 13 of Gutiérrez Solana's (1983: 62–65) classification. See also Pasztory (1983: 164).

72. A detailed description of Subcomplex F_1 is in Appendix 2.

73. See the Offerings Dendrogram.

74. See the rearranged general matrix.

75. Each box is a prismatic monolith with an upper edge raised in order to fit a lid.

76. See the General Plan.

77. Underlining by the author.

78. Grigsby used the pseudonym of Tlaxictlan for this village in order to protect its anonymity. It is a Nahuatl-speaking village in Morelos situated in a valley formed by the intersection of two limestone mountain chains.

79. According to Thompson, it is difficult to determine if this fantastic being with ophidian and fish characteristics is terrestrial or celestial. Nevertheless, it is clear that the God of Number Thirteen is associated with the day *muluc* (water).

80. This ceremony was called *Tsikul T'an Ti' Yuntisiloob* and took place on October 13–20, 1959. Thirteen hens, thirteen candles, thirteen bottles of honey, and thirteen drinking vessels were used during the ritual.

81. The practices of the Tlapanecs of Guerrero, who make bundle offerings that are very similar to those shown in the codices of the Borgia group, are interesting with respect to the repeated use of the number thirteen. In a curing ritual, they offer four bundles of thirteen *zacates* (thatching grass) to obtain "the help of a wealthy spirit." Perhaps this is a way to invoke the Lord of the Mountain who owns the infinite wealth inside the mountains. In another ceremony against evil, they offer a bundle of thirteen zacates and a bundle with fourteen to "the Thirteenth and Fourteenth Seas, from whence evil comes and where it must return" (Loo 1982).

82. In the 1940s, Espejo (1945) divided the offerings of Tlatelolco into two types. Type 1 were objects for personal use and, on occasion, food that served as a mortuary offering in the tombs. Type 2 were cult objects and, at times, human or animal bones that were deposited in the building fill for "ceremonial" purposes. Nagao (1985b: 1–2) thought that buried offerings had the purpose of consecrating the erection of some monument, commemorating a calendric event, consecrating the expansion or the destruction of an edifice, or serving as a gift to a specific divinity or cult. Different from these, the mortuary offerings were meant to serve the deceased in the afterlife (see also López Luján 2001a).

83. Because of the particular circumstances under which offering 29 was discovered, it is probable that it had been partially plundered in the year 1900 during the construction of a drainage system along the ancient street of Escalerillas (E. Matos Moctezuma, pers. comm., Sept. 1990). Moreover, Chávez (2002) discovered recently that the burnt bones from offering 29 are not human but those of an eagle. In consequence, this deposit must be eliminated from the funerary complex.

84. The only contrast that exists among the offerings of Complex E has to do with the number of object types found in each deposit: the poorest offering in the group had only three object types, and the richest had fifteen.

85. *Frequency* is defined here as the ratio of the number of times that a presence state occurs to the total theoretical presences.

86. Several investigators agree that the vase in offering 14 shows the image of Tezcatlipoca. On the other hand, there is uncertainty about the identity of the personage on the vase in offering 10 because it mixes iconographic attributes shared by Quetzalcoatl, Xiuhtecuhtli, Mixcoatl, and Iztac Mixcoatl. It is interesting that the bas-reliefs on both urns are oriented toward the west, so that the two personages are face to face (Aguilera 1987; Matos Moctezuma 1983, 1988c: 106; Nicholson and Quiñones Keber 1983: 95–96; Umberger 1987).

87. Remember that the drawings of this offering correspond to the four levels of excavation, that is, the first one is nearest to the surface, and the last one is the deepest. The description, however, refers to the only real placement level.

88. Durán (1984: vol. 1, 55) commented, "If they burned him in the urn where they threw the ashes, they also cast jewels and precious stones there, no matter how rich they were."

89. The drawings in this offering correspond to the five levels of excavation. The first is the nearest the top; the last ones are the deepest. The description, however, refers to the two real levels of deposition. The first is the deeper, and the second is nearer to the surface. Therefore, the description reconstructs the sequence of the rite and not the archaeological exploration.

90. This mask might well represent the face of Xipe Totec or that of a monkey, with three bells hanging from its chin. It has earplugs in the form of chalchihuitl, topped by four concentric circles like the toponym for Chalco—with rattlesnakes passing through their central perforation. Flores García (1970) reported the finding of a burial similar to those of Tenochtitlan in the Offerings Zone B in Tlatelolco. It was made up of human ashes, flint projectile points, obsidian prismatic blades, Aztec III potsherds, and three small ceramic figures related to the cult of Xipe Totec (see Anon. 1968).

91. In the case of the Maya, Landa (1982: 59) mentioned that cremation was reserved for "the lords and very worthy people."

92. Remember that people who died of causes related to water went to Tlalocan, and babies who died while they were still nursing went to Chichihualcuauhco.
     According to Alvarado Tezozómoc (1949: 244), the soul of Axayacatl arrived eighty days after his death to "Ximoayan, meaning that it was in the deepest part of the enclosure, and dark in all places to the left, *opoch huayocan* in the narrowest part where there were no roads, *yn atlecalocan chicnauhmictlan*, in the ninth hell of the abyss." The souls of Tizoc and Ahuitzotl met the same fate (Alvarado Tezozómoc 1944: 264, 390).

93. It was said that Axayacatl was simultaneously "recumbent and resting in the shadow of the somber meadows of the nine mouths of death, and in the resplendent house of fire of the Sun where his ancestors dwell" (Durán 1984: vol. 2, 296). See López Austin (1988c: vol. 1, 328–30) concerning the divisible nature of the teyolia.

94. See López Austin (1990b: 353–56) for a discussion of this helical voyage.

95. The same information, with a few variations, is found in Las Casas (1967: vol. 2, 458–65) and Torquemada (1969: vol. 2, 521–23).

96. Often the authors of the chronicles called this stone "heart." Sahagún (1988: vol. 1, 221) said that in the case of a *pilli* ("noble"), a chalchihuite was used, and in the case of a *macehualli* ("commoner"), an obsidian or a *texoxoctli* ("a stained stone of low value") was used.

97. López Austin (1988c: vol. 1, 220–21, 322, and 326–27) offered several interpretations of the meaning of this fine stone. On one hand, he discussed two possible Spanish references—that it was used as money to pay for some expense or service during the journey to Mictlan or as a receptacle for the teyolia when the person passed away. On the other hand, the hair on the crown of the head was considered to be a container of the tonalli, a personal connection with the world of the gods. Saving the locks cut at the beginning and at the end of the days of an individual—the limits of the life of the tonalli—would preserve this animic entity.

98. If it was macehualli, it was wrapped in paper (Sahagún 1988: vol. 1, 220).

99. Durán (1984: vol. 1, 55) said that the ashes of burned bodies were buried in the temples.

100. As I will show later, both Sahagún's *Historia general* and the *Crónica X* group stated that the mortuary bundles of nobles were burned at places different from those mentioned by Motolinía.

   When a merchant died during a mercantile expedition, his relatives made an image that took the place of the absent corpse. If the merchant died of some illness, the bundle was burned in the courtyard of his home, but if he had been killed by his enemies, it was burned at the Cuauhxicalco or the Tzompantitlan, both located in the sacred Tenochcan precinct (Sahagún 1988: vol. 1, 256).

101. Among the people sacrificed were slaves, priests, dwarfs, hunchbacks, overseers, and grinders of corn (Alva Ixtlilxóchitl 1975: vol. 1, 353, vol. 2, 188; Alvarado Tezozómoc 1944: 238–39, 390–91; "Costumbres, fiestas, enterramientos" 1965; Durán 1984: vol. 1, 55–56, vol. 2, 248, 295–97, 311, and 392–94).

102. Sometimes the belongings of the deceased were burned and buried with his or her ashes (Alva Ixtlilxóchitl 1975: vol. 2, 188; *Codex Magliabechiano* 1983: fols. 65v and 67v).

   Rich gifts donated by allied nobles and their subjects were buried together with the ashes of the tlatoque. Jewels, fine skins, precious feathers, weapons, mantles, clothing, food, and paper were the most common gifts (Alva Ixtlilxóchitl 1975: vol. 1, 238–39, 390–91; Alvarado Tezozómoc 1944: 264–65, 238–39, and 390–91; "Costumbres, fiestas, enterramientos" 1965; Durán 1984: vol. 1, 55–56, vol. 1, 248, 295–97, 299, 311, and 392–94).

103. Some sources say that the dead person used part of these goods to keep warm and part to offer to Mictlantecuhtli upon arrival at the ninth level of the underworld (*Codex Magliabechiano* 1983: fol. 68v; Sahagún 1988: vol. 1, 221).

104. Alva Ixtlilxóchitl (1975: vol. 1, 353) said that the container with the mortal remains of King Tezozómoc was placed temporarily on an altar next to the image of Tezcatlipoca.

105. According to López Austin (1988c: vol. 1, 322), the purpose of this image was to attract the scattered parts of the tonalli. In this way, they would go to the inside of the box where part of the vital force of the individual would be preserved.

   If it was a tlatoani, the wooden image was dressed, in turn, as Huitzilopochtli, Tlaloc, Yohualahuan, and Quetzalcoatl (Alvarado Tezozómoc 1944: 240–42 and 265; Durán 1984: vol. 2, 298, 311).

106. Nobles were buried in a "crypt in the patio of the house of each lord, where they buried him and his descendants" ("Costumbres, fiestas, enterramientos" 1965).

107. According to Landa (1982: 59), Mayan nobles were cremated and temples built over their ashes. According to Sahagún's (1950–1969: bk. 3, 42–43) informants, the jar with mortal remains was deposited in a hole they called a "cave" located in the house or in the temple of the calpulli.

108. He mentioned "another cu, where the great Mexican lords were buried, which also had other idols, all full of blood and smoke, and it had other doors and figures from hell" (Díaz del Castillo 1982: 195).

109. It is evident that Alvarado Tezozómoc refers to the feet of the idol in these three fragments, not to the bottom of the structure, as some authors have erroneously inferred.

110. Alvarado Tezozómoc (1944: 243) stated that the hearts of slaves were taken to the Cuauhxicalli.

111. As he wrote, "Finally they carried the ash and dust of the king and they buried it at the feet of the king and god they call *Huitzilopochtli*" (Alvarado Tezozómoc 1944: 266).

112. According to Sahagún's (1956: vol. 4, 124) informants, Motecuhzoma Xocoyotzin was burned in the Cuauhxicalco.

113. Palacios (1935) proposed that the southern half of the Temple of Tenayuca was dedicated to Tota, a divinity closely tied to Mixcoatl and to the sun.

114. The first one contained human ashes, dog bones, a conch shell, a *malacate* ("spindle"), piercing-cutting instruments, projectile points of flint and obsidian, and prismatic obsidian blades; in the second, there were cremated remains, fragments of an incense burner, and prismatic obsidian blades; while in the third, there were only ashes.

115. Matos Moctezuma (1984a: pers. comm. Sept. 1990) proposed that they may be the remains of two great captains killed during Axayacatl's unsuccessful campaign in Michoacán territory. This hypothesis is based on (1) the location of the offerings at the place where captives of war were taken to be sacrificed; (2) the proximity of the offerings to the Coyolxauhqui monolith, a goddess slain in battle; (3) the portrayal of armed gods on the funerary urns; and (4) the presence of the glyph *3 Calli* at Stage IVb, perhaps related to 1469, the year of the defeat of the Excan Tlatoloyan by the Tarascan armies. Umberger (1987) suggested that all the ashes of two urns belonged to Motecuhzoma Ilhuicamina. She supports this by citing the placement of the two personages on the urns facing each other, an iconographic arrangement that may indicate legitimation of his succession to power; the depiction of undulating serpents behind the personages, a motif that is associated with dynastic representations; and the presence of the glyph *3 Calli* at Stage IVb, perhaps in reference to 1469, the year of the ruler's death. However, thanks to Chávez (2002) we know now that one different individual was buried inside each one of these two urns.

116. Similar helicoidal beads have also been encountered by members of the Templo Mayor Project at several burial sites at the Sacred Precinct of Tlatelolco (Salvador Guil'liem Arroyo, pers. comm. May 1990).

117. In Tlatelolco, on several occasions, beads in the form of a duckhead have been found associated with human bones and helicoidal beads (Salvador Guil'liem, pers. comm. May 1990).

118. The richness of the offerings making up this complex is shown by the large number of elements, ranging between 49 and 249. Just as important is the diversity of the objects buried in these deposits: all have between twenty-eight and forty different object types.

119. The fusion of Complex A with the other 107 offerings only takes place at the very high value of 47 unshared presences/absences.

120. These thirteen offerings, together with the eleven from Complex A, are characterized by a predominance of materials belonging to the object type Complexes A, B, C, and K. All the offerings have images of Xiuhtecuhtli and Tlaloc.

121. This is composed of a skull-mask, tortoise, sawfish, serpentiform scepters, chicahuaztli, sea urchin, sea sand, oyohualli, serpent, alligator, shark, bone bloodletter, brazier, a miniature atlatl, eagle, hatchet and mace, epcololli, rattlesnake, and the head of an obsidian serpent, a turquoise mosaic, obsidian earplug and scepter, personified sacrificial knife, the skull of a beheaded person, and a projectile point.

122. It should be remembered that the drawings of both offerings correspond to the levels of excavation. Therefore, the first level is the one nearest surface, and the last one is the deepest. The description, however, refers to the actual placement levels. The first of them is the deepest, and the last is nearest the surface. The description refers to the deposition sequence, not the sequence of the archaeological exploration.

123. Each of the offerings in Complex A had one or more remains of alligators, aligned in the same direction as the offering container. The head was found in exactly the opposite direction from that in which the divine effigies who presided over the fifth level had been placed.

124. Each nose cartilage was aligned in the same direction as the offering container. The tip of the nose cartilage was oriented toward the divine effigies that presided over the fifth level.

125. The claws of a puma were found at the corners of offering 23, unmistakable evidence that its skin had been buried in order to cover the top of the whole deposit.

126. These are the front half of a human cranium, representing the god of death. There are perforations in the forehead (perhaps for the placing of thick hair), incrustations of shell and pyrite in the eye sockets, and, at times, flint knives in the nose and mouth openings.

127. Regarding this, see *Die Azteken und ihre Vorläufer* (1986: vol. 2, no. 310) and Heyden (1987: 113–26). According to Heyden, the effigy wears a necklace of *cempoalxochitl* (*Tagetes erecta*), a flower related on one side to the sun and fire and on the other to water and vegetation. She also pointed out that in Tlatelolco, similar receptacles were discovered that contained human skulls instead of copal.

128. To these four objects should be added the representations of divine paraphernalia. These artifacts were relatively scarce; their presence and association varied considerably from one deposit to another. Among them we have the *tzotzopaztli* ("weaving stick") of Ilamatecuhtli; the *xiuhcoatl* ("fire serpent") of Huitzilopochtli and Xiuhtecuhtli; Techalotl's wooden mallet; the *yacametztli* ("moon-shaped noseplate") of the pulque gods; the *epcololli* ("curved shell ear pendant") of Quetzalcoatl and Xolotl; the *ehecacozcatl* ("wind necklace") of Quetzalcoatl and Xolotl; the *anahuatl* ("white pectoral ring") of Tezcatlipoca, Huitzilopochtli, and Paynal; the *oyohualli* ("rattling shell pendant") of the opossum, Tlahuizcalpantecuhtli, and Quetzalcoatl; and braziers with two bowknots. Matos Moctezuma (1982c: 97) thought these small braziers might indicate the symbolic presence of Huitzilopochtli in the offerings at the Templo Mayor.

129. For example, in the *Historia de los mexicanos por sus pinturas* (1965: 37), Camaxtle, the Fire God, used a two-headed deer to vanquish his enemies. The esoteric name for the deer was Macuil Xochitl, a solar deity (González Torres 1975: 60).

130. According to a Huichol myth, the sun shines thanks to the deer (Zingg 1982: vol. 2, 187–208, 330).

131. On a Toltec plaque, a human figure sitting on his heels and carrying a bundle supported by a leather headstrap can be seen. The handle of the staff he carries in his right hand is a deerhead. Just behind the staff, there is an undulating serpent (Fuente, Trejo, and Gutiérrez Solano 1988: 179–80, pl. 142).

132. "Which means looker or place to look because with it the face was hidden and one could look through the hole in the thin gold plate" (Sahagún 1988: vol. 1, 49).

133. Some of the many representations of Xipe Totec with a chicahuaztli are: *Códice Borgia* (Seler 1963: pls. 25, 49, 61); *Códice Tudela* (1980: fol. 12r); *Códice Florentino* (1979: bk. 2, fols. 19v, 20r, 20v, 126r); *Tonalámatl de Aubin* (1981: pl. 14); *Codex Magliabechiano* (1983: fol. 90r); *Códice Vaticano Latino 3738* (1964–1967: pls. 10, 12); and Durán (1984: vol. 1, 96, pl. 15).

134. These knives have flint, shell, pyrite, turquoise, and/or obsidian appliqués, resembling eyes and sharp teeth. Some have polychrome remnants; others were found inserted into balls of copal.

135. This confirms Motolinía's (Benavente 1969: 62) statement that the sacrificial knives were made of flint and not of obsidian.

136. "The quail was the bird that corresponded to the sun as the fourth lord of days...and was particularly sacrificed to this astral body" (González Torres 1975: 60). Quails, together with locusts, butterflies, and snakes, were sentenced to be sacrificed to the gods because they did not predict where the sun would appear for the first time (Mendieta 1945: vol. 1, 85).

137. Five skulls were found in offering 1, three in offering 6, five in offering 11, six in offering 13, five in offering 17, nine in offering 20, two in offering 23, five in offering 60, and one in offering 88. Most of the remaining skulls come from Complex J, which, as I mentioned, is closely related to Complex A: one skull in each of offerings 22, 24, 58, 82, and 5 (?) skulls in offering CA.

138. In a certain way, the quality and distribution of the objects of the three first levels recall the aquatic motifs carved on the underside of the bases of many Mexica monoliths (see Ojeda Díaz 1986: 55, 92–94).

139. One of the earliest findings is the skull of Tlatecomila, in Tetelpan, D.F., dated between 600 and 400 B.C. (Nájera 1987: 172).

140. Commenting on this kind of discovery in the Mayan area, Ruz Lhuillier (1968: 160) noted,

> We have considered them probable burials of sacrifices dedicated to a building (temple or palace) or to stelae (Nebaj), which consist of heads usually with their respective cervical vertebrae, or decapitated bodies or those mutilated in some way. The skulls are frequently placed on plates, in cajetes or jars, or lined up in a row (Chichén Itzá) or in a circle (Nebaj). Only skulls by themselves are found in Nebaj, Uaxactún, Tikal, Baking Pot (with a leg), Dzibilchaltún (with a mutilated body outside the vessel containing the skull), Chichén Itzá, Mayapán, Rio Hondo

and Santa Rita. Beheaded bodies are known from Chiapa de Corzo, Uaxactún, Tikal and Mayapán; and with other mutilations (without hands or feet, decapitated and with neither feet nor legs) in Chiapa de Corzo, Tikal, Dzibilchaltún.

Concerning the rest of Mesoamerica, Ruz Lhuillier (1968: 198–99) added, "There are cases in Monte Albán, Teotihuacan and Cerro de las Mesas, Veracruz, during the Classic period; and in Tzintzuntzan, Michoacán and Tlatelolco (explorations in 1964, under the direction of Francisco González Rul, and later by me)."

Other archaeologists report finding skulls of beheaded people in offerings associated with bases topped with two temples. These are the Templo Mayor of Tlatelolco and that of Tenayuca. Espejo (1945) described the exploration in the former of three deposits (offerings 1, 4, and 5) that contained human skulls with the first vertebrae, flint knives, and other objects. These offerings were found along the central axis that runs through the structure in an east-west direction. Noguera (1935) discovered four deposits (Burials 1, 2, 3, and 4) at the foot of the Tenayuca pyramid, characterized by the presence of human skulls, piercing-cutting instruments, ceramic containers, and other cultural materials.

141. According to the *Historia de los mexicanos por sus pinturas* (1965: 54), the Mexica, upon seeing themselves mocked, captured a maiden named Ahuentizin, sacrificed her, and bloodied the walls with one of her legs."

142. Perhaps because of this there are many sculptures of Xipe Totec holding a human head in one hand. For example, Caso and Bernal (1952: 253–54, fig. 396, 254–55, fig. 400), in their book *Urnas de Oaxaca*, reported two urns with this feature. Vase 15 in Tomb 103 shows Xipe Totec holding a chicahuaztli in the right hand and a head in the left. Urn I in Tomb 58 shows this god holding a ball in the right hand and a head in the left.

143. "Then they took the bodies and the intestines to throw into the Mexican lake…because the heads of these innocent bodies were buried inside the walls." (Durán 1984: vol. 2, 336). According to Sahagún (1988: vol. 1, 186), the heads of those killed in Tlacaxipehualiztli were impaled on the Yopico tzompantli.

144. The future inhabitants of the house used to make omens concerning when the New Fire was to begin (see Bautista 1965; López Austin 1969: 93).

145. Following a strict hierarchical order, the gifts were divided among the lords and nobles of the hostile tlatocayotl, the allied and conquered lords, Tenochca nobles, captains, distinguished soldiers, majordomos, ministers at the temples, the elderly, the poor, and the artisans (Broda 1980).

146. "This happened and began during the fifteenth year of *huehue* (old) Moctezuma's reign" (Alvarado Tezozómoc 1944: 119).

147. These people also brought wood and stone, They first put poles into a square 100 *brazas* (about 1.6 m) on a side. On top of this, they placed a layer of mortar that would serve as the foundation for the building.

148. Tlacaelel referred to the towns of Huexotzinco, Atlixco, Cholula, Tlaxcala, Tliliuhquitepec, Tecoac, Itzocan, Zacatlan, and Yopico.

149. Alvarado Tezozómoc (1944: 298–337); Durán 1984: vol. 2 333–49, pls. 29 and 30); *Códice Azcatitlan* (1949: pl. 21); *Códice Telleriano-Remensis* (1964–1967: pls. 18, 19); *Códice Aubin*

(1979: 73–74); *Códice Vaticano Latino 3738* (1964–1967: fols. 80v, 92r, pls. 120, 121); *Anales de Cuauhtitlan* (1975: 58); Chimalpahin (1965: fols. 103–106, 180v); *Historia de los mexicanos por sus pinturas* (1965: 231); Benavente (1969: 404); and Alva Ixtlilxóchitl (1975: vol. 2, 154–57).

150. The *Crónica X* sources referred to sculptures of Coyolxauhqui, the *tzitzimime* ("demons of darkness"), the *chaneque* ("dwellers"), the *petlacontzitzique* ("holders of the canopy"), the *centzonhuitznahua* ("400 thorns"), the *huitziltzilnahua* ("hummingbird nahual"), and the Coatopil.

151. The prisoners taken to Tenochtitlan to be sacrificed were Huexotzinca, Tlaxcalteca, Atlixca, Tliliuhquitepeca, Cholulteca, Tecoaca, Zacatec, Zapotec, Huaxtec, Tzincoca, Tuzapanea, Tlapanec, and Tamapachca.

152. The priests were dressed as Huitzilopochtli, Tlaloc, Quetzalcoatl, Opochtli, and Itzpapalotl.

153. These priests wore the characteristic costume of Apantecuhtli, Tlamatzin, Toci, Izquitecatl, and Chicnauhecatl.

154. The locations were Coatlan, Tzonmolco, Apauteuctlan, Yopico, Moyoco, Chililico, Naapateuctli, Xochicalco, Huitznahuac, Tlamatzinco, Natempan, Tezcacoac, Izquitlan, Tecpantzinco, Cuauhquiahuac, and Acatliacapan.

155. The number was eighty thousand and four hundred according to the *Anales de Cuauhtitlan* (1975: 58); sixty thousand according to Torquemada (1969: vol. 2, 168); twenty thousand according to the *Códice Telleriano-Remensis* (1964–1967: pl. 121). "If this had been so, calculating twenty places in which they made one sacrifice after another, without stopping, during ninety-six hours, there would have been forty-seven deaths an hour, which means that the Mexica priests were more skillful at killing than the mechanized abattoirs in modern developed countries" (González Torres 1985: 248).

156. According to Alvarado Tezozómoc (1944: 457–61), eight hundred were sacrificed, but Durán (1984, vol. 2, 439–45) said it was twenty-three hundred.

157. These included Tepeaca and its dependencies (Cuauhtinchan, Tecalli, Acatzinco, and Oztoticpac); Tecamachalco; Quecholac; Cuauhquechula and its dependencies (Acapetlahuacan, Atzitzihuacan, Yaotehuacan, Hueyapan, Tetelan, and Tlamimilulpan); Chalco; Atlatlauhcan and its dependencies (Tlayacapan, Totolapan, and another five towns); Xochimilco; Cuitlahuac; Mizquic; Colhuacan and its dependencies (Itztapalapan, Mexicatzinco, Huitzilopochco, and another town); Toluca, Matlatzinco, Tzinacantepec, Calimayan, Tepemaxalco, Tlacotepec and Teotenanco, Metepec, Capuluac, Xochihuacan, Zoquitzinco, Tenantzinco, Malinanco and Ocuilan; Mazahuacan, Xocotitlan, Coatlapan, Xiquipilco, Cuahuacan, Cillan, Chiapan, and Xilotepec; Texcoco and its dependencies (Uexutla, Coatlinchan, Coatepec, Chimalhuacan, Itztapalucan, Tepetlaoztoc, Papalotlan, Totoltzinco, Tecciztlan, Tepechpan, Acolman, Chicunauhtlan, Zacatzontitlan, Oztoyocan, Tecoac, Calpulalpan, Tlatzcayucan, Apan, Tepepulco, Tlalanapan, Tezoyocan, Otompan, Achilhilacachocan, Tzacuallan, Cempoallan, Uitzilan, Epazoyocan, Tulantzinco, Tlaquilpan, Tezontepec, Ueitihuacan, and several other towns), and, finally, Tlacopan and its dependencies.

158. These were Tlaxcala, Cholula, Huexotzinco, Tliliuhquitepec, Michuacan, Metztitlan, and Yopitzinco.

159. These were Xochimilco, Cuitlahuac, Itztapalapa, Colhuacan, Mexicaltzinco, Huitzilopochco, Cuautlalpan, Chiapan, Xilotepec, Xiquipilco, Huatitlan, Mazahuacan, and Azcapotzalco.

160. This beautiful building by Manuel Tolsá is located at the corner of República de Argentina and Justo Sierra streets.

161. Ponce de León's calculations were confirmed by Aveni, Calnek, and Hartung (1988).

162. According to Sahagún's (1988: vol. 1, 82) calendric correlation, Tlacaxipehualiztli began February 22 of each year.

163. "Although Xippe [sic] Totec is not mentioned, they performed the typical sacrifice for this ritual: the *tlacaxipehualiztli* or 'flaying of men'" (Martínez Marín 1978). Cristóbal del Castillo (1966: 85–96) mentioned that during the migration, Tetzauhteotl ordered the Mexica to celebrate the *tlahuahuanaliztli*, or gladiatory sacrifice.

164. Some of the gods represented were Huitzilopochtli, Tlaloc, Quetzalcoatl, Tezcatlipoca, Chalchiuhtlicue, Mictlantecuhtli, Opochtli, Itzpapalotl, Apantecuhtli, Tlamatzin, Toci, Izquitecatl, Chicnauhecatl, Mixcuahuac, Yohualahua, Coatlicue, and Ometecuhtli (Alvarado Tezozómoc 1944: 318 ss.)

165. Broda's (1970) and Graulich's (1982) interpretations of the significance of Tlacaxipehualiztli stand out among other recent interpretations due to their erudition and originality.

166. Paso y Troncoso (1979: 109–10) believed that the two white rhombi on plate 24 of *Códice Borbónico* may correspond to the cocolli. It is interesting to remember that in Mexico today, a braided rhomboidal wheat bread is called *cocol*.

167. The Nahuatl text is "*Auh hualmocueptihui, hualmomalacachotihui.*"

168. Preuss (1903: 200–2) presented a very similar hierogamic interpretation of the sacrifice of Tlacaxipehualiztli. It is interesting that during Ochpaniztli (the symmetrically opposite calendar period that celebrates the fall equinox), the marriage of Mother Earth with the sun to produce Cinteotl, the God of Maize, was reenacted (Broda 1983).

169. Compare this translation by Garibay with the one by Velásquez (*Anales de Cuauhtitlan* 1975: 13).

170. There is convincing evidence about the relationship between Tlacaxipehualiztli and the birth of the sun called *Nahui Ollin*. For example, Sahagún's informants said that the Mexica also lit the New Fire on Tlacaxipehualiztli and on Panquetzaliztli (López Austin 1965). On the other hand, the *Anales de Cuauhtitlan* (1975: 14) said that during the year *13 Acatl*, the war between Tollan and Nextlalpan began, an event that ended in the first festival of Tlacaxipehualiztli. It is relevant to remember that *13 Acatl* is the year of the birth of the Fifth Sun in Teotihuacan, the reason why that date appears on the upper part of the Stone of the Sun.

171. See Nicholson (1972b) concerning the spatiotemporal distribution of the cult of Xipe Totec.

172. Thompson (1978: 132) highlighted the military role of Xipe Totec when he identified him with God Q of the Maya codices.

173. These reliefs have the date *1 Izcuintli* ("dog"), which was the first day of the thirteen-day period dedicated to Xipe Totec and probably served as his calendric name (Nicholson 1959, 1972a).

174. In the *Códice Cozcatzin* (1890: 14–15), Axayacatl was seen dressed like Xipe Totec, defeating Moquihuix during the war with Tlatelolco (see Barlow 1945). In the *Códice Vaticano Latino 3738* (1964–1967), Motecuhzoma Xocoyotzin wore this costume during the conquest of Tollocan (see Nicholson 1959: figs. 9–11). To these images may be added the oil painting with the catalog number CVM 12 (Ex-Bilimek collection), at present in the Nationalbibliothek of Vienna (Fig. 126). It is a painting dated between the seventeenth and eighteenth centuries that pictures Axayacatl in a bellicose way. He is attired like Xipe Totec with the skin of a flayed victim. At the feet of the Mexica tlatoani are the heads of ten decapitated warriors (see Glass 1975: 91 [census 16], fig. 21).

175. One of the most beautiful portrayals of atl-tlachinolli is found on the lower part of the diorite head of Coyolxauhqui at the National Museum of Anthropology. It should be remembered that Coyolxauhqui was decapitated in one of the most famous mythical wars (Pasztory 1983: 152–53).

176. In this ritual, the first ears of corn were sprinkled with blood and pulque (Ponce de León 1965: 127).

177. In this ceremony, the priest subjected the head of the newborn to water and to fire (Ponce de León 1965: 124).

178. A third hypothesis recently proposed by Matos Moctezuma (pers. comm., Sept. 1990) should also be taken into account. He suggested that the body of the fourth base of the pyramid corresponds to the fourth celestial level where, according to the *Histoire du Mechique* (1965: 103), "Tonatiuh, who is the Sun" lived.

APPENDIX 2

1. The offerings in parentheses have the attribute on the left.

2. For obvious reasons, no measurement was made of the vertical dimensions of the offering in the building fill. I only include Z in the offerings deposited in boxes of sillares or stone urns.

3. These are anthropomorphic sculptures characterized chiefly by two protuberances on their heads. To this day, there is an interesting debate as to the identity of these images. Following the majority, I am inclined to relate them to Xiuhtecuhtli-Huehueteotl. From here on, I will refer to them as "Xiuhtecuhtli sculptures." See the discussion about these images in the first section of Chapter 8.

4. See the identification in the first section of Chapter 8.

5. See the first section of Chapter 8, which deals with the different iconographic identifications of this type of anthropomorphic sculpture.

Bibliography

THE FOLLOWING ABBREVIATIONS ARE USED
THROUGHOUT THE BIBLIOGRAPHY:

CEMCA	Centre d'Etudes Mexicaines et Centroaméricaines
ENAH	Escuela Nacional de Antropología e Historia
FCE	Fondo de Cultura Económica
IIMAS	Instituto de Investigaciones en Matemáticas Aplicadas y Sistemas
INAH	Instituto Nacional de Antropología e Historia
INI	Instituto Nacional Indigenista
MNA	Museo Nacional de Antropología
SEP	Secretaría de Educación Pública
SMA	Sociedad Mexicana de Antropología
UNAM	Universidad Nacional Autónoma de México

Acosta, Joseph de. 1962. *Historia natural y moral de las Indias en que se tratan de las cosas notables del cielo, elementos, metales, plantas y animales dellas y los ritos y ceremonias, leyes y gobierno de los indios.* Ed. Edmundo O'Gorman. México: FCE.

Aguilar, Francisco de. 1977. *Relación de la conquista de la Nueva España.* Ed. Jorge Gurría Lacroix. México: UNAM.

Aguilera, Carmen. 1978. *Coyolxauhqui: Ensayo iconográfico.* Cuadernos de la Biblioteca, Serie Investigación, no. 2. México: INAH.

———. 1982. Xopan y Tonalco: Una hipótesis acerca de la correlación astronómica del calendario mexica. *Estudios de Cultura Nahuatl* 15: 185–208.

———. 1987. "Iztac Mixcóatl en la vasija del Templo Mayor." In *Memoria del Primer Coloquio de Historia de la Religión en Mesoamérica y Areas Afines.* Ed. Barbro Dahlgren, pp. 69–82. México: UNAM.

———. 1990. También el sol salió en el Templo Mayor (hipótesis sobre su simbolismo calendárico). *México Desconocido* 158 (Apr.): 49–53.

Aguirre Molina, Alejandra. 2002. El ritual del autosacrificio en el Recinto Sagrado de Tenochtitlan: las evidencias arqueológicas. Bachelor's thesis in archaeology, ENAH, México.

Ahuja, O. Guillermo. 1982a. "La cerámica prehispánica en el Templo Mayor." In *El Templo Mayor: Exacavaciones y Estudios*. Ed. Eduardo Matos Moctezuma, pp. 245–52. México: INAH.

———. 1982b. Excavación de la cámara II. In *El Templo Mayor: Excavaciones y estudios*. Ed. Eduardo Matos Moctezuma, pp. 191–212. México: INAH.

Alva Ixtlilxóchitl, Fernando de. 1975. *Obras históricas*. 2 vols. Ed. Edmundo O'Gorman. México: UNAM.

Alvarado Tezozómoc, Fernando. 1944. *Crónica Mexicana: Escrita hacia el año de 1598*. Ed. Manuel Orozco y Berra. México: Editorial Leyenda.

———. 1949. *Crónica mexicáyotl*. Trans. Adrián León. México: UNAM/INAH.

Alvarez, Ticul. 1982. "Restos de vertebrados terrestres en la ofrenda 7 y conclusiones." In *El Templo Mayor: Excavaciones y estudios*. Ed. Eduardo Matos Moctezuma, pp. 161–84. México: INAH.

Alvarez, Ticul, and Aurelio Ocaña. 1991. "Restos óseos de vertebrados terrestres de las ofrendas del Templo Mayor, Ciudad de México." In *La fauna en el Templo Mayor*. Ed. Oscar J. Polaco, pp. 105–48. México: INAH/Asociación de Amigos del Templo Mayor/GV Editores.

Anales de Cuauhtitlan. 1975. In *Códice Chimalpopoca*. Trans. Primo Feliciano Velázquez, pp. 3–118. México: UNAM.

Anales de Tlatelolco (Unos annales históricos de la Nación mexicana) and *Códice de Tlatelolco*. Fuentes para la Historia de México, 2. 1948. Ed. Heinrich Berlin. México: Antigua Librería Robredo.

Anales de Tula. 1979. Ed. Ferdinand Anders. Graz, Austria: Akademische Druck.

Anderberg, Michael R. 1973. *Cluster Analysis for Applications*. New York: Academic Press.

Andrews IV, E. Wyllys. 1970. *Balankanche, Throne of the Tiger Priest*. New Orleans Tulane University.

Angulo, V. Jorge. 1966a. Una ofrenda en el Templo Mayor de Tenochtitlan. *Boletín INAH* 26 (Dec.): 1–6.

———. 1966b. *Un Tlamanalli encontrado in Tlatelolco, México*. Publicaciones del Departamento de Prehistoria, no. 18. México: INAH.

Anon. 1968. Noticias de los museos. *Boletín INAH* 32 (June): 48–55.

———. 1990. *La Jornada* (Aug. 4): 17–30.

Athié Islas, Ivonne. 2001. La obsidiana del Templo Mayor de Tenochtitlan. Bachelor's thesis in archaeology, ENAH, México.

Aveni, Anthony F., and Sharon L. Gibbs. 1976. On the Orientation of Precolumbian Buildings in Central Mexico. *American Antiquity* 41: 510–17.

Aveni, Anthony F., Edward E. Calnek, and Horst Hartung. 1988. Myth, Environment, and the Orientation of the Templo Mayor of Tenochtitlan. *American Antiquity* 53: 287–309.

Baal, J. van. 1976. Offering, sacrifice and gift. *Numen* 27, fasc. 3 (Dec.): 161–78.

Baer, Gerhard, and Ulf Bankmann. 1990. *Ancient Mexican Sculptures From the Lukas Vischer Collection, Ethnographic Museum Basel*. Corpus Americanensium Antiquitatum, Union Académique Internationale. Basel: Verlag Wepf.

Barlow, R. H. 1943. "The Periods of Tribute Collection in Moctezuma's Empire." In *Notes on Middle American Archaeology and Ethnology*. Pp. 152–55. Washington, D.C.: Carnegie Institution.

———. 1945. "Los dioses del Templo Mayor de Tlatelolco." *Tlatelolco a través de los tiempos*. Vol. 3, pp. 45–55. México: Sobretiro de las Memorias de la Academia de la Historia.

Batres, Leopoldo. 1902. *Exploraciones arqueológicas en las Calles de las Escalerillas, año de 1900*. México: Tipografía y Litografía "La Europea."

Bautista, Juan. 1965. "Advertencias a los confesores de indios." In *Teogonía e historia de los mexicanos: Tres opúsculos del siglo XVI*. Ed. A. Ma. Garibay, pp. 141–52. México: Porrúa.

Benavente, Toribio de (Motolinía). 1969. *Historia de los indios de la Nueva España. Relación de los ritos antiguos, idolatrías y sacrificios de los indios de la Nueva España, y de la maravillosa conversión que Dios en ellos ha obrado*. Ed. Edmundo O'Gorman. México: Editorial Porrúa.

———. 1971. *Memoriales o Libro de las cosas de la Nueva España y de los naturales de ella*. Ed. Edmundo O'Gorman. México: UNAM.

Berdan, Frances F. 1987. "The Economics of Aztec Luxury Trade and Tribute." In *The Aztec Templo Mayor*. Ed. E. H. Boone, pp. 161–84. Washington, D.C.: Dumbarton Oaks.

Bernal, Ignacio. 1979. *Historia de la arqueología en México*. México: Editorial Porrúa.

Blanco, Alicia. 1978. Análisis de los materiales biológicos en las ofrendas a Coyolxauhqui. *Antropología e Historia* 24, series 3 (Oct.–Dec.): 31–38.

Bloch, Marc. 1965. *Introducción a la historia*. México: FCE.

Bonifaz Nuño, Rubén. 1981. *El arte en el Templo Mayor, México Tenochtitlan*. México: SEP/INAH.

———. 1990. Escultura en el espacio: El recinto de los Caballeros Aguila. *Artes de México*, new series, 7 (Spring): 26–35.

Boone, Elizabeth Hill. 1987. "Templo Mayor Research, 1521–1978." In *The Aztec Templo Mayor*. Ed. E. H. Boone, pp. 5–70. Washington, D.C.: Dumbarton Oaks.

Brambila Paz, Rosa et al. 1980. *El animal en la vida prehispánica*. México: SEP/INAH.

Braudel, Fernand. 1974. *La historia y las ciencias sociales*. Madrid: Alianza Editorial.

Broda, Johanna. 1970. "Tlacaxipeualiztli: A Reconstruction of an Aztec Calendar Festival From 16th Century Sources." *Revista Española de Antropología Americana* 5: 197–273.

———. 1971. Las fiestas aztecas de los dioses de la lluvia: Una reconstrucción según las fuentes del siglo XVI. *Revista Española de Antropología Americana* 6: 245–327.

———. 1980. "Intercambio y reciprocidad en el ritual mexica." In *Rutas de intercambio en Mesoamérica y norte de México, XVI Mesa Redonda*, vol. 1, pp. 81–97. Saltillo, México: SMA.

———. 1982. El culto mexica de los cerros y el agua. *Multidisciplina* 7: 45–56.

———. 1983. "Ciclos agrícolas en el culto: Un problema en la correlación del calendario mexica." In *Calendars in Mesoamerica and Peru: Native American Computations of Time*. Proceedings of the 44th International Congress of Americanists, Manchester, 1982. BAR International Series, no. 174. Eds. Anthony F. Aveni and Gordon Brotherson, pp. 145–65. Oxford: BAR.

———. 1985. "La expansión imperial mexica y los sacrificios del Templo Mayor." In *Mesoamérica y el centro de México*. Eds. Jesús Monjarás Ruiz, Rosa Brambila Paz, and Emma Pérez-Rocha. Pp. 433–76. México: INAH.

———. 1987a. "Templo Mayor as Ritual Space." In Johanna Broda, Davíd Carrasco, and Eduardo Matos Moctezuma, *The Great Temple of Tenochtitlan, Center and Periphery in the Aztec World*. Pp. 61–123. Berkeley: University of California Press.

———. 1987b. "The Provenience of the Offerings: Tribute and Cosmovision." In *The Aztec Templo Mayor*. Ed. E. H. Boone, pp. 211–56. Washington, D.C.: Dumbarton Oaks.

Cabrera, Rubén. 1979. "Restos arquitectónicos del Recinto Sagrado en excavaciones del metro y de la recimentación de la catedral y sagrario." In *El Recinto Sagrado de México-Tenochtitlan, Excavaciones 1968–69 y 1975–76*. Ed. Constanza Vega, pp. 55–66. México: INAH.

Calnek, Edward. 1976. "The Internal Structure of Tenochtitlan." In *The Valley of Mexico*. Ed. Eric Wolf, pp. 287–302. Albuquerque: University of New Mexico Press.

———. 1977. "Myth and History in the Founding of Tenochtitlan." Manuscript.

Cantarell, Aquiles. 1984. La arqueología se divorció de la historia. *Información científica y tecnológica*, 6, no. 91 (Apr.): 45–46.

Carlson, John B. 1981. "A Geomantic Model for the Interpretation of Mesoamerican Sites: An Essay in Cross-Cultural Comparison." In *Mesoamerican Sites and World-views*. Ed. E. P. Benson, pp. 143–216. Washington, D.C.: Dumbarton Oaks.

Carramiñana, A. Elena. 1988. Informe preliminar sobre la ofrenda zoológica dedicada a Coyolxauhqui. *Arqueología (México, INAH)* 3: 225–50.

Carrasco, Davíd. 1981. Templo Mayor: The Aztec Vision of Place. *Religion* 11: 275–97.

———. 1987. "Myth, Cosmic Terror, and the Templo Mayor." In Johanna Broda, Davíd Carrasco, and Eduardo Matos Moctezuma, *The Great Temple of Tenochtitlan, Center and Periphery in the Aztec World*. Pp. 124–62. Berkeley: University of California Press.

———. 1990. *Religions of Mesoamerica. Cosmovion and Ceremonial Centers*. San Francisco: Harper & Row.

Carrasco, Pedro. 1979. "Las fiestas de los meses mexicanos." In *Mesoamérica, homenaje al doctor Paul Kirchhoff*. Ed. Barbro Dahlgren, pp. 52–60. México: INAH/SEP.

Caso, Alfonso. 1928. Los jeroglíficos de Tenayuca, México. *Revista Mexicana de Estudios Históricos* 2, no. 5 (Sept.–Oct.): 141–62.

———. 1953. *El Pueblo del Sol*. México: FCE.

———. 1967. *Los calendarios prehispánicos*. México: UNAM.

Caso, Alfonso, and Ignacio Bernal. 1952. *Urnas de Oaxaca*. México: INAH.

Castillo, Cristóbal del. 1966. *Fragmentos de la obra general sobre historia de los mexicanos*. Trans. Francisco del Paso y Troncoso, pp. 43–107. Ciudad Juárez, México: Editorial Erandi.

Castillo Farreras, Víctor M. 1971. El bisiesto náhuatl. *Estudios de Cultura Nahuatl* 9: 75–104.

Castillo Tejero, Noemí, and Felipe R. Solís Olguín. 1975. *Ofrendas mexicas en el Museo Nacional de Antropología.* Corpus Antiquitatum Americanensium VIII. México: INAH/Union Académique Internationale.

Cazenueve, Jean. 1958. *Les rites et la condition humaine d'après des documents ethnographiques.* Paris: Presses Universitaires de France.

———. 1972. *Sociología del rito.* Buenos Aires: Amorrortu Editores.

Cerrillo M. de Cáceres, Enrique et al. 1984. "Religión y espacio, aproximación a una arqueología de la religión." In *Arqueología Espacial: Coloquio sobre distribución y relaciones entre los asentamientos, 27–29 de septiembre.* Vol. 1, pp. 41–54. Teruel, Spain: Colegio Universitario de Teruel.

Cervantes de Salazar, Francisco. 1936. "Crónica de la Nueva España." In *Papeles de Nueva España.* Ed. F. del Paso y Troncoso, vols. 2, 3. México: Museo Nacional de Arqueología, Historia y Etnografía.

Chávez Balderas, Ximena. 2002. Los rituales funerarios del Templo Mayor de Tenochtitlan. Bachelor's thesis in archaeology, ENAH, México.

Chimalpahin Cuauhtlehuanitzin, Domingo. 1965. *Relaciones originales de Chalco Amaquemecan.* Intro. and trans. S. Rendón. México: FCE.

Clarke, David L. 1977. "Spatial Information in Archaeology." In *Spatial Archaeology.* Ed. D. L. Clarke, pp. 1–32. London: Academic Press.

———. 1978. *Analytical Archaeology.* 2d ed. N.Y.: Columbia University Press.

Codex Ixtlilxóchitl. 1976. Ed. J. de Durand-Forest. Graz, Austria: Akademische Druck.

Codex Magliabechiano. 1983. 2 vols. Intro. and trans. Zelia Nuttall. Ed. E. H. Boone. Berkeley: University of California Press [1903 facsim.].

Codex Nuttall: A Picture Manuscript From Ancient Mexico. 1975. Ed. Z. Nuttall. New York: Dover [facsim.].

Codex Selden 3135 (A.2). 1964. Ed. A. Caso. México: SMA [facsim.].

Códice Aubin: Manuscrito azteca de la Biblioteca Real de Berlín: Anales en mexicano y jeroglíficos desde la salida de Aztlan hasta la muerte de Cuauhtémoc (Códice de 1576). 1979. Trans. B. de Jesús Quiroz. México: Editorial Innovación [1902 facsim.].

Códice Azcatitlan. 1949. Ed. R. H. Barlow. *Journal de la Société des Américanistes* 38: 101–35.

Códice Borbónico. 1979. Ed. E. Hamy. México: Siglo Veintiuno Editores [1899 facsim.].

Códice Borgia. 1963. [1905]. Ed. E. Seler. México: FCE.

Códice Chimalpopoca. 1975. Trans. P. F. Velázquez. México: UNAM.

Códice Cospi, Cospiano o de Bolonia. 1964–1967. In *Lord Kingsborough, Antigüedades de México.* 4 vols. Ed. E. Corona Núñez, vol. 4, pp. 5–49. México: Secretaría de Hacienda y Crédito Público.

Códice Cozcatzin. 1890. In *Documents pour servir à l'histoire du Mexique.* Ed. E. Boban, vol. 2, pp. 39–49. Paris: E. Leroux.

Códice Dresde. 1988. Ed. J. E. S. Thompson. México: FCE.

Códice Fejérváry-Mayer. 1964–1967. In *Lord Kingsborough, Antigüedades de México.* 4 vols. Ed. E. Corona Núñez, vol. 4, pp. 185–275. México: Secretaría de Hacienda y Crédito Público.

Códice Florentino: Manuscrito 218–20 de la Colección Palatina de la Biblioteca Medicea Laurenziana. 1979. 3 vols. México: Secretaría de Gobernación, Archivo General de la Nación [facsim.].

Códice Laud. 1964–1967. In *Lord Kingsborough, Antigüedades de México.* 4 vols. Ed. E. Corona Nuñez, vol. 3, pp. 315–409. México: Secretaría de Hacienda y Crédito Público.

Códice Madrid. 1985. In *Los códices mayas.* Ed. T. A. Lee, Jr., pp. 79–140. Tuxtla Gutiérrez: Universidad Autónoma de Chiapas.

Códice Matritense del Real Palacio. 1906. Ed. F. del Paso y Troncoso. Madrid: Hauser y Menet [facsim., orig. 1560–1565].

Códice Mendocino. 1964–1967. In *Lord Kingsborough, Antigüedades de México.* 4 vols. Ed. E. Corona Núñez, vol. 1, pp. 3–149. México: Secretaría de Hacienda y Crédito Público.

Códice Ramírez: Relación del origen de los indios que habitan esta Nueva España, según sus historias. 1944. Ed. M. Orozco y Berra. México: Editorial Leyenda.

Códice Selden (Roll). 1964–1967. In *Lord Kingsborough, Antigüedades de México.* 4 vols. Ed. E. Corona Núñez, vol. 2, pp. 101–13. México: Secretaría de Hacienda y Crédito Público.

Códice Telleriano-Remensis. 1964–1967. In *Lord Kingsborough, Antigüedades de México.* 4 vols. Ed. E. Corona Núñez, vol. 1, pp. 151–337. México: Secretaría de Hacienda y Crédito Público.

Códice Tudela. 1980. Ed. J. Tudela de la Orden. Madrid: Ediciones Cultura Hispánica del Instituto de Cooperación Iberoamericana [facsim.].

Códice Vaticano Latino 3738 o Códice Vaticano Ríos. 1964–1967. In *Lord Kingsborough, Antigüedades de México*. 4 vols. Ed. E. Corona Núñez, vol. 3, pp. 7–314. México: Secretaría de Hacienda y Crédito Público.

Códice Vaticanus 3773. 1972. Ed. F. Anders. Graz, Austria: Akademische Druck.

Códice Vindobonensis (Códice Viena). 1964–1967. In *Lord Kingsborough, Antigüedades de México*. 4 vols. Ed. E. Corona Núñez, vol. 4, pp. 51–183. México: Secretaría de Hacienda y Crédito Público.

Conquistador Anónimo. *Relación de la Nueva España*. 1986. Ed. J. Bustamante. Madrid: Ediciones Polifemo.

Conrad, Geoffrey W., and Arthur A. Demarest. 1988. *Religión e imperio: Dinámica del expansionismo azteca e inca*. Madrid: Alianza Editorial.

Contreras, Eduardo. 1979a. La presencia de Tláloc en el Templo Mayor. *Ciencia y desarrollo* 24: 27–30.

———. 1979b. "Una ofrenda en los restos del Templo Mayor de Tenochtitlan." In *Trabajos arqueológicos en el Centro de la Ciudad de México (antología)*. Ed. E. Matos Moctezuma, pp. 199–204. México: SEP/INAH.

Contreras, Eduardo, and Pilar Luna. 1982. Sección 2. In *El Templo Mayor: Excavaciones y estudios, México*. Ed. E. Matos Moctezuma, pp. 71–102. México: INAH.

Cortés, Hernán. 1967. *Cartas de Relación*. México: Porrúa.

Costumbres, fiestas, enterramientos y diversas formas de proceder de los indios de Nueva España. 1965. *Tlalocan* 2, no. 1: 36–63.

Couch, Christopher N. C. 1985. *The Festival Cycle of the Aztex Codex Borbonicus*. BAR International Series, no. 270. Oxford: BAR

Cuevas, Emilio. 1934. Las excavaciones del Templo Mayor de México. *Anales del Museo Nacional de Arqueología, Historia y Etnografía* (5th series) 1, no. 2: 253–57.

Dahlgren, Barbro, Emma Pérez Rocha, Lourdes Suárez Díez, and Perla Valle de Revueltas. 1982. *Corazón de Cópil: El Templo Mayor y el Recinto Sagrado de México-Tenochtitlan según fuentes del siglo XVI, México*. México: INAH.

Del Olmo, Laura. 1999. *Análisis de la ofrenda 98 del Templo Mayor de Tenochtitlan*. México: INAH.

Díaz del Castillo, Bernal. 1982. *Historia verdadera de la conquista de la Nueva España*. Ed. C. Sáenz de Santamaría. Madrid: Instituto Gonzalo Fernández de Oviedo.

Díaz-Pardo, Edmundo. 1983. "Restos de peces procedentes de la ofrenda 7." In *El Templo Mayor: Excavaciones y estudios*. Ed. E. Matos Moctezuma, pp. 151–60. México: INAH.

Díaz-Pardo, Edmundo, and Edmundo Teniente-Nivón. 1991. "Aspectos biológicos y ecológicos de la ictiofauna rescatada en el Templo Mayor, México." In *La fauna en el Templo Mayor, México*. Ed. O. J. Polaco, pp. 33–104. México: INAH/Asociación de Amigos del Templo Mayor/GV Editores.

Diccionario de la Lengua Española. 1983. 19th ed. Madrid: Real Academia Española.

Die Azteken und ihre Vorläufer: Glanz und Untergang des Alten Mexiko. 1986. 2 vols. Mainz am Rhein: Verlag Philipp von Zabern.

Doran, J. E., and F. R. Hodson. 1975. *Mathematics and Computers in Archaeology*. Cambridge, Mass.: Harvard University Press.

Douglas, Mary. 1972. "Symbolic Orders in the Use of Domestic Space." In *Man, Settlement and Urbanism*. Eds. P. J. Ucko, R. Tringham, and G. W. Dimbleby, pp. 213–21. Cambridge: Schenkman Publishing.

Durán, Diego. 1984. *Historia de las Indias de Nueva España e Islas de la Tierra Firme*. 2 vols. Ed. A. Ma. Garibay. México: Porrúa.

Duverger, Christian. 1987. *El origen de los aztecas*. México: Editorial Grijalbo.

Eliade, Mircea. 1967. *Lo sagrado y lo profano*. Madrid: Guadarrama.

———. 1968. *El mito del eterno retorno*. Buenos Aires: Emecé Editores.

Enciclopedia de México. 1977. Ed. J. R. Alvarez. 12 vols. México: Enciclopedia de México.

Espejo, Antonieta. 1945. "Las ofrendas halladas en Tlatelolco." In *Tlatelolco a través de los tiempos* 5: 15–29. México: Sobretiro de las Memorias de la Academia Mexicana de la Historia.

Espinosa, Guillermo, and A. López. 1980. *Introducción a los métodos jerárquicos de análisis de cúmulos*. México: IIMAS/UNAM.

Espinosa, Guillermo, and Linda Manzanilla. 1985. Consideraciones en torno a la capacidad de los cuencos tron-cocónicos de Arslantepé (Malatya). *Quaderni de la Ricerca Scientifica* 112: 139–62. Rome: Consiglio Nazionale delle Ricerche.

Estrada Balmori, Elma. 1979. "Ofrendas del Templo Mayor de México-Tenochtitlan." In *Trabajos arqueológicos en el Centro de la Ciudad de México (antología)*. Ed. E. Matos Moctezuma, pp. 183–89. México: SEP/INAH.

Florescano, Enrique. 1989. Mito e historia en la memoria mexicana. Inaugural lecture for admission to the Academia Mexicana de la Historia, July 18, 1989.

Flores García, Lorenzo. 1970. Tres figurillas vestidas con piel de desollados. *Boletín INAH* 42 (Dec.): 43–46.

Ford, J. A. 1954. The Type Concept Revisited. *American Anthropologist* 56: 42–54.

Franco Brizuela, María Luisa. 1982. "El tratamiento de conservación en piedra: Tres casos." In *El Templo Mayor: Excavaciones y estudios, México*. Ed. E. Matos Moctezuma, pp. 313–48. México: INAH.

———. 1986. *Conservación del Templo Mayor de Tenochtitlan: Bienes inmuebles*. Bachelor's thesis, Escuela Nacional de Conservación, Restauración y Museografía "Manuel del Castillo Negrete," México.

———. 1987. "Conservation at the Templo Mayor of Tenochtitlan." In *In situ: Archaeological Conservation*, Proceedings of Meetings, April 6–13, 1986, Mexico, pp. 166–75. Century City, Calif.: INAH/The Getty Conservation Institute.

———. 1990. *Conservación del Templo Mayor de Tenochtitlan*. México: INAH/Asociación de Amigos del Templo Mayor/GV Editores.

Frazer, James George. 1956. *La rama dorada: Magia y religión*. México: FCE.

Fuente, Beatriz de la. 1990. Escultura en el tiempo: Retorno al pasado tolteca. *Artes de México*, new series, 7: 36–53.

Fuente, Beatriz de la, Silvia Trejo, and Nelly Gutiérrez Solana. 1988. *Escultura en piedra de Tula: Catálogo*. México: UNAM.

Galinier, Jacques. 1987. *Pueblos de la Sierra Madre: Etnografía de la comunidad otomí*. México: INI/CEMCA.

Gallardo, María de Lourdes. 1999. La conservación preventi va de las colecciones óseas en almacenamiento. Bachelor's thesis in conservation, ENCRYM, México.

Gamio, Manuel. 1917. "Investigaciones arqueológicas en México, 1914–1915." In *Annals of the XIX International Congress of Americanists* (Washington, D.C., Dec. 27–31, 1915). N.p.: Societé des Americanistes, pp. 125–33.

———. 1921. Vestigios del Templo Mayor de Tenoxtitlan descubiertos recientemente. *Ethnos* 1, nos. 8–12 (Nov. 1920–Mar. 1921): 205–7.

———. 1960. *Forjando patria*. México: Porrúa.

———. 1979. "Los vestigios prehispánicos de la 2a. Calle de Santa Teresa." In *Trabajos arqueológicos en el Centro de la Ciudad México (antología)*. Ed. E. Matos Moctezuma, pp. 141–43. México: SEP/INAH. (Orig. in *Boletín de Educación* 1, 1914).

García Cook, Angel. 1978. Rescate arqueológico del monolito circular de Coyolxauhqui. *Antropología e Historia: Boletín del INAH*, 3rd series, 24 (Oct.–Dec.): 18–30.

García Cook, Angel, and Raúl M. Arana. 1978. *Rescate arqueológico del monolito Coyolxauhqui*. México: INAH.

Garibay, A. Ma., ed. 1965. *Teogonía e historia de los mexicanos: Tres opúsculos del siglo XVI*. México: Porrúa.

Gay, Carlo and Frances Pratt. 1992. *Mezcala. Ancient Stone Sculpture from Guerrero, Mexico*. Geneva: Balsas Publications.

Glass, John. B. 1975. "A Census of Native American Pictorial Documents." In *Handbook of Middle American Indians*. Vol. 14, Ed. R. Wauchope, pp. 81–280. Austin: University of Texas Press.

Godelier, Maurice. 1981. *Instituciones económicas*. Panorama de la Antropología Cultural Contemporánea no. 4. Barcelona: Anagrama.

González, Carlos Javier. 1982. "La ofrenda 41, informe preliminar." In *El Templo Mayor: Excavaciones y estudios*. Ed. E. Matos Moctezuma, pp. 213–20. México: INAH.

———. 1987. "Mezcala-Style Anthropomorphic Artifacts in the Templo Mayor." In *The Aztec Templo Mayor*. Ed. E. H. Boone, pp. 145–60. Washington, D.C.: Dumbarton Oaks.

———. In press. Ofrendas excavadas de 1979 a 1982.

González, Carlos Javier, and Bertina Olmedo Vera. 1990. *Esculturas Mezcala en el Templo Mayor, México*. México: INAH/GV Editores/Asociación de Amigos del Templo Mayor.

González de Lesur, Yolotl. 1968. El dios Huitzilopochtli en la peregrinación mexica de Aztlan a Tula. *Anales del INAH* 19: 175–90.

González Rul, Francisco. 1963. Un "cuauhxicalli" de Tlatelolco. *Anales del INAH* 15, no. 44: 119–26.

———. 1979. *La lítica de Tlatelolco*. México: INAH.

———. 1988. *La cerámica en Tlatelolco*. México: INAH.

———. 1997. *Materiales líticos y cerámicos encontrados en las cercanías del monolito Coyolxauhqui*. México: INAH.

González Torres, Yólotl. 1975. *El culto a los astros entre los mexicas*. México: SEP.

———. 1985. *El sacrificio humano entre los mexicas.* México: FCE/INAH.

Gossen, Gary. 1972. "Temporal and Spatial Equivalents in Chamula Ritual Symbolism." In *Reader in Comparative Religion: An Anthropological Approach.* Eds. W. Lessa and E. Z. Vogt, pp. 135–49. New York: Harper and Row.

Graulich, Michel. 1982. Tlacaxipehualiztli ou la fête aztèque de la moisson et de la guerre. *Revista española de antropología americana* 12: 215–54.

———. 1983. Templo Mayor, Coyolxauhqui und Cacaxtla. *Mexicon: Actuelle Informationen und Studien zu Mesoamerika* 5, no. 5: 91–94.

———. 1987. "Les Incertitudes du Grand Temple." In *Les aztèques: Trésors du Mexique Ancien.* Ed. Arne Eggebrecht, pp. 121–31. Hildesheim, Germany: Roemer-und Pelizaeus Museum.

———. 1988. Double Immolations in Ancient Mexican Sacrificial Ritual. *History of Religions* 27, no. 4: 393–404.

———. 1990. "Dualities in Cacaxtla." In *Dualismo mesoamericano.* Symposium at the 46th International Congress of Americanists, Amsterdam 1988. Eds. R. van Zantwijk, R. de Ridder, and E. Braakhuis, pp. 94–118. Utrecht: RUU–ISOR.

Grigsby, Thomas L. 1986. In the Stone Warehouse: The Survival of a Cave Cult in Central Mexico. *Journal of Latin American Lore* 12: 161–79.

Grimaldi, Dulce María. 2001. *Conservación de objetos de concha de las ofrendas del Templo Mayor de Tenochtitlan.* México: INAH.

Guil'liem, Salvador. In press. La presencia de madera en el Templo Mayor.

———. 1999. *Ofrendas a Ehécatl-Quetzalcóatl en Mexico-Tlatelolco. Proyecto Tlatelolco 1987-1996.* México: INAH.

———. 2003. Ofrendas del Templo Mayor de México Tlatelolco. *Arqueología* 30: 65-87.

Guiteras Holmes, C. 1965. *Los peligros del alma: Visión del mundo tzotzil.* México: FCE.

Gussinyer, Jordi. 1968. Hallazgo de estructuras prehispánicas en el Metro. *Boletín INAH* 34 (Dec.): 15–18.

———. 1969a. Hallazgos en el Metro, conjunto de adoratorios superpuestos en Pino Suárez. *Boletín INAH* 36 (June): 33–37.

———. 1969b. Una escultura de Ehecatl-Ozomatli. *Boletín INAH* 37 (Sept.): 29–32.

———. 1970a. Un adoratorio dedicado a Tlaloc. *Boletín INAH* 39 (Mar.): 7–12.

———. 1970b. Un adoratorio azteca decorado con pinturas. *Boletín INAH* 40 (June): 30–35.

———. 1970c. Deidad descubierta en el Metro. *Boletín INAH* 40 (June): 41–42.

———. 1972. Una base para brasero ceremonial tenochca. *Boletín INAH*, 2d series, 3 (Oct.–Dec.): 17–22.

———. 1979. "La arquitectura prehispánica en los alrededores de la catedral." In *El Recinto Sagrado de Mexico-Tenochtitlan: Excavaciones 1968–69 y 1975–76.* Ed. Constanza Vega, pp. 67–74. México: INAH.

Gutiérrez, Isabel. 1982. "Excavación en la Zona Norte." In *El Templo Mayor: Excavaciones y estudios.* Ed. E. Matos Moctezuma, pp. 103–6. México: INAH.

Gutiérrez Solana, Nelly. 1983. *Objetos ceremoniales en piedra de la cultura mexica.* México: UNAM.

———. 1987. *Las serpientes en el arte mexica.* México: UNAM.

———. 1989. Diez años de estudios sobre el Templo Mayor de Tenochtitlan (1978–1988). *Anales del Instituto de Investigaciones Estéticas* 60: 7–31.

Guzmán, Ana Fabiola and Óscar J. Polaco. 2001. *Análisis arqueoictiológico de la ofrenda 23 del Templo Mayor de Tenochtitlan.* México: INAH.

Hasbach Lugo, Bárbara. 1982a. "Restauración de 33 cuchillos ceremoniales policromados." In *El Templo Mayor: Excavaciones y estudios.* Ed. E. Matos Moctezuma, pp. 357–86. México: INAH.

———. 1982b. "Restauración de dos ollas." In *El Templo Mayor: Excavaciones y estudios.* Ed. E. Matos Moctezuma, pp. 369–76. México: INAH.

Hernández Pons, Elsa C. 1982. "Sobre un conjunto de esculturas asociadas a las escalinatas del Templo Mayor." In *El Templo Mayor: Excavaciones y estudios.* Ed. E. Matos Moctezuma, pp. 221–32. México: INAH.

———. 1997. *La Antigua Casa del Marqués del Apartado. Arqueología e historia.* México: INAH.

Hers, Marie-Areti. In press. "¿Rematar el pasado?" In *XIII Coloquio Internacional de Historia del Arte, Tiempo y Arte.* México: UNAM.

Heyden, Doris. 1970. Deidad del agua encontrada en el Metro. *Boletín INAH* 40 (June): 35–40.

———. 1972. Autosacrificios prehispánicos con púas y punzones. *Boletín INAH*, 2d series, 1 (June): 27–30.

———. 1973. "What Is the Significance of the Mexica Pyramid?" In *Attli del XL Congresso Internazionale degli Americanisti* (Rome, Sept. 3–10, 1972). Vol. 1, pp. 109–15.

Genoa, Italy: Tilgher.

―――. 1975. An Interpretation of the Cave Underneath the Pyramid of the Sun in Teotihuacan, México. *American Antiquity* 40, no. 2: 131–47.

―――. 1981. "Caves, Gods and Myths: World-view and Planning in Teotihuacan." In *Mesoamerican Sites and World-views.* Ed. E. P. Benson, pp. 1–35. Washington, D.C.: Dumbarton Oaks.

―――. 1986. "Xipe Totec: ¿Dios nativo de Guerrero o hijo adoptivo?" In *Primer Coloquio de Arqueología y Etnología del Estado de Guerrero.* Ed. Roberto Cervantes-Delgado, pp. 371–87. México: INAH/Gobierno del Estado de Guerrero.

―――. 1987. "Symbolism of Ceramics from the Templo Mayor." In *The Aztec Templo Mayor.* Ed. E. Boone, pp. 109–27. Washington, D.C.: Dumbarton Oaks.

―――. 1988. *México, origen de un símbolo: Mito y simbolismo de la fundación de México-Tenochtitlan.* Colección Distrito Federal 22. México: Departamento del Distrito Federal.

Histoire du Mechique. 1965. In *Teogonía e historia de los mexicanos.* Ed. A. Ma. Garibay, pp. 91–120. México: Porrúa.

Historia de los mexicanos por sus pinturas. 1965. In *Teogonía e historia de los mexicanos.* Ed. A. Ma. Garibay, pp. 21–90. México: Porrúa [orig. 1523].

Historia tolteca-chichimeca. 1976. Eds. Paul Kirchhoff, Lina Odena Güemes, and Luis Reyes García. México: INAH/SEP [facsim.]

Hodder, Ian. 1988. *Interpretación en arqueología. Corrientes actuales.* Barcelona: Editorial Crítica.

Hodson, F. R., P. H. A. Sneath, and J. E. Doran. 1966. Some Experiments in the Numerical Analysis of Archaeological Data. *Biometrika* 53, nos. 3–4: 311–24.

Hubert, Henri, and Marcel Mauss. 1970. "De la naturaleza y de la función del sacrificio." In *Lo sagrado y lo profano: Obras I.* Pp. 143–262. Barcelona: Barral.

Humboldt, Alexander von. 1878. *Sitios de las cordilleras y monumentos de los pueblos indígenas de América.* Madrid: Imprenta y Librería de Gaspar Editores.

Ichon, Alain. 1973. *La religión de los totonacos de la sierra.* México: INI.

Jiménez Badillo, Diego. 1991. "La malacología del Templo Mayor a partir de los datos de la ofrenda H." In *La fauna en el Templo Mayor.* Ed. O. J. Polaco, pp. 171–212. México: INAH/Asociación de Amigos del Templo Mayor/GV Editores.

―――. 1997. *Aplicación de un sistema de base de datos para controlar una colección arqueológica: las ofrendas del Templo Mayor.* México: INAH.

―――. 2004. A Method for Interactive Recognition of Three-dimensional Adjacency Patterns in Point Sets, based on Relative Neighborhood Methods. Ph. D. thesis, University College, London.

Jiménez Badillo, Diego, and Leonardo López Luján. 1989. Informática y arqueología: Aplicación de un sistema de cómputo en el Museo del Templo Mayor. *Interacción, Revista Informativa para la Base Instalada de Hewlett-Packard,* 2d trimester: 13–14.

Keen, Benjamin. 1971. *The Aztec Image in Western Thought.* New Brunswick, N.J.: Rutgers University Press.

Kirchhoff, Paul. 1972. "Dioses y fiestas de los nahuas centrales." In *Religión en Mesoamérica, XII Mesa Redonda.* Eds. Jaime Litvak King and Noemí Castillo, pp. 199–204. México: SMA.

Klein, Cecelia F. 1980. Who was Tlaloc? *Journal of Latin American Lore* 6, no. 2: 155–204.

―――. 1987. "The Ideology of Autosacrifice at the Templo Mayor." In *The Aztec Templo Mayor.* Ed. E. H. Boone, pp. 293–370. Washington, D.C.: Dumbarton Oaks.

Knab, Tim J. 1991. Geografía del inframundo. *Estudios de Cultura Náhuatl* 22: 31–57.

Kohler, Ulrich. 1979. "On the Significance of the Aztec Day Sign 'Olin.'" Paper presented at the XLIII International Congress of Americanists, Symposium "Space and Time in Mesoamerican Cosmovision," Vancouver, Aug. 10–17, 1979. Typescript.

Krickeberg, Walter. 1975. *Las antiguas culturas mexicanas.* México: FCE.

Kurath, Gertrude, and Samuel Martí. 1964. *Dance of Anahuac: The Choreography and Music of Precortesian Dances.* Chicago: Aldine.

Lagunas, Zaid, and Carlos Serrano Sánchez. 1972. "Decapitación y desmembramiento corporal en Teopanzolco, Morelos." In *Religión en Mesoamérica: XII Mesa Redonda.* Eds. Jaime Litvak King and Noemí Castillo, pp. 429–34. México: SMA.

Landa, Diego de. 1982. *Relación de las cosas de Yucatán.* Intro. A. Ma. Garibay. México: Porrúa.

Las Casas, Bartolomé de. 1967. *Apologética Historia Sumaria.* 2 vols. Ed. E. O'Gorman. México: UNAM.

Leach, Edmund. 1978. *Cultura y comunicación: La lógica de la conexión de los símbolos, una introducción al uso del análisis estructuralista en la antropología social.* Madrid: Siglo Veintiuno de España Editores.

Leeuw, G. van de. 1964. *Fenomenología de la religión.* México: FCE.

León-Portilla, Miguel. 1978. *México-Tenochtitlan: Su espacio y tiempo sagrado.* México: INAH.

———. 1981. "Los testimonios de la historia." In José López Portillo, Miguel León-Portilla, and Eduardo Matos Moctezuma, *El Templo Mayor.* Pp. 32–101. México: Bancomer.

———. 1987. "The Ethnohistorical Record for the Huey Teocalli of Tenochtitlan." In *The Aztec Templo Mayor.* Ed. E. H. Boone, pp. 71–96. Washington, D.C.: Dumbarton Oaks.

———. 1988. El maíz: Nuestro sustento, su realidad divina y humana en Mesoamérica. *América Indígena* 48, no. 3: 477–502.

León y Gama, Antonio de. 1832. *Descripción histórica y cronológica de las dos piedras que con ocasión del nuevo empedrado que se está formando en la plaza principal de México, se hallaron en ella el año de 1790.* 2d ed. México: Imprenta del Ciudadano Alejandro Valdés.

Leyenda de los Soles. In *Códice Chimalpopoca.* 1975. Trans. P. F. Velázquez, pp. 119–42. México: UNAM.

Lienzo de Tlaxcalla. N.d. Ed. A. Chavero. México: Artes de México [facsim. of 1892 ed.].

Lock, Gary, and John Wilcock. 1987. *Computer Archaeology.* Aylesbury, England: Shire Archaeology.

Lok, Rossana. 1987. "The House as a Microcosm: Some Cosmic Representations in a Mexican Indian Village." In *The Leiden Tradition in Structural Anthropology: Essays in Honour of P.E. Josselin de Jong.* Eds. R. de Ridder and J. A. J. Karremans, pp. 210–23. Leiden, Netherlands: E. J. Brill.

Lombardo de Ruíz, Sonia. 1986. "La pintura." In *Cacaxtla: El lugar donde muere la lluvia en la tierra.* Pp. 209–500. México: INAH/Instituto Tlaxcalteca de Cultura.

Long Solís, Janet. 1977. *Un enfoque cuantitativo para la clasificación de figuritas.* México: MNA/INAH.

Loo, Peter L. van der. 1988. "Old Models and New Tools in the Study of Mesoamerican Religion." In *Continuity and Identity in Native America. Essays in Honor of Benedikt Hartmann.* Eds. Maarten Jansen, Peter van der Loo, and Roswitha Manning, pp. 42–57. Leiden, Netherlands: E. J. Brill.

———. 1982. "Rituales con manojos contados en el Grupo Borgia y entre los tlapanecos de hoy día." In *Coloquio Internacional Los Indígenas de México en la Época Prehispánica y en la Actualidad,* Ed. M. Jansen and T. Leyenaar, pp. 232–43. Leiden, Netherlands: E. J. Brill.

López Arenas, Gabino. 2004. *Rescate arqueológico en la Catedral y el Sagrario metropolitanos. Estudio de las ofrendas.* México: INAH.

López Austin, Alfredo. 1965. El Templo Mayor de Mexico-Tenochtitlan según los informantes indígenas. *Estudios de Cultura Nahuatl* 5: 75–102.

———. 1967. *Juegos rituales aztecas.* Trans. and comment A. López Austin. México: IIH/UNAM.

———. 1969. *Augurios y abusiones: Textos de los informantes de Sahagún.* Trans. and comment A. López Austin. México: UNAM.

———. 1973. *Hombre-dios: Religión y política en el mundo náhuatl.* México: UNAM.

———. 1979. Iconografía mexica: El monolito verde del Templo Mayor. *Anales de Antropología* 16: 133–53.

———. 1983. Nota sobre la fusión y la fisión de los dioses en el panteón mexica. *Anales de Antropología* 20: 75–87.

———. 1985a. El dios enmascarado de fuego. *Anales de Antropología* 22: 251–85.

———. 1985b. *Educación mexica: Antología de textos sahaguntinos.* México: UNAM.

———. 1987. "The Masked God of Fire." In *The Aztec Templo Mayor.* Ed. E. H. Boone, pp. 257–92. Washington, D.C.: Dumbarton Oaks.

———. 1988a. Las dos posibles interpretaciones de un mito pipil. *Anales de Antropología* 25: 315–28.

———. 1988b. Religión en el México antiguo: Entrevista a Alfredo López Austin. *México indígena* 20 (Jan.–Feb.): 8–12.

———. 1988c. *Human Body and Ideology.* Trans. T. Ortiz de Montellano and B. Ortiz de Montellano. 2 vols. Salt Lake City: University of Utah Press.

———. 1990a. Del origen de los mexicas: ¿Nomadismo o migración? *Historia mexicana* 34: 663–75.

———. 1990b. *Los mitos del tlacuache: Caminos de la mitología mesoamericana.* México: Alianza Editorial Mexicana.

———. 1998. *Breve historia de la tradición religiosa mesoamericana.* México: UNAM.

López Austin, Alfredo, and Leonardo López Luján. 2001. El chacmool mexica. *Caravelle* 76-77: 59-84.

———. 2004. "El Templo Mayor de Tenochtitlan, el Tonacatépetl y el mito del robo del maíz." In *Acercarse y mirar,* Ed. M. T. Uriarte, and L. Staines Cicero, pp. 403-55. México: UNAM.

López Austin, Alfredo, Leonardo López Luján, and Saburo Sugiyama. 1991. "The Temple of Quetzalcoatl at Teotihuacan: Its Possible Ideological Significance." *Ancient Mesoamerica* 1, no. 4 (Apr.): 93–105.

López Cervantes, Gonzalo. 1982. "Informe preliminar sobre los materiales coloniales."
In *El Templo Mayor: Excavaciones y estudios.* Ed. E. Matos Moctezuma, pp. 255–82. México: INAH.

López de Gómara, Francisco. 1870. *Conquista de México, segunda parte de la historia general de Indias.* México: Imprenta de I. Escalante.

López Luján, Leonardo. 1982. Neues aus der Alten Welt, Mexiko. *Das Altertum* 2, no. 28: 126–27.

———. 1983. "Los mexicas, últimos señores de Mesoamérica." In *Gran Enciclopedia de España y América, Los habitantes: Hasta Colón.* Vol. 1. Ed. J. Ma. Javierre, pp. 170–83. Madrid: Espasa Calpe/Argantonio.

———. 1989a. Ausgrabungen in Tlatelolco (Mexiko). *Das Altertum* 4, no. 35: 249–53.

———. 1989b. *La recuperación mexica del pasado teotihuacano.* México: INAH/Asociación de Amigos del Templo Mayor/GV Editores.

———. 2001a. "Offerings." In *The Oxford Encyclopedia of Mesoamerican Cultures,* Ed. D. Carrasco, vol. 2, pp. 403-4. New York: Oxford University Press.

———. 2001b. Arqueología de la arqueología. *Arqueología mexicana* IX, no. 52: 20-27.

———. 2005. *La Casa de las Águilas. Un ejemplo de la arquitectura religiosa de Tenochtitlan.* México: FCE/INAH/Harvard University.

López Luján, Leonardo, and Diego Jiménez Badillo. 1987. Los petroglifos de Los Olivos, Ixtayopan, Distrito Federal. *Revista Mexicana de Estudios Antropológicos* 33, no. 1: 149–66.

López Luján, Leonardo, and Noel Morelos. 1989. Los petroglifos de Amecameca: Un monumento a la elección de Motecuhzoma Xocoyotzin. *Anales de Antropología* 26: 127–56.

López Luján, Leonardo, and Oscar J. Polaco. 1991. La fauna de la ofrenda H del Templo Mayor. In *La fauna en el Templo Mayor.* Ed. O. J. Polaco, pp. 149–69. México: INAH/Asociación de Amigos del Templo Mayor/GV Editores.

López Luján, Leonardo, Jaime Torres, and Aurora Montúfar. 2003. Los materiales constructivos del Templo Mayor de Tenochtitlan. *Estudios de Cultura Náhuatl* 34: 137-66.

López Portillo, José. 1981. "El Templo Mayor." In José López Portillo, Miguel Léon-Portilla, and Eduardo Matos Moctezuma, *El Templo Mayor.* Pp. 23–31. México: Bancomer.

Lorenzo, José Luis. 1979. Sobre el Templo Mayor de México-Tenochtitlan. *Ciencia y Desarrollo* 24 (Jan.–Feb.): 11–21.

Manzanilla, Linda. 1985. Introducción. In *Unidades habitacionales mesoamericanas y sus áreas de actividad.* Ed. L. Manzanilla, pp. 11–18. México: UNAM.

———. 1987. *Bibliografía de la Cuenca de México.* México: Instituto de Investigaciones Antropológicas, UNAM.

Manzanilla, Linda, Luis Barba, René Chávez, Jorge Arzate, and Leticia Flores. 1989. El inframundo de Teotihuacan: Geofísica y arqueología. *Ciencia y desarrollo* 15, no. 85 (Mar.–Apr.): 21–35.

Marín Benito, María Eugenia. 2001. *Casos de conservación y restauración en el Museo del Templo Mayor.* México: INAH.

Marquina, Ignacio. 1935. "Estudio arquitectónico." In *Tenayuca: Estudio arqueológico de la pirámide de este lugar, hecho por el Departamento de Monumentos de la Secretaría de Educación Pública.* Pp. 78–102. México: Museo Nacional de Arqueología, Historia y Etnografía.

———. 1951. *Arquitectura prehispánica.* México: INAH.

———. 1960. *El Templo Mayor de México.* México: INAH.

Martín del Campo, Rafael. 1946. Ofrendas zoológicas en las ruinas del templo de Tlatelolco. *Memorias de la Academia Mexicana de la Historia* 5, no. 4: 406–11.

Martínez-Cortés, Fernando. 1970. *Pegamentos, gomas y resinas en el México prehispánico.* México: Resistol.

Martínez Malo, Luz María. 1979. Algunos métodos jerárquicos y otros subdominantes de taxonomía numérica. Bachelor's thesis, Facultad de Ciencias/UNAM, México.

Martínez Marín, Carlos. 1964. La cultura de los mexicas durante la migración: Nuevas ideas. In *Actas y Memorias del XXXV Congreso Internaticional de Americanistas. México 1962.* Vol. 2, pp. 113–23. México: INAH.

———. 1978. Peregrinación de los mexicas. In *Historia de México.* 13 vols. Series ed. Miguel León-Portilla. Vol. 4, pp. 759–74. México: Salvat.

Mateos Higuera, Salvador. 1979. Herencia arqueológica de México-Tenochtitlan. In *Trabajos arqueológicos en el Centro de la Ciudad México (antología).* Ed. E. Matos Moctezuma, pp. 205–73. México: SEP/INAH.

Matos Moctezuma, Eduardo. 1965. El adoratorio decorado de las calles de Argentina. *Anales del Instituto Nacional de Antropología y Historia* 17: 127–38.

———. 1978. El Proyecto Templo Mayor. *Antropología e Historia* 24: 3–17.

———, ed. 1979a. *Trabajos arqueológicos en el Centro de la Ciudad de México (antología)*. México: SEP/INAH.

———. 1979b. "El Proyecto Templo Mayor: Objectivos y programas." In *Trabajos arqueológicos en el Centro de la Ciudad de México (antología)*. Ed. E. Matos Moctezuma, pp. 13–26. México: SEP/INAH.

———. 1979c. Una máscara olmeca en el Templo Mayor de Tenochtitlan. *Anales de Antropología* 16: 11–19.

———. 1981a. *El Templo Mayor de Tenochtitlan (antología)*. México: Asociación Nacional de Libreros.

———. 1981b. *Una visita al Templo Mayor*. México: SEP/INAH.

———. 1981c. *El Templo Mayor de México: Crónicas del siglo XVI*. México: Asociación Nacional de Libreros.

———. 1981d. "Los hallazgos de la arqueología." In José López Portillo, Miguel León-Portilla, and Eduardo Matos Moctezuma, *El Templo Mayor*. Pp. 102–283. México: Bancomer.

———. 1982a. *El Templo Mayor: Excavaciones y estudios*. México: INAH.

———. 1982b. "El Templo Mayor: Economía e ideología." In *El Templo Mayor: Excavaciones y estudios*. Ed. E. Matos Moctezuma, pp. 109–18. México: INAH.

———. 1982c. "Las excavaciones del Proyecto Templo Mayor (1978–1981)." In *El Templo Mayor: Excavaciones y estudios*. Ed. E. Matos Moctezuma, pp. 11–16. México: INAH.

———. 1982d. "Sección 1." In *El Templo Mayor: Excavaciones y estudios*. Ed. E. Matos Moctezuma, pp. 17–70. México: INAH.

———. 1983. Notas sobre algunas urnas funerarias del Templo Mayor. *Jahrbuch für Geschichte von Staat, Wirtschaft und Gesellschaft Lateinamerikas* 20: 17–32.

———. 1984a. *Guía official: Templo Mayor*. 2d. rev. ed. 1989. México: INAH/Salvat.

———. 1984b. Los edificios aledaños al Templo Mayor. *Estudios de Cultura Náhuatl* 17: 15–21.

———. 1986a. *Muerte a filo de obsidiana*. México: SEP.

———. 1986b. *Los dioses se negaron a morir ...Arqueología y crónicas del Templo Mayor (antología)*. México: SEP.

———. 1986c. *Vida y muerte en el Templo Mayor*. México: Ediciones Océano.

———. 1987a. "Archaeology & Symbolism in Aztec Mexico: The Templo Mayor of Tenochtitlan." In *Trajectories in the Study of Religion, Addresses at the Seventy-Fifth Anniversary of the American Academy of Religion*. Ed. R. L. Hart, pp. 253–70. Atlanta, Ga.: Scholars Press.

———. 1987b. "The Templo Mayor of Tenochtitlan: History and Interpretation." In Johanna Broda, Davíd Carrasco, and Eduardo Matos Moctezuma, *The Great Temple of Tenochtitlan, Center and Periphery in the Aztec World*. Pp. 15–60. Berkeley: University of California Press.

———. 1988a. *Excavaciones recientes en Tlatelolco: Catálogo de la exposición "Tlatelolco: hallazgos recientes."* México: INAH/Secretaría de Turismo.

———. 1988b. *Ofrendas: Templo Mayor, Ciudad de México*. México: Hewlett Packard.

———. 1988c. *The Great Temple of the Aztecs: Treasures of Tenochtitlan*. London: Thames and Hudson.

———. 1989. *Obras maestros del Templo Mayor*. México: Fundación Cultural Banamex.

———. 1991. "Notes on the Oldest Sculpture of El Templo Mayor of Tenochtitlan." In *To Change Place: Aztec Ceremonial Landscapes*. Ed. D. Carrasco, pp. 3–8. Niwot: University Press of Colorado.

———. 1999. *Excavaciones en la Catedral y el Sagrario Metropolitanos*. México: INAH

———. 2000. La ofrenda 102 del Templo Mayor. *Arqueología Mexicana* VIII, no. 43: 80.

———. *Excavaciones del Programa de Arqueología Urbana*. México: INAH.

Matos Moctezuma, Eduardo, and Víctor Rangel. 1982. *El Templo Mayor de Tenochtitlan: Planos, cortes y perspectivas*. México: INAH.

Matos Moctezuma, Eduardo, Francisco Hinojosa, and José Álvaro Barrera. 1998. Excavaciones arqueológicas en la Catedral de México. *Arqueología Mexicana* V, no. 31: 12-19.

Mauss, Marcel. 1971. Essai sur le don. In *Sociología y antropología*. Madrid: Editorial Tecnos.

———. 1972. *Sociedad y ciencias sociales: Obras III*. Barcelona: Barral Editores.

Mazari, Marcos, Raúl Marsal, and Jesús Alberro. 1989. Los asentamientos del Templo Mayor analizados por la mecánica de suelos. *Estudios de Cultura Náhuatl* 19: 145–82.

Mendieta, Gerónimo de. 1945. *Historia eclesiástica Indiana*. México: Editorial Chávez Hayhoe.

Mendoza, Vicente T. 1962. El plano o mundo inferior: Mictlan, Xibalbá, Nith y Hel. *Estudios de Cultura Náhuatl* 3: 75–99.

Mercado, Vida. 1982. Restauración de dos urnas funerarias. In *El Templo Mayor: Excavaciones y estudios*. Ed. E. Matos Moctezuma, pp. 349–56. México: INAH.

Miller, Arthur G. 1973. *The Mural Painting of Teotihuacan*. Washington, D.C.:

Dumbarton Oaks.

Molina, Fray Alonso de. 1944. *Vocabulario en lengua castellana y mexicana*. Madrid: Ediciones Cultura Hispánica [orig. 1581].

Molina Montes, Augusto F. 1987. "Templo Mayor Architecture: So What's New?" In *The Aztec Tempo Mayor*. Ed. E. H. Boone, pp. 97–108. Washington, D.C.: Dumbarton Oaks.

Molins Fabregá, N. 1956. *El Códice Mendocino y la economía de Tenochtitlan*. México: Libro-Mex Editores.

Moser, Christopher. 1973. *Human Decapitation in Ancient Mesoamerica*. Washington, D.C.: Dumbarton Oaks.

Nagao, Debra. 1985a. "The Planting of Sustenance: Symbolism of the Two-Horned God in Offerings From the Templo Mayor." *Res-Anthropology and Aesthetics* 10: 5–27.

———. 1985b. *Mexica Buried Offerings: A Historical and Contextual Analysis*. BAR International Series, no. 235. Oxford: BAR.

Nájera, Martha I. 1987. *El don de la sangre en el equilibrio cósmico: El sacrificio y el autosacrificio sangriento entre los antiguos mayas*. México: UNAM.

Nash, June C. 1975. *Bajo la mirada de los antepasados: Creencias y comportamientos en una comunidad maya*. México: INI.

Navarrete, Carlos. 1976. Algunas influencias mexicanas en el área maya meridional durante el Posclásico tardío. *Estudios de Cultura Náhuatl* 12: 345–82.

Neumann, F. J. 1976. "The Flayed God and His Rattle-Stick: A Shamanic Element in Pre-Hispanic Mesoamerican Religion." *History of Religions* 15: 251–63.

Nicholson, H. B. 1959. The Chapultepec Cliff Sculpture of Motecuhzoma Xocoyotzin. *El México Antiguo* 9: 379–444.

———. 1971. "Religion in Pre-Hispanic Central Mexico." In *Handbook of Middle American Indians*. Eds. Gordon F. Eckholm, and Ignacio Bernal. Vol. 10, pp. 396–446. Austin: University of Texas Press.

———. 1972a. "Aztec Style Calendric Inscriptions of Possible Historical Significance: A Survey." Boston: Harvard University. Mimeograph.

———. 1972b. "The Cult of Xipe Totec in Mesoamerica." *Religión en Mesoamérica, XII Mesa Redonda*. Eds. Jaime Litvak King and Noemí Castillo, pp. 213–18. México: SMA.

———. 1983. "The Iconography of Tepeyollotl: A Postclassic Western Mesoamerican Deity." *Latin American Indian Association Newsletter* 2, no. 1: 3–4.

———. 1985a. "The New Tenochtitlan Templo Mayor Coyolxauhqui-Chantico Monument." In *Festschrift Honoring prof. Gerdt Kutscher*. Vol. 10, part 2, pp. 77–98. Berlin: Amerikanisches Institut.

———. 1985b. "Polychrome on Aztec Sculpture." In *Painted Architecture and Polychrome Monumental Sculpture in Mesoamerica*. Ed. E. H. Boone, pp. 145–71. Washington, D.C.: Dumbarton Oaks.

Nicholson, H. B., and E. Quiñones Keber. 1983. *Art of the Aztec Mexico: Treasures of Tenochtitlan*. Washington, D.C.: National Gallery of Art.

Noguera, Eduardo. 1934. Estudio de la cerámica encontrada en el sitio donde estaba el Templo Mayor de México. *Anales del Museo Nacional de Arqueología, Historia y Etnografía*. 5th series, 1, no. 2: 267–82.

———. 1935. "La cerámica de Tenayuca y las excavaciones estratigráficas." In *Tenayuca*. Pp. 141–201. México: Departamento de Monumentos/SEP.

———. 1968. Ceremonias del fuego nuevo. *Cuadernos americanos* 158, no. 3: 146–51.

———. 1979. "Del México legendario." In *Trabajos arqueológicos en el Centro de la Ciudad de México (antología)*. Ed. E. Matos Moctezuma, pp. 167–68. México: SEP/INAH.

O'Gorman, Helen. 1963. *Plantas y flores de México*. México: UNAM.

Ojeda Díaz, María de los Angeles. 1986. *Estudio iconográfico de un monumento dedicado a Itzpapálotl*. Cuaderno de trabajo no. 63. México: INAH.

Olmedo, Bertina. 2002. *Los templos rojos del recinto sagrado de Tenochtitlan*. México: INAH.

Olmedo, Bertina, and Carlos Javier González. 1986. Presencia del estilo Mezcala en el Templo Mayor: Una clasificación de piezas antropomorfas. Bachelor's thesis in archaeology, ENAH, México.

Orea Magaña, Haydee et al. 1990. Procesos de alteración en los materiales de la zona arqueológica de Templo Mayor y propuestas para su conservación: Informe de la temporada de trabajo, septiembre de 1988–enero de 1989. México: Escuela Nacional de Restauración, Conservación y Museografía "Manuel del Castillo Negrete"/INAH. Typescript.

Orton, Clive. 1988. *Matemáticas para arqueólogos*. Madrid: Alianza Universidad.

Palacios, Enrique Juan. 1935. "La cintura de serpientes de la pirámide de Tenayuca." In *Tenayuca*.

pp. 233–63. México: Departamento de Monumentos/SEP.

Pareyón Moreno, Eduardo. 1972. "Las pirámides de doble escalera." In *Religión en Mesoamérica, XII Mesa Redonda*. Eds. Jaime Litvak King and Noemí Castillo, pp. 117–26. México: SMA.

Paso y Troncoso, Francisco del. 1979. *Descripción, historia y exposición del Códice Borbónico*. México: Siglo Veintiuno [facsim.].

Pasztory, Esther. 1975. *The Iconography of the Teotihuacan Tlaloc*. Washington, D.C.: Dumbarton Oaks.

———. 1983. *Aztec Art*. New York: Harry N. Abrams.

———. 1988. "The Aztec Tlaloc: God of Antiquity." In *Smoke and Mist: Mesoamerican Studies in Memory of Thelma D. Sullivan*. Eds. J. K. Josserand and K. Dakin, pp. 289–327. Oxford: BAR.

Peñafiel, Antonio. 1910. *Destrucción del Templo Mayor de México Antiguo y los monumentos encontradas en la ciudad, en las excavaciones de 1897 y 1902*. México: Secretaría de Fomento.

Peña Gómez, Rosa María. 1978. Análisis de los restos humanos en las ofrendas a Coyolxauhqui. *Antropología e Historia* 24: 39–51.

Polaco, Oscar J. 1982. "Los invertebrados de la ofrenda 7 del Templo Mayor." In *El Templo Mayor: Excavaciones y estudios*. Ed. E. Matos Moctezuma, pp. 143–50. México: SEP/INAH.

———. 1986. "Restos biológicos de la Costa del Pacífico." In *Primer Coloquio de Arqueología y Etnohistoria del Estado de Guerrero*. Ed. Roberto Cervantes-Delgado, pp. 265–75. México: INAH/Gobierno del Estado de Guerrero.

———. 1991. *La fauna en el Templo Mayor*. México: INAH/Asociación de Amigos del Templo Mayor/GV Editores.

Polaco, Oscar J., Ligia Butrón M., and Rolando Cárdenas. 1989. La sala de fauna del Museo del Templo Mayor. In *Trace, Travaux et Recherches dans les Amériques du Centre* 16 (Dec.): 53–69.

Pomar, Juan Bautista. 1964–1968. "Relación de Texcoco (1582)." In *Poesía náhuatl*. 3 vols. Trans. A. Ma. Garibay, vol. 1, pp. 149–220. México: UNAM.

Ponce de León, Arturo. 1982. *Fechamiento arqueoastronómico en el Altiplano de México*. México: Departamento del Distrito Federal.

Ponce de León, Pedro. 1965. Tratado de los dioses y ritos de la gentilidad. In *Teogonía e historia de los mexicanos: Tres opúsculos del siglo XVI*. Ed. A. Ma. Garibay, pp. 121–32. México: Porrúa.

Preuss, Konrad Theodor. 1903. Die Feuergötter als Ausgangspunkt zum Verständnis der mexikanischen Religion in ihrem Zusammenhange. In *Mitteilungen der Wiener Anthropologischen Gesellschaft* 33: 129–233.

Primeros Memoriales [Nahuatl texts of Sahagún's native informants]. 1905. Ed. F. del Paso y Troncoso, vol. 6, part 2. Madrid: Hauser y Menet [facsim.].

Ramírez Acevedo, Gilberto. 1989. Sahumadores mexicas. *Antropología*, new series, 14 (May–June): 18–19.

Rees Holland, Charles Henry. 1989. Instrumentos líticos tallados del Templo Mayor de Tenochtitlan. Bachelor's thesis in archaeology, ENAH, México.

Reyes García, Luis. 1979. "La visión cosmológica y la organización del imperio mexica." In *Mesoamérica: Homenaje al Doctor Paul Kirchhoff*. Ed. B. Dahlgren, pp. 34–40. México: SEP/INAH.

Román Berrelleza, Juan Alberto. 1986. El sacrificio de niños en honor a Tláloc (La ofrenda no. 48 del Templo Mayor). Bachelor's thesis in physical anthropology, ENAH, México.

———. 1987. "Offering 48 of the Templo Mayor: A Case of Child Sacrifice." In *The Aztec Templo Mayor*. Ed. E. H. Boone, pp. 131–44. Washington, D.C.: Dumbarton Oaks.

———. 1990. *Sacrificio de niños en el Templo Mayor*. México: INAH/GV Editores/Asociación de Amigos del Templo Mayor.

Ruz Lhuillier, Alberto. 1968. *Costumbres funerarias de los antiguos mayas*. México: Seminario de Cultura Maya, UNAM

Sahagún, Fray Bernardino de. 1950–1969. *Florentine Codex. General History of the Things of New Spain*. 12 vols. Trans. and eds. C. E. Dibble and A. J. O. Anderson. Salt Lake City: University of Utah Press.

———. 1956. *Historia general de las cosas de Nueva España*. 4 vols. Ed. A. Ma. Garibay. México: Porrúa.

———. 1979. *Codice Florentine*. Manuscrito 218–220 de la Colección Palatina de la Biblioteca Medicea Laurenziana. 3 vols. México: Secretaría de Gobernación, Archivo General de la Nación.

———. 1988. *Historia general de las cosas de Nueva España*. 2 vols. Intro., paleography, glossary, and notes. A. López Austin and J. García Quintana. Madrid: Alianza Editorial.

Salazar Ortegón, Ponciano. 1979. "Bibliografía: Vestigios arqueológicos localizados hasta la fecha en el centro de la Ciudad de México." In *Trabajos arqueológicos en el centro de la ciudad de México (antología)*. Ed. E.

Matos Moctezuma, pp. 269–73. México: SEP/INAH.

Santaella, Yolanda. 1982. "Informe de la sección de restauración." In *El Templo Mayor: Excavaciones y estudios*. Ed. E. Matos Moctezuma, pp. 295–312. México: INAH.

Sarmiento Fradera, Griselda. 1986. Las sociedades cacicales: Propuesta teórica e indicadores arqueológicos. Bachelor's thesis in archaeology, ENAH, México.

Scarduelli, Pietro. 1988. *Dioses, espíritus y ancestros: Elementos para la comprensión de sistemas rituales*. México: FCE.

Schulze, Niklas. 1997. La ofrenda 20 del Templo Mayor de Tenochtitlan: un análisis económico. Bachelor's theses, University of Hamburg, Hamburg.

Ségota, Dúrdica. 1987. Unidad binaria del Templo Mayor de Tenochtitlan: Hipótesis de trabajo. *Anales del Instituto de Investigaciones Estéticas* 58: 47–54.

Séjourné, Laurette. 1957. *Pensamiento y religión en el México Antiguo*. México: FCE.

Seler, Eduard. 1892. "Uitzilopochtli, Dieu de la Guerre des Aztèques." In *Congrès International des Américanistes, Compte-rendu de la huitième session tenue à Paris en 1890*. Ed. Ernest Leroux, pp. 383–400. Paris: Societé des Américanistes.

———. 1899. Die achtzehn Jahresfeste der Mexikaner (1 Hälfte). *Veröffentlichungen aus dem Königlichen Museum für Völkerkunde, Berlin* 6: 58–66.

———. 1903. Las excavaciones en el sitio del Templo Mayor de México. *Anales del Museo Nacional de México* 7: 235–60.

———. 1960a. "Die Ausgrabungen am Orte des Hauptempels in Mexiko." In *Gesammelte Abhandlungen zur Amerikanischen Sprach-und Altertumskunde*. Vol. 2, pp. 767–904. Graz, Austria: Akademische Druck.

———. 1960b. "Mythus und Religion der alten Mexikaner." In *Gesammelte Abhandlungen zur Amerikanischen Sprach-und Altertumskunde*. Vol. 4, pp. 1–167. Graz, Austria: Akademische Druck.

———. 1960–1969 [1902–1923]. *Gesammelte Abhandlungen zur Amerikanischen Sprach-und Altertumskunde*. 5 vols. Graz, Austria: Akademische Druck.

———. 1963. *Comentarios al Códice Borgia*. 2 vols. México: FCE.

Serra Puche, Maricarmen, Jean Pierre Laporte, and Guillermo Espinosa. 1978. Análisis numérico del arte rupestre del Levante español: Un experimento. *Anales de Antropología* 15: 9–31.

Serrato-Combe, Antonio. 2001. *The Aztec Templo Mayor: A Visualization*. Salt Lake City: University of Utah Press.

Signorini, Italo, and Alessandro Lupo. 1989. *Los tres ejes de la vida: Almas, cuerpo, enfermedad entre los nahuas de la Sierra de Puebla*. Xalapa, México: Universidad Veracruzana.

Siméon, Rémi. 1977. *Diccionario de la lengua náhuatl o mexicana redactado según los documentos impresos y manuscritos más auténticos y precedido de una introducción*. México: Siglo Veintiuno Editores.

Sneath, P. H. A., and R. R. Sokal. 1973. *Numerical Taxonomy: The Principles and Practice of Numerical Classification*. San Francisco: W. H. Freeman.

Sokal, R. R., and P. H. A. Sneath. 1963. *Principles of Numerical Taxonomy*. San Francisco: W. H. Freeman.

Solís Olguín, Felipe R. 1985. "Arte, estado y sociedad: La escultura antropomorfa de México-Tenochtitlan." In *Mesoamérica y el centro de México*. Eds. J. Monjarás-Ruiz, Rosa Brambila, and Emma Pérez-Rocha, pp. 393–432. México: INAH.

Solís, Felipe, and David Morales. 1991. *Rescate de un rescate: Colección de objetos arqueológicos de El Volador, Ciudad de México*. Catálogo de las Colecciones Arqueológicas del Museo Nacional de Antropología. México: INAH.

Soustelle, Jacques. 1969. *Los cuatro soles: Origen y ocaso de las culturas*. Madrid: Ediciones Guadarrama.

———. 1982. *El universo de los aztecas*. México: FCE.

Spaulding, Albert C. 1953. Statistical Techniques for the Discovery of Artifact Types. *American Antiquity* 18: 305–13.

Spranz, Bodo. 1982. *Los dioses en los códices mexicanos del grupo Borgia: Una investigación iconográfica*. México: FCE.

Sullivan, Thelma D. 1974. "Tlaloc: A New Etymological Interpretation of the God's Name and What It Reveals of His Essence and Nature." In *Attli del XL Congresso Internazionale degli Americanisti* (Rome, Sept. 3–10, 1972). Vol. 2, pp. 213–19. Genoa, Italy: Tilgher.

———. 1965. A Prayer to Tlaloc. *Estudios de Cultura Náhuatl* 5: 39–55.

Taggart, James M. 1983. *Nahuat Myth and Social Structure*. Austin: University of Texas Press.

Tapia, Andrés de. 1963. Relación de algunas cosas de las que acacieron al Muy Ilustre Señor Don Hernando Cortés Marqués del Valle, desde que se determinó ir a descubrir tierra en la Tierra Firme del mar Océano. In *Crónicas de la Conquista*. Ed. A. Yáñez, pp. 25–78. México: UNAM.

Taube, Karl A. 1994. "The Iconography of Toltec Period Chichen Itza." In *Hidden among the Hills. Maya Archaeology of the Northwest Yucatan Peninsula. First Maler Symposium*. Ed. H. J. Prem, pp. 213–46. Möckmühl: Verlag von Flemming.

Tena, Rafael. 1987. *El calendario mexicana y la cronografía*. México: INAH.

Thompson, J. Eric S. 1975. *Historia y religión de los mayas*. México: Siglo Veintiuno Editores.

———. 1978. *Maya Hieroglyphic Writing. An Introduction*. Norman: University of Oklahoma Press.

Tichy, Franz. 1978. El calendario solar como principio de ordenación del espacio para poblaciones y lugares sagrados. *Comunicaciones* 15: 153–64.

———. 1981. "Order and Relationship of Space and Time in Mesoamerica: Myth or Reality?" In *Mesoamerican Sites and World-views*. Ed. E. P. Benson, pp. 217–45. Washington, D.C.: Dumbarton Oaks.

———. 1983. "Observaciones del sol y calendario agrícola." In *Calendars in Mesoamerica and Peru. Native American Computations of Time*. Proceedings of the 44th International Congress of Americanists, Manchester, 1982. BAR International Series, no. 174. Eds. Anthony F. Aveni and G. Brotherson, pp. 135–43. Oxford: BAR.

Tlatelolco a través de los tiempos. 1944–1956. Pts. 1–13. México: Memorias de la Academia de Historia.

Tonalámatl de Aubin. 1981. Ed. Carmen Aguilera. Tlaxcala, México: Estado de Tlaxcala [facsim., E. Seler, ed., 1900–1901].

Torquemada, Juan de. 1969. *Monarquía indiana*. 3 vols. Intro. M. León-Portilla. México: Porrúa [facsim. of 1723].

Tovar, Juan de. 1972. *Manuscript Tovar. Origines et croyances des indiens du Mexique*. Intro. J. Lafaye. Graz, Austria: Akademische Druck.

Townsend, Richard F. 1979. *State and Cosmos in the Art of Tenochtitlan*. Washington, D.C.: Dumbarton Oaks.

———. 1982. "Pyramid and Sacred Mountain." In *Archaeoastronomy in the American Tropics*. Eds. A. F. Aveni and G. Urton. *Annals of the New York Academy of Sciences* 385: 37–62.

———. 1987. Coronation at Tenochtitlan. In *The Aztec Templo Mayor*. Ed. E. H. Boone, pp. 371–410. Washington, D.C.: Dumbarton Oaks.

Tozzer, Alfred M. 1982. *Mayas y lacandones: Un estudio comparativo*. México: INI.

Tweedie, Ms. Alec. 1901. *Mexico as I saw it*. London: Hurst and Blackett Limited.

Umberger, Emily. 1987. "Events Commemorated by Date Plaques at the Templo Mayor: Further Thoughts on the Solar Metaphor." In *The Aztec Templo Mayor*. Ed. E. H. Boone, pp. 411–50. Washington, D.C.: Dumbarton Oaks.

Urueta Flores, Cecilia. 1990. Presencia del material mixteco dentro del Templo Mayor. Bachelor's thesis in archaeology, ENAH, México.

Vega Sosa, Constanza, ed. 1979. *El recinto Sagrado de México-Tenochtitlan: Excavaciones 1968–69 y 1975–76*. México: INAH.

Veinte himnos sacros de los nahuas. 1978. Collected by Fray B. de Sahagún, trans. A. Ma. Garibay. México: UNAM.

Velázquez Castro, Adrián. 1999. *Tipología de los objetas de concha del Templo Mayor de Tenochtitlan*. México: INAH.

———. 2000. *El simbolismo de los objetos de concha de las ofrendas del Templo Mayor de Tenochtitlan*. México: INAH.

Victoria Lona, Naoli. 2004. El copal en las ofrendas del Templo Mayor de Tenochtitlan. Bachelor's thesis in archaeology, ENAH, México.

Villanueva, G. G. 1987. Los moluscos en asociación directa a Coyolxauhqui. *Cuaderno de Trabajo (INAH)* 6: 23–36.

Villa Rojas, Alfonso. 1985. Nociones preliminares sobre cosmología maya. *Anales de Antropología* 22: 230–49.

Vogt, Evon Z. 1981. "Some Aspects of the Sacred Geography of Highland Chiapas." In *Mesoamerican Sites and World-views*. Ed. E. P. Benson, pp. 119–42. Washington, D.C.: Dumbarton Oaks.

———. 1983. *Ofrendas para los dioses: Análisis simbólico de rituales zinacantecos*. México: FCE.

Wagner, Diana. 1982. "Reporte de las ofrendas excavadas en 1978." In *El Templo Mayor: Excavaciones y estudios*. Ed. E. Matos Moctezuma, pp. 119–42. México: INAH.

Winning, Hasso von. 1987. *La iconografía de Teotihuacan: Los dioses y los signos.* 2 vols. México: UNAM.

Zantwijk, Rudolf van. 1963. Principios organizadores de los mexicas: Una introducción al estudio del sistema interno del régimen azteca. *Estudios de Cultura Náhuatl* 4: 187–222.

———. 1981. "The Great Temple of Tenochtitlan: Model of Aztec Cosmovision." In *Mesoamerican Sites and World-views.* Ed. E. P. Benson, pp. 71–86. Washington, D.C.: Dumbarton Oaks.

Zingg, Robert M. 1982. *Los huicholes, una tribu de artistas.* 2 vols. México: INI.

Zorita, Alonso de. 1942. Breve y sumaria relación de los señores de la Nueva España. México: UNAM.

Index

*Note: numbers appearing in italics indicate figures

174, 193, 200, 216, 242, 250, 251, 252, 256, 258,
275, 278, 281, 282, 286, 290, 323, 330, 336, 347n.
23, 352n. 13, 355n. 42, 369nn. 121, 127, 370n. 137,
370n. 140

sky: in cosmos, 38, 53, 177, 224–25, 350n. 14; and
earth, 38, 66, 71, 72, 192, 218, 221–22, 349n. 12,
362n. 36

slaves, 147, 178, 181, 210, 213, 218, 350n. 18, 367n. 101,
368n. 110

snakes. *See* serpents

Sneath, Peter H., 119

social advancement: rituals for, 76

socles, 57, 58, 59, 60, 61

Sokal, Robert R., 119

Solís, Janet Long, 119

Solís Olguín, Felipe, 2

Soustelle, Jacques, 70

soul of the heart. *See* Teyolia

souls, 176–78, 180, *180*, 183, 205, 209, 366n. 92. *See
also* tonalli

Spanish Conquest, 3, 4, 216

spatial distribution and patterns, 106–11; of Complex
A, 185–86, 238–43; of Complex B, 244–48; of
Complex C, 249–52; of Complex D, 257–59; of
Complex E, 259–62; of Complex F, 262–66; of
Complex G, 270–72; of Complex H, 272–76; of
Complex I, 277–79; of Complex J, 280–82; of
Complex K, 287–89; of Complex L, 289–91; of
Complex M, 292–94; of Complex N, 294–96;
of Complex O, 296–98; of Complex P, 298–99;
of Complex Q, 301–4; of Complex R, 305–6; of
Complex S, 308–9; of Complex T, 310–12; of
offering H, 322–23; of offering L, 325–26; of
offering 9, 337–38; of offering 16, 330–31; of
offering 30, 336; of offering 38, 332; of offering
41, 315–17; of offering 45, 328; of offering 54,
320–21; of offering 64, 324–25; of offering 71,
334; of offering 76, 335; of offering 78, 318–19;
of offering 82, 329–30; of offering 85, 326–27;
of Subcomplex C1, 252–54; of Subcomplex C2,
255–56; of Subcomplex F1, 266–68; of
Subcomplex F2, 269–70; of Subcomplex J1,
282–84; of Subcomplex J2, 286

Spaulding, Albert, 118

spirals, ceramic, 198, *202*, 242, 247, 321, 323

Spranz, Bodo, 360n. 22

springs, 37, 156, 171, 172, 193, 349n. 9; at Tenochtitlan,
65, 145, 348n. 3

Stage I, 51

Stage II, 51, 53, 54, 61, 91–92, *95*, 172, 183, 206; offerings in, 97, 98, 163

Stage III, 51, 53, 91–92, 172; offerings from, 95, 98, 163

Stage IV, 50–52, 53, 91–92, 155

Stage IVa, 51–52, 92, 98, 149, 155, 168, 244

Stage IVb, 51, 53, 91–92, 139, 172, 183, 238, 242, 244;
offerings in, 97, 98, 158–59, 185, 200

Stage V, 51, 52, 53, 57, 60, 91, 162; offerings in, 160–61;
and Sacred Precinct buildings,

Stage VI, 51, 52, 53, 57, 60, 91, 92, 132, 172; offerings in,
91, 160–61; and Sacred Precinct buildings,
49–50

Stage VII, 51, 52, 53, 55, 57, 60, 91, 92; offerings in, 95,
98; and Sacred Precinct buildings

statues. *See* sculptures

Subcomplex C1, 252–54; description of, 252–54

Subcomplex C2, 254–56; description of, 254–56

Subcomplex F1, 263, 266–68, *267*; description of, 168,
266–68

Subcomplex F2, 263, *268*, 269–70; description of,
269–70

Subcomplex J1, 282–84, *283*; description of, 282–84

Subcomplex J2, 284–86, *285*; description of, 284–86

subway excavations, 10

sun, 25, 36, 53, 54, 55, 66, 71, 72, 74, 137, 143, 156, 176,
182, 195, 198, 202, 207, 211, 216, 217, 219–20,
346n. 19, 347n. 22, 348n. 5, 349nn. 12, 13,
350nn. 14, 17, 362n. 35, 366n. 93, 368n. 113,
369n. 127, 370nn. 130, 136, 373nn. 168, 170,
374n. 178

supernatural, the, 33–39

supernatural beings. *See* deities

symbolism, 6, 113, 115, 147–48, 152, 168, 169, 175, 189,
190, 191, 207, 208, 218–19, 224–25; of hills-tem-
ples, 73, 74, 131; of offerings, 36, 132, 167, 183,
195–96, 199, 201, 227, 364n. 69; of Templo
Mayor, 38, 53, 63–79, 139, 216, 218, 350n. 15,
362n. 39; of Xiuhtecuhtli-Huehueteotl,
138–42, 362n. 39

symbols: cosmic, 105, 123, 149, 188, 193, 198; iconic, 37,
120, 191

Tacuba, 72

Tapia, Andrés de, 3

taxonomy. *See* numerical taxonomy

techcatl, 51, 87, 207

Tecoac, 213

Tecpatl glyphs, 52

tecpatl. *See* knives, sacrificial

Teloloapan, 215

temalacatl, 206, 210, 212, 218

Temazcaltitlan, 64

temples: architectural symbolism of, 28, 40, 155; construction of, 205; dedication of, 203, 205; dis-
mantling of, 3, 57; as liminal zones, 38–39

Templo Mayor, Tenochcan, 9, 43

Templo Mayor, Tenochtitlan, 7, *14*, *58*, *71*; astronomi-
cal orientation of, 63–69, 224; burials in,
148–49, 205; chronology of, 52–54; and cosmos,